THE
PREACHERS

THE PREACHERS

James Morris

Illustrations by Tom Huffman

ST. MARTIN'S PRESS   NEW YORK

Library of Congress Catalogue #72-93927
Manufactured in the United States of America
No part of this book may be reproduced without
permission in writing from the publisher.

St. Martin's Press
175 Fifth Avenue
New York, N.Y. 10010

AFFILIATED PUBLISHERS: Macmillan Limited, London
—also at Bombay, Calcutta, Madras and Melbourne

FOR BETTY AND SHARON

Contents

Preface

About 20 years ago I helped erect a Gospel tent and stayed around long enough to watch my first faith-healing service. Since then I have studied many preachers, but those with independent ministries—the one-man "denominations"—have always proved the most interesting. Many of them were faith healers, or mystical snake handlers, or just wandering street-corner preachers. Some of them joined the great revival of interest in miracle healing that swept the county after World War II. Others combined anti-Communism with fundamentalism, a heady brew which still inspires multiplied thousands of supporters. Some of them roamed the land with huge Gospel tents, broadcasting their sermons from radio stations all across the nation. A few became nationally-known television personalities, and civic leaders in their own cities or states.

One of the most perplexing problems I had in preparing this book involved the choice of material. Which of the score or more of well-known preachers with independent nationwide ministries should be included? All have fascinating stories to tell. Some of my personal favorites have been left out to avoid repetition. Those selected are generally the most representative

of the independent preachers, the ones who have had the greatest
social, political and religious impact on grass-roots America. Some
have become multimillionaires as a result of their business acumen;
others are interesting because of their struggles with the postal
authorities or the Internal Revenue Service; and still others because they have developed such original and colorful ministries,
performing such miracles as "seeing" through a plastic eye or causing worn-out lawn mowers to operate by "baptizing" them with
"holy oil." Even the preachers with the smallest ministries have
thousands of supporters and very often are important leaders
in their own regions. Hopefully, *The Preachers* will stimulate
others to study a movement that for too long has been ignored
or dismissed, one that now threatens to become part of the new
religious and political "mainstream" of America.

As much as possible I have attempted to avoid theological
disputes in order to concentrate on the personality of each
preacher and his struggle to build a successful ministry. Also,
it has not been practical to provide documentation for every
important fact, but an effort has been made to include references
for all controversial material.

I am indebted to many persons for advice and assistance at
every stage in the preparation of the manuscript. A list of their
names cannot be included here, with a few outstanding excep-
tions. I am indebted to Dr. John H. George, political science
professor at Central State University (Oklahoma), for use of
his extensive files and for his assistance with regard to preachers
involved in far-right politics. I am also indebted to Mr. Thomas
McDaid for his careful reading of the manuscript and his frequently valuable advice. My particular thanks go to my friend and
editor, Tom Dunne, who made the publication of this book possible because of the skill and infinite patience with which he
guided it through every stage of its preparation. And my thanks
also go to Tom McCormack, President of St. Martin's Press, for
the encouragement he has given this work from its beginning.

TOM
HUFFMAN

I

A. A. Allen

Son, let me tell you something. Do you know when you can tell a revival meeting is over? Do you know when God's saying to move on to the next town? When you can turn people on their head and shake them and no money falls out, then you know God's saying "Move on, son."

—A. A. Allen's message to Brother Marjoe

Except for the threat of high winds or an occasional tornado, late spring and early summer are the best times for miracles all across the deep South and in most parts of the Southwest. For the 1970 season, this proved to be true in a most unusual way. People were being miraculously healed during the services under the Reverend A. A. Allen's big revival tent before he or his associate healers had a chance to lay a hand on them. Even while the congregation was singing, the crippled, the blind and the deaf were rushing to the pulpit ramp declaring they had been healed. God was even filling and cleaning people's teeth during the opening prayer. It was an unprecedented season of many miracles, and no one was happier to report them than radio evangelist Asa Alonzo Allen, who announced he felt like dancing in the Spirit. His broadcasts boasted he was "God's man of faith and power," and he credited the Lord for any growth in his ministry, an increase that often came not only from his tent revivals, but also through his radio broadcasts, television programs, his magazine and books, or the sale of his records.[1]

He wrote that he was especially impressed with the great

3

miracles being wrought in his ministry that spring, an observation that confounded some of his critics, who suggested his ministry already boasted of miracles beyond the belief of a medieval sorcerer: had not an arm instantly grown six inches? What of the baby whose skull had been partly re-created in a moment? A prayer had caused a safety pin to come sailing out of a woman's stomach, and a breast removed by surgery was miraculously restored to one of his female followers. If St. Peter's shadow and St. Paul's handkerchiefs healed the sick and cast out devils, his own ministry could boast quite as much, if not more. Even the dead had been brought back to life.

Allen was also pleased, perhaps for the first time, with the newspaper and magazine articles about his organization, calling them the greatest reporting he had ever read about any ministry. And he must also have been pleased that his autobiography would soon be published. Even *Look* magazine, never especially enamored of faith healers, had helped his ministry, damning him with faint but fancy praise. In October 1969 *Look* Senior Editor William Hedgepeth noted that Oral Roberts had dropped out of the healing business and Billy Graham had become "Richard Nixon's guru-in-waiting." This, he observed, left A. A. Allen the "nation's topmost tent-toting, old-fashioned evangelical roarer." And in spite of the fact that Allen was still a blood-and-thunder fundamentalist, Hedgepeth was willing to concede that the Arizona evangelist was

> . . . at least a practical zealot with a sense of style that sets him apart from that frowzy netherworld of mystical crackpot charlatans, snake handlers, wandering bush-league Bible thumpers, street-corner messiahs and questionable colleagues like the lady evangelist near Waxahachie, Texas, who—when it was learned she'd contracted illegitimate pregnancy—proudly revealed her role in mankind's second case of immaculate conception. In the God business of today, A. A. Allen is a mogul.

Moguls, spiritual advisers to presidents, and others in positions of prominence in every field are expected to appear at their best in public; and true to that code, Allen had always been a natty dresser. But suddenly, as if in celebration of better times, or perhaps in acknowledgement of his new leadership role, the energetic little evangelist burst on the ecclesiastical scene with a "mod" haircut and matching wardrobe, including the latest styles in multicolored shirts and wide ties, and irridescent lavender or camel-colored suits. The new, shaggy coiffure, which featured wispy bangs and locks of his fiery red hair over the ears, gave his usual hard-bitten features a puckish, almost elfin quality. Short of stature and slightly stocky, he was said by many during the early years of his career to bear an amazing resemblance to the late Spike Jones. Others were reminded of James Cagney when they first saw Allen; and in the latter part of the sixties he was often described as a combination of Cagney and Governor George Wallace of Alabama. Controversy swirled around almost every aspect of his miraculous healing ministry, and perhaps the greatest miracle of all was its survival. His critics, who generally denounced his "miracle revivals" as exercises in charlatanry, were in firm agreement on one point: A. A. Allen was the best known and most successful practicing faith healer in the country as the 1970's began.

From headquarters in his own city of Miracle Valley, Arizona, evangelist Allen's religious empire reached out to followers in all the states and many foreign countries. *Time* magazine decided in its March 7, 1969, issue that his faith-healing ministry had for all practical purposes become another sect, and reported, with eyebrows suitably raised, that in the previous year A. A. Allen Revivals, Inc., had grossed $2,692,342—not including the salaries of Allen and his two associate preachers, whose "cut," according to *Time*, was taken in the form of "love offerings" from their field campaigns. His ministry of miracles was flourishing, to be sure, but many who were interested in a faith-healing organization built mainly through the efforts of one dynamic little man, were unaware of A. A. Allen's long struggle to reach the top in the highly competitive business of miracles.

He was born March 27, 1911, the last of seven children of tenant farmers Asa Alonzo and Leona Magdalene Allen, in an unpainted two-room shack perched a few miles from the meandering Black River, in the poverty-stricken, dirt-road hamlet of Sulphur Rock, Arkansas. When he was three, the specter of starvation forced his father from the farm into the nearby town of Batesville, where he found work in a stave mill. As an evangelist, A. A. Allen seemed to enjoy describing his early years, a register of hardships that impressed the rustics who often frequented his tent revivals and aspired to a ministry modeled on his. There was always a jug of moonshine behind their front door, he remembered. And his mother drank almost as much as his father. Even the children drank, much to the delight of the parents, who roared with laughter at their little inebriated capers. Years later, Allen surmised that they probably enjoyed the dubious distinction of being the seven youngest drunks in the state of Arkansas.

It is difficult to exaggerate the degradation of his family in stronger terms than those employed by evangelist Allen himself. Always inclined to extremes, as he grew older he increasingly displayed a propensity for hyperbole, selective remembering, and now and then a fanciful distortion of minute details. According to the evangelist, his mother divorced his drunken father and left all her children except him to marry still another alcoholic, John Bailey of Carthage, Missouri. Later the children were reunited, to share a life of hunger, squalor and privation under the dictatorial whims of their stepfather. His father remained in Arkansas, where he eventually found a drunkard's grave. Young Asa made an abortive attempt to run away from home at the age of eleven and dropped out of school during the eighth grade, sick of the humiliation of attending class in his bare feet. He soon entered what he described as the "swirling rapids of sin," working where he could and living by his wits. After a few years of drifting, his health in shambles, he rejoined his mother on a small farm outside Carthage. Although he was still a very young man, Asa Alonzo was already old in the ways of the world. He had started smoking at the age of six, had his first woman at the age of twelve, and at eighteen lived with a common-law wife. By the time he was twenty-three he claimed the reputation of worst sinner in that section of Missouri, having added stealing and a stay in jail to his list of early offenses against society. But drink was the family's greatest weakness. Years later Allen remembered that

> . . . If we had had a coat of arms, the beer bucket and the gin bottle would rightly have been emblazoned upon it. Drunkenness was a family trait. My mother had gone through one divorce and was destined for another. I had a loveless father in Arkansas, a loveless stepfather at home. . . . I had four wild sisters and I was an ex-bum, a drinking, carousing, smoking, stealing sinner. . . .[2]

And then the church touched his life. He was helping his mother run a dance hall roadhouse at the farm, selling home brew boiled on the cookstove and tested by the cupful as it drained out of their little still. He later wrote that a friend on the next farm invited him to a revival in the local Methodist church, and much to his own surprise as well as his friends, he agreed to go. Later he would view it as the hand of God moving him. He was saved during the second night of the revival and knelt at the altar under the prayer of a Sister DePriestes. But within two weeks he had left the Methodists for a Pentecostal church in the same neighborhood. The whole of the matter surrounding this sudden change is not entirely clear. Allen said it stemmed from a disagreement over the mode of baptism and the weakness of his pastor "in conviction and knowledge of the Bible." Critics have pointed out that this statement contradicts an earlier one, in which he lamented that, at the time he joined the church, he was completely ignorant of things Scriptural, including even who or what Jesus was.[3] Still another reason was advanced in his May 1968 newsletter, when he recalled that

> Thirty-three years ago the Lord saved me in a Methodist Church when I repented of my sins, and accepted Jesus Christ as my Savior. But I soon parted company with the Methodist Church as I saw it going backward into liberalism, socialism, and modernism! Any church is a good place for a sinner to start for heaven, but no church

is good enough to continue in unless it is going forward, onward, and upward with God.

Considering his own description of his education and lack of church background, it is doubtful that he knew the meaning of such words as "socialism" or "liberalism" at the time of his conversion. Even if one grants the young Allen an ideological awareness, it is still difficult to believe he "saw it [the Methodist Church] going backward," since he only remained in it two weeks. Later he stated that at the time of his conversion he knew he was meant to preach, because an inner voice commanded him to spread the gospel, "an insistent, clear voice." Out of the welter of conflicting testimony, it is probably safe to speculate that he possessed a craving for respectability, a burning ambition to find something more from life.

A short time after his conversion, Allen attended a tristate camp meeting at Miami, Oklahoma. Here he found the baptism of the Holy Ghost, which had so far eluded him. In ecstasy, he spoke in tongues and lay prostrate in the sawdust until after midnight. That experience convinced him that he wanted to preach. And for the next year and a half he studied while he worked on a ranch in Colorado. Later he applied for admission to a Bible school. Having no money, he offered to work for his tuition or pay it later. Years afterwards, he noted, somewhat bitterly, that his proposal had not been accepted: "God's word at that particular school was taught only on a cash-in-advance basis."

Without a church to pastor, he went on the road, an evangelist willing to go where a revival preacher was needed—mostly little churches in backwoods communities. The offerings were small and living conditions often harsh. He praised his wife for her help in those early days. She bore him four children and worked without complaining, even when there was little or no food. "Thank God," he wrote later, "for a woman who will stand by a man!" But he was frankly discouraged with the results of his ministry. He longed for big meetings, but ". . . no matter how many I led to Christ, I was never satisfied. The crowds, too, were usually heartbreakingly small, and even among the minuscule number who came, too many failed to see the light." He wanted to help the sick and allowed two hours during each revival for divine healing, but "many left the meetings still racked with pain, still in the coils of demons, as hopeless as when they had come to the service." He wanted to perform miracles. "Lord, why can't I heal the sick? Why can't I work miracles in your name?" he pleaded. He was unhappy and discouraged. He had by that time received his license to preach and an ordination in the Assemblies of God Church. Ambition was his terrible master, under whose lash he chafed impatiently:

> . . . I was still a backwoods, backwater evangelist, and I didn't feel I was serving the Lord as I should. . . . My ministry hadn't caught fire, and long years of small meetings in small town after small town appeared to be my fate. . . . I wasn't seeking fame for myself, but from the moment of my conversion I had seen a vision of a sea of faces, massed throngs before me eagerly listening to my preaching, and hundreds, thousands coming forward at each altar call. . . .

Finally, he reported that a long-sought special message from the Lord arrived. On his knees in his prayer closet, Allen wrote on the top of a cardboard box thirteen requirements God demanded in return for "power over all the power of the enemy." Later he would publish a number of versions of the revelation, but all contained the essentials of the agreement between God and A. A. Allen. The evangelist called the requirements, two of which he considered too personal to reveal, "the price tag for the miracle-working power of God."

Asa Allen's ministry started getting some results, but not in the impressive manner he had hoped for, and he decided to accept the pastorate of an Assemblies of God church in Corpus Christi, Texas. In the past he had tried almost everything to attract people to his ministry. He spent long hours learning to play the accordion, piano, organ and the guitar. He even made chalk pictures as prizes for those who brought the most people to his meetings. He advertised in the newspapers and started a direct-to-the-prospect mailing service. At the start of his min-

istry, he firmly believed that a preacher should not talk about
money, that a minister with two suits was a sinner, a pastor with
a new automobile, an obvious hypocrite. But living on the edge
of poverty had tempered those beliefs somewhat. Now he wanted
to raise money to construct a new church building, but the board
of deacons cautioned him against saying too much, lest "people
think you are just out after money." If we decide that money
is really needed, they remonstrated, the church can go to the
bank and borrow it. Allen was adamant, persuaded that his
people had "plenty of money." Why, the head deacon was the
biggest contractor in the state. And the deacon's son-in-law was
one of the richest men in the city. The people had jobs: "I intend to preach it out of them." If he was convinced his way
was the right one, the deacons were equally determined: they
reminded him they had directed the church before he came
along and would continue to run it after he was gone. In a
little while Pastor Allen was once more preaching revivals.[4]

A little earlier in the fateful year of 1951 he had traveled with
a pastor friend to attend an Oral Roberts healing revival in Fort
Worth, Texas. He said later that he had not much wanted to go,
since he had previously been quite critical of the big-time independent faith healers. But when he and his pastor friend were
permitted to sit on the pulpit platform as special guests, and he
watched the long line of sick and afflicted wait for a touch from
the famous right hand of the Reverend Oral Roberts, he suddenly discovered that the Lord was interested in A. A. Allen's
becoming a faith healer. The Lord spoke to him: "If you had
done what I asked you to do years ago, then you could be doing
what this man is doing tonight." Allen's reply to the Lord suggested that he might have been secretly thinking about the same
thing:

> But Lord, how can a little man like me with no name and no repu-
> tation start out now? Oral Roberts has been in the healing ministry
> for five years, and Jack Coe longer than that. Then there are O. L.
> Jaggers, Dale Hansen, and about a hundred other Voice of Healing
> evangelists already on the field. They all have a head start on me,
> and I wouldn't have a chance.

He went on to explain to the Lord about Brother Branham and the other famous healers who already had their own magazines to which thousands of people subscribed. They also had large tents which could seat a congregation of ten thousand. "I thought there was just too much competition . . . I was so far behind I just knew I could never catch up. . . ."

Allen believed that a great revival had broken out in 1950, a faith-healing renaissance of the Latter Rain movement. The evangelists drawing the largest crowds were those using big canvas tents, but tents and the items of accessory equipment were extremely expensive. "Yet I wasn't going to permit a mere lack of money to stand in the way of doing His work under a tent," Allen declared, because ". . . I felt the Lord wanted me to have a tent, too. . . ."

The big healers were attracting national attention in the early 1950s, but not all of it was favorable. Some critics noted that among the professional healers the competition often centered on the subject of whose tent was the largest. Jack Coe, the big Dallas healer, was moving into a new tent some three feet larger than any in the land. With Coe moving up a notch, his old tent would be for sale, and Asa hurried to see it. "I longed for it," the evangelist said, "as I had longed for new shoes when I was a youngster." Coe wanted $8,500, but agreed to take $1,500 down and $100 for every night Allen used the tent. That part was fine, but he would need trucks to transport the tent. Allen hurried back to his congregation. Coe had hired trucks to move his tent, but Asa Alonzo had made up his mind: "I wanted my own trucks . . . was I asking the Lord for too much?"

In 1951 he incorporated his operation in the little town of Brooks, Oregon, under the name of A. A. Allen Revivals, Inc., and claimed tax-exempt status as a nonprofit, religious organization. On July 4, 1951, the old Jack Coe tent went up for business under new management. Allen considered it such a special day of celebration that he lapsed into a rhapsody over his canvas auditorium: it was "an eagle with outstretched wings against the good, clean, cotton-white clouds of Yakima, Washington." None of the larger tents he would later own would mean so much. It was a turning point, "my maiden voyage with Christ under my own canvas."[5]

The people came by the thousands and the miracles began to pour forth in a steady stream that would in time become a veritable Niagara. Allen's raspy, rapid-fire Ozark baritone voice gave his sermons a distinctive flavor. The big healing platform was made to order for his nervous pacing style. With a microphone in his hand and his coat discarded, he prowled the platform like a caged tiger, his visage as fierce as that of an Old Testament prophet. When he wanted to, he could whisper of the goodness of God Almighty and the sweet love of Jesus, only to become a raging Savonarola an instant later, screaming of the terrible wrath in store for sinners, threatening with the awful consuming fire reserved by almighty Jehovah. His gestures were dramatic, first crouching, then pointing, waving, his red hair flying, his jutting jaw fixed sternly. He tried to preach the devil out of every congregation he faced.

His healing technique was not unlike that of most professional healers, except that he often was more dramatic. He could lay a gentle hand on a poor cancer victim in a stretcher, but he could also fasten a double-handed grip around the head of an ambulatory patient strong enough to shock him out of a psychosomatic fixation. He might bend, grapple, feint, pull, wrestle or twist his wheel chair patients, but he could also gently and slowly help them to their feet.

Sometimes he paused to remind the congregation to come to the platform with donations or to make pledges, or to purchase his books, long-playing records or sermon aids. If not all could be induced, he might send his ushers, with brightly colored plastic pails, to collect offerings from among those who remained seated.

But he was soon back to the sick, sweating through his shirt as he worked on, often for many hours. He believed that medical doctors were unable to cope with the demons which caused sickness, and sometimes he would cast out seven or eight demons from one patient, even though it required a half-hour. He hated to leave even one demon, and considered himself too clever to be fooled when a patient began speaking in an unknown tongue, since it was often another demon, not the patient, who was speaking.

At various times he lined up all who wished for a "touch." Down the long line he would move, slapping each sinner on the forehead. Some fainted, others sobbed or moaned. Often the "slain of the Lord" might be so numerous as to cover a large part of the tent floor, a battlefield of bodies slain in the Spirit, sprawled grotesquely, in deathlike trances.

After a propitious shakedown in Yakima, he sailed forth to storm "citadel after citadel of sin" across the country. It was his "juggernaut for Jesus," grinding down the demons of sin next in Nampa, Idaho, then in Memphis and finally in St. Petersburg, Florida, just before winter set in.

He set up headquarters in Dallas, Texas, and interest in his miracles grew so rapidly that in less than a year he needed more space. Here he processed his mail and started "The Allen Revival Hour" on radio and, later, television. He also began publishing his monthly *Miracle Magazine,* which he sent to those who requested it, just as independent evangelists all over the country were doing to advertise their ministries. Allen claimed his magazine was sent ". . . to those who want a bare-knuckled Christian publication in their homes, to those who seek news of our forthcoming revivals and to those who say amen while reading the endless, inspiring testimonies of people who've been healed through contact with our ministry." And what testimonies they were! But critics who regarded his ministry as a money-making side show pointed to his demurrer in fine print at the bottom of a page in each issue of the magazine.

. . . Utmost care has been taken to assure the accuracy of all testimonies before publication and A. A. Allen Revivals, Inc. and "Miracle Magazine" assume no legal responsibility for the veracity of any such report, nor do they accept responsibility as to the degree or permanence of reported healings, deliverances or miracles since the Bible itself declares that for those who do not continue to live for God, even worse things may come (John 5:14).

Critics meant little to A. A. Allen. There were too many signs and wonders being manifested in every city. That was what in-

terested the faithful, and he reported his miracles at every opportunity. In Knoxville, Tennessee, a woman testified that she
closed her eyes while he was preaching, and when she opened
them, Reverend Allen was gone. In his place stood Jesus, his
arms reaching out from a glistening white robe. A fifteen-year-
old boy saw Christ walk up and down the aisles. In Minneapolis
the crowd gasped when a cross of blood dramatically appeared
on Allen's forehead. Getting the jump on his critics, he cautioned
the scoffers to keep quiet. Acts 2:19, he pointed out, had promised such things.

There seemed no end to the wonders he could report. The
lame left their wheel chairs, people leaped from stretchers, the
sick were healed and the blind could see. And when he received
a phone call from a man threatening to burn his tent, the evangelist demonstrated his faith to his followers by refusing even to
worry. He was able to report that, instead of the arsonist's torch
that night, God sent a sign, a huge ball of fire in the sky. Week
after week, month after month, the big tent crisscrossed the
country, fighting the devil and taking up offerings for the Lord.

Then, on October 21, 1955, in Knoxville, Tennessee, trouble
struck like a Jovian thunderbolt. It was hardly the devil this
time, unless one counts "that old devil, demon rum." The wire
services carried the story to every part of the country: evangelist
A. A. Allen, the healer, had been arrested for drunken driving.
His supporters groaned in disbelief; his detractors nodded knowingly. The County Clerk's office was deluged with requests—
from Arizona, California, Texas, North Carolina—for certified
copies of the court proceedings. Others merely asked, was it
really true?

According to reports in the Knoxville *News-Sentinel*, Tennessee
state troopers arrested Allen in the Knoxville suburb of Bearden,
shortly after the state patrol office received calls complaining
about his driving. Two troopers on the alert for the evangelist's
car spotted it as he drove through a traffic light. He was taken
to the city jail, where a drunkometer indication of .20 was recorded, well above the .15 reading necessary to charge a person
with drunken-driving.

Money in bills, checks and coin was taken from the trunk of

his car. While at patrol headquarters, Allen challenged reporters to print anything about his arrest. "Come on, tell me I'm drinking," he yelled. "I'll look you in the eye and tell you you're a liar."

When a photographer took his picture, he shouted, "I rebuke you in the name of the Lord." He explained to the officers that his arrest was a "trick of the devil," but quickly added, "don't get me wrong, I don't think you are demon-possessed." He pounded the desk and shouted to the reporters, "Hallelujah! I dare you to print the truth."

His bond was set at $250 and his hearing scheduled for October 25, 1955. But his attorney insisted he needed time to secure depositions and requested a continuance of the case. Attorney General Hal Clements agreed, provided Allen's bond was increased to $1,000. A new hearing date of October 29 was arranged for the case (No. GSC A 12322), but when that date arrived, A. A. Allen had already departed Knoxville, and he failed to return for his day in court. On January 7, 1956, Judge Arthur Alexander certified the bond for forfeiture, and Allen's attorney, L. C. Ely, and the State Bonding Company paid the $1,000, plus an additional $18.85 in forfeiture costs on January 9, 1956.[6]

Almost immediately the Assemblies of God Church recalled Allen's credentials of fellowship, pending the outcome of his trial. The Tennessee District of the Assemblies of God later recommended that Allen be dropped from membership in the national organization. The evangelist was summoned to appear in Nashville, Tennessee, on May 7, 1956, for a hearing. His membership was terminated when he failed to appear.[7]

A final footnote must be added to the Knoxville affair. Two nights after the evangelist's arrest, Knoxville *Journal* reporter Al Webb was thrown out of the services when some of Allen's men noticed he was taking notes. Webb later revealed that outside the tent his escorts had slugged him twice on the head and warned him: "Don't ever come back."

On February 20, 1956, A. A. Allen's canvas caravan was rolling toward Fresno, California, to meet a February 24 revival date. Unknown to the evangelist, a group of clergymen, representing 45 Fresno Pentecostal churches, was gathered in a solemn assembly to decide whether they wanted to be associated with his ministry. They weighed his entanglement with the law in Knoxville and his dismissal from the Assemblies of God Church, and refused to endorse his healing revival.

After Fresno his "Jesus juggernaut" was scheduled for a March 28 opening in the San Francisco area. Assemblies of God ministers, aware that Allen planned to set up his tents in Alameda on land owned by the United States Maritime Commission, successfully petitioned the Commission to revoke the agreement to rent tent space to Allen. A spokesman made public the ministers' concern that the controversial healer's reputation might lead people to think the whole religious community was part of a racket.

Ever the resourceful field general, the energetic little evangelist quickly revised his strategy and directed his miracle entourage to pitch tents in Sacramento. Unknowingly, he was moving toward one of the greatest confrontations of his career. From the time Allen tightened his tent ropes on Stockton Boulevard outside the city, reporters from the Sacramento *Bee* newspaper were monitoring virtually his every move. They had, in fact, decided to do a number of articles on his activities, and the opening paragraph of the first piece set the tone for the entire series:

> Is it an age of miracles we live in? . . . A snapping eyed little bantam rooster of an evangelist, A. A. Allen, out of Dallas, is huckstering a carnival tent full of them . . . Or so he says . . . But not, evidently, for the cold eye of a news camera.

The reporter referred to the work of the *Bee* photographer who quietly snapped Allen in the process of exorcising a demon from a young stretcher-borne victim of encephalitis. The pictures caught the frenzied antics of the healer as he grasped the sobbing, emaciated boy and shrieked at the demon. The writer reproduced for his readers the various healing "commands:" "You foul, filthy demon, I rebuke you . . . evil spirit, I command you to leave this boy . . . Thaynnnun kewjeeezuss!" Allen screamed, jumping up and down, "Thaynnnnun kewjeeezussus!"

Allen's men spotted the photographer as he attempted to film the offering service and ordered him to leave. The evangelist's Knoxville ordeal had evidently convinced him the press would be forever hostile, and he would henceforth bar all snooping reporters from his services. Outside the tent his men surrounded the photographer and demanded the film from his camera. He gave them instead an undeveloped roll and escaped to carry back a warning that the tent should be considered dangerous territory for newspapermen.

At his services the next day Allen denounced the newspaper and its reporters. He explained to the congregations pouring into his three daily sessions that everyone knew reporters were possessed by demons trying to tear down God's work. As a matter of fact, he happened to have proof of that statement. His own photographers, who took pictures for *Miracle Magazine* and shot footage for his TV shows, had taken a picture of a *Bee* reporter, and when it was developed, three demons could clearly be seen clustered over his head!

Now it was the reporters' turn, and they carefully monitored the sick who lined up in front of the platform during the afternoon service. They watched a tall, 60-year-old cancer victim, Tom Jennings, as he walked through the line. Jennings was one of those given a card admitting him to Allen's healing line in the evening service. They reported he was later taken behind the healing platform to the smaller "invalid" or "prayer" tent, where a variety of wheel chairs and wheeled ambulance stretchers were kept. During the evening service Allen dramatically pointed to Jennings, who waited in a wheel chair with a blanket wrapped around his legs. That man, the healer cried, has only six weeks to live; he has a cancer demon and we're going to heal him God willing! For some ten minutes Allen worked on Jennings, twisting his legs and screaming at the demon. Then he ordered him to get up and walk. Jennings walked down the sawdust aisle to a deafening roar of Glory! Hallelujah! Praise God! When he returned to the platform, he found a smiling Allen sitting in his wheel chair. The drama ended with Jennings pushing a triumphant Allen down the aisle, waving his arms to acknowledge the victorious praise of the congregation.

The April 3 edition of the paper revealed that reporters had interviewed both Jennings and his doctor. The doctor stated, and Jennings verified, that the cancer patient had never been told he had only six weeks to live. Jennings, the doctor said, would probably live for several years and was definitely able to walk.

It was inevitable that the reporters would scrutinize Allen's collection of books and tracts, especially a booklet entitled *Demon Possession Today and How To Be Free* and a paperback called *Invasion From Hell*. These works were advertised to prove "the reality of demons, uncover their master plan to bind, vex, oppress, possess and eventually destroy humanity." The newspaper carried the unusual story under the headline of "Demons—Faith Healer Has Them Right There in Jars."

> Grotesque animal organisms, pickled in embalming fluid, are a mainstay in the freak tents of shabby, fly-by-night carnivals, up and down the back roads of rural America. Demonologist Asa Alonza Allen, the evangelist camped just outside Sacramento, goes them one better. His glass-jarred specimens are evil spirit demons.

Allen neutralized the newspaper attack by explaining to his congregation that although the specimens in the glass jars might look like strange animals or reptile bodies, that was just a ruse of the devil. This thing might look like a frog to some people, he said, but it was actually a cancer demon that had come out of a woman's body. It had simply taken the form of a loathsome toad to deceive and get demon power over people. And of course this was just one of the many types of special demons. Some caused cancer or arthritis, others epilepsy or sugar diabetes. He had it on good authority from a nurse in Phoenix that in most operations the doctors who operated for tumors or cancer actually cut out living things in the forms of snakes and toads and other things which were truly demons. She had told him about the case in which the doctors cut out this thing—you and I know it was a demon—that looked something like a tadpole, only it weighed 15 pounds. It had one eye, right in the middle, and little ears and a mouth. It had a tail 15 feet long wrapped around its body.[8]

The miracle evangelist decided he did not care what the paper printed, since it had amounted to about $5,000 worth of free advertising. And as for the reporters, "I'd hate to be in their shoes. You just don't fool around with a man God has anointed. He will get them one of these days. Do you believe me?" He warned the reporters that he had just driven a cancer demon out of a man who had flown all the way from Hot Springs, Arkansas, to be healed. That same demon would return to strike the reporters. They had attacked a man of God, and "they live in fear and trembling. It'll strike them, maybe not today, not tomorrow, but sooner or later it will strike them." Amens went up from the congregation.[9]

The newspaper responded by featuring the evangelist in a lead editorial entitled "No Racket Should Enjoy Immunity From The Law." Referring to Allen's methods as "a burlesque and a parody of true religion . . . redolent with claims of healings which are purely imaginary yet made to appear plausible to the credulous by wile and deceit. And all in the sacred name of Christ and Him crucified." Revealed too were the efforts the District Attorney's office had made in searching the statute books, only to find nothing in California law which could be used to "hail Allen and like charlatans into court."

The editorial writer was somewhat more restrained than the reporter who wrote about Allen and money. He described the evangelist as the "mendicant miracle man in a Palm Beach suit" and declared that Allen's greatest miracles occurred three times each day when he separated "bills from billfolds." He saw testimony to the evangelist's miracle power with money everywhere: in the expensive, late-model cars Allen and his troupe drove; in the sleek, aluminum house trailers they traveled in; in the powerful new truck vans which transported the tents and chairs. He noted that with his tax exemption, Allen had reported a 1954 income of $214,267. Inquiries at the federal income tax office revealed that his evangelistic ministry was considered a cash operation, which tax officials screened on a basis of net worth. They computed an operation's increase in the value of ˙bank accounts, stocks and bonds and property holdings from one year to the next. The increase was considered the annual gross income. The reporter concluded that only Allen could know "the exact take in this kind of cash business."

A spokesman for the 70 churches that constituted the Sacramento Council of Churches condemned the "exploitation of human suffering and ignorance in the name of religion," and said manipulated "miracles" at a price had no place in the program of the church. The *Bee* had already printed a statement from the Chancellor of the Monterey-Fresno Diocese of the Catholic Church, who referred to the revival as a "circus," where healing claims were made to raise money. And a statement by the pastor of an Assembly of God church emphasized that, while his church believed in faith healing, he was "shocked and dismayed" at Allen's activities. The paper also quoted the American Medical Association and a variety of experts on the excesses of faith healers. The Baptist churches, preparing for an areawide revival, released a long statement which said in effect that they believed in divine healing but not in divine healers, and wanted it made clear their own revival had no connection with A. A. Allen's. The evangelist lashed back, remarking on "these pale, deadwood pastors and their pink tea socials, their Sunday School building funds and their watermelon cuttings . . . where are their miracles, their signs and wonders?" The newspaper called his remarks "spiels filled with sneering, sardonic ridicule."

The evangelist's wife, Lexie Allen, entered the fray. She "thanked" the paper for the free advertisement already extended, and she ventured that the attack on her husband's ministry was "Communistically inspired." The Sacramento *Bee* was in league with the devil, she stated, and was trying to quiet Allen for the paper's "Communist purposes," because of its "Communist control." And she took exception to a quote from the American Medical Association that the paper had printed. The AMA statement made reference to the many faith healers who carried "shills" as part of their entourages. At regular intervals the shills would be miraculously healed in the tent service, throwing away their crutches in a dramatic, faith-building paroxysm of praise for the healer.

Even the Reverend Robert Schambach, Allen's right-hand

helper, felt constrained to give his opinion of the *Bee*. He maintained God would render judgment on the newspaper—and in
fact already had: "We told you that within 10 days someone
would be carried out feet first! Well, just look at the *Bee*. It says
here that the 'circulation chief of Fresno *Bee* dies.'" He was
referring to the circulation chief of the Fresno *Bee*, a sister paper
that had been active in the revival controversy. While he was at
it, Schambach also gave Asa Allen credit for the earthquake
which struck the California city of Eureka two years earlier, and
the flood which damaged the same city in December 1955. He
claimed those events had been brought on because the miracle
man had been denied the use of the municipal auditorium in that
city.

On April 10 the Fresno *Bee* sent the Sacramento newspaper
a report of their follow-up on the faith healer's claims in their
area. After Allen completed his three-week revival, the Fresno
Bee's reporters began the difficult task of checking on all those
who claimed they were healed or helped by Allen during his
stay in Fresno. Traveling more than 400 miles through three
San Joaquin Valley counties, they interviewed ministers, doctors,
nurses and many of those who had visited Allen's revival for
healing. The results of their survey showed that while a few
people still claimed to be healed, no case of healing attributed
to Allen's miracle ministry could be confirmed by a competent
medical authority or physician. They also found that a number
of illnesses had been self-diagnosed, ranging from cases of arthritis to ulcers and cancer. Several persons who had permitted
Allen to use their cases as examples of his healing ability later
admitted that their ailments had either returned or had never
left them.

Perhaps the most damaging example was that of J. Clides
Bennett, a Colorado rancher who traveled more than 1,000 miles
to be healed of cancer in Allen's Fresno revival. He was ministered to by the evangelist on March 7, while television cameras
documented the event before some 2,000 people. Bennett later
revealed to a reporter that he had learned of Allen through the
evangelist's radio programs and had induced his son-in-law to

drive him to Fresno after a physician told him he had only a few weeks to live. He returned to Colorado following his miraculous cure, and two weeks later a Colorado physician certified that he had died of cancer of the liver.[10]

Allen left Sacramento, but not without observing that it was a city that needed a "holy shaking" as much as any he had ever known. His canvas caravan rolled on toward cities where the citizens would perhaps display a higher regard for his miracle ministry. He had long since made it clear that he cared not a whit what any critic said or wrote. And he seemed more determined than ever to succeed. Since the opening of his headquarters in Dallas in November 1953, the number of employees required to process his mail and send out tracts, books, healing aprons anointed with miracle oil, and his *Miracle Magazine* had been increased to thirty. The sale of his books and other publications had brought in some $200,000 in 1955. His "Miracle Ministry Broadcast" was heard daily on 35 radio stations, and his healing programs were broadcast on four television channels. He had begun describing his ministry as an international movement, and one of the first missionary fields he selected was the Philippine Islands. That missionary endeavor, like many others, generated a shrill cry for funds and a flood of sensational tracts and booklets. One rather bizarre booklet was entitled *Bitten by Devils!* and was promoted as "the true story of Clarita Villanueva, a 17-year-old girl, who was repeatedly tortured and bitten in Bilibid Prison, Manila. See actual photographs taken during her seizure. See doctors examining teeth marks—as many as 25 bites in one attack." In the States his nationwide campaigns reported ever more wondrous miracles. The ball of fire that once hovered over the giant tent had now become a number of dazzling balls that danced over the healing platform. There were also flames that appeared to sparkle and dance in the air, and towering spires of smoke circled the tent poles. The cross of blood that formerly appeared on the evangelist's forehead now appeared on others, miraculous mystery oil dripped from the hands of the faithful and sometimes demons could be heard threatening his congregations. And his television advertisements were as blatantly frank as words could make them:

SEE! HEAR! ACTUAL MIRACLES HAPPENING BEFORE YOUR EYES. CANCER, TUMORS, GOITERS DISAPPEAR. CRUTCHES, BRACES, WHEELCHAIRS, STRETCHERS DISCARDED. CROSSED EYES STRAIGHTENED. CAUGHT BY THE CAMERA AS THEY OCCURRED IN THE HEALING LINE BEFORE THOUSANDS OF WITNESSES.[11]

Asa Allen had also brought back the old-time camp meetings. Ordinarily they lasted for several days, a sufficient time to "generate emotion for the Lord." The worshipers lived in tents or some form of temporary housing, and the services were held either in the open air or in his tent, which he could now advertise as one of the largest in the world. In January 1958 he scheduled his second such meeting in Phoenix, Arizona, and named it the "Second Great International Miracle Revival Training Camp and Solemn Assembly." It would always be remembered by Brother Allen as the place where the Great Miracle occurred.

During the Phoenix camp meeting, a rancher named Urbane Leindecker donated his 1,280-acre ranch in southern Arizona to Allen, who was so pleased he almost sang with joy. He called it the Great Miracle and made reference to it in many of his later writings. But there does not seem to be an account revealing what happened to Leindecker in later years: whether or not the Lord compensated him twofold, or a hundredfold, as Allen often promised for such generous donations. The evangelist did write that at least once during the time that Leindecker wrestled with God's order to make the donation, the rancher had attempted to sell the land. Allen explained this occurred because Leindecker had not clearly understood what God wanted him to do, and when a prospective buyer was ready to sign the sale papers, God struck him blind! Thus was Leindecker made aware that God's hand was against any transaction that did not put the land in Brother Allen's name.

The evangelist carefully noted that at 4:47 P.M. on January 9, 1958, the deed to two square miles of "newly sanctified Arizona land" was recorded. He felt the Lord had wanted him to have a place where he could build his own community. It would be his Miracle Valley. But he needed donations of all kinds. First, he wanted money to buy the 52 head of white-faced cattle and one Black Angus bull already on the ranch, and he needed another large well dug to irrigate the land. The Lord sent him to his congregations, and they gave.

And he needed building materials, much lumber and at least a million concrete blocks. Blocks were eight cents each, but a brother knew of a block-manufacturing machine that might be available cheaply. They could make their own blocks. God spoke to him again and said,

> Son, if another can sell you a block for eight cents and make money, you can make that block and save money, because you can do what anyone else can do, and even better, with my help. I have already washed the sand and the gravel for this purpose and deposited it where you will need it.

Later, as he was preparing to leave for a missionary crusade in the Philippines, he received a call from Jerry King, his new foreman at the Miracle Valley ranch. King related what Allen called "the greatest news since Urbane Leindecker donated his 1,280 acres": another two square miles of adjoining land was theirs! Their offer to purchase the land at what Allen called a "generous price" had been accepted. Now he had some 2,500 acres of "reverent ground." And, most amazing, a sand and gravel pit was found on this new adjoining property, just as the Lord had prophesied. Next he needed workers, and his plea for help blanketed the nation. Soon volunteer workers from many states, even some from Canada, began arriving.

He called his new city "a Zion for eternity." To most of the natives, it was a flat area that lay between Bisbee and Fort Huachuca, Arizona, but he described it in more picturesque terms: "Among the purple mountain majesties the holy city stands, shimmering under indescribably beautiful sunsets and desert nights illuminated by silver starlight." He was away at revivals a good part of each year, but he returned to Miracle Valley at every opportunity "to revive my own spirit."

While he was away, his religious oasis would be well cared for. He had long since brought a number of his family under the sheltering umbrella of his empire. A great change had come over the sisters he once considered "wild." Ruby had made her peace with the Lord and went to live, and later die, in Miracle Valley. Allen reported that Eunice had married "Carthage's most prominent bootlegger, who died in Los Angeles in 1967, yet another victim of alcohol." But she had since found the road to salvation and eventually joined the remaining family at Brother Allen's ranch. His other sisters, Lee and Zan, left burlesque to marry. Lee became the wife of Gerald King, and after they joined the organization, Gerald was rewarded, for his hard work and loyalty, with the title of Tent Engineer. Soon he was elevated to vice president and executive director of A. A. Allen Revivals, Inc., and Asa Allen called him "my dearest associate."

As the 1950s drew to a close, Allen's ministry had become one of the best-known faith-healing organizations in the country. A few were larger and more prosperous, but that of the peppery little evangelist was not far behind. His tent revivals were as active and well attended as any on the road; his broadcasts could be heard in most parts of the country; and if other faith healers had prosperous ranches, his own was even larger. His ministry was prospering and growing at such a rate that he turned toward a wider ministry and announced that God had given him the whole world! Most of the time he ignored his critics, but occasionally he lashed out at articles that denounced him as a wild money-monger. He reminded his congregations that the newspapers had not been around to write his story in the early days of his ministry, when he was struggling even for food:

> Nobody then said anything about offerings and trucks and tents. The newspapers didn't say then, "They're making so much money there ought to be a law to prevent it." They had better shut their mouths now, too. God will bring everyone of them before the judgment bar to give an account of every word they have said. Our motives are just the same today.[12]

There was no indication that any newspaper took the evangelist's advice or even heard it. But one government bureau, the Internal Revenue Service, did take notice of the revivalist. Having noted deficiencies of some $74,000 in his organization's income taxes for the tax year ending in 1958 and of more than

$247,000 for 1959, the IRS questioned whether A. A. Allen Revivals, Inc., was exempt under section 501 (c) (3) of the tax code, as a corporation "organized and operated exclusively for religious and educational purposes with no part of its net earnings inuring to the benefit of any private shareholder or individual."

This was a serious financial threat, and A. A. Allen reacted to the ruling by filing a lawsuit against the IRS. In the Federal Tax Court in Fort Worth, Texas, the IRS contended that Allen's religious and educational activities were merely incidental to his "miraculous healings" and commercial operations such as the production and sale of his magazine, books, pamphlets, Bibles, music records, tape recordings and pictures. And, most important, for it struck at the heart of the professional faith-healing business, the IRS submitted that "miraculous healing" did not represent a religious function and that the money derived from it should be as taxable as the income received from healing by doctors, dentists, osteopaths and chiropractors.

The case received very little publicity, and few outside the ranks of radio preachers, religious broadcasters and independent faith healers followed its progress. Most of those critical of the healers who used the air waves observed that, whatever its outcome, it would be a landmark decision from the standpoint of the health and longevity of thousands, perhaps millions, of Americans.

On October 11, 1963, the court found in favor of the petitioner, A. A. Allen Revivals, Inc., declaring in somewhat stilted language that divine healing was a basic tenet of a number of religious organizations. The court based its finding on several prior decisions, including a tax-exemption petition won by the occultist Saint Germain Foundation.

His critics could view the outcome of the tax case however they pleased; to Brother Allen it was a triumph, and he quickly raised its status to that of a miracle. In his November 1963 letter to his followers, he revealed that God had miraculously taken care of a number of his problems. Faced with what he called "a million dollars worth of trouble," he had solved his problems by making a one-hundred-dollar pledge to God. When his followers made a pledge to God, the actual routing of the money was simple enough: it was mailed to the Allen organization. Just how Brother Allen paid his one hundred dollars to God was not explained. His followers were invited to make a pledge just as he had, because God was challenging them. They could give gifts or make pledges to Allen and then write what they wanted from God on the little pink "Prayer-Promise-Partnership" forms he had thoughtfully provided.

In addition to the income tax problem, the evangelist mentioned he had been sued on a charge of libel. He assured his followers that God had solved that problem without even making it necessary to go to court.

For some time Allen seemed inclined to adopt some of the arguments of the "anti-Communist ministries" which had built strong radio followings with their blend of fundamentalism and extreme right-wing political doctrines. It is understandable that such doctrines would appear more palatable than his demon theories to some people and would be useful in explaining opposition to his ministry, but it was undoubtedly a tactical mistake to move so far from his successful strategy of many years. The right-wing doctrines were ordinarily employed by middle-class fundamentalist groups who were, for the most part, decidedly opposed to not only the A. A. Allen ministry, but to all forms of faith healing. Also, the various conspiracy theories required to propagate such doctrines were often extremely complicated, requiring a considerable degree of political sophistication and education on the part of those who wielded them. Unfortunately, Allen and his organization had never displayed this level of political astuteness, to say nothing of his rank-and-file followers. He was aware of the average American's fear of Communism and had not hesitated to indict it as a terrible enemy of the church. But for many years he had not found a need to distribute political extremist literature.

Thus, it is somewhat understandable that when he began to quote from extremist publications, he chose perhaps the worst possible source material available. He had found a booklet distributed by a race-agitating, anti-Semitic organization located in Denver, Colorado. The organization claimed its document was adapted from a dangerous Russian textbook on "psycho-politics," a blueprint for the destruction of America. Perhaps because it mentioned faith healers, Allen liked the document so much that he quoted from it in a number of issues of his magazine and stocked it for sale at one dollar a copy. His ministry had always opened its doors to all people, especially blacks. That he would now sanction such a booklet can only be explained on the grounds of gross ignorance. There is no evidence that he ever was aware that the booklet had been exposed from the floor of the United States Senate as a complete hoax.

In the March 1958 issue of *Miracle Magazine* the topic of the Communist danger to America appeared in connection with a group known as the Freethinkers of America. Allen's magazine noted that ". . . The methods being used by the 'Free Thinkers' of America coincide perfectly with the methods taught by the Psychopolitics teaching of the Communists . . . What is the connection between Communism and the 'Free Thinkers' of America?"

Whether he received answers to that question from his followers is not a matter of record, but it is known that on June 25, 1958, while his tent was at Broad and Patterson Streets in Philadelphia, he was served with a set of papers that had a great deal to do with it. It was a complaint in trespass, which the Freethinkers of America explained in the headline of the August 1958 issue of their magazine, the *Age of Reason*: "Freethinkers of America File $500,000.00 Libel Suit Against Fake Healer A. A. Allen." [13] As mentioned previously, Brother Allen made a pledge and was later able to settle the case out of court.

Perhaps because of the libel case he soon returned to demons and miracles, resorting to conspiratorial or Communist theories only in extreme circumstances, and then only in guarded phrasing, usually without publishing the names of persons or organizations. By 1965 his revival organization was so strong that Allen placed an increased emphasis on his worldwide evangelism. His radio program, "The Allen Revival Hour," covered the nation and was heard in several foreign countries. It was broadcast to the 7,000 islands of the Philippines, where he had opened a branch office and a Bible school. In England no radio station would accept his programs, but they were broadcast over Radio

City London, a "pirate" station that avoided government control. He had ministers in Mexico, Africa and South America. In Miracle Valley his Bible school was progressing nicely, and an independent development corporation sold homes to followers who wanted to live near him in his valley of the sun. Taking advantage of the climate of fear generated by the Cuban missile controversy between the superpowers, the evangelist advertised that "the experts declare that in case of a nuclear blast, this part of Arizona has the lowest atomic fallout in the world! Here is a safe place for YOU!"

Through his *Miracle Magazine* he pounded away at readers all across the country with an ever-changing variety of Biblical passages. From the book of Isaiah he extracted "Command ye me," and his readers were encouraged to send a contribution and command what they wanted from God. Later he found a companion passage, "decree a thing," from Job 22:28. Using these commands, one could pretty well ask for anything. Of course, as he explained in his February 1964 issue of *Miracle Magazine*,

> . . . if you want to receive a hundredfold in lands and goods and possessions here, there comes a time when God asks you to put everything on the altar and be willing to forsake all. Not only pay your tithes, and not only put in an offering, or make a pledge of ten dollars, or put a five-dollar bill in an envelope and mail it to the Allen Revival Hour, but make a hundred-dollar pledge. . . .[14]

The Surgeon General's report in 1964 condemned cigarettes and tobacco as a health hazard, and the evangelist promptly started an American Rescue Operation against tobacco, alcohol and drugs. He was years ahead of most organizations that would later sound an alarm over the scandal of drug abuse. And despite the fact that he integrated the rescue mission with his regular financial plans, this operation, which he continued for a number of years, unquestionably did much good. Oddly enough, he seemed at times to accept scientific explanations for some diseases, even though he continued to insist in his literature that sickness was a result of demon possession.

In 1964 he clarified his position on taking offerings from the

poor he ministered to overseas and in Latin America. Some
pastors had remonstrated with him about making the very poor
pay. But Allen insisted it was Scriptural: "You don't get too poor
for God to tell you to bring to Him and to give!" What about
those who were totally destitute—would they be able to receive
his ministry without paying? No. Not even those in a condition
of absolute want were exempt: "If you have nothing to give,
you're still not too poor to have God's blessing like Jacob. If
you have nothing to offer the Lord, you're broke, have no job,
and if you are in trouble, you can still promise God something
in the future, and God's blessing will come upon you." [15]

Brother Allen had always promised prosperity as one of the
fruits of generous giving. Later he upgraded that exchange and
promised the giver real wealth. From the Old Testament Book
of Job, he quoted, "Thou shalt have plenty of silver," to his
followers, many of whom were from the lowest income groups.
What was the secret of this power to get wealth? He explained
that the Lord had directed him to Acts 19:11-12, where it was
made clear that it was Scriptural to send a blest handkerchief to
drive out the demons of poverty from his followers' lives. Also,
in some cases, poverty was a disease caused by demons. To
exorcise this demon, it was necessary for those who were already
prospering to send an offering of one hundred dollars over and
above the regular ten percent tithe. Those who had no money
could make a pledge.

The evangelist found a way to supplement this miracle program by using his old white-top revival tent, which was due to
be replaced. On July 5, 1964, he heard from Heaven concerning what he should do with the old tent. God said, "Don't you
know that this tent is saturated and impregnated with My
Power? I want you to cut these strips of canvas into little prayer
rugs and send them to your friends who are your partners in
this ministry." That made a lot of sense to Allen; after all, night
after night for the past five years the power of God had come
down upon the thousands who were saved, healed and delivered
in the tent. Coming down from Heaven, the power had to pass
right through the canvas of the tent. For a pledge of one hundred
dollars a "Power Packed Prayer Rug" from the old tent would

be sent by return mail. Smaller pieces, suitable for carrying in a billfold, were called "Prosperity Blessing Cloths" and could be substituted for a regular healing cloth.[16]

Allen had also begun a great "Miracle Restoration Revival" that would continue for years, and he was urgently requesting everyone to make a one-hundred-dollar pledge to get the special revival underway. Building was continuing at Miracle Valley, and he was pleased to announce that a Pool of Bethesda had been opened for the hundreds who were coming to bathe and be healed. Water from his Pool of Bethesda would also be sent to anyone in the world: "People are being healed instantly while they sip it as an act of faith." Vials of dirt from Miracle Valley were also sent around the world. It was not clear how the dirt could be used, but one follower reported sprinkling it in his shoes to relieve the ache in his feet. A Dial-a-Miracle service was set up to permit those with burdens or emergencies to telephone for a prayer at any hour of the day or night. Telegrams could also be sent to Miracle Valley or to Allen himself, if the supplicant knew what city he was compaigning in.

In every way, the evangelist appeared to press for ever more sensational miracles. In late 1965, in the midst of one of his many sermons which denounced denominational churches, Allen demonstrated that he was still the master of the unusual. Shouting, "I believe there's more of God in my shirt tail to heal the sick than there is in some whole denominations that bitterly fight, oppose, make fun of and ridicule and brand God's Miracle Revival as 'fanaticism!' I've just torn a piece off my shirt tail. Ushers, bring me that woman on that wheelchair."

A large black woman was wheeled up his healing ramp. Brother Allen explained that the woman had been struck by a speeding car and that the fractured bones in her legs had never healed. She also suffered from spinal injuries and had no control over her kidneys. "You know what I am going to do tonight?" Allen asked his congregation.

I'm going to put a piece of my shirt tail on this woman's legs, and I'm going to ask God to make her every whit whole for the glory of God! . . . I believe my shirt tail has more of the power of God in it than some of these long black robes and collars backwards. And I believe that it's got more of the power of God in it than these silver chains hanging around necks, with images and crosses on them! . . . Now, God, I'm putting a piece of my shirt, Lord, on each horrible scar . . . Don't fail me, Jesus! . . . She's getting up! Start walking, in the name of Jesus! Here she comes! Come on! There she goes down the ramp! This is the woman doctors said would never walk again! [17]

In April 1965 an article in his magazine strongly hinted that he was about to introduce a radically new program. Having quoted at length from an issue of *Look* magazine on the success of American doctors in resuscitating patients who were "clinically" dead for a few minutes, Allen declared it would be a shame if raising the dead had to be introduced to the church by earthly, worldly men, instead of preachers: "Are we going to leave it up to medical doctors to preach us the gospel?" He disclosed he had recently had a vision that touched on the very subject, and the same God who said, "Heal the sick, cleanse the leper and cast out demons," had also said "raise the dead!"

It was almost a year before he seriously inaugurated a "raising the dead" program, and he may have been encouraged to get the campaign underway because of still another magazine article, entitled "How the Russians Bring Their Dead Back to Life." Whatever the reason, he dramatically announced in March 1966 that two children at his Miracle Valley headquarters had been miraculously returned from the dead. The following month he continued to comment at length on what appeared to be a sensational new outreach of his ministry.

But a few weeks later he was calling a halt to the program. In a cautiously-worded statement, he notified his people that ". . . in the past, testimonies of the dead being raised have been published. Perhaps in the future, *Miracle Magazine* will publish other testimonies of the dead being raised to life through prayer, when there are sound, reliable witnesses." He urged them to research the subject in the Bible. There were, he counseled, several conclusions to be drawn. First, most of the dead who were raised in biblical times were restored a very short time after death. Only one man had been raised as long as four days after his death.

Finally, Jesus never meant for His ministers to raise all the dead. That would happen at the Second Coming. Meanwhile, every man had an appointment with death.

Why had he suddenly drawn back from this latest and most sensational type of miracle? Apparently the problem stemmed from the laws, which in most states, prohibited holding the dead beyond a reasonable period of time. There were also laws which prevented individuals from moving the dead, he cautioned. His organization would not knowingly encourage any person to do anything that was unlawful or unscriptural. And perhaps to insure that his people would not ship bodies to Miracle Valley, he pointed out that even in those instances in the Bible when people were raised from the dead, the minister was either present or went to the scene of death. "In no case was the dead body transported to another place for prayer. It is against the law!" [18]

It had become a regular practice each winter for Allen and his revival teammates to travel overseas. He recruited thousands of converts from among the poor of the Philippines and the Caribbean. And his radio programs reached into the United Kingdom and part of northern Europe. The volume of mail from England showed a good response to his broadcasts, although there had been such a spate of articles on the decline of church-going in that country that he decided the English had become pagan. In 1965 he mounted a revival sweep of Britain and Wales and part of the Continent making a first stop in Cardiff, Wales, where a great number of people came to the revival, even a number of Pentecostal preachers. But over-all, he found the people religiously cold, "bound in religious rituals and tradition."

He moved on to Finland, where a group of Full-Gospel pastors borrowed $4,000 to rent the Messuhall, Helsinki's huge "Fair Hall," the scene of many great national exhibitions and Finnish folk dances. On opening night in Helsinki, he noticed that most of the people assembling were women, and everyone seemed burdened and sad. These people needed to hear the gospel! He read his text: "Ye are cursed with a curse: for ye have robbed me, even the whole nation . . . In tithes and offerings." God, Allen concluded, could never bless and revive a people whom He had cursed, because they were thieves and robbers in His sight. These

Finns "could never get healed or even blessed in their condition."
They needed to give God some money.

The evangelist was shocked at the negative response to his
offer. The Finns had a state church supported through their taxes.
He may have felt a greater shock the next morning when a
newspaper headline read, "A. A. ALLEN CHARGES PEOPLE
THREE HUNDRED MARKS TO GO TO HEAVEN." Another
screamed, "PAY ALLEN THREE HUNDRED MARKS OR GO
TO HELL." "Outrageous lies," Allen fumed. "It was a cleverly
printed lie of Satan to stir up stingy, covetous, grasping people."

No doubt, the evangelist reasoned, the "skeptics, unbelievers
and dead church members" in Finland were easily convinced
that newspaper reports were true. Many might be damned because they believed the evil reports. Finally, he decided the
articles had been written by one of the Pentecostal "big-boys" in
Helsinki. The news items warned that since the sponsors of the
revival had departed from the respectable Pentecostal denominations, they were "breaking laws and committing a criminal act
in taking an offering from the people in a public auditorium."
Until the matter could be settled in court, the pastors were to
observe the "no offering" law, and if they did not, all the preachers and ushers "would be arrested on the spot as criminals."

The Finns may have a reputation as great fighters, but were
they aware of the resourceful opponent they were facing? Allen
turned the congregation over to the local pastors, who ordered
their people out of the public hall. Three abreast they marched
through the streets of Helsinki, accompanied by a police escort,
to Pentecostal Zion Church. Cars stopped and people stared in
amazement as the "religious freedom march" sang all the way to
their church, where Allen and the Pentecostal pastors took up an
offering.[19]

If the Allen evangelistic team was shocked by the response to
their fund-raising methods in Finland, it was but a harbinger of
what awaited them in England. They knew something of the
opposition of the British to American evangelists and hardly expected to be greeted with open arms. On the other hand, they
could not have foreseen that their campaign would precipitate
demonstration, riot and sensational headlines.

They held revivals in Southampton and Stockport without a great deal of publicity, but word of Allen's activities was spreading. In mid-June he opened in Birmingham, and the Birmingham *Planet* greeted his revival with a news item that insured his stay would not go unnoticed. Under a banner headline of "THE 'MIRACLE MAN' FROM ARIZONA," the *Planet* trumpeted:

> Evangelism 1965. An old and blind Jamaican woman is led up the Town Hall steps by her two tiny grandchildren. She prays that a miracle will restore her sight . . . Evangelism 1965. A 60-year-old cripple throws away her sticks and trots around . . . This is evangelism 1965 being played out three times a day in the centre of Birmingham until June 20 when A. A. Allen Revivals, from Miracle Valley, Arizona, depart for pastures new. But like most evangelistic crews they are surrounded by a thin group of faithful adorers and move in a welter of public doubt, mistrust and disbelief. They are a globe-trotting band—and have got to have globe-trotting funds . . . And the faithful few who are following Brother A. A. Allen . . . are keen to give what they cannot really afford under the exhortations of the ministers. Or can they afford it? Are they really hired by the group to stimulate proceedings? [20]

It was the old charge of shills. In Britain the critics were generally quicker to object to Allen than were their counterparts in the United States; although in both cases the objections were essentially the same. While many of his critics apparently did not believe in any type of faith-healing, they were largely unconcerned that it was practiced. There was no religious bigotry on their part, but a belief that those who could least afford it were being bilked of their money, money which all too often came indirectly from the critics' own pockets in the form of welfare payments. There was also a humanitarian concern that many who sought out the healers might grown more gravely ill or even die because they were delayed or diverted in seeking help from legitimate medical services.

The Allen theory that adverse publicity insured a good crowd at his revivals seemed to hold in Birmingham. But part of his first congregations consisted of young people and students from Birmingham University who violently objected to Allen's taking any money out of their city. Outside the Town Hall pickets marched with signs reading "ALLEN WE DON'T WANT YOU." "UNIBRUM [Birmingham University] SAYS ALLEN OUT," and "OUR ONLY QUARREL IS WITH ALLEN AND HIS METH-ODS."

The following night Allen was ready for the demonstrators. The Town Hall balcony, the students' favorite heckling spot, was closed. Outside, a large contingent of police barred anyone from entering except those who had tickets issued by the revival team. A police van stood at the ready, and a police inspector directed his men to keep a pathway open to admit worshipers to the hall. They turned some 200 students away, even though the protesters insisted they only wanted to discuss the issue with Allen. Finally the police banned the demonstration, after the students reported that one of their number had been assaulted by an evangelist. The services then proceeded without interruption, and those outside could hear the jangle of the tambourines and the shouts of hallelujah. No one attempted to halt the associate evangelist who addressed the congregation as he prepared to take up an offering:

> One thing the devil does not like is for us to give of our offerings to God. That's what we are going to do just now . . . Tonight we are going to pay the rent on this auditorium. Isn't that fair? I read in the paper this afternoon that some of the students accused Brother Allen of running a confidence game. You wouldn't support this, if you thought Brother Allen was one great big crook, would you? [21]

The revival continued in Birmingham's Town Hall, swollen with large numbers of West Indians from the Midlands area. On the final night of the Birmingham rally, pandemonium broke out again in the midst of the congregation. Allen stopped the service and called the police. The audience of some 1,200 people were asked to leave the building and be readmitted by showing their tickets. About 80 students and other young people who had entered without tickets refused to leave their seats and were forcibly removed by the police and Allen's men. A student explained to a *Sunday Mercury* reporter that "it was never the intention of the students to cause trouble." They were only mounting a silent protest, he insisted, against someone attempting by dubious means to take money from the naive and the sick.

Asa Allen wanted very much to include London in his revival itinerary; however, all his efforts to secure a large hall proved futile. But his English supporters, in particular the Reverend Peter Hawker of Feltham, Middlesex, kept up their efforts and were successful at last in leasing Wimbledon Town Hall. It was a miracle! Allen celebrated with a touristlike burst of rhetoric: "LONDON, capital city of a worldwide empire! The city of Her Majesty Queen Elizabeth, of famous Big Ben and the ancient London Bridge has discovered with amazement that revival news has spread along its narrow streets, across the Thames, and into the suburbs and countryside."

More than 500 people attended the opening service of the evangelist's six-day Wimbledon campaign. The reporter for the Wimbledon *News* was particularly impressed by those who were "slain of the Lord"; he apparently had never heard of the people who fainted as the evangelist walked along slapping them on the forehead. He headlined his column, "Fainting, Hysteria at Town Hall," and wrote that

> Women fainted and went wildly hysterical at the Town Hall, Wimbledon, on Tuesday. Men writhed, shuddered and shouted. All rejoiced. . . . The congregation queued up to be touched on the forehead by the "man of God" from Miracle Valley, Arizona . . . A number of people collapsed as they shuffled through the gauntlet of his ministers. They were hauled up and passed on.

The Wimbledon campaign had hardly started when some 40 of the Birmingham students appeared. Denied entrance, they immediately began a sitdown protest outside, where they were joined by the Vicar of Wimbledon, the Reverend Clifford Smith, who sympathized with the students but urged them not to cause further trouble. Asked to comment on the revival, the vicar observed that the publicity material supplied by Allen's revival showed there was no evidence that the message Allen preached had anything to do with the Christian gospel as understood by the Christian Church. Other published comments were even less hospitable: "His message seems a throwback to 1,000 B.C. Faith in God is automatically rewarded by deliverance from present troubles and by future prosperity. The rich are blessed. The sick and the poor are afflicted by demons which Mr. Allen offers to cast out."

By June 27, 1965, the newspapers had made Allen's name well known, and the reporters, often barred from the services, were becoming increasingly hostile. The independent *Sun* headlined Allen as "Preacher With the 'Rich' Gift." The Sunday *Citizen* used double headlines to ask DO WE WANT THIS MAN HERE? DO WE WANT THIS YELPING WONDER? The *Citizen* of June 27 called Allen "the man from Miracle Valley who "jumps, shouts and jiggles," and asked, "Does anyone in Britain really want the presence of a well-dressed, tubby, ranting, miracle-claiming American evangelist named Andrew [*sic*] A. Allen? His services resound with yelps, leaps, exhortations and tambourine slaps." Noting that Allen had left his "motel-equipped pasture of Miracle Valley" to bring his "three shows daily" to Britain, the paper quoted the Chairman of the Council of Churches, the Vicar of Wimbledon: "We denounce what Mr. Allen is doing. We deprecate this sort of meeting. I informed the police that these meetings were taking place. He induces an atmosphere of mass hysteria, using his powers of rhetoric." Also quoted was the Reverend Robert Hughes, chaplain at Birmingham University: "He used unpleasant techniques to get the crowd worked up, so that 300 people were eventually surging round the platform waiting for him to decree a miracle."

The reporters also noticed how difficult it was to obtain a direct quotation from Allen, who chose to answer their questions with such remarks as, "I never talk to strangers." Piqued, they began to describe him and his clothes in lurid phrases: He was a gum-chewer; he whistled; he wore checked trousers; he was tubby. Writer Robert Adam, one of the many confused about the evangelist's name, wrote that "Andrew Allen is a small, stockily built American, florid and getting on for being fat. He wears a pink shirt, a blue suit and a black tie. He does not look anything like a preacher—but that is what he says he is." And they were amazed at the ritual in his services. Reporter Michael Brennan wrote:

Five hundred in the hall. Mostly coloured people. Many infirm, many pathetic. Whipped to frenzy by Allen and his team . . . 40 minutes nonstop bellow and tambourine "Clap Your Hands for Jesus" chorus. Three women at least in shuddering trance. Allen jumps, jiggles like a beat group idol, urges audience to shout. Checks his wrist watch frequently.[22]

It was "Riot or Revival," Allen declared after leaving England. In his report to his supporters he compared his troubles in England with the difficulties experienced by Jesus and the apostles. Nowhere was there such coldness, such narrowness of tradition, such hatred for his message. His fury was unchecked when he spoke of the British reporters; one, he wrote, "was so drunk, he had to be literally taken out of the Birmingham meeting." He recalled that the British Broadcasting System would not accept his radio or television programs, but when his meetings were picketed, God used the demonstration to give him publicity on the BBC in the form of news. Riot, Allen said, was a sure sign of Scriptural revival, and in England Miracle Revival brought riot from the devil.

His photographer filmed the demonstrators in action both inside the meeting hall and on the street. Strange figures similar to fingerprints were visible on the pictures. He published a number of these pictures in his August 1965 *Miracle Magazine*, asking his people to notice the peculiar figures on the film. Some appeared closer to the camera than others; some were dark, others white. Were they photos of demon spirits? "Was this demon possession on parade?" Allen complained that even though he had always used Scripture as a basis for his sermons, his critics still accused him of using "psychology and Hitleristic" methods to swindle money. If he were to be inspired like Elijah and were to ask a widow for her last piece of bread, he was sure the public would be "informed of the new hoax that is swindling widows out of their last three-pence."

In a short time he seemed to have forgotten about England, and in a return to his optimistic reports, he announced wonderful progress on almost every evangelistic front. By 1967 his Philippines campaigns were so successful that he asked his sup-

porters for a helicopter. It was the only way he could reach the
unevangelized in remote islands before the Communist Huks
did. It could be useful in the States also, and there were facilities
for it at his Miracle Valley airport, where he kept a private
plane. His telegram and dial-a-prayer program was a resounding
success. Very often these calls for prayers were emergencies, in
which people asked for help from his Miracle Valley Prayer
Band before calling for medical aid, an ambulance or even relatives and friends, and that was the way the evangelist wanted
it—give God the first place! His miracles continued apace, and
he reported the healing of many types of diseases. Some extraordinary cases highlighted almost every campaign. On the Philippine island of Mindanao his prayer even lengthened a young polio
victim's leg three inches in view of thousands.   ,

Mark Twain once said that sorrow can take care of itself, but
good news must be shared. Evangelist Allen had shared so much
of his good news that it seemed doubly cruel to his followers
that he should be compelled once more to share a portion of his
sorrow with the public. It was the ubiquitous newspaper reporters again, this time in Cleveland, Ohio, where the revival team
was enjoying a rousing response from large congregations. Into
an atmosphere of religious joy stepped Joseph Eszterhas, a reporter for the Cleveland *Plain Dealer*. He asked a lot of questions, poked around a great deal, purchased some literature and
deposited a quarter in the collection bucket "for the show."

The *Plain Dealer* published his story on June 16, 1967, under
a headline of "SPIRITUAL BLAST RATTLES ARENA AS
GREAT 'HEALER' PLIES HIS TRADE." Eszterhas saw the revival as a "honky-tonk kind of spiritual blast," since there was
an amplifier, a screeching electric organ and a boom mike. Also
the star of the show was thumping hard on a tambourine.

> His audience was in blissful red-faced frenzy. A young girl was moan-
> ing and throwing herself from her chair. On stage, torsos were twist-
> ing and some members of the group were gyrating their hips and
> moving their feet to the beat.

The revival reminded Eszterhas of a performance he had witnessed a year earlier in the same arena, a wild musical extrav-

aganza by the Rolling Stones which caused young girls to moan and throw themselves from their chairs. Brother Asa Alonzo Allen, whom he described as a "56-year-old revivalist, beating his tambourine and moving his short body to 'Save for Sweet Jesus'," was unlike the Rolling Stones in one vital respect. He presumed to raise the cancerous half-dead to life, to make the crippled walk, to perform all manner of miracles. The Rolling Stones would never think of claiming such power.

Allen is a nervous man. He is a combination of George Wallace and James Cagney. He rants, raves, bellows, screams—but never speaks. He runs back and forth before his altar. His secretary introduces him as 'a man who walks in the shadow of God.'

Eszterhas listened to a warm-up speaker prepare the crowd for the healing service. The preacher jumped up and down and screamed, "Can God? CAN GOD? Yes, I say God can! GOD CAN!!" The congregation prepared, Allen advanced to heal a critically ill young boy who he claimed had been rushed there from a hospital and would be rushed back if "Jesus does not have mercy." When Allen struck with his healing touch, the boy leaped from his stretcher and ran out of the service. The reporter hurried after him for an interview. He found the boy with his mother, who told Eszterhas the boy's name was Jimmy Adkins and that he had been in the Lutheran Hospital. Before he could ask more questions, an Allen helper rushed mother and son into a rest room. The reporter also attempted to enter the emergency section behind the altar to speak to a man freshly healed of emphysema, but one of the ushers ordered the "reporter sinner" out and followed him through the parking lot to make sure he left.

Eszterhas decided to check further on Allen's patients and on the healer himself. He began with the Lutheran Hospital, where authorities told him there had never been a patient named Jimmy Adkins in their hospital.

Eszterhas raised once more the old charge of "shill game," and worse, his research unleashed an unprecedented explosion over the head of evangelist A. A. Allen, for his article not only included an account of Allen's drunken-driving fine in Knoxville,

Tennessee, but it also revealed that the evangelist had been convicted of drunkenness charges in Laguna Beach, California, and in Las Vegas, Nevada.

The Arizona healer denounced the *Plain Dealer* writer for an "extremely critical, prejudiced attitude" and for "defaming statements," but he seemed even more incensed at the *National Informer*, a Kansas City, Kansas, religious paper published by a Pentecostal church, the Church of God in Christ. The *Informer* published a column entitled "A. A. Allen Revival in Cleveland Exposed," giving a summary of the Allen article published in the *Plain Dealer*. No mention was made of Allen's convictions for drunkenness, but the article ended in a note of veiled piety that hinted at terrible scandals:

> . . . Other things were related in print that we dare not print . . . because charity rejoices not in anything that is not right. We regret to hear of anything derogatory about any minister, the ministry has too much now to live down.

Allen had been warring with various Pentecostal churches since the day his name was dropped from the rolls of the Assemblies of God organization. He had rebuked them in his magazine and sermons, and denounced them in more than one of his books: He called the Pentecostal leaders "blind leaders of the blind" in his *Prisons with Stained Glass Windows*; he referred to their ritual as "Godless religion in the Christless church" in his booklet *Bargain Counter Religion*. If anything could upset him more than hostile reporters, it was a Pentecostal leader who criticized his ministry. He told his followers that

> Some preachers have been so anxious to try to destroy another man's ministry, I have seen them eagerly join hands with drunken, lying, atheistic, newspaper reporters. I have known some who went so far as to furnish false reports and information to the news media that were lies to be reported in the papers. . . .[23]

Reporters were generally dismissed as drunken atheists; preachers were another matter. He finally decided the principal reason for their opposition was rooted in their envy of his success, of his money. He revealed that a highly placed friend of his ministry told him: "Brother Allen, I believe all your opposition across the country from preachers can be summed up in one word, 'Money!' I hear them say again and again, 'Allen is getting rich.'" He no longer attempted to deny that great volumes of money flowed into his Miracle Valley headquarters, although he sometimes protested that few of his critics realized how many bills his organization paid each month. As his wealth increased through the years, his philosophy slowly changed from a young minister's belief that affluence corrupts to a rock-hard defense of wealth. "It isn't a sin to have money," he preached. "The blessing of the Lord maketh rich and addeth no sorrow with it," he quoted. Why, the Bible was just full of examples of men God blessed with riches. God said to Solomon: "I will give thee riches and wealth." He gave Job twice as much as he had before his affliction. What about Abraham, Isaac, Jacob, David, Joseph of Arimathea? They each were rich as a gift of God!

As far as Allen was concerned, the preachers who indulged in "evil surmising" about his money were condemned by God's word. They were always quoting Scripture out of context to prove that the rich would not get to Heaven, especially the passage in the tenth chapter of Mark about how it is easier for a camel to go through the eye of a needle than for a rich man to enter into the kingdom of God. Preachers just didn't understand that passage. Rich men don't go to hell because they have money. It's because they don't put their trust in God! He had no sympathy for the jealous preachers who were talking about him. They had "garbage-can" ears and were anxious to have everyone dump trashy reports about A. A. Allen into them. Apparently forgetting the many times he had begged for donations, he ridiculed those "desperate radio preachers" who could be heard pleading for funds to stay on the air. They weren't preaching the full Gospel or God would give them money. He didn't believe anyone should support them.

As for the critics who endlessly talked about his property at Miracle Valley—his office buildings, the school buildings, the dormitories, the cathedral with a Plexiglas dome, the farm, the cattle, the cafeteria, the machinery and television and radio equipment, the printing presses, the record manufacturing plant,

the airport, the plane and helicopter, even his own post office—
they should know that it all belonged to the corporation, which
was operated in strict compliance with the Internal Revenue
Service regulations for tax-exempt religious organizations. "I have
nothing to hide! . . . Why should I attempt to keep the blessings
of God a secret? . . ." [24]

His critics were far from assuaged, noting that the Internal
Revenue Service was unable to rigidly monitor his income or that
of any other similarly structured religious organization. "Love
offerings," or direct gifts, of any amount can be kept by any
preacher whose ministry is approved as a tax-exempt religious
organization by the IRS. Money to pay salaries and other types
of expenses may also be approved as necessary to an organization's activities. Allen claimed even the house he lived in was
not his own; it was provided by the corporation. But his critics
wondered why it should be a 12-sided mansion of cut stone and
wood, with an expensive swimming pool covered by a simulated
stained-glass canopy. [25]

Regardless of the degree of affluence his ministry enjoyed, it
could hardly afford to stand still. There were always expenses, and
the volume of incoming funds had to be maintained, if not increased, in the face of competition for the fickle faith-healing and
prosperity dollar. Great changes were taking place. There were
fewer big tent revivals. Many independent ministries were using
halls and auditoriums, and all successful ones were using radio as
much as the Allen ministry did. New gimmicks cropped up on
all sides, religious fund-raising innovations that were beginning
to make some of the standard Allen techniques appear conservative.

Since the end of World War II many of the independent radio
ministries, especially those which emphasized faith healing, had
relied heavily on blacks in their congregations, and preachers designed their ministries to fit a "salt-and-pepper" constituency. As
the revival fires dimmed toward the close of the fifties, most independent faith healers were ministering to congregations that
were overwhelmingly black. Some of the lesser-known white faith
healers began tailoring their revivals exclusively for Negroes and
scheduled revivals in the hearts of large city ghettos.

While A. A. Allen always counted on an element of white support, in many of his revival campaigns in the late sixties the blacks sometimes filled all but a very few of the seats in his tent. And Allen kept in step with most of the changes; he added a black singer to his team and encouraged blacks to attend his Bible school and become ministers. He tilted his prosperity sermons toward the blacks and instituted a system of vows or pledges as the most practical means of obtaining sizable donations from a large mass of low-income followers. Vow and give to get God's blessings of health and prosperity. Make a pledge and keep it! This was Allen's message to the blacks. Critics noted that the more his empire expanded, the harder his financial whip lashed the backs of his followers. His need for money apparently could not be satisfied. Vow and pay and still greater blessings will be yours! You can even decree your own miracle! But first you must give your money to God. By 1968 the Arizona evangelist had refined his peculiar money doctrine into a perverted form of hyper-Calvinism which taught that wealth was a sign of God's blessing. He could not abide followers who remained poor, for that was certain evidence they were out of God's will. "As far as I'm concerned, those who die in poverty, die in shame," he preached. In the thirteenth chapter of the Book of Proverbs he found a passage to gird his philosophy: "Poverty and shame shall come to him that refuseth instruction." To those who posed the question, "What instruction?" Allen's answer was unequivocal:

. . . God has set me aside to give His children instruction. Everyone of you will have to confess that the instruction that I give is Biblical and Scriptural. You see, Friends, I'm free! I'm not bound! I'm free to preach the whole Word of God! I haven't got any deacon board to tell me that I can't preach it, and to tell me that I'm preaching too much about money.[26]

To those who refused to respond properly to his call for tithes and special pledges, he applied object lessons derived from the experiences of those who withheld their money. One of his favorite examples involved a couple who attended a camp meeting in Arizona. God spoke to the wife to give a hundred dollars. Her husband insisted that if it really was God talking, he could tell them tomorrow. Day by day they procrastinated until the camp meeting was over. As they were driving back to Los Angeles, their camper turned over and burned. Locked inside the camper was all their money, some $800. While they watched it burn, God spoke to both of them: "There is a sore evil which I have seen under the sun, namely, riches kept for the owners thereof to their hurt."

If Allen prodded the blacks to pledge more money, the stormy little religious petrel reciprocated by shaping his services more to their liking. Special music and dancing had slowly become a major feature of his meetings. "God states time after time that He wants enthusiastic, noisy worship!" he exulted. Singing and dancing before the Lord, shouts, praises and hand-clapping were all Scriptural. As the organ boomed and the tambourine jangled, the black congregations caught the spirit by shouting, waving, howling and dancing. A reporter from the Greensboro, North Carolina, *Record* watched a service and described it as an "undulating conga line." More than one reporter commented on the moaning, shrieking women who danced until they collapsed in the dirt. And to those who inquired what dancing had to do with music in the church, Allen answered that "it has to do with the kind of music that will be found in the church that worships according to the Scriptures!"

The new music, often called "miracle music," soon evolved into "prophetic music." It improved attendance, but in the meantime, the new radio ministries featuring "discernment" as a form of mind reading were growing tremendously popular, and Allen hardly knew how to cope with it. Discernment as a test of whether spirits were true or false had long been a legitimate religious doctrine of many Pentecostals, but these new radio preachers were using it along with the "gift of knowledge" to expand their faith-healing ministries. When a cancer victim approached the Allen ministry in hopes of being healed, he normally attended an early morning or afternoon service to obtain a card admitting him to Allen's prayer line during the evening service. If a sick person said he had cancer, Allen healed him of cancer. The cancer may never have been diagnosed by a licensed physician; indeed, a large element of those seeking help from faith healers joined the prayer line with self-diagnosed illnesses. With the new discernment technique, the applicant for healing could have his ailment diagnosed and healed at the same time. Not only would time be saved, but many people who "just felt sick" were also interested in having someone tell them what their trouble was. The spectacle of uneducated preachers diagnosing illnesses on radio programs apparently did not cause so much as a ripple of concern on the part of those who sold them time on the air. These new "doctors" seldom were able to pronounce medical terms, so they generally limited their diagnoses to diseases they could pronounce or couched their "discernments" in general terms, such as, "Lady, you've got female trouble; you've also got bad blood, real bad."

In time the vagueness of the discerner expanded into a net so broad that thousands of potential contributors could be snared with one "discernment." God always spoke to Asa Allen, but as the evangelist was quick to point out, the Lord had always taken the trouble to be specific. When Allen heard one of the new radio preachers say, "Right at this moment, the Lord shows me there are two people listening who have a twenty-dollar bill in their billfolds. God wants you to send it to me right now!", he called that preacher a "phony," because there were probably thousands of people listening who had twenty-dollar bills in their billfolds. This was a perilous situation. These preachers were not playing fair, and he warned his people to detect charlatans who got on the air and said something like

> I discern there is someone listening to me who has an infirmity and desires to be healed. The affliction is an internal disorder. It has you worried and upset, filled with anxiety and distressed. The Lord shows me that you have a large amount of the Lord's tithe still in your possession. God is showing me that if you mail these tithes to me now, you will be healed of your infirmity immediately.[27]

By 1968 A. A. Allen had the largest faith-healing organization in the country. However, there was hardly time for accolades. A burgeoning occult movement was already pressing in from all sides, pulling his people into an endless number of "sin traps" with exotic names like telepathy, spiritism, metaphysics, precognition, fortunetelling, witchcraft and ESP. Allen gave abundant evidence in his sermons and literature that neither he nor his associates possessed anything more than the most rudimentary knowledge of the occult world. He was apparently never able to understand clearly what extrasensory perception was or that telepathy clairvoyance and precognition were merely elements of psychic phenomena within the parapsychological orbit of ESP. Perhaps because he was so woefully unprepared to cope with the occult, he concentrated his fire on witchcraft, the most feared and despised segment of the occult. In the latter part of 1967, while campaigning in the Philippines, the Allen team found themselves almost at the center of a worldwide pilgrimage to the Philippine psychic healer Anthony Agpaoa. While Allen was traveling half-way around the world to take faith healing to the people of the Philippines, Americans and Canadians were flying there in char-tered planes to seek miraculous cures from a Philippine psychic healer. Allen received mail from Agpaoa's followers, and many of the evangelist's people expressed their concern and confusion about the two different types of miracle healing. Allen called the psychic healing counterfeit, lamenting the confusion it had caused his people, who were unaware that another form of miracle heal-ing enjoyed a worldwide following larger than that of their own variety of faith healing. Indeed, his own prosperity doctrines were, unknown to him, borrowed in part from the psychic healers who had refined them from the "New Thought" theories of the "power of positive thinking" cults. The whole occult movement so startled the Arizona preacher that he found himself playing the role of his early critics. He published a booklet called *Is It Religion or Racket?* and perhaps felt rather "orthodox," thanks to an opportunity to label a whole variety of movements "reli-gious rackets." [28]

In the midst of his struggle with the occultists, he found him-self the victim of a dastardly attack by another fundamentalist faith healer. He always spent much of his time and energy en-couraging people to make vows, and after they signed a pledge, he continually pleaded, cajoled and remonstrated to make sure they paid. Now a preacher, using what Allen called "Satan's latest gimmick," was contacting Allen's people and convincing them he had a miracle mandate from God to release them from their vows. Of course, the preacher expected something in the way of a donation for exercising his release power, but it was always far less than the amount of the original pledge. Furthermore he guaranteed that no harm or curse could later be placed on them.

Brother Allen was very upset. He reminded his followers of the promise that Jonah made so God would bring him out of the whale's belly: "I will pay that which I have vowed." Again the peppery little evangelist found himself beating off charlatans with words strangely reminiscent of some hurled in his own direction twenty years earlier:

> One pathetic thing about racketeering preachers is that they prey upon babes in Christ who do not yet have sufficient spiritual maturity and knowledge of the Word to discern what is happening. Also they deceive persons who do not know the Scriptures and cannot discern between a human gimmick and a divine gift.

Miami, Florida, had a reputation for being tough on faith healers, despite the fact that some of the biggest crowds in the country regularly turned out there for tent revivals. And it was in Miami in November 1969 that Allen showed he still had his old quick-tempered fighting spirit. A thousand people poured into the tent on November 1, not a bad crowd considering that the Miami *Herald* included the story of his Knoxville drunken-driving record in their report of his previous night's service.

Allen blessed an old woman and started to pray. Suddenly he grabbed the microphone and, pointing to a man in the congregation, shouted: "Are you the reporter who wrote these lies in this morning's *Herald*?" A thousand heads turned in surprise. When the reporter refused to obey an order to leave the tent, Allen summoned his helpers to throw him out. Explaining that the newspaperman was "demon-possessed," the evangelist scanned the tent for more reporters. His fierce, snapping little eyes spotted a photographer. Three of his assistants demanded the photographer's film and camera. When he refused, they pinned his arms behind his back and threatened him with bodily harm. They wanted his pictures: "We'll take it from you by force. We've done it before." [29]

Early in 1970 Allen's autobiography, called *Born To Lose,*
Bound To Win, was published. It was an interesting, well-written
work, but many important events and people, including his wife
and children, were not mentioned. In 1962, in a suit for divorce
filed by the evangelist, he asked that his wife be enjoined from
filing insanity proceedings against him. His complaint, charging
cruelty, said that Mrs. Lexie Allen had filed such proceedings ,
twice, but both actions were dismissed, according to Allen, upon
judicial determination that he was mentally competent. But if he
neglected his family, he did not forget to devote a chapter to his
critics. Perhaps he saw it as an opportunity to return some of the
criticism which had been poured out against his ministry over
the years. Calling himself "the world's most persecuted preacher,"
he denounced the press and the intellectuals. And it was clear
that after almost 15 years he still felt the sting of the Sacramento
Bee. The "word of Satan working overtime," he called it. After
he had declared that California harbored "an army of religious
bunco men and con artists," he attacked the *Bee,* demanding to
know by what authority its editor presumed to judge what "true
religion" was. Such was the contradictory nature of much of his
caustic and wide-ranging criticism.

Allen was elated by the completion of his life story in early
1970, and he was pleased with some of the newspaper articles
about his ministry. But, according to his associate minister Don
Stewart, he complained that he was very tired during the latter
days of May. He continued to feel worse, and in Mobile, Alabama, he told Stewart that he no longer had the energy he once
had. Rumors of his illness mushroomed into reports of his death.
An Associated Press news story disclosed that his associates were
trying hard to convince his supporters that Allen was very
much alive. He took a short rest and later joined the revival team
in Wheeling, West Virginia. But in the middle of the campaign
he suddenly decided to fly to San Francisco. The Reverend Don
Stewart later wrote in his autobiography that he knew then that
A. A. Allen was dying.[30]

From the Jack Tar Hotel in San Francisco, Allen ordered a
special taped message included in his radio programs when the
rumors of his death continued. The announcement began, "Here

is Brother Allen interrupting this program for an important bulletin."

> This is Brother Allen in person. Numbers of friends of mine have been inquiring about reports they have heard concerning me that are not true. People as well as some preachers from pulpits are announcing that I am dead. Do I sound like a dead man? My friends, I am not even sick. Only a moment ago I made reservations to fly into our current campaign where I'll see you there and make the devil a liar.

On June 11, 1970, Asa Alonzo Allen lay dead while his radio programs continued to carry a message insisting he was alive. He was found in his room in the Jack Tar Hotel. A United Press International report quoted a spokesman at the Miracle Valley headquarters who said, "the cause of death was apparently a heart attack suffered about 8 P.M." [31] An Associated Press release revealed that police went to Allen's room when an associate reported that the evangelist did not respond to telephone calls. The faith healer was found clad in his underwear, slumped at a table. The police found several vials of pills and $2,309 in his billfold.[32]

Even as they reeled under the impact of the sad news, many of his followers continued to receive Allen's letters several days after his death. An Associated Press release of June 19, 1970, reported that "The Reverend Dr. [sic] Allen wrote the letters days before he died, to deny rumors of his death circulated after he entered a hospital for treatment of an arthritic condition."

His critics were interested in knowing whether Allen had sought help from doctors, recalling that he had written in his book *Does God Heal Thru Medicine*, "The gift of healing needs no help from doctors for it is all-powerful to remove a cancer or a tumor." On June 25, 1970, the U.P.I. news service released a story headlined, "Coroner Says Evangelist Died From Alcoholism":

> San Francisco (UPI)—City Coroner Dr. Henry Turkel said Wednesday evangelist A. A. Allen, found dead in a Jack Tar Hotel room June 11, died of "acute alcoholism and fatty infiltration of the liver." . . . Turkel gave his findings after a 12-day investigation. He did not elaborate.

Miracle Valley headquarters apparently made no comment on the coroner's report, but did note that among the devout listeners to his radio program rumors circulated that Brother Allen had risen from the dead. The New York *Times*, a newspaper that still waited for a kind word from Brother Allen, gave his obituary a full column. It was a very sympathetic story and included the information that his organization employed 175 people and that *Miracle Magazine* went regularly to 350,000 homes.[33] Other news stories noted that the volume of literature leaving Miracle Valley totaled more than 55 million pieces a year.

A. A. Allen Miracle Revivals, Inc., continued. The Reverend Don Stewart became the new chief evangelist; the Reverend H. Kent Rogers became the new president of the corporation. But most of Allen's followers agreed that things would never be the same. No one could replace Brother Allen. Gerald W. King, executive director of the organization and Allen's brother-in-law, soon left. Shortly after Allen's death King wrote:

> . . . While some preachers are sitting around lusting for a chance, so to speak, to pick up the pieces, wondering how they can go about it, the man whom God has chosen is already a long way down the road. Brother Don Stewart didn't just happen to be ready. . . .[34]

The revivals would be a bit more youth-oriented with a young evangelist as the preacher. Don Stewart had dropped out of school and had gone through the usual hard times before joining the Allen team. But he came from a family that believed in faith-healing, and his father had once faith-healed a milk goat.[35] Stewart was more inclined to meet the press and strive for a good public image than Asa Allen had been. In early 1971 he accepted the invitation of TV station WJCT in Jacksonville, Florida, to answer questions on a "call-in" show. He made clear what position Miracle Valley headquarters had adopted on Allen's death when a caller asked, "Is it true that A. A. Allen died of acute alcoholism?" "No," he answered.

> I know that there was a report in newspapers. The first report that I received was that it was an apparent heart attack. Then, two weeks

later, they came out with another report. I was not with him at the
time, so I couldn't answer that question other than what I believe.[36]

Was Brother Allen destined to be controversial even in death?
Was his past fated to be that of the repentant woman of whom
the great Ibo poet Pol Ndu wrote . . .

> Take past events as the repentant woman's past,
> Always forgotten and always retold.

So soon, and yet already the rumors harden into legend. A
woman from Tucson thought she saw him in a grain field as she
drove along the Miracle Valley road. His arms were filled with
sheaves. And it was rumored that high up in the shimmering,
snow-capped Huachuca mountains that guard his holy Zion, some
hikers saw him, at twilight, stretching forth his arms. Some saw
a mighty fountain flowing down the hills to Miracle Valley into
the arms of those precious ones who believed his message.

II

Oral Roberts

Yet despite how much every person wants to be accepted by the establishment and leaders of the nation, I have known deep within that this could never be for me. God called me to a ministry to the needy and not to those with plenty. . . .

—Oral Roberts, *The Call*, 1972

Up from Faith-Healing: The Miracle Ministry of Oral Roberts

If there were any indications in the spring of 1946 that a great Pentecostal faith-healing crusade was about to begin, they went unheralded by the reporters and religious observers of the day. Even some of the leading Pentecostal evangelists were surprised by the first reports of a great new healer moving through the land. Only two years earlier, the charismatic Aimee Semple McPherson, the most recent in a long line of famous healers, had been laid to rest in an ornate casket equipped with a live telephone; and some Pentecostals, as well as other believers in miraculous cures, considered it too soon to expect another great healer.

But a sudden resurgence of interest in fundamentalist faith-healing began in early May of that year, after an obscure preacher named William Branham received a command from an angel to take a healing ministry to the people. A few weeks later his message reached as far as St. Louis, and by the middle of summer the impact of his crusade had been felt throughout most of the South. Members of various Pentecostal churches from many parts of the country, together with some fundamentalists from other religious

57

bodies, were soon making pilgrimages to meet the new healer, who scheduled his spectacular campaigns in as many cities as possible.

Among the visitors to Branham's services were Pentecostal evangelists and pastors eager to watch the new man of miracles perform. Some had started their own healing campaigns when they first heard of the widespread public response to the Branham ministry, and they visited the services to learn as much as possible about his methods. Others came mainly to witness the miracles which had stirred so many members of their congregations; but after observing a Branham performance, they hurried home to resign their pastorates and start assembling a faith-healing team. The Reverend O. L. Jaggers attended one of the early Branham services and later established a healing ministry that eventually became an independent church. When Branham arrived in Portland, Oregon, full-gospel minister T. L. Osborn was captivated by the remarkable healing of a little deaf-mute girl. When Branham snapped his fingers and the girl appeared to speak and hear perfectly, Osborn heard voices saying, "You can do that . . . that's what God wants you to do!" [1] He left his church and started an overseas healing ministry. Another Pentecostal minister, the Reverend Gordon Lindsay, visited a Branham campaign in Sacramento, California, and was so impressed that he not only started his own miracle ministry, but also became the official chronicler of the Branham crusades. And so it went all across the country: Branham met preachers who had either learned of his remarkable success and started their own faith-healing ministries, or attended his services to study the Branham technique before striking out on their own. Some of them would become famous and wealthy, while others would return to the relative obscurity of their little congregations.

And one day Branham and his entourage met a Pentecostal preacher whose fame as a faith healer would later become so great that he would virtually dominate the entire world of Pentecostal-style miracle healing and whose international evangelistic association would become so well known that the ministry of William Branham would be all but obscured. Gordon Lindsay wrote of that meeting in one of his best-selling books: "After an interval of time, we converged on Kansas City, Kansas, for a campaign in the city auditorium. Here we meet for our first time Brother Oral Roberts. . . ." [2]

Since the early 1950s, the name of Oral Roberts has been synonymous with faith-healing for millions of people in the United States and countries all around the world. Many became his supporters because of Roberts' far-flung network of radio and television faith-healing programs. In more recent years he has reached out to other millions with his more modern television specials, hour-long programs which skillfully blend religion with musical entertainment provided by many of America's leading motion picture and television performers. More than faith healer and television star, Roberts is known also as educator, banker, college president and Chamber of Commerce director. After more than twenty years in the religious spotlight, it is safe to say that except for Dr. Billy Graham, Oral Roberts is better known to the general public than any other preacher in America.

But Brother Roberts, as he is affectionately or reverently called by many who know him well, has apparently paid a heavy price for his success. In climbing so high in such a relatively short time, he has garnered more than the usual number of critics. *Time* magazine, whose reports on Roberts have generally been objective, has called him "one of the country's most flamboyant and most criticized faith healers." [3] Many of his critics are opposed to faith healing, and they include not only some atheists and agnostics, but millions of deeply religious people. This fact Roberts has not hesitated to confirm: ". . . for years in our crusades local congregations of the Churches of Christ in that city [New York City] would take out full-page ads in the newspapers attacking my ministry and challenging me to a debate. One of their most repeated ploys was usually, 'If Oral Roberts can heal, why doesn't he empty the hospitals?' " [4] Other critics, some of whom may be more than a little envious of Roberts' success, seem to believe that he has had almost unlimited access to millions of dollars from both public and private sources, money with which he has indulged his every whim. Some of the resentments against Roberts are often expressed in the form of questions. How does the son of a poverty-stricken farmer become the head of a giant international evangelistic association? How could a college drop-out become the president of his own university, a $30-million, 500-acre campus in Tulsa, Oklahoma? Why should a provincial faith healer who became a preacher by merely having a prayer said over his head be allowed to escape military service in World War II when he did not have the education to qualify for the Chaplain's Corps? How does a preacher enjoying special tax exemption become a board member of the National Bank Corporation?

These are only a few of the questions asked about Oral Roberts, who admits there have been "plenty of critics." [5] In his latest autobiography, *The Call*, he has published one such critical attack on himself, a newspaper article entitled "How Scripture Shark Makes Holy Hysteria A Lucrative Gimmick." Excerpts from that article provide an indication of the harshness of some of the attacks on Roberts:

> When a shameless shyster known as "Rev. Oral Roberts" takes the stage to perform, one of the comic strip character Marrying Sam's most expensive weddings pales beside his performance . . . The fake cures, the Bible screaming, the exhortations to repent—all are only masks for the cunning mob manipulator who deftly slides in his pitch when he judges the time is right. . . .[6]

But the famous evangelist insists that he knows "better than anyone else how many tens of thousands have been saved and healed and are still being reached through this ministry. I know, too, the integrity of this ministry and the high standard of ethics we have maintained." [7]

Brother Roberts has also reported a variety of other criticisms, including those which picture him as a man of great wealth. To understand why such arguments rage about him, it is helpful to know something of his early career, especially the period during which he left his church to become an independent healer. Behind much of the criticism of Roberts is the belief that he has been more successful in using faith-healing as a means of personal aggrandizement than any other healer since the sick line queued up at the Temple of Asclepius in Greece, some 2,500 years ago.

In 1946, the year that saw the beginning of the great resurgence of interest in Pentecostal faith-healing, Oral Roberts was 28 years old. He served as pastor in a Toccoa, Georgia, Pentecostal Holiness Church for a few months that year before returning to his native state of Oklahoma, where he enrolled in Phillips University, a Disciples of Christ school in the city of Enid. He had evangelized throughout the South for some 11 years, holding revivals and pastoring, but apart from the satisfaction of having saved souls and generated spiritual good will, he had little to show for the years of work. He later wrote that he and his family had barely managed to eke out a living. He seemed almost desperate in his frantic attempt to be somebody, to be a success; and he may have thought for a time that formal education was the answer to his problems. But he soon needed a job, and at the end of the first semester he accepted an offer to pastor a local Pentecostal Holiness church, while continuing to carry a full schedule of college courses.

Brother Roberts soon became discouraged with conditions in Enid. In his earliest pastorate he had been paid ten dollars a week. Now, 12 years later and with a family to support, he was struggling to exist on $55 a week. And he was distressed because he could not draw large crowds. His family was forced to live with one of the church members, and after enduring several months of this arrangement, his wife, Evelyn, threatened to take the two children and go home to her mother. But Oral told his problems to the members of the church board, and they arranged for him to buy a parsonage.[8]

He was still not content. He wanted to undertake a new kind of ministry, but some of his church members opposed the idea. He wrote later, "But though the church I pastored was filled with wonderful people, I sensed that enthusiasm and faith for the kind of ministry I was interested in was at a low ebb."[9] During this time an evangelist conducted meetings at another church in Enid, and Oral attended the services. According to Brother Roberts, the people in his own church were much disturbed by the meth-

ods used by the visiting faith healer, but Roberts claimed that he
"kept an open mind and received benefit."

He was by this time determined to begin his own independent
faith-healing ministry, for he wrote later that "Two men I knew
in Enid came to me and said 'If you are going into this racket,
we want in on it.'" Oral asked where they had gotten such an
idea, and the two men replied that they had heard about "all the
money this evangelist raised." Brother Roberts told his two visitors, "I want you men to know that my vow to God is to touch
neither the gold nor the glory. I am sure God will meet the needs
of my forthcoming ministry in an honorable way, and all funds
will be handled in the highest manner." [10]

When his wife heard of the proposition the two men had made
to her husband, she observed, "Oral, this is a trick of the devil.
He knows God is going to do a great work through you or he
would not be attacking you so early." Eleven years later, in another autobiography, Evelyn's speech had been rewritten to express her concern in language slightly more sophisticated: "If
you do what is right, God will bless you despite what some uninformed critics might say." [11]

Brother Roberts resigned his pastorate and started his own
healing ministry, but only after he tested the Lord to be sure he
had been "called" to do this new work. He rented an auditorium
in downtown Enid and prepared to hold a public service. He
promised God that if it proved successful in terms of attendance,
finances and miracles, he would resign his pastorate and "enter
immediately into evangelistic crusades."

He felt God responded adequately to his three requests, and
he withdrew from his church and moved to Tulsa, Oklahoma.
In Tulsa he arranged with the Reverend Steve Pringle, a Pentecostal Holiness minister, to take over the pulpit of Pringle's revival tent for a week. Oral later wrote that the revival was so
successful that it was continued for two months. During that time
the name of Oral Roberts became known nationwide.

Brother Roberts' performance under Pringle's tent probably
included some of his better sermons, for a number of people were
saved and enough miracles were counted to keep the tent filled.
There are at least two other good reasons for the success of his

first campaign. One had to do with the publicity provided by a stranger who strongly objected to the revival. One evening while Roberts was preaching, this man, whose name the police did not reveal, stood across the street and opened fire on the revival tent with a revolver. The police arrested the gunman, but could find no motive for his actions. He was later released without providing a coherent explanation for his odd behavior. Thanks to the wire services, which found the story interesting, Oral Roberts' name was printed in newspapers all over the country, a king's ransom worth of publicity for his new crusade. Although he was not aware of the shooting incident until his healing service was over, Brother Roberts placed the incident high on his list of important biographical data and referred to it as "my first brush with death as an evangelist of God." He also claimed that "overnight I was labeled a controversial evangelist." [12]

Another reason for the success of the first Oral Roberts campaign can be traced to the genial Steve Pringle, the minister who offered Oral the use of his tent. Pringle was one of the best-known preachers in Tulsa at that time. Thousands knew him because of the popularity of his early morning radio program. Accompanying himself on the guitar, he opened his show with a favorite hymn, "The Man From Calvary," and a cheerful "Hello, folks, this is your friendly parson, Steve Pringle!"

Somewhat surprisingly, in his biographies Oral Roberts has made only brief references to Steve Pringle in connection with that first campaign in Tulsa, and apparently never mentions his name in any other manner, in all the volumes he has published. Today Pringle lives in the limbo of semiretirement in the general area of Prague, Oklahoma, loved and remembered by many, but there is apparently no communication between him and the preacher he helped make famous.

The Roberts ministry was off to a very good start, and soon he was able to negotiate for his own tent, which he christened the "Canvas Cathedral." He moved his crusade into the little towns of Kansas and Oklahoma, where he gathered both "love offerings" and experience in faith-healing. Writing about the Roberts' ministry in *American* magazine in May of 1956, John Kobler noted that six months after setting up headquarters in Tulsa, Roberts had "collected $14,000 in love offerings, persuaded banks to loan him money, a local radio station, a printer, and an advertising agency to extend him their services on the chance of future profits. He has been expanding ever since."

In the early days of his new ministry Brother Roberts was concerned with the publication of Scriptural literature, tracts and other printed materials so essential to a revivalist. He often based his sermons on his own experiences, and as in the case of most rural preachers, the story of his conversion and victory over the devil proved to be very popular. During most of his long career Oral Roberts has made at least one of his many autobiographies available to the public. He called the first one *Oral Roberts' Life Story As Told By Himself*. He also sold his wife's autobiography, *I Married Oral Roberts*. And one of his best sellers was a paperback written by his parents and entitled *Our Ministry and Our Son Oral*. In this little book, which provided much of the hagiographic foundation of her son's earliest days, his mother revealed that she had asked the Lord to give her a son who would become a minister, that she had once made a vow to give her unborn son to God in return for the healing of a neighbor's child who was dying of pneumonia, and that the baby Oral walked on the sides of his little feet until she took the problem to the Lord.

Roberts' ministry grew rapidly, and he started a career as a radio preacher as early as 1947, when he began broadcasting on two stations. And at an early date he saw the value of advertising. When Brother Roberts arranged with L. E. "Pete" White of the Tulsa Advertising Company to handle his publicity, he made probably the single most important decision of his career. White, an old hand at preacher promotion, stayed with him until 1955, when he moved across town to join the staff of Billy James Hargis' Christian Crusade. Pete White is credited with transforming the back-water healing ministry into a multimillion-dollar enterprise and Oral Roberts into a nationally-known personality. There are still many long-time residents of Oklahoma towns and cities such as Holdenville, Pryor or Muskogee who remember the "old" Oral Roberts before he became the more modern, sophisticated personality known around the world today. They remember him as rather typical of Pentecostal Holiness preachers, many of whom are puritanical enough to condemn dresses that reveal a woman's armpits, cosmetics that color her face and hair styles that bob or cut her biblical "crown of glory." Brother Roberts was opposed in those days to attending the theater, dances, circuses and fairs. With the more sophisticated image came an increased friendliness toward other sects and creeds; no hostility was expressed toward another church. As late as 1962, long after he had convinced most of the press that the new Oral Roberts was a permanent image, a reporter who was interviewing him for a story in *Harper's* magazine surprised him by asking about one of his early pamphlets, *The Drama of the End-Time*. A quotation from that vintage-1941 document provides a rather graphic picture of the early Roberts thinking, as well as syntax.

> The average preacher is so mixed up on what he believes until it is hard to say what it is. They do not preach the Christ of Calvary, to a lost and dying world as Christ has commissioned, but are busy walking the Milky Way, turning somersaults in the Big Dipper . . . The rising of false prophets, such as Father Divine, Mary Baker Eddy, etc., is just a preliminary to that vast horde that shall precede Antichrist and prepare the way for him.

When the reporter asked if the evangelist still felt as he did when he wrote the pamphlet, the startled Roberts answered, "I respect the Christian Scientist people very much!" [13]

Some of his early publications were revised or dropped as the new Roberts image slowly emerged. The title of his wife's autobiography, *I Married Oral Roberts*, while suitable for the rural, gingham-dress circuit, was reissued as *Whither Thou Goest* when the Roberts ministry became more national in scope. And as he transformed his image from country preacher to urban minister, parts of his autobiography obviously required updating. There were other reasons too. Reporters from the national magazines often combed his literature to flesh out their stories with any interesting quotations, some of which often cast Brother Roberts in the role of half-educated country bumpkin. His second autobiography, bearing a copyright date of 1961, was called simply *My Story;* for many years visitors to his beautiful Abundant Life Building in Tulsa received free copies of this publication. In

1967 he brought out *My Twenty Years of a Miracle Ministry,* an autobiography supplemented with a large number of photographs. His most recent effort, entitled *The Call,* was published in a hardbound edition by Doubleday and Company in 1972. Judging by their enthusiasm, many reviewers who received copies of this book were apparently unaware that much of the information it contained had already been distributed to the public many times. But like all the autobiographies which preceded it, *The Call* contained some new data to bring the Roberts story up to date, as well as some old information slightly revised.

Why has Brother Roberts published so much literature about himself? One answer to that question can probably be found by examining the careers of some of the most famous and successful fundamentalist faith healers who preceded him. John Alexander Dowie, an Australian who found fame and fortune while practicing faith-healing around Chicago, owed much of his success to the use of the proper literature. Although not Pentecostal in the strictest meaning of that word, Dowie's ministry strongly influenced the Pentecostal movement during its early, formative years, shortly after the beginning of the twentieth century. The Reverend Mr. Dowie demonstrated that acceptance of a charismatic leader's claim to healing power is usually based on the ability of the would-be leader to convince the religious rank and file that he has been specifically and divinely selected to act as God's agent on earth. Dowie's remarkable career showed that the most important literature a faith healer can place in the hands of a potential follower is not a Gospel tract, but an account of his own life, filled with stories of his conversion, visions, miracles and messages from Heaven.

Much the same case can be made for the ministry of the great, charismatic faith healer, Aimee Semple McPherson. Sister Aimee's book *This is That,* published in 1923, remains a classic in the hagiographic literature of fundamentalist faith-healing and miracle ministries, as important as the work of the great Dowie, who had preceded her by some 20 years.

But in some respects the autobiographies of Oral Roberts form a class by themselves, since he is the only leading faith healer who has published the same general subject material a number of times during a period of about 20 years. Using his autobiographies to trace some of the important events in the life of the famous evangelist, we find that all of them contain some of the following information about the early years of Oral Roberts. He was born January 24, 1918, on a farm near the town of Ada, Oklahoma. He was the youngest of five children born to Ellis and Claudius Roberts, God-fearing members of the Pentecostal Holiness Church. Ellis Roberts, now deceased, was part Indian, a farmer who turned to preaching shortly before Oral was born. His mother, who is also part Indian, is today the most famous resident of Oral Roberts' Retirement Village in Tulsa, Oklahoma. They named the future healer Granville Oral Roberts, but called him Oral, a rather ironic choice, as Brother Roberts has since observed, because through most of his youth he stuttered and stammered very badly. Oral was extremely awkward and shy. In some of his biographical material he recounts how he was humiliated by schoolmates who teased him because of his inability to speak fluently. He tried both fighting and running away to rid himself of his tormentors. Roberts says that on one occasion the laughter at his affliction became so embarrassing and painful that he hid under the house until the guests had departed.

At age sixteen he left home, glad to escape parental discipline and a religion he had never accepted, but went no farther than the nearby town of Atoka, where he found a handyman's job and a place to live in the home of a judge. Access to the judge's law books kindled an ambition to become a lawyer and even governor of Oklahoma. He worked in a grocery store on Saturdays, delivered papers, maintained a high grade average in school and still found time to indulge his political dreams by working in the campaigns of local candidates. Even after he had become a well-known figure in the world of religion, some of Brother Roberts' literature still hinted that he could have reached the governor's seat had he not responded to a higher calling.[14]

His dreams were shattered before his seventeenth birthday, when he collapsed on a gymnasium floor in the final minutes of a basketball game. Unconscious, with blood hemorrhaging from his mouth, he was taken directly to his parents' home. Unlike some Pentecostals, who leave all healing in the hands of the Lord,

the elder Roberts and his wife placed their confidence in both
the Almighty and medical science. The diagnosis was advanced
tuberculosis in both lungs, and the doctors advised that he enter
a sanatorium at once. While he waited for a hospital bed to become available, relatives and friends concentrated on prayer for
his salvation and healing. In time he came to believe that the
devil had afflicted his body, and he prayed at length to be saved,
promising finally, "Lord, I will preach the Gospel." Soon afterward, he felt "the presence of Jesus Christ enter my feet and my
entire body began to quiver." Still very ill, he had found his salvation.

Sometime later, his older brother Elmer rushed to his room
with news of a tent revivalist in Ada who was healing the sick
in a most remarkable way. With the help of the parents, Elmer
carried his brother to a car and started over the rough roads
toward the revival tent.

On the way, Oral Roberts later testified, he heard the voice
of God. "He was speaking to me. He spoke in a clear and audible
voice: 'Son, I am going to heal you and you are to take the message of my healing power to your generation.' " [15]

Under the revival tent, propped up with pillows in a rocking
chair, Roberts waited for the evangelist. When his turn came,
the faith healer prayed briefly and touched him on the head, trig-
ering a series of events that are apparently still unfolding. Oral
Roberts later wrote, "A blinding flash engulfed me and that light
was all I could see for several moments. Like the night I was converted, I felt light as a feather, only this time it was in my body
that I felt the sudden impact of divine power." Unassisted, he
leaped from his chair and raced back and forth on the platform,
waving his arms and shouting, "I am healed! I am healed!" [16]

Throughout his long career Roberts has steadfastly maintained
that he was healed instantly; somewhat less important but equally
miraculous, he found that his stuttering was also cured. A Roberts
autobiography indicates that during the two months following his
dramatic recovery his father obtained two negative reports on
samples of young Oral's spittle sent to the State Hospital in Oklahoma City; the book also reveals that fluoroscope tests taken
after his recovery indicated his lungs were normal.[17] But there

does not appear to be any published account containing the names of the doctors who diagnosed his illness. Neither is there a facsimile in any of his autobiographies of a positive spittle report indicating that he was tubercular. Today sputum records are retained in Oklahoma City for five years. During that period access to records requires a signed release from the patient. At this late date probably only Roberts himself would be able to publish the type of document or report that would establish beyond question that he was tubercular.

A few weeks after his recovery, young Roberts was ordained in the Pentecostal Holiness Church and began conducting a summer revival with another young preacher. Upon what formal education or training the ordination was based is not revealed in his autobiography, but one can assume there was none, since he was only 17 years old. At summer's end he joined his father to form an evangelistic team and later reported a good response to their Gospel message. When his father accepted the pastorate of a church in Westville, Oklahoma, Oral carried on in the evangelistic field alone. In 1936 he met his future wife, Evelyn Lutman, in Sulphur, Oklahoma, where she was playing guitar at a camp meeting. They were married on Christmas Day 1938 in his father's church in Westville, and the Reverend Oral Roberts took his beautiful bride and went back to the life of an evangelist.

As related previously, Oral Roberts spent some eleven years moving through the South, conducting revivals and serving as pastor of small churches before returning to college and a pastorate in Enid, Oklahoma. Then, about a year later, he resigned his pastorate to become a professional faith healer. In his autobiographies Brother Roberts stresses that the year immediately preceding his entry into an independent faith-healing ministry was a period of preparation, a time of mighty miracles, of anguished striving for God's anointing. According to the famous faith healer, he experienced an unusual number of signs that finally culminated in his receiving power from God to heal the sick and cast out demons.

Oral Roberts wrote that he first realized that his "hour" was approaching in 1946, when he was pastoring in Toccoa, Georgia, shortly before leaving for college in Oklahoma. He received a phone call from Clyde Lawson, a deacon in his church. Lawson had been injured by a heavy motor which dropped on his foot. With Bill Lee, another deacon, Roberts rushed to the Lawson garage. There is some conflict concerning the details of this story. In a small book published by Brother Roberts some years later, *God's Formula For Success and Prosperity*, he wrote in a short summary of his life that actually Lawson's wife made the phone call.

When Oral arrived at the garage, he found that Lawson's foot was crushed. "I could see blood running out of his shoe, which was nearly cut from his foot. He was in such pain that he was thrashing about on the floor. He could only point at his foot in an unspoken plea for me to pray."

Oral touched the end of Lawson's toe with his right hand and cried, "Jesus, heal!"

Clyde Lawson stopped rolling in agony and asked, "Oral, what did you do to me?"

"Nothing, Clyde, except pray," Roberts answered.

"I'm healed!" he cried.[18]

Oral told the story of the Toccoa miracle in detail in his 1961 autobiography: "In amazement I saw him take his shoe off, stand up, stamp his foot on the floor, with no swelling or pain left. I saw with my own eyes that his foot had been instantly restored. Bill Lee saw it, too."

Brother Roberts observed that he had always believed such a miracle could happen. And he later considered what Deacon Bill Lee said that day to be a prophecy: "If you could have God's power to pray like that all the time, you could be used of God to bring a revival to the world!"

It was a very great miracle, one that helped Brother Roberts to believe he had been selected by God to do a great work. He observed,

> When a man moves in God's will, the events and incidents of his life have a way of falling into place. A pattern develops, according to the divine plan. From my birth in 1918 when Mamma gave me to God, through 1946 when Clyde Lawson received his healing through my prayer, the plan of God had been shaping me to reach the place where God could fully use me to bring the message of His healing

power to my generation . . . From late 1946 to early 1947 one idea possessed me. Bill Lee's words that God could use me to bring a revival to the world kept ringing in my mind. When I left Toccoa for Oklahoma, I felt destiny had me by the hand and soon the big thing would happen to me which would lead me into the stream of God's healing power.[19]

Roberts' 1961 autobiography established a tie between the Clyde Lawson miracle prayer in 1946 and the fact that Oral's Mamma had given him to God when he was born. It was all part of a pattern that he saw developing "according to the divine plan." [20]

But some observers have wondered why Brother Roberts spent more than eleven years as an ordinary Pentecostal preacher, praying for the sick without effecting any dramatic miracle cures, if the Lord meant for him to specialize in healing. And why did he suddenly remember those old prophecies and understand their meaning just when Pentecostal preachers all across the country were putting up canvas tents to find fame and fortune in the great resurgence of interest in faith-healing after World War II? [21] He faced those questions when he published his 1967 autobiography. "I could not understand the complete meaning of God's command. Twelve years were to pass before I would begin to understand. During this time I evangelized, pastored churches and attended college. . . ." [22]

His autobiography [23] continued to reveal page after page of new signs that the big moment was at hand. The reader is gripped in a seeming eternity of suspense as one supernatural event follows another. Brother Roberts emphasized that his mind remained filled with the experience of Clyde Lawson's healing and the prophetic words of Deacon Bill Lee. This is an interesting point since this was the last autobiography in which the miracle of Clyde Lawson's smashed foot was used. Later versions, in 1967 and 1972, are silent about what he considered an important prophecy and healing miracle of the first magnitude in 1961. The story can be found in summary form, but neither Clyde Lawson nor Bill Lee is mentioned by name. Brother Roberts felt he was hearing God's voice in his mind as he had first heard it in 1935, when God healed him. He reported that his think-

ing and believing were rapidly approaching a climax: "I had
the feeling that I was near God's time for me to enter his healing stream. A flame was in my heart. . . ." He had a firm conviction that God was going to make His move soon:

> . . . Destiny had carried me this far along, and I thank God for
> providentially arranging people and places and things to help me on
> my way. But my moment of trial was imminent. Soon I would be at
> grips with THE FORCE which controls all life. It would be a de-
> cision which I had to make alone—a decision that would forever alter
> my life and affect the lives of millions in my generation.[24]

Still holding his readers in suspense, he revealed that "In early
1947, I knew the miraculous power from God was within finger-
tip reach." Here Brother Roberts avoided hints and half-state-
ments and said clearly that what he was reaching for was power
from God to perform miracles. But he revealed in his very next
sentence that he had still not reached his victory: "Yet I was
unable to break through the invisible barrier which kept me
from experiencing it in the measure which I knew I must. God
had reserved some important lessons for me to learn." [25]

He decided that God was not quite ready to give him miracle
power. However heartbreaking it must have been for him, he
was determined not to give up.[26] He studied and prayed. Then
he decided to fast. He felt the Scriptures make fasting a secret
between God and man, so he was unable to tell anyone about it,
but he lost a great deal of weight.[27]

During those crisis days, he also made a special study of parts
of the Bible, and his autobiography showed how that project
led to what he called his "great discovery." He was leaving the
house early one morning, in a hurry to get to a college class,
when he realized he had not taken time for his daily guidance
—a passage of Scripture and a prayer to God for the day, in which
he spoke to Him and listened for His answer. Brother Roberts
wrote that "I returned to the house, opened my Bible at random
and began to read where my eyes fell." The passage he saw was
John 3:2, "Beloved, I wish above all things that thou mayest
prosper and be in health, even as thy soul prospereth." He read
the passage over and over; he could see the hand of God mo-

tioning him forward. He would always believe that providence prompted his discovery of the passage, ". . . for what I read that morning was one of the final touches to the concept of abundant life which has changed the thinking of millions of people and given them an answer to life." He called his wife from the kitchen and had her read the verse aloud. He was tingling all over. How could he have overlooked it in all his reading of the Bible? Perhaps, he suggested, he wasn't supposed to have noticed it before or hadn't been prepared to receive it. The college class was apparently forgotten as he read and reread the passage and saw new horizons opening. He saw that John 3:2 and other passages like it contained God's wish for man: "He wishes us to prosper in our daily living and to be in health, body, mind and soul. The measure of our prosperity and our health is to be equivalent to our spiritual well-being. . . ." [28]

It is probably shocking to some fundamentalists when critics point out that Brother Roberts had introduced the occult practice of stichomancy, a form of divination performed by opening a book, especially the Bible, and hoping that a random passage will provide guidance or inspiration. Among the more emotional and superstitious the practice of stichomancy is still followed, even though William Branham refused to believe in it. [29] Brother Roberts' critics also point out that by equating health and wealth with spiritual well-being, he had arrived early in his career at a quaint form of hyper-Calvinism, perhaps without being aware of it.

In his search for special power from God, Brother Roberts revealed that he had almost reached his goal, only to be delayed a little longer. He said that God still had things to show him, and he emphasized the suffering he endured throughout this final period. For example, he would awaken at night and find that he had been walking in his sleep. One night his wife discovered him in the corner of a room; he was on his knees, sobbing and praying. When she sought a reason for his strange action, he explained, "The cause of my being so upset at this time is a dream God has been giving me; it has been the same dream night after night, and it distresses me."

What was the dream?

"I dream that God shows me mankind as he sees them and as
he hears them. What I see and hear takes my breath away.
Evelyn, I did not know this before this dream, but most of the
people in the world are sick or afraid in some way. God lets me
see them and hear them."

"Well, what do they look like?" his wife asked.

Have you ever gone into a hospital and heard the moans and groans
of the dying? Have you ever seen a person so sick and emaciated he
looked like a skeleton and heard him gasping his last breaths? That
is how mankind appears when you see them as God sees them. Even
people who appear normal and well to us generally have something
seriously wrong, some ailment in their bodies, some fear in their
minds. Evelyn, I did not know it before, but these people are lost
and helpless! They must have healing from God.[30]

Dreams, visions and trances have long been important to those
who rely on faith-healing to the total exclusion of medical science, and perhaps for that reason considerable space was given
to such subjects in some of the Tulsa healer's autobiographical
data.

Oral wrote that he was now 29 and a half years old and was
finally ready to answer the calling of God, whose pattern had
been revealed to him. But not just yet, for still another thought
had suddenly become dominant in his mind: "I must have God's
anointing to pray for the sick." He wrote that he knew there
would be many difficulties, serious criticisms, unhappy mis-
understandings. But he felt he had reached the point of no
return. He had to make direct contact with the Lord "to hear
His voice again and receive my instructions." [31]

And he complained that the people around him knew something was about to happen and some could not let him alone,
and this was hindering his search for God.[32] To escape these
distractions and get on with his search for God, Brother Roberts
went to his church and locked himself in the study. He proceeded to address the Lord:

Today is the end of my searching. I am going to find You. I will
lie down on this floor before You and start praying. I will never rise

until You speak to me . . . Suddenly, God spoke to me in an audible voice. He spoke like a military commander, words of crisp command, clear and strong: "Stand upon your feet." I stood and found myself facing the door. "Go and get in your car." In the car I sat with my hand upon the wheel . . . Then God said, "Drive one block and turn right." As I turned at the corner, which was the direction of the parsonage, God said, "From this hour you will heal the sick and cast out devils by My power." [33]

After that unprecedented conversation, he drove on to the parsonage, dashed into the house, hugged his wife and said, "You can cook for me now!" She replied with a question, "Oral, the Lord has spoken to you, hasn't He?"

Brother Roberts had come to the end of his long preparation period at last. He had God's promise that he would be able to heal the sick and cast out devils. His description of his encounter with God was much quoted and remarked upon by critics who interviewed him for the large national periodicals several years later, when he had become famous. Writers from magazines like *Time, Harper's* and *Newsweek* found the story of his meeting with God in Roberts' first autobiography, *Oral Roberts' Life Story as Told by Himself.* In 1961, when he published *My Story,* some of his earlier descriptions of God's voice, such as "He spoke like a military commander," or "as a general would speak to a buck private," were missing. And some of the childlike threats contained in the earlier version had been removed and replaced with somewhat more modest statements; "I will never rise until You speak to me" had become "I told the Lord I had come to the end of myself and that I would not leave him [sic] until he [sic] spoke to me." Later, in his 1967 publication *My Twenty Years of a Miracle Ministry,* this was further modified to "I told God I was going to settle it once and for all. He would have to give me His power or deny me." By 1972, when Doubleday and Company published *The Call,* Brother Roberts had so subdued the onetime dramatic encounter with God that it was scarcely recognizable: "I saw that God was good, that it was His will to heal and to make whole, and that He was the source of abundant life. He spoke to me and left me without any doubt that He had called me to take His healing power to my generation." [34]

Before deriding Brother Roberts for publishing the story of how he pouted on the floor while waiting on God, one should consider that Roberts' account bears a resemblance at many points with those found in hagiographic literature distributed by faith healers since the beginning of the Pentecostal movement at the start of this century. Turning, for example, to the celebrated John Dowie, one finds that the most famous of the very early fundamentalist faith healers discovered his power by threatening the Lord with a daring ultimatum: "Now, Lord I pray that Thou wilt heal me, or I will never believe You again!" [35]

The personable and articulate Aimee Semple McPhersen also received her commission to heal the sick directly from Heaven. She said, "When I was a girl seventeen years of age the Lord spoke these words plainly into my startled ears, as I was alone in my bedroom praying one day. It was a solemn time when He ordained me there to preach the gospel." Hers is perhaps the only example of a major fundamentalist faith healer receiving a divine commission made up of verses from the Bible. The message from God to Aimee consisted of passages from the Book of Jeremiah (1:4–9), but oddly enough, when she published them for her followers, some of the words from these verses were omitted and replaced with ellipsis marks. Whether the words were omitted when they were spoken to her from Heaven or whether Aimee for reasons of her own decided to delete them, is not known. Whatever the case, the ordination message clearly established that she had been predestined to her leadership, and the verses selected seemed eminently appropriate to her youth and limited education. Here is her divine commission, with the deleted words replaced in parentheses:

> The word of the Lord came unto me, saying, Before I formed thee (in the belly) I knew thee; and before thou camest forth (out of the womb) I sanctified thee and I ordained thee a prophet unto the nations. Then said I, Ah! Lord God! behold, I cannot speak; for I am a child. But the Lord said unto me, Say not, I am a child; for thou shalt go to all that I shall send thee, and whatsoever I command thee thou shalt speak. Be not afraid of their faces; for I am with thee

to deliver thee. Then the Lord put forth His hand, and touched my mouth, and said unto me, Behold, I have put My Words in thy mouth.[36]

It was fortunate indeed that the message to Aimee ended with Jer. 1:9, for the following passage, Jer. 1:10, boldly declares: "See, I have this day set thee over the nations and over the kingdoms, to root out and to pull down, and to destroy, and to throw down, to build, and to plant."

Evangelist T. L. Osborn, who started his healing ministry shortly after the Roberts crusade began, followed much the same procedure Oral had used in getting a message from God. Osborn shut himself in his bedroom for two days and nights before the Spirit spoke to him. His commission also differed somewhat from that given Brother Roberts. Osborn was granted additional power —that of raising the dead. And while Oral was to take a healing message to his generation, Brother Osborn was commissioned to go to all nations and peoples.[37]

Finally, the ordination message of a healer who directly preceded Oral should be considered. And there is perhaps no better example than that of William Branham, the man who started the renascence of interest in fundamentalist faith-healing, for the message he received no doubt indirectly influenced the Oral Roberts ministry. Branham's great moment was different from that of many ministers in that he did not hear directly from God; instead, his message was delivered by an angel. Branham later commented that, considering how angels are usually described, the angel seemed very large, as big as a 200-pound man. Except for his garment and long hair down to his shoulders, he might have been taken for a man off the street. But Preacher Branham did not notice many details of the angel's apperance; he was far too excited about the message from Heaven:

Fear not. I am sent from the presence of Almighty God to tell you that your peculiar life and your misunderstood ways have been to indicate that God has sent you to take a gift of divine healing to the peoples of the world. IF YOU WILL BE SINCERE, AND CAN GET THE PEOPLE TO BELIEVE YOU, NOTHING SHALL STAND BEFORE YOUR PRAYER, NOT EVEN CANCER.[38]

Following that most unusual delegation of heavenly authority, the angel added a number of technical details concerning the power given to Branham, a power which resided basically in two "signs." According to author Julius Stadsklev, an admirer of Branham, the first of these signs was a gift in his left hand, with which Branham would be able to detect and diagnose all diseases and afflictions: when the gift was operating, by taking the right hand of the patient Branham could feel various vibrations or pulsations which indicated to him the diseases from which each patient was suffering. Stadsklev added,

> Germ diseases, which indicate the presence and working of an "oppressing" (Acts 10:38) spirit of affliction can be distinctly felt. When the afflicting spirit comes into contact with the gift it sets up such a physical commotion that it becomes visible on Brother Branham's hand, and so real that it will stop his wristwatch instantly. This feels to Brother Branham like taking hold of a live wire with too much electric current in it. When the oppressing spirit is cast out in Jesus' name, you can see Brother Branham's red and swollen hand return to its normal condition. If the affliction is not a germ disease, then God always reveals the affliction to Brother Branham by the Spirit. This first sign usually raises the faith of the individual to the healing level; but if not, the second sign does.[39]

The second sign was a gift permitting Brother Branham to discern the thoughts, sins and past events in the patients' lives. "He even tells some their thoughts while they are coming to the platform or before they come to the meeting." And why should the signs be repeated for a person who came forward for healing when he had seen them displayed for someone else? The logic of that deduction was amply demonstrated to Branham's followers when they saw that many were healed while sitting in the audience. But this could not take place without Brother Branham knowing it. "He feels it as distinctly as you would if I should pull on your coat . . . he even points out the individual whose faith is touching Christ." [40]

With the power of his signs operating, it is little wonder that Branham's faith-healing efforts were soon widely heralded as a miracle ministry. Word radiated in every direction that all manner of diseases and afflictions were healed instantly by the little Indiana preacher. Even cases of raising the dead were published.[41] By the end of his first summer of revivals, he was already so famous that more than 25,000 people from 28 states and Mexico gathered at the relatively little-known city of Jonesboro, Arkansas, to attend his services. And Branham was setting other standards of performance difficult for a newcomer to emulate. Revivalist Jack Moore of Shreveport, who helped arrange a Branham revival in Louisiana, wrote that a steady stream of traffic had wound its way through the Arkansas hills and Louisiana valleys on revival day, "reverently tracing the path of this Twentieth-Century prophet, whose prayers could cause diseases to be accursed, broken homes to be reunited, drunken fathers to repent, prodigal sons to return, feuding churches to stack arms and make peace, and lukewarm Christians to be rekindled by the fire of their first love. . . ." [42]

While William Branham had received the sign in his hand at the same time power to heal was bestowed upon him, Brother Roberts was not given special power in his hand until some five months after God spoke to him like a military commander in Enid, Oklahoma. However, there is no record indicating that he was embittered or that he felt slighted by the Lord. For that matter, he has never been given Branham's second-sign power of reading minds, although God has often spoken to him in an audible voice. Brother Branham was also credited with raising the dead, a power apparently withheld from Oral, but Brother Roberts can claim time-delay healings, cures that occurred a long time after he placed his hands on a sick person. And, of course, he has great power over demons.

Brother Roberts got his special hand gift when he was conducting a one-night service in Nowata, Oklahoma. While praying for a small boy who was deaf in one ear, he heard God speaking as if He were standing by his side: "Son, you have been faithful up to this hour, and now you will feel My presence in your right hand. Through My presence, you will be able to detect the presence of demons. You will know their number and name; and through my power, they will be cast out." [43]

Oral immediately tested his hands. He noticed there was

warmth—a feeling of God's presence—in his right hand, but very
little or none in the left. When he discussed this phenomenon
with his wife, she stated emphatically that it was a sign to him,
and reminded him that certain men in the Bible had been given
signs by God for their spiritual ability to help the people, such
signs as Moses' rod, Samuel's horn of oil, David's slingshot and
Peter's shadow.

Demons had always presented something of a problem to
Brother Roberts. During the first days of his ministry, at the
age of seventeen, he had felt only one fear as he prayed for the
sick and that was praying for those who were "demon possessed."
His father had warned him to be careful when praying for such
people, because the demon might be cast out only to enter
someone else. Said Oral, "He told me never to pray for any of
them until I felt a special anointing of God's power. His warnings
frightened me so that I prayed for only a few in my early
ministry." [44]

Many years later, in the early 1960s, he discussed demons with
a writer collecting material for an article on his ministry. Brother
Roberts told him that demons cause man to become whatever
they themselves happen to be. "If the demon is an epileptic
demon, he transfers his violent convulsive nature to the person,"
he explained, adding that he possessed the personal power to
recognize and exorcise demons, which he believed to be the cause
of sickness. When the writer asked him precisely how he went
about recognizing demons, Brother Roberts explained: "First, I
feel God's presence, usually through my hand; then I catch the
breath of a person—it will have a stench as of a body that has
been decayed; then I notice the eyes. They're—they're like snake
eyes." [45] In a little book entitled The Fourth Man, Brother Roberts explained in more detail how he discerned demons. He
claimed that when a demon possesses a human being, that person's breath gives off such a stench that it is unlike any other
odor one has ever smelled. Not just bad breath, it is much more
powerful and disagreeable. The eyes of a demon-possessed person
take on a luster which is uncommonly bright and remind one of
the eyes of a poisonous serpent, he said, adding, "It is an un-

forgettable experience to see the leering eyes of a demon-possessed person."

When Brother Roberts received the special warmth, the sign of God's presence in his hand, he was also given another special gift. This was the ability to feel God's presence in what was called a "point of contact." Through this point of contact, Brother Roberts and other people could release the faith for healing power.

When God spoke to him and gave him this new gift, Oral said the first thought that went through his head was, "This is the thing I have been needing." Evangelists had been working with people for many years, striving to increase their faith. Brother Roberts pointed out that one's faith did not need strengthening. What was needed was a way to release faith in any quantity, to release it toward God. It sometimes proved to be a hard point to grasp. Oral explained, "My point of contact is God's presence in my hand." Then he gave some illustrations.

A point of contact is something you do; and when you do it, you release your faith toward God, just as turning on a faucet makes the water come out, or turning on the switch makes the light come on. It is not enough to have faith; you must release the faith you possess . . . You may go to the store for a loaf of bread. You have the money in your pocket to pay for the bread, but unless you release the money, the storekeeper will not give you the bread.

Oral associated the point of contact with a physical act which in turn released one's faith toward God. But it caught on most quickly when he suggested people could lay their hands on their radios as a point of contact while he was praying. In later years this concept was widened to include the use of the home television receiver. Critics claimed that the so-called point of contact had been around long before the Roberts' ministry used it. One such critic was the late Brother Earle Ivy, a revivalist who operated for many years in the Tennessee-Kentucky area and who conducted a radio ministry out of Houston, Texas, in the 1960s. He claimed in his radio broadcasts that he had originated the term "point of contact" in connection with radio receivers in the early 1930s, and he often seemed upset because he had not received credit for coining that phrase. It may not be possible to establish who originated the expression or the act, but one theory for its longevity does seem reasonable. This is the folk theory of electrical ground, which has been advanced by a number of observers. Because of the ignorance of many regarding the operation of radio receivers, especially the first models operating on the superheterodyne principle, there existed a widespread belief that if a hand or other part of the body touched the case of a radio receiver, it would affect the reception of the broadcast signal. By placing a hand on, or even near, the receiver, it was often possible to add enough capacitance to a circuit to alter its operating frequency. In some instances, this resulted in a strengthened output or an increased volume from the radio. This result, perhaps more than anything else, induced some listeners to believe that laying a hand on the receiver made an invisible bond between the hand and the person speaking in the broadcast studio. The introduction of taped broadcasts has not appeared to diminish this curious belief, and critics point to such facts in their attempts to explain how Brother Roberts has been able to use the point-of-contact concept so successfully for most of his long career. On the other hand, Oral has explained in a little book called *101 Questions and Answers* that the laying of hands on a radio or television is definitely not a superstition and should be regarded as biblical. He has included the point-of-contact theory in many of his publications, including one small book entirely devoted to that subject. Called *How to Find Your Point of Contact With God,* the book was popular enough to warrant a revised edition in 1966.

The Oral Roberts healing ministry was incorporated in 1948 under the name of Healing Waters, Inc. It published a monthly called *America's Healing Magazine.* Its theme song was "Where the Healing Waters Flow," and one of its first publications was *If You Need Healing Do These Things.*

Roberts' ministry was discovered by the national news media in 1951. In its May 7 issue, *Life* magazine called him "a new revivalist," and noted that "tall, 33-year-old Oral Roberts, the loudest and flashiest revivalist to appear since the advent of

Billy Graham," was packing his 10,000-seat tent night after night in Atlanta.

Brother Roberts had not been the first of the Pentecostal-turned-independent preachers to hit the highways with his tent and folding chairs, but he was in first place—the king of the faith healers—at the beginning of 1952. He was drawing the biggest crowds, had more employees, mailed out more literature, sold more books and tracts and was on more radio stations than any other faith healer. Right behind him was the big Dallas healer, Jack Coe. For a time, Coe could even boast of the largest tent, a mountain of canvas that could cover 25,000 people. Somewhere further back in terms of outreach and income were O. L. Jaggers, A. A. Allen and William M. Branham, who, more than anyone, had started the whole movement. T. L. Osborn was also in a leadership position, but his ministry, like that of Tommy Hicks, was outside the continental United States.

In the 1950s Roberts' empire continued to expand, thanks in part to good advertising and public relations activities. Faith-healing was a subject which generated a great deal of interest and controversy. Many of the articles in national periodicals treated the Roberts' organization objectively, and some were quite favorable, referring to the Tulsa evangelist as a "handsome, snappily-dressed Oklahoman," and "the U.S.'s newest religious comet." Roberts had been on radio since 1947 and was soon covering most of the nation; in 1954 he began developing a television program, and the next year his TV coverage expanded so rapidly that he pulled sharply ahead of his competitors.

By the mid-1950s the number of articles that took harder, probing looks at the Roberts ministry was on the increase. Early in 1956 a reporter for *American* magazine found that Brother Roberts' Healing Waters corporation was expanding so rapidly that its large headquarters building could hardly accommodate all its activities. It had taken in $3,000,000 in cash the previous year; it employed 287 workers to handle a huge volume of mail, maintain a complex bookkeeping system and promote the sale of books and tracts; it had produced a feature-length film called "Venture into Faith," which had already shown a $150,000 profit. Among other items, it sold thousands of "Jesus Heals" lapel pins and albums of Oral's sermons and songs. It was growing so fast that Roberts had purchased a 175-acre site outside of Tulsa for $250,000, and there he hoped to erect a whole "City of Faith." [46]

Oral Roberts is usually described as being about 6-feet-1 and weighing around 190 pounds, of swarthy complexion with dark black hair. Often called handsome, especially in the earlier part of his career, he has also been described as a "dapper fellow with a good-natured, mobile face." Among his competitors, O. L. Jaggers, a West Coast faith healer, has also been considered very handsome, but has never been as well known as the Tulsa evangelist. There have been a few "sour-grape" observers who insisted that Brother Roberts' eyes are set a bit close together and that his nostrils flare excessively when he preaches. A few have unkindly downgraded his sermons because they found them plagued with a high-frequency whistle, but far more have described his voice as very pleasing. He has always dressed well; indeed, he has often been described as a "natty dresser." And most important of all, he has never been troubled with a weight problem. Thus, he has always presented a very clean-cut appearance, a youthful, tall, dark and quite modern father-figure, generating a great deal of middle-class trust. He has always projected a friendly image toward the public and has enjoyed the advantage of never being considered an intellectual, a certain kiss-of-death in the fundamentalist faith-healing world.

In the mid-fifties money was pouring into his organization's coffers. His own reported $25,000 salary was bolstered by one day's offerings out of the usual six in each campaign, a "love offering" which improved his income by some $40,000 in 1955. And royalties from his books brought him another $80,000. [47] He was reported to be indulging his boyhood dreams of becoming a dashing cowboy on a beautiful horse.

He bought a 280-acre ranch some 15 miles south of Tulsa, and named it Robin Hood Farm. The ranch house alone was estimated to be worth $60,000 and was described as "seven super-gadgeted, wall-to-wall-carpeted, lushly-paneled rooms." He stocked the ranch with purebred Aberdeen-Angus cattle, and maintained, "The Lord owns our cattle." He also made room on the farm for a runway for his 12-passenger Aero Commander executive airplane.[48]

When the writers and photographers from the big magazines came, he was ready with his cowboy regalia and his favorite steed. In early 1956, for example, he posed for *Cosmopolitan*, wearing a string tie and Stetson and plunking on a guitar. He made it clear that if he had not become a minister, he would have been a singing cowboy. He told a reporter from *American* magazine that Western stories constituted his favorite reading, that he favored hearty ranch food like pinto beans, sorghum molasses and fried chicken.[49] And he may have let himself go too far. The reporter quickly fitted Oral with the image of a likable hillbilly parvenu who was overly impressed by signs of wealth and power. He also attributed a host of cowboy expressions to him: "When ah preach, ah perspire freely," "Ah have a pretty fair business sense," "Ah am jest God's humble instrewment" and "Some of you highfalutin society folks loosen up and clap your hands."[50]

To remove the rustic tarnish on his image and neutralize the criticism he had attracted in his role as cowboy-gentleman rancher-preacher, Brother Roberts sold his prize cattle and moved to a more modest, five-acre retreat.[51]

In December 1953 he had announced that God had instructed him to win a million souls by July 1, 1956. In partial fulfillment of that directive, which later formed part of a ten-million-soul master plan, the famous Tulsa healer extended his overseas ministry to include Africa. *Time* magazine observed that "almost 2,000,000 people in the U.S. and South Africa have already heard Roberts' orotund voice and been exposed to his high-pressure evangelism. He has conducted 20 successful crusades, set up regular programs on 223 radio and 98 TV stations throughout the U.S., gone into the publishing business with books, tracts and two magazines; total circulation 5,000,000."[52]

Brother Roberts conducted open-air services for thousands of whites in Wembley Stadium in Johannesburg, South Africa. And he ministered to thousands of blacks, frankly admitting that he cringed from laying his hands on the many black lepers who

sought miracle healing. His African crusade was deemed a
success, and an office was established and a committee formed
to work toward the saving of 100,000 souls in South Africa
during 1955.

The Dark Continent, as some evangelists still describe it, has
always been one of the favorite mission fields of the leading
fundamentalist faith healers. Long before Oral Roberts invaded
Africa, John Alexander Dowie sent missionaries there from his
theocratic community of Zion City, Illinois. Unfortunately, the
results of the faith healers' African campaigns have been uniformly poor. The exotic products of the faith-healing seed
Dowie's missionaries planted, for example, are little short of
amazing. As a result of his evangelizing, the word "Zionist" remains a popular church name among the African Bantu peoples,
such as the Zulu, who continue to emphasize healing by faith
and the efficacy of the Holy Spirit, but often with strange rit-
ualistic forms. Like Oral Roberts, William Branham made a
journey to Africa with his faith-healing team. There is no evidence to suggest that either Roberts or Branham was ever aware
that visions, trances, speaking in tongues (the sudden manifesta-
tion of the Holy Spirit which caused those affected to speak
in a foreign or unknown language), and miraculous cures were all
part of many African religions thousands of years before evangelists thought of going there. And the visits by faith healers such
as Dowie have accomplished little more than to teach such
groups as the Zulu Zionists to perpetuate the Protestant scandal
of divisiveness.

The doctrines taught by Dowie's missionaries were long ago
blended with the remnants of the old Zulu beliefs to form a
syncretism condemned by the old church denominations and
supported almost totally by the black servant classes. Worship
is now often conducted in a circle on the ground representing
the round world—the kraal—of the old traditional Zulu life. They
dance in colorful garments appliquéd with moons, stars and
crosses, "heating up" the circle to create a propitious atmosphere
for the coming of the Holy Spirit, which is identified closely with
the old Zulu worship of the spirits of the dead. The Holy Spirit

is suggested in the wind and in the ocean, to which the worshipers descend periodically for purification and rebaptism in the Holy Spirit. Before entering the surf, the Zulu Zionists stand on the beach confessing their sins to one another. Those particularly impure purge themselves in the traditional manner by vomiting into a hole in the sand. It is covered over, and two candles are lit above it. Then, singing Christian hymns together with the old regimental songs of the Zulu warriors, the Zionists enter the ocean in search of the Holy Spirit. This, so far, has been the legacy of the faith healer's missionary effort. But while Dowie's fundamentalism has been melded into a new paganism in less than two generations, it has somewhat ironically managed to forge for the Zulu Zionists a weekly release from their world of social deprivation.[53] On the other hand, the Roberts missionary effort may prove in time to be a lasting victory for Christianity in Africa.

Toward the end of 1955 the Oral Roberts Crusade team headed for Australia, planning to hold campaigns in Sydney and Melbourne early in 1956. There was every reason to believe the Australians would welcome the Roberts team. Instead, the crusade was abruptly halted in the middle of the Melbourne campaign, the tent was dismantled, and Brother Roberts returned to the U.S. saddened and embittered.

The Tulsa faith healer devoted two chapters to the "great Austrialian crusades" in his 1961 autobiography, *My Story*. He claimed that while in Australia, he was "the object of the greatest controversy of any minister of modern times. The persecution I had faced up to that time seemed as nothing in comparison." It was, he said, the first time he had failed to enjoy "religious freedom," but he maintained he would make the decision to go there again if God gave the word.

Who opposed his ministry so cruelly in Australia? Who denied his revival team religious freedom? The famous healer took pains in *My Story* to make clear it was not the churches of Australia. He stated that he and his team went there at the invitation of a group of ministers representing the Full-Gospel churches of that country.

These good people welcomed us with open arms. We were met at the airport by the largest delegation I had ever seen . . . We found the pastors and their people to be some of the finest Christians we had ever met. They were hospitable and courteous—Christians in every sense of the word—and they were receptive to the message of deliverance as I preached it.[54]

Brother Roberts also praised the city fathers of both Sydney and Melbourne for granting him free use of their parks in which to erect his big tent.

But trouble was brewing. As Roberts later wrote: ". . . acting under some strange influence, some of the daily newspapers of the two cities had determined that we would not have successful meetings in Australia. Obviously prewritten stories greeted us as the crusade swung into action." [55]

He also wrote that in Sydney the reporters who visited his tent were disrespectful of public worship, and the newspaper photographers remained crouched in front of him, waiting to photograph an unfavorable expression. He added that one of the local pastors had "caught one of the reporters back of the platform trying to pour an alcoholic beverage into my glass of water." And he quoted one reporter as saying. "We are not writing what we want to write but what we are told to write." Another was said to have admitted that his orders were, "Get Roberts!" [56]

But Brother Roberts called his Sydney crusade a victory, despite the opposition of the newspapers. Melbourne was a different story. It was, he said, unlike any situation he had ever known.

. . . the Melbourne newspapers launched an all-out attack against me personally and the crusade. The articles were anti-God, anti-Bible and anti-American. They referred contemptuously to America, the base of my ministry, as the "Bible Belt." They pointed out time and time again that I was an American evangelist. Their familiar cry was, "American, go home." [57]

Hecklers were in his tent congregations, yelling and screaming at him and his converts. Roberts wrote, "Well-known Communist agitators were recognized moving about, directing the mob attack. Ushers and sponsoring pastors tried to quiet them, but were immediately surrounded and threatened with physical violence." He decided that "the press attacks had emboldened the Communists to the point that they were conducting an organized campaign of heckling, hoping that they would find some excuse to start open violence and a riot." [58] Even though he had been cursed by the reporters, and the mob had screamed physical threats against his life, these were not the main points of the disturbance to Oral Roberts. Most important,

I knew that thousands were being doomed by the Communist mobs that had been inflamed by an unfair press. C. H. Montgomery, Editor of *Abundant Life* magazine, who accompanied us on the trip, has said "As for the papers themselves, we did not have to worry about their judgment. We knew they had released the very force that would one day destroy them. They would have their reward, and it would be of their own doing, for the press that releases mob fury and aids and abets the evils of Communism inevitably loses what it cherishes most—freedom to write and publish the truth." [59]

Each night the mob grew larger and wilder. A truck was set on fire, and a tent rope was cut. Said Roberts, "I was told later that sharp-faced men, with cockeyes and cigarettes dangling from the corners of their mouths, moved purposefully from one [worker] to another. The cell members were doing their dirty work trying to whip those fine young people into a killing frenzy, to mold them in the Kremlin's own image." [60]

Roberts wrote that while he was asleep that night, his team made the decision to close the crusade. He and his wife left early the next morning for the United States. He was warmly welcomed home and reporters in Tulsa wrote sympathetic accounts of his adventure in Australia. "I was invited to address the Tulsa Chamber of Commerce and at the close of my talk I was given a standing ovation." In time he could even view the Melbourne crusade as having a victorious ending: "The full responsibility of the *debauch* was thrown into the laps of the newspapers who stirred up and supported the Communist mob . . . We lost but we won, because it brought to light the fact that the Communist minority in Australia wanted to destroy religion. . . ." [61]

Had Brother Roberts stated all the facts surrounding what he called his "persecution in Australia"? Those who wished to read the story as presented by his Australian persecutors were under a severe handicap. None of the universities in the state subscribed to Australian newspapers.

If no Australian newspapers were available, what of the American press? Of the national news magazines, only *Time* and *Newsweek* provided the kind of coverage that indicated there was a story other than Oral Roberts' to be told. In a short news item entitled "Trouble for Oral" in its February 13, 1956, issue, *Time* observed:

> In the U. S., the Rev. Oral Roberts is somebody. He regularly conducts faith-healing meetings over 300 radio and 115 TV stations, and draws crowds wherever he pitches his revival tent. Since Australia usually welcomes visiting U. S. performers with open arms, his campaign down under should have gone well. But even before he landed in Sydney, a group of Australian preachers denounced him as a "fraud and impostor."

Preachers? But Brother Roberts has made it unmistakably clear in three different autobiographies that the churches were on his side. It was not the churches, he emphasized, but the newspapers with their Communist helpers who had opposed his ministry. But a review of the major Australian newspapers of that period reveals that the people he described as meeting him with "open arms" when he arrived in Sydney also included reporters. They were there to get his reaction to the activities of the Open Air Campaigners, an Australian preaching organization which distributed more than 10,000 copies of a booklet describing Oral Roberts as a "fraud and impostor" during the week before his arrival in Sydney. According to the Sydney *Sun-Herald*, the Open Air Campaigners enjoyed "wide support in Protestant Churches." In referring to the Roberts' faith-healing ministry, the Open Air Campaigners emphasized that they were "concerned and distressed at the possibility of many uninstructed Christians being caught up in the snare of this delusion." When

Oral was asked by reporters if he would read the booklet, he replied: "I never take any notice of such people or what they say." [62]

The criticism steadily increased throughout most of the press: "SALVATION CIRCUS COMES TO TOWN," headlined one paper. Oral was called "at best a big blabbermouth" by the national weekly *Truth*. And when reporters discovered that he had checked in at Sydney's swanky Glen Ascham Hotel under an assumed name, they published Brother Roberts' explanation: "Christ has no objection to prosperity." [63]

It is understandable that Roberts might emphasize the role of the Communists in his Australian troubles. The waning McCarthyism of that period still gripped many minds; if any group was charged with being associated with Communism, the effectiveness of its programs would be neutralized if the American public became convinced of the truth of the charges against it. There can be no doubt that the Communist element which attended his rallies delighted in Brother Roberts' problems and would have rejoiced in his or any other revivalist's failure. And it is true that the Tulsa healer was careful never to claim that the Australian press and the Communists were allies. But he did assail the press for its anti-Americanism and claim that the Communists were "used" by the newspapers. He also accused the press of "aiding and abetting the evils of Communism."

In retrospect, Oral's attempts to attack the Australian press through guilt by association with Communism seem completely uncalled for. It also seems clear that he went too far in claiming so much support from the churches and religious bodies of Australia. As noted previously, he referred to the group which met his plane in Australia as ". . . the largest delegation I had ever seen. . . ." But the Sydney *Sun-Herald* of January 15, 1956, stated there were only 250 people to meet him. And the president of the Baptist Church of New South Wales, the Reverend A. C. Prior, was quoted in the *Daily Telegraph* of January 17, 1956, as saying that "the recognized churches did not support Mr. Roberts' visit." [64] The Reverend Mr. Prior described the Pentecostals as very good people, but added that "what boogie-woogie is to music Pentecostalism is to religion."

Oral accused the Melbourne newspapers of attacking him in articles which "were anti-God, anti-Bible and anti-American." Yet he did not cite any examples. To be accurate, he should have said the newspapers were anti-Oral Roberts. He claimed the Melbourne press had "referred contemptuously to America, the base of my ministry, as the 'Bible Belt,'" and he insisted that the familiar cry of the Melbourne newspapers was, "American, go home." Unhappily, this is Brother Roberts as he is not often seen. Most of this criticism shows the famous faith healer during one of his most unhappy periods, straining to use patriotism to win when his cause could not prevail on its own merits. A review of the stories published about the Roberts campaign shows the Melbourne newspapers did not publish anti-God or anti-Bible articles. Some of their articles about the Roberts ministry were reprints of earlier stories that had appeared in *Time* magazine or in New York newspapers. There were no cries of "American, go home," but there were plenty of cries which said in effect, Oral Roberts, go home. In Melbourne men and women shouted, "You ought to be tarred and feathered," and "We aren't a mob of hillbillies, why don't you have a go at healing yourself?" [65] And a man who shouted, "It's all a matter of pounds, shillings and pence!" was ejected from the Roberts tent at Yarra Park.[66] The *Argus*, a newspaper in which Oral had bought large advertising space, devoted the first page of the *Weekender*, its Sunday supplement, on February 4, 1956, to an article entitled "Bibles, Ballyhoo in the Big Top." The page carried a subtitle of "Lord, How The Money Rolls In." And on February 9, 1956, the same newspaper reported that Roberts had quit talking about demons. Probably most important, the *Argus* quoted the Roberts ministry on what was behind much of their trouble. Roberts knew "a certain religious organization had organized the demonstrations against him, and had even brought some people down from Sydney with the purpose of breaking up the Roberts show." [67] Thus, to the Australians, it was a church organization trying to break up his campaign; to the people in the United States, it was the Communists and the newspapers who were guilty. The Australian newspapers centered their attacks mostly on Roberts and the money he collected. They also published the reactions of people in the street to his compaign. An example can be found in the Sydney *Sunday Telegraph* of January 22, 1956, in an article entitled "They'd Give Oral the Big Heave-Ho."

> Many Sydney people think fast-talking U.S. hot gospeller Oral Roberts should be put on a fast boat to China—or anywhere else. They doubt Oral's claim that he is a God-appointed agent for curing the sick. The Sunday Telegraph yesterday asked 25 people their opinion of Oral. Of these, 16 thought Oral's departure would be Sydney's gain. Six didn't care if he stayed or went—so long as they didn't have to listen to him. Two people said, "Give him a go," and one man hadn't heard of him.

The whole truth of the matter is probably not to be found in the extreme position of Oral Roberts, nor in the wild, *ad hominem* attacks the Melbourne newspapers were guilty of. But in the final analysis, Brother Roberts should bear part of the blame. At the invitation of a tiny minority, the Full-Gospel churches of Australia, he attempted to propagate his beliefs among the majority, many of whom considered his faith-healing tenets unscriptural and his advertising methods overly commercial and culturally untoward.

Perhaps the greatest mistake made by Oral and his team was their failure to recognize the quite different attitude of the Australians toward religion. This might be explained by describing the recent experience of the Reverend Raymond Payne, a Baptist minister from Oklahoma, who set up a church in Australia in 1969. In an interview published on April 30, 1972, Payne had this to say about his experience in taking religion to the highly individualistic Australians:

> It's very hard. Australians look upon me as an outsider and they are very reserved about religion. They have a term here—"sticky-beaking"—which means prying into others' affairs, and that's how they look on my visits.[68]

If Brother Roberts has never stopped publishing accounts of his "persecution in Australia," he has hardly commented at all about the domestic opposition that greeted him a few weeks after his return to America.

On February 19, 1956, Jack Gould, TV and radio critic of the *New York Times*, mounted a strong attack against the programming of television faith-healing shows, particularly those of the Reverend Oral Roberts, whose style of presentations, he concluded, were "a matter of fundamental policy for the broadcasting industry." Observing that Roberts was then seen or heard over more than 400 radio and TV stations and seemed to be edging out non-faith-healer Billy Graham for first place in the popularity polls, Gould questioned whether the religious programming standard of a station should be determined by a faith healer merely because of his ability to pay for time.

Gould began his carefully-worded criticism by noting that no one would dispute that faith could play an enormously vital role in hastening recovery from bodily ills. Neither, he said, need there be a question concerning the existence of miraculous recoveries that seemingly cannot be explained by medical science. But it was quite another thing, he insisted, to display miracles on a regular weekly basis and claim, "without even the most rudimentary proof, permanent cure of an endless variety of ailments."

Mr. Gould observed that faith can come to men in many ways, but faith-healing is quite another matter. To allow the enormously influential medium of television to be used week after week to show undocumented "miracles," with all "their implied aspersions on the competency of medicine," seemed to the columnist to be contrary to the spirit, if not the letter, of the code governing mature and responsible broadcasting. Gould called for an enlightened partnership between the clergy and the medical profession, an arrangement that had nothing to do with "a gospel preacher making his own extemporaneous medical diagnoses and claiming magic results unsupported by the slightest shred of rational evidence." Brother Roberts, Gould noted, carefully avoided rigid comparative tests before and after his miracles. The columnist insisted he was all in favor of trying to heal a man's soul and restore his faith. But for Roberts to ask television viewers to hold up their babies in front of their screens while he extended his hand to the camera, with a "crystal-clear inference" that such a maneuver would heal the infants of bodily ills, was hardly an edifying use of a mass communications medium. The columnist concluded that "if Brother Roberts wishes to exploit hysteria and ignorance by putting up his hands and yelling 'Heal,' that is his affair, but it hardly seems within the public interest, convenience and necessity, for the TV industry to go along with him." [69]

Two days after Gould's column was published, a circular letter from Oral Roberts to his "partners" went out from his Tulsa headquarters. Requesting his followers to register a protest to the *New York Times*, Brother Roberts made it clear that he considered Jack Gould's effort a "very unfriendly article concerning the Oral Roberts television program." He suggested that Gould had "departed entirely beyond the realm of unbiased criticism which is the true activity of such a columnist." Coming so soon after the Australian trouble, this new threat may have frightened Brother Roberts more than it ordinarily would have. He warned his "true friends" that there was a definite possibility that "the influence of such articles might in the none-too-distant future jeopardize our religious freedom in praying for the sick."

In noting the response to his request for protest letters to the *Times, Newsweek* began a report on the evangelist's activities with a quotation from the March 1956 issue of Roberts' magazine: "It is wonderful to be honest and to know you are free from insincerity." *Newsweek* observed that Brother Roberts had been having a trying time of it, but like Job, to whom he had compared himself, he faced such problems "ostensibly undaunted." The Tulsa faith healer's request for mail to the *Times* had quickly brought in some 1,500 letters overwhelmingly protesting Gould's column. The *Newsweek* article also included a report of possible trouble from another quarter: "Last week, a commission of the National Council of Churches, in an obvious though indirect reference to preachers like Roberts, condemned the sale of TV-radio time to religious groups or individuals and requested adequate free time for 'representative churches.'" [70]

If *Newsweek* reported on Oral's activities with seeming tongue-in-cheek, a number of publications were more critical. The Catholic weekly *America* made no attempt to pull its punches:

> There is certainly a reasonable doubt that these programs are in the public interest. Of their very nature they play on the hopes and fears of the credulous and ignorant. There is no positive proof that some of the "cures" are not rigged. At any rate, standard medical treatment seems to be flouted. We can wonder how many, viewing such programs in their homes, are impelled to neglect ordinary medical treatment.[71]

Brother Roberts should not have felt singled out for persecution. By early 1956 the excesses of some of the leading independent faith healers were being brought to the public's attention, and the revulsion in some quarters against professional faith healers was now beginning to reach significant proportions. A short time after Gould's attack on Oral Roberts' TV programs, the Reverend Jack Coe of Dallas was suddenly involved in the thorniest problem of his faith-healing career. Next to Roberts, Coe was probably the most successful healer in the country and vastly enjoyed hanging on long lines behind his pulpit the discarded crutches and braces of those he healed—a grim but convincing testimony to his healing prowess. In a Miami, Florida, campaign, he removed the leg braces from a three-year-old polio victim who had been carried through the healing line by his mother. In his usual style, Coe smeared a fresh batch of oil on his thumb, pressed it against the boy's forehead, raised his hooded eyes to the sky and shouted: "Jesus, heal this boy!" He then ordered the mother to remove the braces and turned to the next health-seeker. For three days the child stumbled and fell, but the mother worriedly refrained from applying new braces, lest her lack of faith rob her son of the miraculous healing. Finally she took him to the family doctor, who found irreparable bone damage. She called the police, and the County Solicitor ordered Brother Coe's arrest on a charge of practicing medicine without a license. Pictures of the Reverend Jack Coe behind prison bars were featured prominently in most of the country's large newspapers, along with stories on the extent of his financial empire. The court revealed that in five years he had amassed holdings of more than $500,000.[72]

Another of the leading preachers, Orval L. Jaggers, was also feeling the lash of criticism. Orval felt very strongly that a minister should be well-dressed and appear prosperous, and boasted of never paying less than $40 for a shirt. Flying back to his big ranch from a revival, he opened his brief case when the stewardess was passing his seat. Glimpsing the container stuffed with bills, she suggested to the pilot that he might be a bank robber. At the airport the police detained Brother Jaggers for several hours before he could convince them that the $70,000 was really his own money. There was criticism, too, from many of his followers, who felt he had gone too far by identifying flying saucers as the cherubim and seraphim of the Bible. Reporters revealed that Jaggers continued to insist that, like Lazarus, he had been raised from the dead.[73]

A widely-quoted critic of the faith healers, the Reverend Carroll R. Stegall, pastor of the Shalimar Presbyterian Church of Shalimar, Florida, went further than most critics and declared after a long and detailed investigation of the healers that he had never witnessed a single legitimate cure. He stated categorically that apparently successful healings were the results of careful selection.

> Most of the big healers hold screening sessions the day before the service. They say they have to pick out the people who are spiritually enlightened. . . . What they really do is restrict their choices to those suffering from functional ailments: arthritis, rheumatism, migraine, high-blood pressure. These are the professional faith healer's favorite subjects. Those suffering from genuine organic illness he smoothly sidesteps.

Calling the professional big-time healers frauds, Stegall stated that the egos of such men are enormous. "They swell upon the admiration of crowds. They are astute enough to make a great show of giving God glory, but one glimpse of their publicity will show what the 'main attraction' is." Deriding their claims to have recovered the apostolic gift of miraculous healing, Stegall wrote:

They have, instead, manufactured a new cult, using the age-old tricks of suggestion and psychological cant. So far from glorifying God with this, they cause His name to be blasphemed among the worldly by their excesses. So far from curing, they often kill. Far from blessing, their arrival in a city is rather a curse, a misery, a racket, a destruction of faith in simple people.[74]

At one time in the mid-1950s Stegall was considered Oral Roberts' most aggressive critic. He attended several of the Roberts healing campaigns and interviewed many of the people who came to the services. He watched a four-year-old girl, a polio victim, as she removed her braces at Roberts' command. "I was within a few feet of the healing line and saw the little shriveled leg unchanged. She was not able to walk; but Roberts told her parents not to put the braces back on or it would be a lack of faith and would ruin the 'healing.'" In the same service, according to Stegall, Oral told a middle-aged woman to remove her hearing aid and never wear it again. She was completely deaf in one ear and hard of hearing in the other. The woman could hear Oral clap his hands but could hear no words. Stegall reported that Roberts shouted, "She's cured, but the demon is resisting; she's getting it and she's losing it. You wait over there and I'll come back to you." He never did.[75]

There were also others who warned of the dangers involved in faith-healing, and since Brother Roberts was the widely-acclaimed "king" of the healers, it was his ministry which most often came under attack. In an article called "Supersalesman of Faith Healing," W. E. Mann visited several healing campaigns and wrote that "the guilt feelings called forth in those who were not healed were spiritually and physically destructive. The disappointed ones could easily reason that, 'If faith heals and I am not healed, then I am at fault. I am being punished. What's wrong with me?'"[76]

Still more tragic, many critics argued, were those deluded ones who, believing they had been miraculously healed, threw away their medicine or refused to keep their appointments with their doctors. These believers in illusions often found their names moved up to the top of the grim reaper's list.

Brother Roberts came under attack following an incident in a 1959 campaign in Detroit. Believing she had been healed, a diabetic woman threw away her insulin, even though all her life she had required daily shots to keep her diabetes under control. She telephoned her parents to tell them the good news. The next day she was taken to a hospital, where a doctor reported she was in a diabetic coma. She died later that day.[77]

Brother Roberts was very concerned when he read of the tragic incident. He said he did not remember praying for her specifically: "I had no particular feeling that this woman had or had not experienced a significant improvement, yet it was not for me to determine. That was a physician's responsibility." [78]

A similar experience involved a Mrs. Mary Vonderscher, age 43, of Burbank, California. She testified on one of the Oral Roberts television programs that she had been cured of cancer of the spine, even though doctors had considered her condition hopeless. Three days after her testimony was recorded, her relatives were on their way to her funeral.[79]

The argument continued, and spokesmen for the large Protestant denominations began announcing official positions. In June 1955 the Presbyterian Church in the U.S. (Southern) voiced its concern about faith healers. Two years later the same church pointed to faith healers who "distort the Scriptures to buttress their brand of personal 'cures.'" In May 1960 the Presbyterian Church in the U.S.A. (Northern) warned its more than 3,000,000 members against "faith healing cults and healing evangelists motivated by self-glorification and publicity." In February 1962 the United Lutheran Church in America alerted its 2,500,000 members to steer clear of the healers. "Faith healers," its report said, "are often less concerned with the spiritual and physical well-being of people than with the demonstration of their personal power or the attainment of prestige and financial gain. This is religious quackery."

The American Medical Association took the position that all reported miraculous cures could be explained as faulty diagnosis, spontaneous remission or suggestion. During the height of the debate over faith-healing, the AMA isued a widely-quoted statement which said, in part,

The medical profession recognizes the power of faith on the individual mind as a factor that may affect the condition of sick people. There are occasional instances in which diseases generally regarded as uniformly fatal reverse themselves without any explainable medical cause, whether or not the patient has had the ministrations of so-called healers. If such a phenomenon were to occur to an individual under "treatment" by one of these healers, the likelihood is that he or she would take the credit. But the medical profession does not recognize that "faith healing" as such has any accepted merit whereby it can be regarded as having remedial or curative effect in persons who are actually victims of organic disease.[80]

In the 1950s faith-healing grew to towering levels in other countries, often under names and frequently as a form of occult or psychic healing. In Brazil and the Philippines it reached pandemic proportions and was often related to the practice of spiritualism. In France the number of faith healers of various types was believed to be almost equal to the number of licensed doctors. In 1956 the Church of England asked the British Medical Association to do an impartial study of faith-healing. The May 23, 1956 issue of *The Christian Century* reported that the British doctors found that while "many aspects of healing are still outside our present knowledge and this we should honestly and humbly admit," enough of the "miracles" investigated proved susceptible of natural explanation that the doctors concluded there was little room left "for miraculous cures of organic disease by the methods of spiritual healing."

What effect did these learned conclusions produce in the ranks of the faith healers? In South America the American Tommy Hicks continued to draw crowds of 60,000 a night. In the Netherlands the strife in the Dutch royal family, which began as a household disagreement over Queen Juliana's reliance on a faith healer, had grown into a marital conflict of throne-shaking proportions. The Queen had originally consulted the healer in a desperate attempt to cure little Princess Marijke's near-blindness. In England the psychic healer Harry Edwards and other spiritualists had a following estimated at more than 10,000,000. And in the United States, the big healers grew richer, and in little towns and communities all across the country thousands of people started healing ministries each year, often in their own homes. By 1955 an estimated 5,000 evangelists roamed the country, most of whom had some type of healing ministry.[81]

Brother Roberts apparently paid little attention to most of the arguments generated by the foes of faith-healing. It was his policy not to answer critics. He was more famous than ever. Pictures of him meeting with national leaders from all over the world helped make his name a household word. A former governor of his home state was present at the ground-breaking ceremonies for a new headquarters building. Another governor attended the dedication of the seven-story Abundant Life Building, which became a Tulsa showplace as soon as it was completed.[82]

In the late 1950s the Roberts ministry was reaching out to millions of people. Among those ministered to were the Indians on reservations in the United States and Canada.[83] Pictures of Oral visiting the Indians are featured in his autobiographies. In one picture he is shown praying for a papoose; in another he is wearing an Indian war bonnet and is mounted on a horse, alongside two Crow Indian chiefs. In still another picture he is surrounded by Navajo children to whom he has presented Gospel literature. In 1963 he was named "Outstanding American Indian." When the award was presented to him at the American Indian Exposition in Anadarko, Oklahoma, Oral commented, "I am of Cherokee descent and have a burden on my heart for the salvation of my people. One of our Eight World Outreaches is our ministry to the American Indians."

Some critics have depicted the famous healer's relationship with the Indians in a rather bad light, in seeming contradiction to Brother Roberts' declaration of love for his red brothers. Gordon H. Fraser, the Director of the Southwest School of Missions in Flagstaff, Arizona, has written a critical eyewitness account of an Oral Roberts Navajo Crusade at Window Rock, Arizona, from August 17 to 19, 1959.

According to Director Fraser, the evangelistic and healing campaign at Window Rock was attended mostly by Navajos, along with a few Apaches and Hopis. In response to widespread advertising, so many of them brought their crippled and sick to be prayed for by Brother Roberts that they filled the 5,000 seats at the fairgrounds race track. Roberts did not preach very much, since the emphasis throughout the campaign was on healing. In general, the Navajos' health has always been poor. Many suffer from eye diseases, and a congenital deformity of the hip joints is very common.

The Oral Roberts team began distributing prayer cards to large numbers of Indians at the first service. But the climactic healing service was scheduled for Wednesday afternoon, the closing day of the crusade, when all prayer-card bearers who had not previously been cared for would get an opportunity to be prayed over by Oral Roberts.

On Wednesday, when the preliminary functions were completed, the holders of prayer cards were directed to assemble in front of the grandstand. They were instructed to form a single line around the one-mile track. The sick ones hobbled around the enclosure in the hot afternoon sun until a solid line was stretched around the entire track, except for a short distance in front of the stands. Many were unable to walk around the track and returned to the starting point, hoping that they would eventually be able to get Brother Roberts' attention there. Fraser estimated that between 1,800 and 2,000 were in the line.

All was in readiness for the Reverend Roberts, who proceeded to announce his authority as a healer. He read from Luke, Chapter 4, Verses 16-19, in which Jesus stated that he had been anointed to heal the sick. Brother Roberts added, "I, too, have this anointing."

The movie and still photographers began to get into position to take pictures. They concentrated on the first Indian in line, a young man with his foot in a cast. To make a more spectacular shot, two old crippled Navajo women, hobbling on homemade crutches, were posed in front of the young man with the cast. Oral assumed his characteristic healing posture, and the cameras rolled. The two old squaws were then allowed to return to their places, and Brother Roberts worked his way down the long line, laying his hands on each head, as the camera car paced alongside.

Fraser was accompanied by a missionary to the Navajos and a native Navajo evangelist. They followed Roberts at close range about one-fourth the distance around the track. "He offered no audible prayers and no results were seen," observed Fraser. "Those who had hobbled around the track on sticks went away on their sticks; the blind were led away still blind. There was a look of dismay on most faces . . . It was quite apparent that all of them came expecting results. . . ."

Brother Roberts continued along the line, laying hands quickly on the heads until he reached the far corner of the track. At that point, Fraser noted, he was picked up and whisked away to the nearby airstrip. In a few minutes his private plane was disappearing overhead, leaving some 250 people still waiting in line, prayer cards in hand.

In a little while there were only a few members of the Roberts team remaining, and they were loading the paraphernalia on the truck. No one paid any attention to the hundreds still waiting to be prayed for. Crushed and shredded prayer cards began to appear all over the track, and the disillusioned Indians wandered off one by one. Soon the truck was loaded, except for the folding chairs used by the old cripples. They had to be placed on the ground so the chairs could be loaded. The invalids then began to gather up their blankets and leave. Fraser wrote, "A spastic boy was carried away by his mother. An old blind man who had entered every line possible for three days was led away by his wife . . . An old man on a crooked stick eased his way along the rock retaining wall, resting every few steps. . . ."

Fraser summarized the results of the campaign at Window Rock: there were no healings and no apparent healings. And probably no conversions. The Navajos went back to their hogans. But what did Brother Roberts get out of it?

Cash offerings probably amounted to several thousand dollars, and several thousand of Roberts' books were sold, at a handsome profit, to Navajo Indians—ninety-eight percent of whom cannot read English. The Roberts party also went away with a wealth of publicity photos such as could not be gotten anywhere else than among the Navajos. These will perhaps be shown on the screen and in publications throughout the country as a great triumph of the gospel in Navajo land.[84]

❈   ❈   ❈

As early as 1955, the Oral Roberts television programs were being broadcast regularly to much of the nation, and the response was overwhelming. Roberts' mail tripled, and he became so famous that he wrote, "I was recognized by children, taxicab drivers, business people and almost everybody." The number of Abundant Life monthly publications he mailed out soared to over one million. He felt his life had reached a new dimension. It was, he said, simply "God working." But it was apparently too good to last very long: "About this time we were confronted with a new wave of opposition which, in some instances, amounted to outright persecution. Organized religious pressure groups asked the local television stations to put us off the air . . . Beer and cigarettes were on the air and were not protested, but religion was!" [85]

The Tulsa healer wrote that while he had received praise from some quarters, many newspaper columnists vilified his work. "Controversy raged everywhere," he complained, adding that he was accused of using shills to stage fake healing and of hypnotizing people, and some insisted that those who claimed to be cured would find their healing would not last. Some Catholic leaders eventually instructed their people not to attend his campaigns. But despite criticism from almost every quarter and direction, he could report, "The masses were excited and thrilled, and they thronged our crusades and made our mail heavy." [86]

Probably the most common criticism of Oral Roberts had to do with the subject of money. "I was accused of supposedly getting millions of dollars from my ministrations of prayer," he said. "This collapsed when it was learned that the Oral Roberts Evangelistic Association was controlled by a board of trustees which was in absolute control of all finances and that all I received personally was about what any successful minister is given." [87]

Perhaps because many people seemed to believe that he was getting rich by praying for the sick, Roberts reserved a relatively large amount of space in some of his autobiographies to discuss his finances. He explained, ". . . I became increasingly aware that I needed to be scrupulously responsible with my personal finances as well as the ministry's. If there was any hint of taking personal advantage of people in need, it would be a deep black mark on my work as well as my conscience. The best way to do this, I felt, was to organize the ministry so that others would share in the financial decisions." [88]

> In July of 1948 I felt it best to incorporate into a nonprofit religious organization. . . . Absolute and final authority over all financial matters was put into the hands of a board of trustees. These were dedicated Christian businessmen who had not only an effective Christian witness but good business sense as well.[89]

One of the first decisions made by the trustees had to do with the salary Brother Roberts would receive. It was customary, he had pointed out, for ministers in his denomination to be paid by a "love offering," so the trustees recommended that he live by freewill offerings instead of a salary. Oral agreed to accept one offering in each crusade, or approximately one per week. And he reaffirmed his rule of not accepting any gifts.

> I could not afford to allow people to equate healing prayers with money. I have often offended people because I refused the money they tried to put in my hand after I had prayed for them. I had promised God I would not touch the gold or the glory. I meant it.[90]

And even though some critics continued to discredit the practice of accepting love offerings, Brother Roberts never questioned the propriety of that system. In the 1950s several articles stated that love offerings alone were bringing Oral at least $30,000 per year. But preacher Roberts said that he knew how much the offerings really were, and they amounted to a lot less than the critics estimated them to be. He continued taking the love offerings until about 1960. He observed, "By this time our assets had become substantial, although not anything like reported. However, it was large enough for me, a minister, to feel uncomfortable. It had been gained through incomparably hard work, through being at home an average of eight days a month and through helping people at the point of their need." He also noted that the Roberts' holdings consisted mainly of real estate. He had never had much cash, he said, "for it had been our policy to give generously, pay our living expenses, and invest the rest by making a down payment on a piece of property and then paying the balance in installments.[91]

In 1962, Evelyn and I divested ourselves of our holdings and gave the money to help Oral Roberts University get off the ground. I also made arrangements so that royalties from any books I wrote would go into a trust for my children, or directly to the University. I felt especially strong about providing some resources for my children because of the burden they had borne as a result of the misunderstanding of this ministry and my constantly being away from home.[92]

In 1969 one of Tulsa's national banks named him to its board of directors. Roberts observed in *The Call* that such positions are normally held by men of personal wealth. Because of Oral Roberts University's "increasing significance in our community," the bankers felt it would be "good business for them and for us to have a representative of the college on their board of directors." Brother Roberts did not name any other college presidents in the Tulsa area who were directors, but he did seem delighted to report that

> . . . they also felt quite certain that I was personally wealthy. When I turned in my certified financial statement, the bank's president could hardly believe it, for much to his surprise, I lived on a salary with no substantial financial worth. He said, "People need to know this." It was a witness I was proud to make.[93]

In the past, the financial affairs of the Oral Roberts Evangelistic Association have been criticized for the manner in which they have been presented to the public. As the laws of the State of Oklahoma require, the Articles of Incorporation for the Roberts ministry are filed with the Oklahoma Secretary of State, and are accessible to all who wish to inspect them. The original Articles were filed on April 29, 1948, under the name of Healing Waters, Inc. The incorporators were Oral Roberts, Evelyn Roberts and L. V. Roberts, the last apparently being Oral's brother Vaden. The Articles have been amended several times, and the name of the corporation has been changed to the Oral Roberts Evangelistic Association, Inc. The last amendment included changes in the original document which led Brother Roberts to declare that "absolute and final authority over all financial matters was put into the hands of a board of trustees."

The articles of incorporation for the Oral Roberts Evangelistic

Association, Inc., are generally similar in outline and content to those filed by many nonprofit groups. Article Six states, "The number of Trustees of the Corporation shall be not less than three (3) nor more than forty-one (41). . . ." And Article Seven provides that "Members present in person pursuant to a regular or special called meeting shall constitute a quorum of the Members for the transaction of business of the Corporation, and a vote of a majority of such quorum shall be sufficient to transact any and all business properly before such meeting." A perusal of these articles reveals that unless the Board of Trustees has some other authority over the financial matters of the Oral Roberts Evangelistic Association, Inc., than that which is delegated to it by the Articles of Incorporation, the Board's control over financial matters is far from "absolute and final." It is in fact possible for Oral Roberts alone to constitute a majority of a voting quorum under certain conditions. As we shall see shortly, on at least one occasion Roberts has threatened to close ORU; this is a fair indication of his power to control the Oral Roberts Evangelistic Association, Inc.

A national periodical which published an objective news story about the Roberts ministry in the 1950s took a closer look at his organization in the early 1960s. Noting that Oral Roberts was seldom openly criticized by churchmen or doctors because to many it might seem to be an attack—however oblique—on faith itself, *Life* magazine took careful notice of "the uproar of the spectaculars that Ringmaster Roberts runs under his crowded and hysteria-filled tent." [94] *Life* focused its attention on several aspects of the Roberts empire, but especially on Oral's way with money:

> In a Kansas crusade he dreamed up a fund-raising gimmick called a "blessing pact" which still accounts for far more than the old-fashioned collection plate. He asked his followers to pledge a certain amount of money each month for his work, and told them that they'd receive the same amount and more from a completely unexpected source within one year.

Brother Roberts assured the donors that if they did not receive a windfall, he would gladly repay them. And he did pay a few times, but over-all the Blessing Pact worked so well that in a little while Oral dropped the refund guarantee. He just asks for the money and gets it, *Life* observed, adding, "It goes into the Oral Roberts Evangelistic Association, which is a nonprofit organization that does not have to divulge either Roberts' salary or a breakdown of its multi-million-dollar budget."

Brother Roberts explained it a bit differently. His first television programs were on the air in 1954 and were stimulating multitudes of people to write to him for literature and prayer. But the programs seemed to lack the kind of quality he wanted. Encouraged by his friend, the Reverend Rex Humbard of Akron, Ohio, he located a company which agreed to try to film the healing line right in the tent. But the cost was some $42,000 above his budget. How to get that much quickly was the problem. "I began to study the Bible for a way to get at this problem. After much wrestling and praying, I felt I had it. I named it the Blessing Pact." [95]

He called a special service to explain that the Lord had given him a plan to enter into Blessing Pacts with those who would become partners with him in carrying on his ministry. He had found some examples of this in the Bible and cited people like Barnabas and Dorcas, who assisted the Apostles financially. Then, "I dropped a bombshell into their thinking. I knew it would shock everyone there except those with great faith." He asked 420 people to make a pledge of $100, promising that if the Lord had not returned their gift from a totally unexpected source within a year, he would refund their money. The response to his request was an audible gasp in the audience. Even Brother Roberts had to admit that the audacity of the plan had shocked him. But he said he had carefully thought it through and believed the Lord would bless these people. "As a matter of fact, I believed it would be the key to unlimited financial blessing for many of them. It would open the doors of their minds to thinking and believing for bigger things in their own lives." [96]

The Blessing Pact worked so well that Brother Roberts continued to use it. And in time it accounted for about half of his association's income. The dedicated pledged $10, $15, $25 or more each month for a year, for which money the donors could claim tax deductions. Robert sponsored a system of free luncheons in various cities to secure annual renewal of the Blessing Pact pledges.[97] Some critics consider the Blessing Pact as a special application of the Oral Roberts success and prosperity doctrine. It also can be called a special form of tithing, a sort of spiritual withholding act. From one standpoint, the only thing novel in the Blessing Pact system is the nerve required to put the plan into action. From the early phases of his faith-healing ministry Brother Roberts had relied heavily and with remarkable success on the prosperity doctrine. He had claimed as his "great discovery" that the measure of one's prosperity and health is equivalent to one's spiritual well-being. And by an occult procedure, he had found the Biblical passage of John 3:2, which he has used endlessly: "Beloved, I wish above all things that thou mayest prosper and be in health, even as thy soul prospereth." This isolated verse formed part of what he called the "concept of abundant life which has changed the thinking of millions. . . ."[98] He eventually would name both his monthly magazine and one of his headquarters buildings "Abundant Life."

Even though Brother Roberts had a Biblical verse to use as a foundation for his success and prosperity doctrine, he was heavily criticized for using a tool which had long been considered the property of some parapsychology and occult groups. Some fundamentalist preachers had, of course, used bits and pieces of the doctrine for years, but not in the wholesale manner of Brother Roberts. One of his most successful books, *God's Formula for Success and Prosperity*, was published in 1955 and was reissued in 1966. It consists of some 15 chapters, each one telling the story of an Oral Roberts friend who found prosperity and success through his faith. Chapter V, for example, is the story of "God's Manufacturer"; Chapter VIII deals with "God's Plumbing Supply Man"; and Chapter XV, the last chapter, is reserved for Oral Roberts, "God's Man For This Hour." Chapter XI is the story of Jack Linn, "God's Poultry and Real Estate Man," who called on his "divine business Partner for guidance" after entering a national "Chicken of Tomorrow" contest. Said poultryman Linn, "He reminded me that since He had created the chicken to begin with, it was no problem to Him to create the kind of bird we needed to win this contest." What Linn called "the amazing result" was the creation of the "Golden Broad." "God gave me the formula for breeding it," said Linn. Through further guidance of "our great Partner" the Linn Hatcheries also developed the formula for the "Silver Broad" chickens.[99]

Brother Roberts' use of the success and prosperity doctrine was widely copied, especially by radio preachers, even though it was roundly condemned by critics whose ranks included churchmen from many denominations. In an article which appeared in *The Pentecostal Evangel* of March 5, 1967, Howard Carter, a leader in the Assemblies of God Church, attacked the myth of Scriptural support for the prosperity doctrine. In his article, entitled "The Call to Poverty," Carter made his position clear without referring to any evangelists or faith healers.

> Wealth offers a clear path to self-pleasing. It affords protection against the evil day of sickness and starvation. It also raises its possessor to a pedestal in the community . . . We who prefer to follow the Christ should consider the course He took. He chose to be poor . . . Not one of the disciples had money.

The Tulsa healer believed that by equating prosperity and health with spiritual well-being, he had helped explode the common theory that to be spiritual one must be in poverty. And he told an interviewer that he made "no apologies for buying the best. God doesn't run a breadline. The idea that religious people have to be poor is nonsense."[100]

The year 1962 was a watershed of sorts in the fabulous Roberts career. Taking a look backward, he found he had ". . . faced bullets, mobs, stink bombs, tornadoes, fire, hatred, libel, character assassination and need in every form. But we had only grown stronger."[101] It seemed a good time for summing up, because this would be a year of change, when there would be less planning and more action in complying with God's orders to enter the new phase of his ministry.

The healer's dream of building a college went back a long way. Critics who brought up the old Southern saying, "Most fundamentalist preachers never find peace of mind until they can call themselves 'Doctor' or start their own Bible school," could be shown that Roberts had announced his decision to build a university as early as 1961. God had told him to build it. He had also told him what to name the university. Declaring that the ministry must be continued even after Oral's death, God said, "Give it your name, that it may be forever identified with healing. Your name has become synonymous with healing in the world. . . ." God also showed him the university would have two parts, one a School of Evangelism and Graduate School of Theology and the other a liberal arts university.[102]

The biggest problem he had in getting started was finding enough money, but Oral kept praying for a solution. "Finally, God let me know that I should start with the same thing He used when He made the universe—NOTHING! . . . all I knew was that I felt God wanted me to build it."

He had the first three buildings ready for use by 1963, and in the fall of 1965 some 300 students started their college careers. By 1967 seven beautiful buildings were clustered in the heart of the 500-acre campus. Soon a magnificent 200-foot, eternal-flame-tipped prayer tower dominated the mushrooming complex of academic buildings and high-rise dormitories. A vast network of fountains, sidewalks and beautiful sunken gardens spread out to connect the central prayer tower with other structures. Each year more new buildings sprang up in the same style of ultra-modern architecture. A large triangular learning center with its towering colonnade, a field house built in the shape of a giant white bubble, and triple-winged dormitories combined spectacular size and breath-taking beauty to remind some visitors of a trip to a world's fair. Since ORU has never stopped growing, it is difficult to estimate the cost of the university plant. In 1969 it was referred to as a $21.5 million campus; in 1972 Brother Roberts called it a $30 million institution.

The university was to be a blend of the old and the new. It would seek the most innovative in educational techniques while remaining ". . . definitely old-fashioned when it comes to Christian morals." And it would have a specially picked faculty that would reflect "the motifs" of Robert's ministry. It would be a university that would keep Oral's ministry in the spotlight.[103] There would be no student protests or rioting, and both on and off the campus the students would present a middle-class image of neatness and respectability that would reflect great credit on ORU. Neckties would be required for classes, and women would be forbidden to wear slacks and miniskirts. Students would have to attend church and refrain from smoking, dancing or using alcohol.

But there would be nothing old-fashioned about the educational equipment at Oral Roberts University. There would be closed-circuit television in the classrooms, and elaborate dial-a-lecture library on video tape, and electronically graded examinations that provided students with their grades at the end of each class.

It is such an outstanding university that less than six years after it came into existence it was given full regional accreditation. The Tulsa power structure, especially the daily newspapers, are very proud of Brother Roberts' university, and not only because it has become a first-class tourist attraction. One editorial beamed,

But there's something more yet—the ORU atmosphere. The kids who leap forward to hold the door open for you. The smiles. The unashamed prayers. The aura of decency and good humor. Maybe these, too, have something to do with a university's ability to make a contribution to its times.[104]

On March 13, 1972, the Tulsa *Tribune* published a lengthy article entitled "Private Schools Must Get Money or Die." The article reported on a decade of financial struggle that had led almost every private college and university in America into retrenchment, and half of them into extinction. Some 364 private educational institutions had filed for bankruptcy since 1968. State-supported colleges also were in trouble in many states. Operating on reduced budgets, many colleges were forced to drop classes and sharply limit outside activities.

Things were different at ORU. The local newspapers described Roberts as being determined to build a nationally recognized basketball team.[105] There was much comment in the press about his drive to recruit better players. Late in 1972 *Sports Illustrated* decided that "Oral Roberts has recruited everybody but Marjoe. . . ." [106] And Dana Lewis explained in the May 1972 issue of *Sport* magazine how Oral Roberts University applied "pressure tactics" to keep him from breaking his scholarship and transferring to the University of Tulsa: "When they heard I was thinking of leaving, one of the vice-presidents got in touch with my mother (who is very religious). He said he had just talked with the Lord and He'd said it was His will that I stay at Oral Roberts University." [107]

What was the source of ORU's apparent financial security? Roberts provides only hints: "This institution was built by the prayers, the dedicaiton and money of men and women who love God, who believe the Gospel and who believe the Bible is the Word of God." That could mean that ORU was built with considerable private backing. And Brother Roberts has said that he has obtained much help from his prayer partners, which has allowed him to keep the tuition cost at his school fairly low. He also has observed that he received some help from the federal government: "As we were building the physical plant at Oral Roberts University in the early Sixties, we applied for a federal construction loan." [108] Across Tulsa, the Reverend Billy James Hargis has spiced some of his radio broadcasts with reports of the millions of dollars of government money Oral has obtained to build his school. Not all of the agencies through which federal educational funds are transmitted make their records public. But enough information is available to disclose that Oral Roberts University secured a federal loan in the amount of $2,985,000. And under the authority of Title I of the Higher Education Act of 1965, a grant of $520,707 to ORU was approved on October 7, 1965. This gift from the taxpayers was used in the construction of a Brother Roberts showpiece, the ORU Learning Resources Building.

On April 2, 1967, the dedication of ORU and the investiture of Oral Roberts as president of the university took place before a crowd of some 20,000 visitors. The Reverend Dr. Billy Graham, the world's best-known preacher, was the dedicatory speaker. And when that glorious day was over, the newly-installed president of ORU could be called "Dr." Oral Roberts.

Following the dedication of his university, the Tulsa faith

healer began to initiate a number of changes in his ministry. He decided to start phasing out his televised faith-healing programs. He dropped half the stations in 1966 and went off the air entirely in May 1967. He did not return to television until March 1969. Gone was Oral the faith healer. The preacher who had been quoted 13 years earlier as saying, "Ah consider Hollywood and all its works unclean," was now the star of his own Sunday TV series and superstar of quarterly prime-time specials, topflight musical productions with a patina of piety, featuring some of the biggest Hollywood names. Starring along with him were his son Richard and Richard's wife, Patti. Brother Roberts has written that he feels strongly about providing for his children, since they have suffered because his ministry has been misunderstood. Therefore, it was not altogether a surprise to learn that Richard and his wife would get the leading roles. They quickly became such a vital part of the World Action singing groups that their names were featured in the Oral Roberts ads. Their "Now" sound helped the Oral Roberts show capture a very large television audience.

The same year Oral dropped his faith-healing programs he also closed out another part of his original ministry. After some 20 years, the tent crusades ended, and his big tent came down for the last time in Anaheim, California, in 1967.

But the most dramatic change in the history of his ministry occurred on April 7, 1968, when Oral Roberts joined the Boston Avenue Methodist Church in Tulsa. His leaving the Pentescostal Holiness Church to become a Methodist created a shock wave of such seismic proportions that it almost closed down his ministry. Oral described the unexpected intensity of opposition his decision created, and he noted that if he had known what a furor his joining the Methodist Church would cause, he might never have taken the step. Apparently he had been considering the change for some time. Bob DeWeese, one of his closest associates and one of the very few people who had advance knowledge of his decision, encouraged him to make the move: "Oral, besides your feeling that God wants you to do it, the structure of the Methodist Church will allow you the freedom you've wanted these nearly twenty years I've been with you. We're with you all the way." [109]

But others who worked with the famous healer were not so enthusiastic. Roberts observed that when word leaked out that he was about to announce his move to Methodism, rumors started flying in all directions. Some years later he told the editor of the Texas *Methodist* that "most of my staff was appalled. They knew that many who had supported me would not understand that the move was a response to what I felt was God's will. They would think I was compromising what I believe." [110]

To announce his decision Brother Roberts wrote a two-page letter to his supporters, his prayer partners. He explained, "The Lord has been dealing with me for several months about accepting ordination in the ministry of the Methodist Church. God has revealed this to me to be His will and that I should make this step of faith now." He emphasized that he had not changed his faith in any way and that his radio programs and publications would "go on exactly as before." To reassure those who feared ORU would be taken over by the Methodists, Bishop Angie W. Smith of the Methodist Church told reporters that Oral Roberts University would remain independent and never become a Methodist satellite.

When reporters interviewed Bishop J. A. Synan, the General Superintendent of the Pentecostal Holiness Church, he commented on Oral Roberts' decision to become a Methodist: "We don't understand fully why, but it is our opinion that he is moving perhaps more toward the ecumenical movement, and that the people of the Pentecostal Holiness Church will not follow him in this." Bishop Synan verified that Roberts had remained a member of the Pentecostal Holiness Church for many years, although his activities had "been along an independent line for a long time. There have been no charges preferred against him, although because of things he emphasized and his methods, he has been a controversial figure."

According to reporters, the news of Roberts' decision took many leaders of the Pentecostal Holiness Church in Oklahoma by surprise. The director of the Church's Board of Evangelism told of his shock and disappointment: "There never has been any official action taken against Brother Roberts. In fact, the feeling was the best it had been in many years. Pentecostal people have given him millions of dollars. We feel they've been unusually kind to him."

Another state Pentecostal leader, the Conference Superintendent, observed, "I think to most of us it is a regrettable thing for him to have this change of attitude toward the doctrines he has been preaching. There's a strong feeling of desertion, of people forsaken in a cause." [111]

Despite all of Brother Roberts' assurances that he had not changed his faith in any way, there were indications that many Pentecostals believed otherwise. Especially alarmed were some of that persuasion on the ORU faculty. Brother Roberts had recruited teachers from various denominations in order to keep his university independent, but apparently some Pentecostals considered it very much their school. After all, approval of faith-healing and speaking in tongues was written into the University catalogue, and wasn't Brother Roberts himself a Pentecostal?

Another ingredient was suddenly added to the boiling cauldron of suspicion and misunderstanding when reporters discovered a dissenting voice within the ranks of the ORU faculty. Dr. R. O. Corwin, the dean of the ORU Graduate School of Theology, told the press that Evangelist Roberts had fired him after they had differences of opinion about Christian theology. Dr. Corwin said that Roberts told the faculty, "either he [Corwin] is removed as dean or I will close the school. . . ." That statement alone intrigued those critics who insisted that Oral Roberts, not a Board of Trustees, held power over all segments of his evangelistic association. But it paled into bland insignificance beside the next statement attributed to Dr. Corwin. Oral Roberts, the dean volunteered, had been leaning toward Christian existentialism and had read about fifty volumes on that subject.

When word of Oral's decision to join the Methodists leaped the fences around his university, it spread quickly. Roberts complained that ". . . some radio preachers low on material zeroed in on me. I was charged with having gone liberal, turning Communist and being a backslider. They claimed inside information that I had made a deal to become a bishop, and in return ORU would belong to the Methodist Church. Nothing was further from the truth."

The Tulsa faith healer was entering the Methodist camp through the gates of the Boston Avenue United Methodist Church, the grandest church in perhaps the whole Southwest. The pastor there was a staunch friend who had once defended both Oral and his university against the attacks of a radio preacher.[112]

The Reverend Dr. Braxton B. Sawyer's resonant voice, an unusual blend of Ozark and Alabama cultures, vibrated radio speakers in a half-dozen states around his headquarters in Ft. Smith, Arkansas, with the news that Oral Roberts had departed the little peoples' church. A more dynamic speaker than many radio preachers with nationwide ministries, he has almost always been first for more than twenty years with the news his radio audience wants to hear. Often enough he perks up his programs by praying for an old-fashioned revival, a "cotton-stocking, gingham-dress, sawdust-trail revival that can fight the devil and lift people from the garbage can of sin and put our feet on a solid rock." But when the news about Oral started to break, he supplied his listeners with daily reports while he worked on a comprehensive written summary of the Roberts story. He received such a response to his broadcasts about the Tulsa faith healer that he named one of his broadcasts "Pentecostal Holiness Day." Never, he said, had he heard from so many wonderful Pentecostal Holiness people. One of them was a minister, and Dr. Sawyer wanted to share his letter with his people in radioland.

Dear Brother Sawyer: I am a Pentecostal Holiness minister, semi-retired. I'm 76 years old. I've been listening to your programs for a long time, and I'm very much concerned over the latest report concerning Oral Roberts. I knew Oral and Evelyn, his wife, before they were married. I was pastor of our church in Ada, Oklahoma. Oral joined the Ada church while I was there, so I guess I was his first pastor. I have kept in contact with Brother Roberts through the years and have witnessed his rise to become a great world envoy and president of the university here in Tulsa. I have always had a very deep respect for Brother Roberts and his work. . . . Now this latest move of Brother Roberts to the Methodists comes as a complete surprise and a shock to me. I am most interested in the work you are doing, and I want a report when you finish. . . .

Dr. Billy James Hargis demonstrated why he is known as a dynamic radio preacher. He does not believe in faith-healing, but his anti-Communist organization enjoys a certain amount of support from rank-and-file Pentecostals. Over his nationwide network of radio stations he commented on the millions of dollars he claimed the little Pentecostal people had poured into Roberts' coffers. And those fifty books that Oral was reported to have read on existentialism! Authors with strange-sounding names like Sartre and Heidegger and Kierkegaard. With his genius for getting right to the heart of a matter, Dr. Hargis summarized the change in Oral Roberts for his listeners: it's modernism, my friends, that's what it is!

While the suspicion that Brother Roberts might be some kind of secret intellectual was incubating among some Pentecostals, there was also bitterness against him. This came largely from ministers and other personal friends he had worked, lived and attended school with.

But the opposition sparked outside of Methodism is still hard to understand in retrospect. The intensity of it and the bitterness of many was far and above anything I had imagined. And the difficult part of it is that most of it came from men whom I counted as my close friends. A lot of it was from men and leaders in the church to which I had formerly belonged . . . when I received letters of vilification from men I had grown up with and known so closely, it was a shock to say the least.

When he moved to the Methodist camp, Oral went because he said it would "open a wider door" for his ministry. Did he not have a wide-open door in the Pentecostal Holiness Church? Had that little Church been so restrictive? Had he not been virtually independent?

His move opened up the discussion of Pentecostalism, and Oral made his views public as he perhaps had never done before. As he saw it, "Pentecostal" meant an experience, not a church or organization. At the turn of the century the various Pentecostal churches had reclaimed a valid biblical experience—"the Baptism of the Holy Spirit and speaking in tongues." But opposition to speaking in tongues was such that many people were forced out of the historic churches. Those people founded the many Pentecostal churches we have today. And, Roberts said, "Speaking in tongues became a badge of identification. Anyone who spoke in tongues sooner or later gravitated to one of the Pentecostal denominations."

> However, in the forties and fifties when the impact of my ministry began to reach into other denominations, many people began to affirm not only the healing ministry, but the ministry of the Holy Spirit, which included speaking in tongues. Very few of them saw any need for leaving their own churches.[113]

Thus, Brother Roberts believed his ministry had been so well received by members of non-Pentecostal churches that "A gradual division between these 'new' Holy Spirit people and those of institutional Pentecostal denominations occurred." These new people wanted to believe in healing and speaking in tongues while remaining in their own churches—Baptist, Methodist, Presbyterian, etc. But the traditional Pentecostals felt that these new believers should leave their churches and join a Pentecostal church. Had Oral Roberts insulted the traditional Pentecostals by spurning them to move up the social ladder? Had he deserted their cause to join the ranks of a hated social class which, according to many Pentecostals, had always held them in derision? According to this theory, Brother Roberts had, in effect, fled the emotionalism of the Pentecostals to settle across the tracks with the sophisticated, the educated and the wealthy. He had been one of the few nationally-known ministers they could point to with pride, even though he was controversial. And they liked him because he had made faith-healing more respectable and had forced some of the big "main-stream" denominations to reconsider the Biblical promise of healing. They loved him so much that they were willing to believe him every time he declared that God had told him this or that, no matter how silly it sounded or how much it cost them, until God finally told him to desert their cause and join the ranks of their social betters. They were mostly poor people who had stood by Brother Roberts when he was poor. They remembered when they had to take up a special collection one night in Muskogee to buy him a pair of pants that would match his coat. Now he seemed to be using the word "charismatic" as he had once used "Pentecostal." They watched him as he chatted and smiled on television with Dinah Shore or chatted and grinned on the fairway with Bob Hope. And they watched him hurry to what he called "America's largest pulpits and outstanding pastors," and they wondered if he was truly happy now that he was free.

While Brother Roberts was weathering the storm caused by his decision to become a Methodist, he lost many of his regular supporters, his prayer partners. In a few months his income had dropped to a dangerously low level. It was a very serious financial crisis. He began to fear for the survival of ORU, his overseas offices, his publications and his radio programs. In this time of great anxiety, he turned once more to a study of the Bible.[114] And the Lord guided him to the discovery of the principles of "Seed-Faith."

According to Brother Roberts, there are three key principles which constitute Seed-Faith. The first of these is that God is a person's source: "God is your supply!" During the grave financial crisis that had overtaken his evangelistic association he had analyzed his condition and was shocked to realize that he had not been thinking of God as his source:

I was beginning to think of people as my source. Inadvertently, I was looking to people to pay the bills. I was depending on people to help us take the steps of faith we needed to take. I decided then and there that first I was once again going to claim God as my source. . . .[115]

Next he discovered the second key principle of Seed-Faith, which he thought was best expressed in Luke 6:38, where Christ said, "Give and it shall be given unto you." And he found in Gal. 6:7 that "whatsoever a man soweth, that shall he also reap." With a few other passages from the Scriptures, he was led straight to the third key principle of Seed-Faith: "Expect a Miracle."

In short, Seed-Faith meant giving. ". . . In our lives we have to give something to God first before he can multiply it back to us," Brother Roberts explained. And giving is like sowing seed, which introduces all the thought of the Seed-Faith concept, especially its third great principle: Expect a Miracle. If you give to God, you can expect your miracles.

Just as he was formulating the great principles of Seed-Faith, Brother Roberts had an opportunity to test them. A small evangelistic association expressed an interest in a large piece of equipment his organization was planning to sell. God told Oral, "Don't sell them this equipment. Give it to them." He gave the equipment to the group, and "the very next month, January, we had our first upturn in income in eight months. . . . Support for our outreaches doubled in less than two years. It was a miracle!" [116]

Oral found such a warm response to his explanation of Seed-Faith that it seemed only natural that he would want to write a book explaining it to others. He called the book *The Miracle of Seed-Faith*. It has now surpassed in circulation all of the more than forty books he has published.

When many of the Pentecostal people withdrew their support after Brother Roberts joined the Methodists, he turned his attention to a somewhat different audience. While he tried to win back many of his departed flock, he carried his new Seed-Faith principles to as many new people as possible. Who were these new people?

Although they were generally in opposition to the fundamentalist faith healers in the 1950s, some clergymen and a number of well-known writers of that period still retained a strong belief in miraculous cures. They deplored the excesses of the itinerant healers and refused to be associated with services in which people shouted, screamed, rolled in the dirt and talked in "unknown tongues." On the other hand, they believed that the subtle relationships between sin, sickness, psychotherapy and prayer had only begun to be explored. They believed there was so much evidence for remarkable cures that the phenomenon ought at least to be taken seriously. In fact they had reason to believe that a wholly skeptical attitude toward miraculous healing was actually unscientific.

While these believers in miracles were one in their opposition to most fundamentalist healers, there were definite divisions in their own ranks. All objected strenuously to the term "faith-healing," but no agreement could be reached on the best name for miraculous healing. Some preferred to use the term "divine healing." Others had adopted various occult theories, such as belief in clairvoyance, telepathy or other elements of ESP, and preferred "paranormal healing" or "psychic healing." One of the most popular names, "spiritual healing," was also used by the spiritualists; the usage posed no problem in most countries, but often aroused opposition in the United States. There were other schools of miraculous healing, some different only in name, that clamored for recognition now that faith healers like Oral Roberts and A. A. Allen had shown that a large segment of the public was interested in miracles. Mystic fire, radiesthetic diagnosis, Divine Presence, magnetic healing, and Cosmic Force were other names for miraculous healing; so were the residual energy of cosmic creativity, and the coiled energy in man called the Kundalini in India. The metaphysical school of healing known as Christian Science had evolved from magnetic healing through the work of Quimby and Mary Baker Eddy. And Christian Science could claim a famous decendant in Unity, the organization built by Myrtle and Charles Fillmore of Kansas City, Missouri, into what has been called "the largest mail order religion in the world."

Earlier Brother Roberts had set about to spy out the land around Lee's Summit, Missouri, the home of the Unity School of Practical Christianity, which by 1969 was dealing in more than 700,000 prayers a year. Unity has held some things in common with the Oral Roberts Evangelistic Association: it prefers modern evangelical terms like "outreach," it deals heavily in prayer for the sick, and its annual income is measured in millions of dollars. Charles Fillmore, grandson of Unity's founder, recently told an interviewer, "The Reverend Oral Roberts came up here with his staff and studied our *Daily Word*, and six months later God told Oral Roberts to publish a devotional magazine and it's just like *Daily Word* except that the Bible verse appears at the bottom of each page instead of at the top. Well, we don't mind." [117] Brother Roberts didn't seem to mind that Unity and ESP lived in harmony; nor was it mentioned that "Seed-Faith" is a widely-advertised concept in the occult magazine *Chimes*.

With the widespread acceptance of Seed-Faith and the continued growth of his Evangelistic Association, Brother Roberts turned his attention to a project he had long dreamed of. He had always promised to care for his mother, and if he built her a home, why not build a whole retirement center? Thus, University Village Retirement Center was born. It is a complete residential facility, offering a choice of cottages or leisure apartments. To a person 62 years of age or older, it offers the finest in community living in a secure and protected environment. There are craft and hobby rooms, outdoor plazas, gardens, a library, lounges, medical services, a nurse on duty around the clock, and a religious center with a chapel and lecture room—a dream in retirement living that was constructed at a cost of $4.5 million.

Oral Roberts called it "a bold new idea . . . one of the brightest stars on the retirement-home horizon." For a reasonable amount of money each month, a retired person can live in total comfort near Oral Roberts. There is only one difference between moving into University Village and retiring in any other place. At Brother Roberts' retirement village one must "sponsor" a residence. This is accomplished by making a "sponsorship gift" for the type of apartment desired. For the smallest unit, an efficiency, the sponsorship gift is $10,500. In addition to this initial cost, a resident couple must pay a monthly rent of $330, which includes most living expenses. For a larger apartment, the monthly rate is of course higher, and the sponsorship gift is also increased. For example, to move into a four-room, two-bath apartment, with a rental of $500 per month, one must make a gift of $28,000 to University Village. Does the outlay of this much money in the form of a sponsorship gift mean that one owns the apartment or has an investment in it? Unfortunately, no. The money is a gift only, but of course it is tax-deductible. What happens if a person becomes too ill to continue living in his apartment, or dies? In either case he is removed from the apartment.

In theory the sponsorship gift does not mean that only wealthy or financially secure people can afford to live in Brother Roberts' retirement center. The literature distributed by University Village discloses that if one cannot make a sponsorship gift, the retirement center "will endeavor to find a sponsor." Prospective retirees are give a "Preapplication Questionnaire" to complete. It is not legally binding, and the prospective retiree is assured that all information is held in strictest confidence. In addition to being questioned about his health, a prospect is also asked about the social security or pension benefits he receives and about his insurance and property and the amounts of money he has invested in stocks, bonds, mutual funds, real estate and savings.

Anyone meeting the age requirements may apply for an apartment in Brother Roberts' retirement village. After his preapplication questionnaire has been graded, the applicant may expect to receive a reply from University Village. If he has little or no income or savings, he can expect a letter telling him that the retirement center is "making your situation a very special matter of prayer." It may go on to say,

> In all fairness, I must tell you that we have received many thousands of requests from folks interested in living at University Village. In fact we have many waiting for openings . . . I hope you will pray for the possibility of providing more of these units . . . Please let us know if you want us to send an application for the waiting list which is growing daily . . . May the Lord make it possible for more housing for the aging to be provided . . . and may He keep you!

Since University Village represents itself as a charitable, non-profit corporation, a person placed on the waiting list may be hard pressed to understand why a more affluent retiree's questionnaire elicits such a different response from University Village.

An applicant whose preapplication questionnaire indicates that he has a relatively large amount of property and savings can generally expect a long-distance phone call followed by a personal letter. Oral Roberts has divided the United States into regional areas. A minister is assigned to labor in each of these vineyards, and a potential University Village retiree in good financial standing can expect to hear regularly from Brother Roberts' representative as long as there is a chance he will move to the retirement center.

A visit to Oral Roberts' Retirement Village is instructive. Talking with some of the people who have sold their homes to live near Oral leads one to suspect that many who place their trust in miracle healing may also believe that its efficacy is directly related to the distance from the healer, a doctrine of propinquity that draws them almost inexorably to University Village. Perhaps many have not considered that they might become so ill that they could be moved out of their apartments. One group of visitors to the Village in 1972 witnessed an old woman being transferred from her place to the Health Center. She cried to be allowed to return to her apartment. If her health did not improve enough to allow her to live in an apartment once more, or if she died, her sponsorship gift would remain the property of the University Village, and her apartment would be readied for another retiree.[118]

*   *   *

In 1968 Dr. Louis Rose, a British clinical psychiatrist, announced the results of a long study of miracle healing: "After nearly twenty years of work I have yet to find one 'miracle cure'; and without that (or, alternatively, massive statistics which others must provide) I cannot be convinced of the efficacy of what is commonly termed faith healing. . . ." In making his report public, Dr. Rose noted that he had found nothing to contradict the findings of two earlier authoritative studies of miracle healing conducted by the Archbishop of Canterbury's Committee in 1920 and the British Medical Association in 1956.[119]

The English reports generally parallel the findings of many studies made in the United States since World War I. Yet in 1973 the appeal of the miracle healer is greater than ever. Some churches that persistently resisted the faith healers in the 1950s have since somewhat revised their attudes toward miraculous cures. Many state medical associations no longer include faith healers in their files on quacks and charlatans. The United States State Department now includes faith healing as an alternative form of medical practice on its physical examination questionnaire form. And Herbert W. Armstrong, head of the Worldwide

Church of God, has recently begun to discuss his position on healing over the largest network of radio and television stations in Gospel broadcasting. Always opposed to the noisy fanaticism which he associated with Pentecostal faith-healing services, he apparently believes that public attitudes toward miracle healing have changed so drastically that it is now in the best interests of his Church to reveal the "quiet, dignified" healing services it has been conducting for many years.

It is too early to estimate how much credit for the changed attitudes toward miracle healing history will assign to the dynamic preacher from Tulsa. But few who have followed his career closely would dispute that the ministry of Oral Roberts has done more than any other in history to make miracle healing respectable. At the same time he has dramatically altered his own image. Carefully-barbered sideburns and tailored suits have replaced the short hair and the tattered dress of a tent revivalist. The backwoods healer who paced up and down a preacher's platform now promises millions in his television audience that "Something good is going to happen to you!" His is now the best-known name in Tulsa, and he ranks almost as high on many lists of prominent television personalities. Addressing the Democratic National Convention in 1972, he called on God to "heal America" with as much fervor as he once displayed in driving demons from the sick. As irrationality grows more attractive to a world filled with turmoil and despair, and as an increasing number of people turn seriously to the occult and the mystical, time and the currents of history appear to be placing Oral Roberts in the enviable position of sower ("Expect a Miracle!") and reaper of a potentially enormous harvest of new adherents to his philosophy.

TOM
HUFFMAN

III

C. W. Burpo

If I don't ask for money, I don't get any. I love you.
　　　　　　　　—Dr. C. W. Burpo, March 2, 1972 broadcast

. . . People call me a fascist pig, [and] I get mad. I admit it. I wouldn't advise some of you to do that again.
　　　　　　　　—Dr. C. W. Burpo, Nov. 15, 1971 broadcast

Dr. Burpo and His
Bible Institute of the Air

Of the myriad faith healers, Gospel-politicians and miracle-workers privileged to stake out ministries on the public's radio waves under the benevolent suzerainty of the Federal Communications Commission, only a very few can be classified as "general practitioners" of radio religion. Some specialize in interpreting the Bible in terms of extremist politics, while others feature messages based on old-time fundamentalism, end-of-the-world prophecies, or success and prosperity through prayers and positive thinking. One radio reverend promises to intercede with God to have his supporters' corns, bunions and aching feet massaged with Heavenly love, and another claims to effect miraculous weight reduction with a piece of red string. Following the trend toward ever greater specialization, some preachers advertise that their prayers and related ministrations have filled dental cavities, mended broken marriages, made hair grow and brought the dead back to life. And one has reported good results in repairing broken-down lawn mowers and motorcycles with a splash of his "holy oil." Almost all are specialists, their radio programs restricted by fierce competition and high operating costs to the messages or miracles they do best. Only a limited number have attempted to include in their radio ministries the variety of religious, medical and social services offered by the Reverend Dr. C. W. Burpo, founder and president of the Bible Institute of the Air, Inc., of Mesa, Arizona.

Mark Twain delighted in telling the story of a man who set out to write a best-selling book. When his investigation indicated that most successful books of that day were about doctors, Abraham Lincoln and dogs, the would-be writer proceeded to write a book about Lincoln's doctor's dog. The Reverend Dr. Burpo has also been concerned in reaching the widest possible audience, and although he may never have heard of Twain's story, he has applied much the same logic to the building of his nationwide radio ministry. A more specialized service would almost certainly have been less of a burden to Burpo, who has faced problems that might have destroyed an ordinary ministry. He has suffered painful financial reverses and endured the attacks of his ideological enemies to provide his supporters with a wide-ranging ministry compounded of such elements as a unique radio communion service, a faith-healing program that has repeatedly cured the Doctor himself, a fundamentalist interpretation of most of the Scriptures, various bits and pieces of positive thinking, a medley of Gospel-integrated right-wing politics, snips and snaps of eschatological and millenarian doctrines, and an overflowing abundance of love, sweet love!

Like some other nationally known radio preachers, Charles W. Burpo is a native of Oklahoma. He grew up in the rugged farm country of southern Oklahoma and attended school in the town of Madill, a cotton and oil center near the Texas border. He came from a large family so poor that the future faith healer knew what it was to chop cotton for a dollar a day. He enjoyed no special training in a Bible school, but picked up a little theology from a correspondence course put out by a St. Louis, Missouri, school. And he learned a lot of "Bible" through preaching in little country churches. When in 1967 a reporter from an Arizona newspaper, the Apache *Sentinel*, asked him about his education, Burpo revealed that he held an honorary Doctor of Divinity degree from a St. Louis school, but refused to reveal to the reporter the name of the school![1] While such behavior might appear more than a bit strange to some people, Burpo has never refrained from calling himself "Doctor," nor has he named the school which bestowed the title on him. Some of his followers also know him as "Brother Burpo," but he apparently prefers the title of "Doctor," especially on his books and important papers.

Most of the pages of his early ministerial record appear to be blank, an arrangement he seems to prefer, since he has carefully avoided public reference to a church in which he served as minister for some six years. On a radio broadcast in 1970, he indicated that he began his ministry in the Methodist Church.[2] If this meant that he was ordained to preach in that church, there does not appear to be a record supporting such a statement. According to official church records, C. W. Burpo was ordained in the Church of the Nazarene in the Western Oklahoma District in 1934. He served in Guthrie, Oklahoma, until 1938, when he moved to Beaumont, Texas. In 1940 Burpo surrendered his credentials and withdrew his name from the Church of the Nazarene, and his name was dropped from that church's Assembly Roll.[3]

Why would Burpo suddenly withdraw not only from his ministry, but even from membership as a Christian in a church he had served so long? The General Secretary of the Church of the Nazarene, B. Edgar Johnson, does not refer to Burpo by the title of Reverend or Doctor, and obviously does not enjoy discussing the background of that onetime minister in his church. In response to an inquiry about Burpo from a professor at Southwest Missouri State College, Secretary Johnson limited his remarks to one short sentence.[4] Since Burpo apparently will not mention his service in the Church of the Nazarene, it behooves the leaders of that eminently respectable church to make public the details of his resignation. To do less would only add fuel to the fires of gossip that already burn fiercely.

After leaving the Nazarenes, Dr. Burpo became an itinerant evangelist for a time. He needed new credentials and turned to an organization called the International Ministerial Foundation in Fresno, California. The head of that foundation, William E. Opie, advises that he only issues ordination certificates to ministers who have been previously ordained.[5]

Burpo had surrendered his Nazarene credentials, but since he had once been ordained, he qualified.

He was now a preacher with a certificate and an honorary title of "Doctor" from a school he would not name. All he needed was a cause worthy of his talents. He held evangelistic campaigns in the Angelus Temple in Los Angeles during the early 1940s and attracted some large congregations. He has fond memories of those campaigns, and now and then while broadcasting, he refers to the days when he preached in a "great temple." Once he even referred to the temple by name. The beautiful Angelus Temple was built by famous faith healer Aimee Semple McPherson and is still the headquarters of the church she established, the International Church of The Foursquare Gospel. That church reveals that while Burpo held campaigns in the Angelus Temple, he was neither a graduate of their L.I.F.E. Bible College nor a minister in their church.[6]

After a time Burpo moved eastward. He had many friends in Oklahoma, and some of them encouraged him in a plan to hold an evangelistic campaign in Peoria, Illinois, where their friends had a revival church. There, in a successful revival conducted in a large tabernacle, he prayed down a miracle so big he would remember it years later. As the good Doctor recalls, a little woman came to him and said, ". . . I heard you on the radio this morning and I believe that God has given you the power to send the Word. . . ." She described her daughter who was then several hundred miles away, in Florida suffering from rheumatoid arthritis, heart trouble and arthritis of the spine. She was also pregnant. The mother insisted that if Dr. Burpo would only send the "Word," her daughter would be healed.

Burpo was overwhelmed: "I told the audience over the loudspeaker what she said and I asked if they would stand with me because God had been working miracles there. . . ."

He learned of his answered prayer by means of an airmail letter the young girl wrote to her mother. The young girl had, it would appear, been completely healed in a matter of five minutes. Reverend Burpo urged her to come before the congregation to show the people what he and God had done. She came to Peoria, and everything turned out wonderfully, ". . . not because Brother Burpo is great, but because Jesus is!" [7]

Indiana was very important to Burpo's career in at least one other respect, for it was a little woman from Indianapolis who willed him the money to start his radio ministry. It was only $2,925.00, but it was enough to put his message on one radio station while he broadcast pleas for support. He taped his first sermon in the cramped little 35-foot house trailer that he and his wife called home in southern California. On December 8, 1953, his first radio message was broadcast over station KBYE in Oklahoma City, Oklahoma. Sometime later he bought a small house in Oklahoma City and set up an office in a storage room built onto his garage. In later years the Doctor was fond of recalling that he made his first broadcast in Oklahoma City while sitting on a five-gallon bucket in that little room.

Almost from the beginning, his radio ministry included a great deal of faith-healing with an old-fashioned fundamentalist message. This was an era of rapid growth for many of the nationally known faith-healing ministries, such as those of Oral Roberts and Jack Coe. But it would not be correct to classify Dr. Burpo in the same category with those famous healers. For one thing, faith healing was never the whole of his message, and more important, he seldom indulged in exaggerated claims or attempted vulgar displays of his healing prowess. He usually referred to only a few specific miracles in which his prayers had been instrumental. He seemed to prefer discussing his own miraculous recoveries from various dread diseases to stimulate the faith of his radio congregation. Thus he announced at the beginning of his radio ministry that through the use of his own Aesculapian healing wand he had been miraculously cured of sugar diabetes and cancer.[8]

Only once did he halfheartedly attempt a dramatic encounter with God, in the manner made famous by Oral Roberts. This was in connection with the healing of his little granddaughter. As Burpo later recalled, he went to the trouble of explaining the case in some detail to the Almighty before adding: "Lord, I don't want you to misunderstand me; but my *will* is that this child receive her healing for the glory of God." Then, more pouting than threatening: "If this child is not healed, I will never have the courage to go before the microphone and preach another message on healing. . . . And one day, not long ago, God delivered the child. . . ." [9]

Miracle healing would play a very important part in Rev. Burpo's ministry, but his was only one voice in a savagely competitive cacophony of faith healers operating from almost every point on the broadcast band. From KBYE in Oklahoma City, one of the "gospel" stations springing up in most large cities, the Doctor asked his listeners for help.

> We began to tell the great listening friends on KBYE that we had a desire to enlarge our program and we wanted them to help us, and they did. We spread from there to KFMJ in Tulsa, Oklahoma, then to KGRC in Miami, Oklahoma, and to a small 500-watt station in Newton, Kansas. . . .[10]

By 1959 C. W. Burpo's voice was boosted all the way to Canada by the 50,000 watts of power KFAX radiated out of San Francisco. Then he went on another powerful West Coast station in San Diego. Next his ministry spread to Ohio, Pennsylvania, Washington, D. C., and down into Alabama. And when he bought time on XERF, the giant 250,000-watt Mexican station, his voice could be heard all over the United States during most of the seasons.

With the help of his new friends, he enlarged his ministry in a very short time. But his new supporters not only wanted his fundamentalist doctrines spread as widely as possible, they had something else they hoped the Doctor could blend with his faith healing and Fundamentalism: an extreme right-wing political message. Had they approached the wrong preacher? If any radio preacher knew less than C. W. Burpo about right-wing political ideology, he had not bothered to display his ignorance over a network of radio stations in the United States. Still, the Doctor seemed to recognize his shortcomings and was willing to learn. And he was grateful to his new, politically-oriented friends for giving him a chance to become nationally known, and for years he thanked them at every opportunity, even to the extent of calling their names on the air. To the religiously-oriented listeners who insisted that he stick to religion and leave politics alone, Doctor Burpo pleaded that his political message was necessary to wake up the people and help save the country.

And so another modern version of Peter the Hermit, which the state of Oklahoma has produced in such colorful profusion, emerged from the cotton gin and strode onto the religious-political stage to pray down a revival, preach up a standard and lead a crusade to save the souls of those who could save the country. For almost two decades he has fumbled lines, forgotten names, contradicted major and minor premises, cited incorrect references, borrowed material, discussed family problems on the air and still muddled through. At times, unknown to the good Doctor, his comedy of errors has attracted listeners not ordinarily interested in faith-healing, religion or right-wing politics.

As his ministry grew, Dr. Burpo took to meeting his listeners at rallies and get-togethers in cities where he enjoyed especially strong followings. He complained at one such rally that listeners who had never seen his picture expected him to be a little old fat man. But he surprised them, for Dr. Burpo was always concerned about his appearance. In the early 1960s he was of medium size, weighing no more than 165 to 170 pounds. The exercises he often boasted of had apparently kept his girth within bounds, but seemed to do little for the folds of stored fat under the jaws and on the sides of his neck. He steadfastly refused to divulge his exact age to his listening audience, but he appeared to be somewhere on the sunny side of sixty. Except for a few stray wisps of hair, he was nearly bald, though enough remained on the sides to complement a little Prussian-style mustache trimmed so carefully it sometimes appeared to be a third eyebrow pasted below his huge horn-rim glasses. When Dr. Burpo smiles, as he constantly does in public, his little brown eyes seem to soften rather than flash, and furrowed crow's-feet that start at the corners of his eyes reach almost to his little puckered mouth. He is neat and trim and always well turned out in expensive-looking suits. If one hesitates to describe him as dapper, the word "pleasant" would certainly not be misunderstood. He could pass for the local school superintendent or perhaps the owner of a small-town hardware store or funeral home.

Part of the magnetism the Bible Institute of the Air radiates unquestionably derives from Burpo's unique personal approach. He has a wholly unorthodox microphone presence and is usually not only relaxed, but downright casual. Some mornings he is overly fussy about irrelevant details, an old maid scolding to mask her joy at being noticed. Another time he may spend an extra minute of radio time convincing the last cynic that he really does care for little stray dogs. But one of his trademarks—his daily insistence that "God loves you, and I do too!"—produces a mixed response. No doubt it has evoked hymns of joy from many lonely old women, but it has also irritated a few listeners. And although he can always be counted on to turn a neat phrase with just a hint of a Scottish burr, he sometimes comes off rather badly with his "I love you!" gambit. To some it apparently has an insipid flavor, but many more must consider it meaningful and sincere, for Burpo has never given up using it.

It does not seem unfair to speculate that Burpo's discussion of his family problems attracts to his radio show many listeners who might otherwise be enjoying daytime television. Most often the audience hears about his wife, Margaret, whom he has praised and petted on the air as "that little tyke!" He frequently mentions that her opinions are important, saying, for example, that "Margaret says I shouldn't mention this on the air, but I'm going to just this time anyway." In the pictures he sends to his listeners, Margaret appears the docile housewife, a small figure, her eyes almost disappearing into her thin face as she smiles. It has never been clear just how much power she wields in influencing a given course for the Bible Institute, but from the earliest Burpo radio programs she has been an officer in the corporation and has drawn a salary. She rarely speaks to the radio audience, but Burpo, who often declares that she is absolutely indispensable to his ministry, keeps them posted on her whereabouts and reminds them each year when her birthday is approaching.

The four Burpo children are now all grown. The oldest of the three sons, Jim, is rarely mentioned on the radio show or in Rev.

Burpo's printed messages. The other two, Chet and Charles, have played important roles in the history of the Bible Institute of the Air. The daughter, a handsome woman named Virginia, now appears infrequently on the Burpo shows, but there have been a few times when she has not only taken an active part in the radio programs, but has also helped to write the monthly newsletter, the Bible Institute *News*.

From the early days of his radio ministry, C. W. Burpo has tried to integrate a great deal of right-wing material from all the traditional sources into his scriptural messages. Until he gained a great deal of experience, this approach often produced very poor and uneven results. Without suitable transitional material, it was rather difficult, for example, to move directly from a discussion of the Old Testament prophet Amos to a view of the Civil Rights Act as a piece of dangerous legislation. But after Burpo learned enough about right-wing political issues, he was able to do a reasonably good job, provided he could find all his references, remember his subject, wasn't interrupted by a phone call and didn't forget to turn on the proper switches and keep an eye on the studio clock.

There is a great quantity of right-wing literature available everywhere in the United States. Much of this material has never been copyrighted and may be used by anyone without cost, and it is an excellent source for anyone interested in starting a crusade. Also available is a vast body of literature produced by organizations which permit reproduction of their material if a suitable acknowledgement is made. There are also many anonymous writings, mostly in the form of pamphlets and tracts. This literature often contains undocumented accusations and fake quotations designed to alarm prospective followers and stampede them into the extremist camp. All such literature is potentially useful to Dr. Burpo, and from this vast right-wing "public domain" he has culled a variety of the most popular tracts, pamphlets and booklets for his own followers. As he discusses a particular subject, Burpo often suggests that his listeners write him for additional information. At the same time, he usually reminds his radio congregation that he has no sponsor and that his program is kept on the air by the thoughtful "love offerings" sent in by the wonderful people in radioland. And if they are concerned enough to write for his literature, they can hardly forget that he is busy saving a country, a task that requires a considerable amount of financial help.

In 1963 Dr. Burpo suddenly pulled up his Oklahoma City stakes and moved the Bible Institute of the Air to Mesa, Arizona, a community on the outskirts of Phoenix. With a steady growth in the number of stations that carried his message and an increasingly prosperous ministry in his home state, it is not entirely clear why he wanted to move to Arizona. Perhaps there were reasons for moving that he did not wish his followers to be burdened with. In any case the Bible Institute headquarters were again established in a suburban residence, although the new home in Mesa was a somewhat larger house.[11] But before he departed Oklahoma City, Dr. Burpo made a broadcast that gained him his first measure of nationwide publicity.

Rumors of impending national catastrophes were unusually rife in 1963, especially in that vast American subculture known as the "far right," elements of which formed part of Burpo's listening constituency. As a result of the manner in which Washington handled such crises as the Bay of Pigs, the Soviet missiles in Cuba, and the United Nations intervention in Katanga, the confidence that may religious conservatives still retained in the Kennedy administration was badly eroded. Even worse, some lived each day in a sort of quiet desperation because of "special" reports not available to most Americans, reports circulated by right-wing organizations. Due to these alarming rumors, thousands of Americans believed in mid-1961 that some 250,000 Red Chinese troops were stationed in Cuba. In 1962 similar reports placed 150,000 troops from the same army in Mexico, with thousands more dragging their guns up from the beaches every night. At about the same time a frightening rumor concerning the Russians in South America was being circulated by the far right. The Soviets were said to be building the largest series of airfields in the world on the Bolivian Altoplano, the vast three-mile-high plateau that stretches some five hundred miles through the Andes. When completed, the network of bases would give the Russians undisputed military control over all of Central and South America.[12]

Early in 1963 a new rumor began circulating through the hundreds of right-wing groups and conservative camps. It started after the U.S. Army announced the last in a series of three training maneuvers to be conducted in rural Georgia. A number of foreign nations who were members of the United Nations were invited to participate in the military exercise, known as Operation Water Moccasin III, and that fact alone was enough to arouse hostility and opposition from many people. But the rumor about Operation Water Moccasin III gained strength after speculation altered it to include the participation of black troops from Africa. Soon these blacks were further identified as Congolese troops. Could they be some of the same troops who had murdered and raped Christians in Katanga? And was it really true that U Thant of the United Nations was establishing a command post in Georgia? Would the South, and perhaps the rest of the country, be subjugated by the infamous United Nations, with help of our own United States Army troops?

No one could say with absolute certainty who was the first to start the rumor; like Topsy, it just grew. It was given wide dissemination by hundreds of individuals and groups, many of whom bombarded their congressmen with inquiries and furnished them "documented" information on the terror that already seemed to be at their very gates. It was also spread by several radio "call-in" programs, in particular "Party Line," an audience-participation show broadcast over KWKH, a 50,000-wat station in Shreveport, Louisiana. "Party-Line" was a regular evening program that served, to a great degree, as one of the principal transmitters of right-wing fears and rumors. Seldom was a voice of moderation heard that might temper the fears or request source documentation for the wilder statements regarding Operation Water Moccasin, and so rumors grew to truly shocking proportions. Many of these rumors, from various sections of the country, were mailed or telephoned to trusted conservative congressmen in Washington, D. C., and some of them formed the basis of the February 27, 1963, newsletter that the late Congressman James B. Utt, Republican from California, sent out to his constituents and friends. One of those friends was Dr. C. W. Burpo.

Congressman Utt's report on Operation Water Moccasin III was grist for any right-wing broadcaster's mill. It began with a tone guaranteed to gain the reader's attention:

> NOW HEAR THIS AND LISTEN WELL! By the time this Washington Report reaches you, there will be under way one of the most fantastic and, to me, truly frightening military maneuvers ever to be held in the United States. It is called "Exercise Water Moccasin III," and is just as deadly . . . We do not know whether African troops will be involved or not, but we do know that there is a large contingent of bare-foot Africans that have been moved into Cuba for training. . . .[13]

Congressman Utt also based some of his fears on the testimony attributed to a thirteen-year-old girl who was said to have recently escaped from Cuba. She described the Africans many believed to be training to invade the United States: ". . . I was terrified of them. They're savages. . . . They're always barefooted and they wear short skirts that come just above their knees. They have big rings in their ears and noses. They talk funny . . ."[14]

Who had brought these Africans to Cuba, the congressman asked. "Was it the United Nations? Was it Russia? Or was it the United States?"[15]

With Utt's *Washington Report* in his hand, Burpo hurried to alert his followers on his next broadcast. He quoted from the congressman's newsletter and warned, "We have to face this one thing . . . that our country is threatened and that Operation Water Moccasin could mean something ominous to our country . . ."

The heavy flow of congressional mail reflected the fear C. W. Burpo and many other right-wing commentators had evoked from their followers. At first many congressmen and Defense Department leaders were puzzled, but when the deluge of inquiries continued, some of them took steps to see what was behind the great scare. On May 2, 1963, Republican Senator Thomas H. Kuchel of California addressed his colleagues from the Senate floor. In his opening remarks he noted that ". . . the American people are keenly aware of the grave and evil hazards to our freedom and to our way of life which international Communism is eternally dedicated to destroy." The Senator noted that everyone in America except a handful of "traitorous zealots" in the ranks of the Communist party were unalterably committed to defeat any attempt to take away our freedom. He rose, he said, to speak of another danger, one just as offensive and evil to all reasonable, rational and free American citizens. It was a danger of hate and venom, of slander and abuse, generated by fear and heaped indiscriminately upon many great Americans by a group of zealots in the ranks of the self-styled "I am a better American than you are" organizations. He asked,

> How hysterical and idiotic can one get? I am afraid to answer, until I have seen tomorrow's mail. Leaflets, of course, are not the only cause for hysteria. Lunatic columnists, apostles of hate and fear on radio and television, and even loony letters to the editor provoke their share of fright mail. The curious fact is that the fright peddlers, from the simpletons to the wretched racists, all claim to be conservatives. They defile the honorable philosophy of conservatism with that claim as thoroughly as the Communists defile the honorable philosophy of liberalism.[16]

Senator Kuchel denounced by name many of the leading rightists who had played a part in rumor-mongering, including Dr. C. W. Burpo. Kuchel sympathized with his constituents who, he said, were "honestly bewildered and confused by the trash of the right-wing extremists." But he had "nothing but seething contempt" for the originators of the hoaxes and swindles, the leaders of all the several hundred self-styled patriotic groups.

> They are anything but patriotic. Indeed, a good case can be made that they are unpatriotic, and downright un-American. For they are doing a devil's work far better than Communists themselves could do.[17]

Dr. Burpo made his broadcast using the fright material supplied by Congressman Utt before he moved to Mesa, Arizona. Later that year a television network made the scare generated by Operation Water Moccasin the subject of a documentary. Several of the people most heavily involved in making Operation

Water Moccasin a national issue declined to participate in the documentary, but Dr. Burpo was more than willing to face the cameras, and his listeners from coast to coast had an opportunity to see him perform right in their living rooms.

The fear of snakes and barefoot troops in rural Georgia had hardly been forgotten when C. W. Burpo found himself at the center of another storm, this time within the center of his own right-wing world. He could hardly be faulted for errors in the religious portion of his shows, and some listeners would no doubt applaud his efforts in the political realm. But professional right-wingers are often purists at heart and cannot abide sloppy scholarship. There was little hope that Burpo's political faux pas would go unnoticed by such experts; his friends could only hope that his blunders would be overlooked as the peccadilloes of a beginner. That may well have been the case for a time, but in early 1965 his efforts came under the ban of the John Birch Society leadership. Dr. Burpo had opened his network microphones late in 1964 to one Kilsoo Haan, a representative of the Sino-Korean Peoples League, which conducted certain Korean Underground work. The series of programs featuring Mr. Haan was well received, and Rev. Burpo decided to publish the most interesting portions in a paperback. And early in 1965 *The Impending Storm,* by C. W. Burpo, D. D., rolled off the press, and thousands of copies marched out like little soldiers to help slow America's wild slide toward the garbage heap of history. Copies were even sent to every member of Congress.

One day Dr. Burpo's little book may be recognized as a unique work among the thousands of right-wing books that flooded the country during the sixties. Among the many interesting statements that Mr. Haan presented and the Doctor accepted and publicized over the air and in print was a rather novel set of facts concerning nuclear-powered aircraft. Haan declared that Russia had at that time some 150 nuclear-powered bombers. These bombers could fly at an average speed of 2,500 miles per hour; they could cruise nonstop for 90 days; and they could fly at a height of 85,000 feet. They could also penetrate the Radar System without detection. Without so much as a wink at the world, Dr. Burpo went right on explaining about the new Russian nuclear bombers, apparently convinced that he had "scooped" the whole right-wing movement. And not only did his book reveal that the Soviets had nuclear-powered aircraft that could remain in the air for 90 days, but it also said that the bombers had actually flown over California, New York and the Hawaiian Islands during 1964. And if that were not revelation enough, he added for good measure that each of the Russian planes carried "what is known as a phantom box, two feet by six feet, which performed the feat of neutralizing any and all radio and radar detector systems."

The wrath of the great Birch leader was not directed against news of the Russian aircraft nor even Burpo, as much as it was against another radio commentator who had "sponsored" Kilsoo Haan, whom Robert Welch, the Birch chieftain, considered "a lifelong enemy of Syngman Rhee." In a memorandum he sent to his Section and Chapter leaders on February 25, 1965, Welch said: "No really informed anti-Communist with careful judgment would touch Kilsoo Haan with a ten-foot pole." This indirect anathema stirred Dr. Burpo to tell his listeners on March 26, 1965, that "Mr. Welch is wrong by all standards" and to reassure them that "Mr. Haan is a true American." That should have done it, for he had already written in the introduction to *The Impending Storm* that Kilsoo Haan was "a true Christian . . . a true Methodist . . . I know this man to be for real." But just in case, Dr. Burpo added in his letter to his prayer partners that "The John Birch people are among the finest patriots I have met. . . . I have defended the Birch Society."

During the 1960s Burpo's influence continued to grow. In addition to his constant pleas for financial assistance to get on more radio stations or to purchase new equipment, pleas which usually took up part of each broadcast, Burpo periodically sent long letters to his "prayer partners," "co-workers," or just plain "Christian Friends." Besides containing urgent requests for money, the special letters were reserved for certain grim "truths" that he declared he could not utter over the radio. Dr. Burpo has a special talent for tantalizing and tormenting his radio audience with tidbits of information. The remainder, the succulent parts, are usually promised when he visits them at a rally, where he claims to be able to confide in them personally.

Over the years he has made steady progress in getting his message to an ever-increasing audience. He has done this mostly through his own efforts, although he has always had the help of Margaret and a number of hired office assistants. It is difficult to call his Institute a "Mom and Pop" operation, for his income in 1963 was a whopping $212,000. In 1964 it increased to $233,800; and in 1965 to $257,400. Still he continued to plead for financial help, and by 1966 his income had increased to $308,500.[18] By 1972 his income for the previous fiscal year had reached $557,263.

In the December 1966 issue of his newsletter, C. W. wished that he had enough money to do some missionary work in Africa and Mexico. He wanted very much to go to West Africa, but lamented that ". . . it would take $1800.00 to make the trip and, of course, we don't have it." The next month he reported happily that a man from California had sent $2,000 for a plane trip to Africa! Wonderful, except that he was suddenly receiving invitations to speak to conservative groups in Europe. He told his "partners" that he had prayed about the trip and felt that God was in favor of his journey. He would now go to the Berlin Wall and broadcast right across from East Germany, which, he noted, was "Communist territory!" Then in his best Marco Polo fashion, Dr. Burpo explained, "Someone must reach these world capitals and bring back the truth. In this trip, if God permits, I want to visit Paris and Rome and then on down to Accra, Ghana. . . ." [19]

But suddenly there was trouble in his own back yard. His neighbors were taking legal steps to have him removed from the neighborhood because he was operating a business in a residential district. "Well," observed Dr. Burpo, "God's business *is* business, but this is not a commercial enterprise. Well, I prayed and I got up and went down into the front of our office building and told the girls that I got desperate before God." [20]

A month later he was still in his headquarters and did not seem too concerned about having to move. He was still planning his overseas trip and had added Syria, Israel, Turkey, Italy and France to his official itinerary. He would not reveal the exact date on which he would leave, because of "security reasons," nor would he disclose all the stops he planned to make. He would simply go down to the airport around the first of March, and ". . . board a giant jet airliner and take off with the arms of God supporting me and, of course, your most earnest prayers." And just before he boarded the plane, Dr. Burpo revealed a tiny bit more of his plans: his personal doctor (his physician) had ordered him to make a two-day stopover in Nice on the French Riviera.[21]

Was Dr. Burpo guilty of an error in judgment in revealing that he had a personal physician? After all, many of his listeners relied on faith-healing rather than medical science to cure them of their diseases and afflictions. And was it wise to mention the two-day stopover in Nice?

Dr. Burpo sent his first trip report back in time to make the April 1967 issue of his newsletter. He was then about to leave Berlin, and he included a word of warning that would surely spike any wrong thinking that might be going on in the ranks of his supporters: "I assure you that this is not a vacation. Not one step of this trip has been any kind of a vacation.. I have worked every moment that I have been awake and will tell you much more of what happened when I get home." That should have taken care of anyone with ideas about ratatouille in Nice or the *joie de vivre* in Paris. Traveling about Europe so rapidly, he did not know exactly how things were going back in Arizona, but he had heard that the mail had been running behind and he hoped everyone would write as soon as they had read his newsletter.[22]

When he returned to Arizona, Dr. Burpo had enough information and conversation to fill up many broadcast tapes and monthly newsletters. At first, his descriptions of places and events seemed rather commonplace, but as time went by he seemed to remember more and more details, and finally the things that happened to him were so exciting and tinged with adventure and danger that it was hard to believe a man of his age could be that full of courage and derring-do.

But the thrill of telling about his adventures in exotic lands was fated to end all too soon. The problems inherent in a country-saving operation such as he was running can become a real

burden at times. He had gone off on the trip, leaving the threat
of eviction from his headquarters unresolved, and instead of disappearing, that problem continued to worsen. Faced with the
prospect of having to go into court "regarding our right to operate
as a church in our humble little Home Office," he confessed to
his prayer partners that the neighbors who wanted him to move
were not very nice people:

> Such hatred I have never experienced by neighbors. They are not
> really "neighbors" at all. I think it is the work of the enemies of this
> broadcast . . . It is now in the hands of God and the Court. Trial
> will be held in July. Brethren, pray for us! [23]

He vowed never to rent another headquarters, but the cost of
building one was almost prohibitive. And although Dr. Burpo
still held out hope of victory to his co-workers, his vision of the
future was grim and called for the greatest possible sacrifice:

> I will be very frank with you in my closing words. I am tired, but
> not discouraged. I am perplexed, but not dismayed. I know that in
> the end, we shall win. I expect severe persecution right here in the
> United States. Imprisonment is possible to those of us who contend
> for Bible living and Constitutional Government. . . .[24]

By the end of the month there had been no final disposition of
the Bible Institute headquarters problem, and Burpo was worried, but he girded himself for another trip to Washington, D.C.
He was pleased that his latest call for financial help had resulted
in such a good response: "Now that we have taken care of a lot
of bills that were pressing us, let's keep the mail up each month;
then we will never have to make an appeal again." But Dr.
Burpo usually made some sort of financial pep talk before heading out on a trip. This time he said he planned to go to the
Federal Communications Commission while he was in Washington "to have a good visit with the men on that Commission and
lay our entire program before them." So far he had not received
so much as a letter from the FCC, but he explained that he knew
through his "personal correspondent in Washington" that the
FCC had received "many letters against me, as well as several

others who are fighting this battle." [25] That was so like Dr. Burpo, always ready to go right to the heart of the problem. Once when he was upset at the National Educational Association, he threatened to go right into their headquarters in Washington, D.C., and have it out with them. And he was especially interested in the FCC. In 1966 he had even notified his prayer partners when a new chairman had been appointed to the FCC. He called it a real victory, for according to Burpo, the new chairman "happens to be a conservative. So let's pray for him and ask God to give him compassion on those of us who are trying to do a job for God and country."

While he waited for the court's decision on his home, he kept working at his mail and the unending task of preparing tapes for his programs. Suddenly he was in the midst of another imbroglio as a result of one of his broadcasts. And people in all parts of the country were probably laughing at him.

This time the trouble started when a woman sent him an article from the editorial page of the San Jose *Mercury*. It was written by the syndicated columnist and humorist Russell Baker of the New York *Times*, and published on August 15, 1967. Already well-known for his hilarious tongue-in-cheek articles, Baker set out in this article to report on the "true" identities of black militants H. Rap Brown and Stokely Carmichael. These were only the undercover names of two men hired by the federal government to deliver inflammatory harangues wherever racial animosity threatened to erupt into violence, Baker soberly reported. The appearance of these well-known radicals at a riot would help reduce public support for the civil rights movement and would let the taxpayer off with only a bill for providing prison accommodations for agitators caught crossing state lines, the straight-faced Baker continued. These men were considered invaluable by congressmen. The "Black Power!" slogan with which Carmichael, whose real name was Peter Mulligan, so effectively cooled the egalitarian ardor of white liberals had actually been the inspiration of Senator Eastland of Mississippi! [26]

On his broadcast of September 27, 1967, Dr. Burpo began with the Russell Baker story. "Now, when we talk about perturbed Americans, I want to read you a letter—it's an article that was on the editorial page . . . it said . . . 'Many persons have been infuriated this summer by the demagogic virtuosity of H. Rap Brown, but very few know Rap Brown's true identity. His name —his real name—is John Green, and he's an undercover outside agitator on the payroll of the Senate Appropriations Committee.' "

It was a news story so strange that even the Doctor seemed truly upset, afflicted as it were, with more than his usual amount of grunting, uh-ing and oh-ing. "That's hard to believe, you know, but the paper said it," Burpo ventured. "Russell—um, uh, um—where is it—yes, um, Russell Baker of the *New York Times* wrote it and . . . a Senate aide who insists on—uh being, uh— well, he didn't want to be known, he wanted to be anony- mous. . . ." And he went on to quote more of the strange article before pausing to let his followers know how perturbed he was.

You know, when you know the background of this man and know what it means to be yelling "Black Power" all the time—no wonder some of us get perturbed. If I were to say anything like these men as a white man, I would be in prison now. You know, I think this ought to be investigated. If the Senate actually has to stoop that low to get things done, I think it's time we looked at some of our legis- lators.[27]

Charles R. Baker, executive director of the Institute for Amer- ican Democracy, a clearing-house for information on the activities of both the far left and far right, was the first to notice that Burpo had been taken in so completely by the joke. Through his *Home- front* bulletin, Baker shared the Burpo blunder with the rest of the country.

In the past Dr. Burpo may have quoted the wrong people, but he had certainly never before turned a mistake into an entire radio program. Earlier that year he had approvingly quoted Harry A. Overstreet, apparently unaware that author Overstreet had long been the bête noire of the Birchers.[28] Also, he still didn't seem completely to understand that pesky Federal Reserve issue. After all this time, he still seemed ignorant about certain aspects of the far-right ideological spectrum, of important distinctions between the overt and covert racists, the religious non-racists, the conspiratorial psychotics and the anti-Semites. Some listeners were concerned about his recent interview with a congressman who denounced Senator Goldwater "and his new traveling buddies such as Richard Nixon" for supporting the Consular Treaty.[29] And he had insulted some right-wing Catholics by dwelling on the fact that Communist leaders had been received by the Pope. and asking "Will there be a Union between this religion and the atheistic Communist regime?" [30] Now his latest blunder was being called the "Burpo Blooper." This had to stop before some listeners started seriously to question his lack of judgment.

Invidious remarks about the Doctor's gullibility could still be heard when the official hearing to decide the fate of the Bible Institute headquarters finally ended. The decision was a crushing blow to Dr. Burpo, who nevertheless faced the tide of adversity with courage and a certain serenity. In his most unflappable manner he prefaced his report to his prayer partners with a passage from the eighth chapter of Romans before revealing the bitter news:

> We lost! We were framed from the beginning. I was not permitted to read our Articles of Incorporation, nor to read the book on zoning and what was permitted in this area. The Zoning Board ignored even the statement from proper authorities in Washington as to our being a church. In other words they were determined to stop us.[31]

What had happened to make Burpo suddenly believe that he had been framed? Until the board's decision was handed down, he had seemed to treat the problem as little more than a zoning dispute between neighbors. Now he declared, "They ignored the law and became a law unto themselves. This happened in America, not Russia." [32]

The little Doctor from Arizona had been quiet long enough; now he would stand up to his enemies, who were frustrating his efforts to save the republic. And he was ready to reveal some of the details of the insidious plot hatched against him and his work.

> Last year there was a meeting held in Mesa by a group of liberals who thought they were alone. A friend of mine was there, thank God. In the meeting, they said, "We want to get Burpo, no matter what we have to do." Now we have the end results; we have to move out. I have upheld the Constitution of our Country, namely, that this is a Country of law, and not one of the law of man. Gradually this

procedure is being changed. It is now the law of man, and not the Law of the Country.[33]

Despite Dr. Burpo's convoluted syntax, his message came through loud and clear to his followers. There definitely had been a plot to destroy his country-saving work. A dastardly plot by a group of liberals. But he was on the job: he had known of their plans all along, even though he had not mentioned it before. Now, at last, the facts were out in the open. And he would probably proceed to lay the evidence discovered by his infiltrator friend before the Zoning Board and ask for a new hearing. Strangely enough, Burpo didn't do that. He did not even disclose the name of his infiltrator so his friends could thank him. He revealed instead that he had already been negotiating for a larger place, one with twice the space. He would go on radio and television and "win over this cruel frame-up." And he planned an extensive tour of the nation: "I want to bring truths to you in person that we are not allowed to bring on radio." Prayer partners and listeners should get their contributions in as soon as possible; he would ask for donations to build a new headquarters twice as large as the old one. That would show them. That would expose the liberal clique and the Zoning Board to the whole world for what they really were! [34]

Dr. Burpo went immediately into action. He hurriedly got out a special letter to his "dear friends," a letter in which he reviewed the loss of his headquarters. "Cruel and angry men are responsible for this," he said, adding that "we are guilty of nothing except standing up for God and Country." He reported that "one of the biggest businessmen here" had called to tell him, "Doctor, they are out to get you." It was probably an oversight that he forgot to mention the businessman's name, but he did promise that "I am going to Washington as soon as possible and have it out with certain people. We don't have to be harassed as if we were living behind the Iron Curtain." That was Burpo at his best, standing right up and slugging it out with certain people in Washington. He explained that he wanted a place where he could expand, because he had "only just begun to fight for God and this Republic." And then, most important, he added, "I believe that our program can help guide this Nation in the crucial days ahead." He would, of course, need help. Actually, he needed about

$40,000. He would leave it up to each person to decide how much to give.

By November 1967 Dr. Burpo could report progress on the new headquarters. The cost of the lot and building had gone up to approximately $65,000, but now he would have adequate room in which to operate. The beautiful new headquarters complex would be completed around January 1968. It would contain some 4,500 feet of floor space and would be a long, rambling ranch-style complex, with the outside landscaped with cacti and palm trees. Money continued to come in to the building fund. One woman even sent money to build a small chapel on the south end of the building. In fact some $80,000 above regular contributions had come in, and now the number of radio stations could be increased.[35] In time there would be a little acreage nearby which Dr. Burpo could call his "ranch." Here in his home he could escape the pressures and burdens piled on him at his headquarters studio. It would also be a refuge for the animals he loved to tell his listeners about: Smokey, the little black d-o-g, who couldn't stand to be called a dog; that lovable doll, Miss Ethan the goat; Rosita that Pest, the donkey; Fancee-Nancee, Margaret's pet horse; and the Doctor's pride and joy, Rokir the Arabian pony.

After the formal opening of the headquarters in January 1968, Dr. Burpo revealed some of his thinking for the future. He was planning to have two of his sons and his daughter Virginia join him during 1968 ". . . on the broadcast and in the heavy responsibilities involved in this work." If something happened to him, the family would carry on the work. Of course, his voice would continue to be the principal ". . . one heard bringing thundering messages of truth; but behind the scene, our attorney son and our second son will be working on the legal aspects of strengthening this work and, of course, Virginia will be with me quite a bit on radio." [36]

By the late 1960s Rev. Burpo and the Bible Institute of the Air could definitely be called successful. C. W. was familiar enough with the pertinent right-wing issues of the day to be described as a vocal leader of the American right, if not something of an expert. He had perfected his "doomsday for America" approach until there were few right-wing broadcasters who could outclass him. He never deviated from his winning combination of much stick and a little carrot: when his listeners could tolerate no more of his frightening predictions for Christian America, Dr. Burpo would quickly switch and show them a hint of light at the end of the tunnel—hope through prayer. When he had them so worked up, so enraged at their enemies and detractors that they seemed ready to take their guns from secret hiding places, he would insist that they go to their knees in prayer to find victory for America. Fatigued in spirit, they would lapse into prayer only to find the Burpoian cry of alarm driving them back to their gun turrets once more. And Dr. Burpo never seemed to run out of new threats and fears. Each month he mailed them a new collection of terror in his Bible Institute *News*. Between articles on faith healing, he pelted them with such headlines as "The Worst Is Yet To Come . . . Unless," "America Is Lost, Unless," "America Is Tottering," "Has America Forsaken Sanity?" and "Pray or Perish." And he could supplement these warnings with Scriptures in a most remarkable way. For example, when he wanted to warn about gun registration, he quoted Matt. 24:23: "But know this, that if the good man of the house had known in what watch the thief would come, he would have watched, and would not have suffered his house to be broken up." That passage, Rev. Burpo decided, explained the evil efforts of some men to bring about the registration of guns in America: "The disarming of America is underway. The people who are fighting hard for a gun law, a bit of legislation, and they're going to get it from the way it looks to cause everyone of us to register our guns. Then later on when the enemy wants to take over, [they] come and pick up our guns, cut off our electricity, beat us to our knees and this country is gone. . . ."[37] And in those rare times when he felt it necessary, Dr. Burpo was not afraid to advise his followers to arm themselves: "My advice to you is to be prepared to defend yourselves in more ways than one. Our Pilgrim Fathers went to Church with a Bible in one hand and a gun in the other. God forbid that we have to do these things, but we just can't be run out of our own homes without a protest."[38]

C. W. Burpo rarely became so pessimistic that he did not reserve a spark of hope for his supporters. Toward the end of the 1960s there was genuine disagreement among some of the leaders and spokesmen for the far right about whether America was a "sick" country. Dr. Burpo's usual approach was to emphasize that the blackness was fast closing in on America, but prayer could still reverse the trend. But in the September 1968 issue of his newsletter, he got on both sides of the argument at the same time. First he decided that the world had entered upon the last phase of its history, and the doom had already begun: "The fact of the matter is, this nation is dying. It is sick unto death . . . The world hangs over an abyss, fearful to contemplate, and it hangs by a thread that only Divine Grace and Mercy keeps from breaking!" That seemed clear enough, but five pages later in his eight-page newsletter, the Doctor commented, "You hear a lot of talk these days about our country being sick. I don't buy it. America is still the greatest country in the world. America hasn't failed. . . ." [39]

But the Arizona faith healer didn't mix things up that badly very often. He usually played it safe by looking at the blackest side of things. And at times he even claimed to know what was causing the trouble: "We all know that there is something going on, and has been going on ever since World War II ended, right up to this moment. There is some hidden force, some hidden power, or something that is influencing our people. They do not act like Americans." [40] Would Dr. Burpo be more specific and identify this hidden force? No, he couldn't explain it fully without getting kicked off the radio, but he would say this much: "If we get our people straightened out, we then will see the menace that is facing us today in Communism is just a front for a gang of gangsters and one-worlders that hope to take over. You don't dare name them as a non-profit corporation or off you'd go." [41]

At times, no quotation seemed too wild or undocumented to escape Burpo's printing press, if it promised to heighten his listeners' fears about world conditions. He demonstrated his faith in the fraudulent "Communist Rules for Revolution" by publishing them after they had been discredited.[42] He used the fake Edmund Burke quotation, "All that is necessary for the triumph of evil is for good men to do nothing," long after the Birchers had publicly admitted it could not be attributed to Burke. And he found a very scary quotation, which he attributed to one Dimitri Manuilsky, and published it in a special, undated edition of his newsletter.

The frightening quotation became known as the "Manuilsky clenched-fist quotation," and was used by any number of far-right organizations. It stated that

> War to the hilt between Communism and Capitalism is inevitable. Today, of course, we are not strong enough to attack. Our time will come in twenty to thirty years. To win we will need the element of surprise. The bourgeois will have to be put to sleep. So we shall begin by launching the most spectacular peace movement on record. There will be electrifying overtures, and unheard-of concessions. The capitalistic countries, stupid and decadent, will rejoice to cooperate in their own destruction. They will leap at another chance to be friends. As soon as their guard is down, we shall smash them with our clenched fist.[43]

Burpo apparently had not spent much time searching for documentation for the dreadful Manuilsky quotation, but fairness dictates that we assume he would not have published it had he known that scholars had traced the fabrication to a onetime Communist, Joseph Zack Kornfeder, who was paid for testifying at investigations.

There were many other fake quotations available, and the Doctor used some of them, but he did not always rely on material filtered through the printing presses of other organizations. Sometimes he developed his own program material from literature sent in by his listeners.

In one of his most effective stories, Dr. Burpo said that as he drove down to the studio from the ranch one morning, God had given him the answer to the Vietnam problem. "The answer," Burpo said, "is to do exactly what my son Charles said that General George Patton did in World War II: advance and win. . . ." He also had another approach to that war. He asked, "How do we expect to defeat something that we're actually financing and promoting?" He was not the first to accuse the U.S. government of backing both sides in the Vietnam war, but it was the first time he had made such a radical accusation on the air.

The American public had not taken his various suggestions to heart, and Burpo threatened that "conditions will continue to get worse and worse until the Communists decide it's time for them to do their destructive work and destroy from fifty to seventy-five million of us, just like they have openly threatened to do . . . why wait to see if it will happen? [44] Such terrible speculation seemed to stimulate Dr. Burpo to reveal still more of his thinking, ideas capable of frightening many into supporting a far-out ideology.

I was thinking this morning on the way down from the ranch, uh, about something . . . suppose that there are young people and children in your home right now, and a few years ago those precious boys dying in Vietnam were around your knees. Did you tell them about the history of our country, or will you tell them that you were too busy making money, or playing golf or going fishing to be interested in any religious or patriotic movement or to read the truth published at great personal sacrifice?

Or will you just have to look your children in the face and admit you were brainwashed by lies and deception, the Doctor continued. What will you say, Mother, to your little girl when she cuddles up to you saying, "Momma, I'm afraid."? What will you say if you are forced to take your children to the embarkation point and you see them, perhaps for the last time, as they are being shipped off for indoctrination in some foreign land?

What will you say when they ask if they should say their prayers before they go to bed? You say, Brother Burpo, what are you talking about? I'm talking about what has happened in other lands . . . we are almost to the point of no return. I want you young parents to look at your children. If they're asleep, walk in tonight and look at them—peaceful, innocent and trusting. What are you going to do to prevent the possibility of such a terrifying event from occurring?

Dr. Burpo was pressing in on his listeners with his very best sermon. They were worried now, and it is a part of the Burpoian virtuosity that he will only take time from his initial thrust to shore up his own credibility:

Oh, I know—don't think I can't stand here before this microphone and get the reaction of people to this type of message. They're saying, "That guy Burpo is off his rocker. He's a nut!" Well, they called, uh, Paul a nut. They called Christ a fool. They killed every one of the twelve apostles but one. China when the Communists took over murdered 20,000,000 Christians [sic]. The same fate is awaiting this nation . . . Mothers and fathers of America, if you sit by and do nothing now, what will you tell your children when it happens? . . . we're not up against a namby-pamby bunch of religious club members who belong to, uh, uh, a, uh, big, rich, aristocratic church. We're up against a group of people, we're up against a conspiracy that intends to put you and me under their heels. There'll be no church bells ringing in America if Communism takes over; there'll be no altars in your church where you can go and weep your way through to God. There'll be no Christian funerals, no Christian marriages, no open Bibles—it will be all underground if this nation perishes.

The Doctor ended his sermon with an unusually strong plea for financial help, asking for thirty-dollar contributions. And for those who had trouble spelling his address, "Mesa is spelled M-E-S-A. M as in Margaret. . . ." [45]

No one, not even the Doctor, could hope to maintain such a disciplined guard against the forces of evil and darkness without suffering untoward reaction. He was, after all, only human, and as Shakespeare wisely observed in *Antony and Cleopatra*, "The nature of bad news affects the teller." As early as February 1967, Burpo warned his supporters to have double locks installed to guard themselves and their property. He was already equipped with locks, a shotgun, two pistols and a dog. He was surrounded by an eight-foot cement-block fence, and he promised to blast any crook who tried to get in his headquarters. [46] In early 1968 Doctor Burpo announced he was taking the advice offered him by a congressman to secure two bodyguards to accompany him on a trip to Washington, D.C. He reported that "You can almost see the dark clouds of Armageddon hanging low over the world," but he bravely went on to the nation's capital. And he reported that in May of that year a threat had been made on his life. [47]

By 1970 he had become even more concerned. He noted that people were writing to him to say that they were afraid to become identified with his organization for fear of persecution in the future. And he seemed increasingly fearful that the enemy was closing in on his well-guarded fortress: ". . . You see the bars over the windows of my Institute here," he explained to a guest on a broadcast. "You saw me lock every door when we came in here. I've had threatening phone calls all day long today, from people under assumed names wanting to get in. I know why—they want this [program] hushed . . ." [48] In March 1971 he reported that he had installed a burglar alarm system in his home. Twice the Sheriff's department had sent men out, the Doctor noted, "because the alarm was set off by people trying to cut the lines and break in." [49] Things seemed even worse by the end of 1971. A man stopped by the Institute headquarters and said he had heard the place was for sale. Burpo told his followers he was convinced the man was an "enemy plant." [50] C. W. seemed almost at the end of his rope at the beginning of March 1972. He confessed, "Many times I've awakened, shaking with a nightmare of young hoodlums surrounding me with long, slender-bladed knives, dancing, showing their teeth, threatening me. It was a nightmare, because I had been studying and I had been reading our newspapers." [51]

After "America is in danger" sermons and appeals for financial contributions, the next most popular subject on Bible Institute programs has probably always been faith-healing, or divine healing, as the Doctor prefers to call it. C. W. Burpo has never been one to spend time and effort recording the names and ages of those healed through his prayers and ministrations; neither has he been guilty of carrying faith-healing to the commercial extremes that some preachers have. But the Doctor is quick to proclaim that he has himself been miraculously healed many times. And after having conducted healing programs as part of his ministry for many years, he came to endorse virtually all types of miracle healing early in 1970.

A few weeks later, on June 13, 1970, while riding high above the clouds in an airplane one hour out of Washington, D.C., on the way to Phoenix, he was stricken with a severe urological attack. A short time after landing he was in the emergency ward of the Lutheran Hospital at Mesa, Arizona, and following a series of tests, he underwent corrective surgery. It was more than a month before he was able to return to his regular office routine.

And it took an equally long time before he wrote a letter to his prayer partners and co-workers explaining why he had undergone surgery instead of relying on the faith-healing he had been recommending to his listeners.

Without doubt, the situation called for the very best explanation C. W. could provide, so he went to the Book of Job to locate a set of circumstances that paralleled his own somewhat unique trouble. He came away with a very interesting, but far from original, explanation for seeking help from a physician rather than the Lord. Said Dr. Burpo to his radio audience,

> I was stricken, and thirty minutes after I landed at Sky Harbor Airport in Phoenix, I was in the emergency ward at the Mesa Lutheran Hospital. And after some very extensive tests, I had to undergo surgery—according to my two surgeons—if I were to live. I wondered about that and I prayed about it. I've always practiced, uh, faith in God, and I turned to the twenty-second chapter of Luke, verses 31 and 32, and I read: "Satan obtained you by asking that he might sift you as wheat. But I have made supplication for thee that thy faith fail not. . . ." Well, Satan never gave up and he afflicted Job, but in the end God brought him out. Well, I took comfort in that. . . .[52]

He had only begun his explanation, and two days later he broadcast some additional information. This time he did not dwell on the similarities between his own affliction and the problems of Job, but he did surround the operating table and the surgeons with as much sanctity and holiness as possible.

> You know, when I told my doctors—they said don't give our names— I said I am going to ask the Master Surgeon to guide your hand as you operate, and tears came up in their eyes, and they said, "Thank you, we'll need it." And they came through, thank God, and according to all reports, I'll be around here a long time to minister to you and to help you. And you know something? I wanted to tell you about this, but I was told not to. Because of another great problem which has caused me agony of heart, and I will tell you about that as soon as possible. They said—my advisers—don't tell the people about your going to the hospital until it's all over and you're well. But

I do want to thank you—some of you the Lord revealed it to—and all of you knew that something was wrong and you prayed.[53]

Once committed to the Job analogy, Dr. Burpo apparently decided that he should stay with it. And he tried improving it at every opportunity. By September of that year he had even found a way to scold some of his doubters by inventing a clever little dialogue with Satan:

> Every time since I've had my recent trouble that I go to make, uh, bring a message on, uh, divine healing, Satan attacks me, and says, "Well, why didn't God heal you?" And I said, "Obviously, Satan, you haven't been listening, 'cause I gave the reasons from the first and second chapters of the book of Job. Now, I know that God has healed, I know that he does heal, and whether or not, uh, d—, uh, people will have a tendency to doubt. All of us need our faith built up.[54]

It appeared that the Doctor had a real job on his hands trying to explain why he had sought help from medical science after claiming miraculous cures so many times and strongly recommending faith-healing to his supporters. And it seemed almost impossible that he would be able to re-establish his old miracle-healing programs that had been so successful. But Burpo realized he would have to move very slowly, and many months passed before he took to reporting that he had been miraculously healed of something again. Two years later the Doctor was still discussing his surgery, and by then it almost seemed that he had made a greater sacrifice by going under the surgeon's knife than if he had waited for a miracle.

> . . . God showed me why he let me go through surgery. . . . And God told me, through the Spirit, in the hospital, right there in the Lutheran Hospital in Mesa, "I have given you your lovely headquarters; I've healed you of a malignancy that the doctor was gonna operate the next morning in Santa Monica, California, in 1956; I've healed you of a heart condition when you'd strained your heart, and it was enlarged and now it is normal! I've healed you of diabetes, and Satan is still coming to accuse the brethren . . ." And He told me that the reason, that, uh, uh, that was he [Satan] said you've,

you've been too good to him. Let me at him. Let me fix him. Well, God let him. But He said [to Satan] to spare his life. I prayed and . . . I said, Lord, if anything is ever going to disgrace this work that you've entrusted me with, I want to die . . . But there's not—I want to live! Maybe it's the coward's way out, but I can't stand it . . . I saw my doctor recently and he said, "Amazing!" He leaned back against the wall and looked at me with a smile: "Amazing, I never thought you'd make it." And I said, "The Lord thought I would." . . . And I'm so happy I'm going to sing. . . .[55]

And Dr. Burpo's melodious voice pealed forth the first beautiful lines of "My Father is Omnipotent" after he dedicated it to a sweet little lady somewhere deep in the heart of Texas.

The Arizona preacher continued to explain the deeply religious significance of his going to the hospital, even after his faith-healing program had returned to the usual format. Everything seemed to be progressing well: the number of stations broadcasting his program continued to increase, his new hairpiece had come to look natural, and he wrote that somebody said he looked like the movie star David Niven!

But there was one other problem, one he had hinted at when he first explained the details of his surgery in a special letter to his supporters on July 28, 1970. He said then he could not reveal the details of the trouble, except that it was very serious, that the enemy was harassing him and trying to still the voice of the Bible Institute. As week after week went by, Dr. Burpo continued to prepare his listeners with hints that his latest heartache involved a member of his family, a son who had betrayed him in some manner. The problem also appeared to involve some agency of the federal government, for he revealed in September 1970 that "Many of you have requested that I tell you the problem that I am going through. Most of the letters seem to indicate that it is the FCC that is giving me trouble. But, such is not the case." He explained that his attorneys had advised him not to state exactly what he was going through until it was all over, "but I think you can read between the lines and get my meaning," he wrote.

There are forces in this government that do not want non-profit organizations such as ours to continue the hard-hitting messages that we are bringing. This is why we are under heavy surveillance. Every word that I utter on the radio is monitored, and they are searching for something to use against me in trying to get our non-profit corporation cancelled.[56]

In December 1970 Dr. Burpo sent out his seventeenth anniversary letter, which revealed his message was being heard on 65 half-hour radio programs each day, including those on FM stations and several stations that played his sermon twice daily. It was his dream to push the number of stations up to an even 100. He referred also to his special problem:

When this trouble that I have mentioned came up, I immediately called my son Charles, who has four active attorneys working for him in his office. Also, we have a very prominent attorney in Phoenix. My total outlay of money at this time has been $20,000, which has been used to protect us. When you write us, do your best to help us get this money back into the Institute so that we can pay up all of our bills.[57]

The following month, in January 1971, Burpo's regular newsletter revealed that his supporters were criticizing him severely for not telling them the whole story of his harassment by the federal government. He explained that the Bible Institute was waiting until the enemy had been defeated entirely before telling all about the battle they were going through. Since his request for $20,000 a month earlier, some $11,000 had come in, and the Doctor was most appreciative. He commented that one "sarcastic lady" asked why, if the Bible Institute had that kind of money, the listeners were being bothered for contributions. Since many people may he unaware that a national radio ministry involves very big sums of money, Dr. Burpo might have been unwise to discuss precise amounts, but he usually knows best how to handle such things. The money had been borrowed, he explained.[58]

Burpo continued to agonize on his broadcasts about the cruel heartache he was enduring because of the harassment by the government, and in March 1971 he announced that his attorneys were allowing him to write a letter to his prayer partners to outline some of the details of the terrible persecution he and Margaret had been going through.

His letter was entitled "Special Personal Report" and was marked, in large letters, CONFIDENTIAL. And the Doctor started right off with the bad news. It involved Chet, his second son.

My son Chet, who at one time worked with me in this office with the promise that he would give himself to God and never drink again, terminated his work with me through getting so completely saturated with liquor after seven months that I had to let him go . . . Nine times I put him in the Franklin Alcoholic Hospital in Phoenix to dry him out and finally took almost the last dollar I had and put him through a real estate school and prepared him to make a very handsome living. Instead of doing this, he turned to the bottle again. For weeks upon weeks he remained drunk. And then one day he and his wife called me on the phone and said that if I did not give them $80,000 in cash they would go to the Internal Revenue Service and tell every conceivable thing possible about me and how I was hiding away large sums of money and would see that I was put behind bars.[59]

Dr. Burpo's most difficult problems have always seemed to involve members of his family, perhaps because he has always wanted them with him in his radio ministry. More than once he has discussed turning the program over to one or more of his children in case he should be called away to Heaven. As far back as 1963 he had attempted to move his son Chet into the business. At that time he told his listeners some "wonderful news."

Our second son, Chet Burpo, received a call to the ministry some years ago. For some reason God did not open the door for Chet at that time. But he never lost his faith in God nor doubted at any time that God had called him. Recently while I was so ill I called upon God for the answer. Immediately the Lord showed me that He had kept Chet for this very purpose. We called him and he broke down and cried, saying "Dad, I am greatly honored that you would want me to join your staff, but I will." [60]

Burpo went on to promise his listeners that they would be hearing Chet on the broadcasts as he began taking over some of the programs. He spoke glowingly of his son's qualifications and reported that "Chet is a happily-married man with a lovely wife and one teenage daughter."

After a while there was no further mention of Chet in connection with the Bible Institute. But some years later, in 1968, Dr. Burpo again had fond hopes of bringing Chet and others of his family into the Institute. He told his radio audience that summer, "Now that Chet is with us and doing a valiant job—he's out of the studio and I can talk about him—he has a new glow on his face, a new consecration in his heart. And soon there will be Virginia, and then Charles Jr. Pray for us and never give up the fight. . . ." [61]

Now that he despaired of bringing his son Chet into his organization and was revealing the details of their trouble, would he tell the listeners how Chet had gotten the idea that the Doctor was able to pay blackmail of $80,000? Not exactly, because he didn't know how Chet could have come up with that idea.

Chet worked with me in this office, and each day I would show him what came in. At the end of the month I would show him the radio bills and all the other bills, and I also showed him how at one time I had to borrow several thousand dollars to catch up. He knew that all he told was untrue and his lies were unfounded, but the Internal Revenue Service took his word against mine. They have been investigating us for nearly a year . . . I believe that this is political as well as tyrannical and a last effort to disgrace my ministry and stop this great work that YOU and I have built together. [62]

At the time of his special letter C. W. Burpo had not been indicted, but the IRS was investigating him carefully, and thousands of his prayer partners and co-workers had written to tell him they had been questioned. He told them that Margaret's heart was broken and that he knew how the Apostle Paul felt when he was pressed out of measure. He felt he could have endured the pain much more easily had it been laid on him by an outsider. "But when you have given your all to a child, and then he turns against you and curses you and goads you and threatens you with the penitentiary, then you can understand how broken I am." His doctor had told him that this worry was the greatest source of the illness he was now enduring. But his son Charles Jr. was coming soon to lift most of the responsibility of the work from his shoulders. Charles would also do much of the broadcasting, but the Doctor's voice would always be heard. He was certainly not going to quit. He had many plans, including some which involved missionary work. And he still had faith that God would spare America. Right at that very moment he had a burden for the people in the earthquake area in California: "Even though it has been prophesied by scientists that one day Los Angeles and San Francisco could be shaken loose from the country and fall into the sea, I have prayed that it will not happen." He had confused the scientists with the occultists, but Burpo meant well by the Californians. He still loved Chet, though he had changed his earlier opinion of Chet's wife.

> Now, after having read this, I want you to tear this letter up so that the enemies of the Lord will not get hold of it. I still love Chet and wet my pillow with tears every night because of him. He has a vicious wife that he should have let go a long time ago; but since both of them drink, all we can do is pray for them. . . .[63]

The long battle with the IRS continued. Dr. Burpo continued to tell his partners as much as possible over the air and through his newsletter. He warned them that his programs were monitored and that he was watched. He would have to save the most important information until he could visit them personally at rallies. And the Doctor did not mean to give up without a real fight.

> Not only has the blackmail attempt hurt us, but the truth of the matter is that orders came from the Justice Department of Washington to prosecute this case. If they do, I am going to go to Washington and pick out three powerful Senators who have promised to stand with me. We will then face this thing through—even if we have to carry it to the White House.[64]

He was advised by his personal physician to retire completely from the Bible Institute ministry, but that he refused to do. His health was very poor, and Margaret also had health problems, but Burpo reported, "We are depending on God to heal her body and also to get me over this infectious hepatitis soon." [65]

On every side there seemed to be trouble and misfortune. Even his loyal son Charles Jr., who had been so much help, was ill. And Chet and his wife were continuing in their sinful ways. But Dr. Burpo kept up the fight. He continued his faith-healing work, but he had become so disgusted with the wild claims of some radio healers that he almost refused to talk any more about miracle healing. Also, he had come to believe that there was a "great offensive attack being launched on those of us who believe in Divine Healing." He based this on an article which appeared in the June 1971 issue of *Reader's Digest* and which attacked commercialized faith-healing.

And even though the IRS continued to investigate his work, the Doctor undertook the added burden of going on the rally circuit. He asked his people to locate meeting places in their cities—auditoriums, not churches. Burpo was certainly not against churches, but he had found that "so many people will come to a school auditorium, or an auditorium in some hotel, where they will not come to a church." [66]

But he seemed to be trying too hard to please his followers at the rallies. What were once slight overstatements now became wild distortions. His stories of his 1967 trip to the Berlin Wall became altogether too vivid. He even told an audience that a general stationed in Berlin had promised to send a tank down to Checkpoint Charlie if the Communists tried to hold him in East Germany. And he was using that old favorite, the Federal Reserve Conspiracy fable, entirely too often and in much the wrong manner. In one rally, for example, the Doctor claimed he had recently gone to the office of Representative Wright Patman, Chairman of the Banking and Currency Committee, to tape an interview. Burpo said that because there was a "strange-looking man" in Representative Patman's office who listened to everything that was said, he decided to postpone the interview until the following day. The next morning Representative Patman took him aside and whispered that he had been warned by the Federal Reserve people not to tape an interview with Dr. Burpo. All this, Burpo promised, could be verified by writing Representative Patman's office.

At his rally in Oklahoma City's Little Theater on September 27, 1971, a group of college students copied down the Doctor's remarks about the Federal Reserve and Representative Patman. Burpo was apparently unaware of their special interest in his little story, nor did he realize their tape recorders were running throughout his performance. Taking him at his word, some of them contacted Representative Patman, who greatly appreciated having his attention drawn to the Doctor's remarks. He noted that he could find no record of ever having promised Burpo an interview; in fact he had never met him nor heard of him. "Furthermore," wrote Representative Patman, "the content of the alleged statement attributed to me is ridiculous on its face." [67]

Now it was late in 1972, and still the investigation by the IRS continued. The Mesa faith healer had become so frustrated that one day during a broadcast he screamed: "I've been hounded like a dog by a government agency." [68] He found it necessary to keep up a constant plea for financial assistance from his radio flock, and he had become more outspoken about money. He told one lady who had spent $1,800 trying to secure healing from a certain religious organization that she would have done better to use the $1,800 for his radio expenses and let him pray for her. And he had also become more openly critical of other ministries. He no longer hesitated to advise his people about giving to other preachers: "Do be careful where you put your money. These exaggerated statements made over radio saying that you will be healed if you give a 'prove-me offering' are not Bible." [69]

Burpo had also lost his shyness about mentioning the IRS on his broadcasts.

In mid-1972 he began sending out three articles "on the tyranny in the Internal Revenue Service" which described the harassment of taxpayers by that agency. And despite the insistence of some listeners that he ought to stick strictly to religion and leave politics alone, he continued to speak out on almost all subjects. He was especially upset that President Nixon had gone to visit Red China. And he had come all the way back to his old faith-healing programs. God had recently healed him again, this time of hepatitis, and now his service to his people in the faith-healing department promised to be bigger and better than ever.

In January 1973, Doctor Burpo had some good news for his followers. He confided that two specialists had wanted to operate on his throat, but "God beat them to it and took the nodules off my vocal chords and larynx. My voice is being restored." Some listeners had not been aware that the Doctor was suffering so acutely until the next month when, for some unexplained reason, he surprised them with more information about his miracle cure. Perhaps it was because some listeners had heard he had gone to a hospital or perhaps it was simply because his latest miracle healing was so unusual, that he decided to share a few more details about it. Whatever the case, some listeners discovered for the first time how worried he had been:

> At first when I lost my voice I was terrified. Then I began to quiet down and reason the thing out. The devil was making another attack on me as he did in June of 1970. I simply resented it and pulled off to the side of the road on the way to the hospital and Margaret and I joined hands, as I have already told you, in prayer . . . The next morning at 11 o'clock when they put me under anesthesia, and opened my throat and put the equipment there to hold it open and went down through my vocal chords and larynx, the nodules were gone. Praise God! So, my voice is almost back to normal . . . Aren't you happy that we have such a good and wonderful God!

What an unusual example of faith healing! A miraculous cure had occurred after part of the operation had been completed!

Most of Dr. Burpo's other news was encouraging. Margaret was feeling better and the bloom was returning to her cheeks. He also promised that "very soon I am going to tell you of a secret that I can't repeat right now." And he needed about $1,800 for a cassette recorder. C. W. Burpo assured his flock that "Our work is not for sale, money cannot buy our mailing list nor our building. Your names are protected from everyone. Men come in and say I want to see your mailing list. They are promptly shown the back door because this is a Church. You are my sheep and I am going to protect you." [70]

IV

Rev. Ike

You can't lose with the stuff I use, and the stuff I use is mind power.
—Reverend Ike, January 1973

Reverend Ike—
Apostle of Green Power

Sunday afternoon church services in the ornate, elegant, magnificently decorated Palace Auditorium of Reverend Ike's United Church Center are always spectacular, but when they fall on Christmas Eve, they become a colorful yuletide festival as well as the usual joyous celebration evoking the muse of material success. Promptly at three o'clock on Christmas Eve of 1972, a musical ensemble rose phoenixlike from beneath the dais to sing hosannas while the Rev. Dr. Frederick J. Eikerenkoetter II (who tells everyone he is better known as "Reverend Ike") poured out benevolent greetings to his followers. Beaming a transcendent smile of love, the most flamboyant preacher in the nation moved slowly through the vast auditorium packed with 5,000 of his followers. He walked a dozen steps and paused to stretch out his arms as if to embrace a whole group of his people, who responded by throwing their arms out toward him. With his dark, half-hooded eyes sparkling almost as brightly as his diamond stickpin and the rhinestones on his lapels, Reverend Ike tossed his pompadour of black wavy locks pomaded shiny-bright. Slowly he began to close his outstretched arms, folding them about his own body until he was quite literally hugging himself. After a moment he moved on to repeat the cycle of gestures to other parts of his congregation until he had spread a mantle of love over all the auditorium.

Reverend Ike slipped from sight behind the banks of flowers to reappear a moment later onstage. He glided past magnificent triple-tiered candelabra, past great decorative urns and two awesome scarlet- and gold-embroidered thrones. He moved to a microphone half hidden behind a long, low row of poinsettias flanking two organs and a group of musicians. As the footlights brightened, the handsome, 38-year-old preacher swung himself about to give the whole congregation an opportunity to gaze at his chiseled profile. He moved slowly, holding the chin high, rotating his profile to a new angle as he modeled the latest creation in his famous wardrobe, a Reverend Ike trademark that reportedly costs his supporters $1,000 each week. He continued to pose, smiling, resplendent in a rose and fuchsia floral-patterned blazer, Prussian-blue flare slacks and high-heeled patent leather jodphurs. Still beaming joy and happiness, he motioned to the congregation to join in the beat he was tapping. Softly he began to lead them in singing, "A-men, A-men, A-A-Amen!"

Only seven years ago Frederick J. Eikerenkoetter II was a struggling fundamentalist preacher on the lowest rung of the spiritual ladder—the world of black storefront religion. The son of a Baptist minister from Ridgeland, South Carolina, Eikerenkoetter decided in 1965 to leave hellfire-and-damnation preaching behind and become Reverend Ike, the apostle of the Good Life here on earth. His father was of Dutch-Indonesian extraction, and Reverend Ike's flashily handsome face has been described as cocoa-colored, tawny, creamy-brown and coffee-colored. He speaks slowly and carefully, masking any hint of a Southern accent, as he addresses vast and mostly black congregations.

As the top-ranking black radio preacher, Reverend Ike is heard on a nationwide network of some 80 stations. His regional television specials have been viewed by millions. And his newsletters and full-color magazine called *Action!* are mailed to approximately a million and a half followers. It has been claimed that he draws more people than any evangelist but Billy Graham. Few independent ministries can boast such a large headquarters congregation. As pastor of the United Church in the Washington Heights section of Manhattan, Reverend Ike ministers to a congregation that has grown so rapidly it now requires a number of associate ministers. Although Ike's United Christian Evangelistic Association is supported by many whites in his far-flung radio audience, most of his United Church congregation in New York City is black. They pack his 5,000-seat sanctuary every week, prosperous conservatively-dressed middle-class blacks, a congregation dominated by matrons in furs and wide-brimmed hats. One finds few bearded men or young men and women in Afro hairdos. The United Church does not cater to the avant-garde or the social activists. Reverend Ike makes it clear that he has no truck with Black Power. He is militant about just one thing—money. It is Green Power that Reverend Ike preaches about, along with a bit of faith-healing. He is the first non-denominational radio preacher with a nationwide ministry who has dared to abandon the traditional preachments of heaven and hell, and offer instead a Gospel based blatantly on money. He has been pictured as the latest and most brazen addition to a growing tradition of rich, flamboyant black religious leaders like Sweet Daddy Grace or Father Divine. In one sense that estimation of Reverend Ike is true, but the Rev. Dr. Frederick J. Eikerenkoetter II is already better known than his famous predecessors and now seems destined to become the most controversial and famous black preacher in the history of American religion.

The flamboyant New York minister has propelled himself to fame and fortune by means of the Blessing Plan, his version of an old method of increasing a preacher's income. Far from being a complicated fiscal arrangement, the Blessing Plan is the very essence of simplicity. In just three words, Reverend Ike has explained his plan as a way of "(1) Believing, (2) Giving, and (3) Prospering. . . . The Blessing Plan is the idea of success and prosperity, working in your mind, moving you to give." [1] The first two steps in the Blessing Plan are in operation the moment a person believes enough to give money to Reverend Ike's ministry. The third step—prosperity for the giver—might take longer, but Reverend Ike furnishes volumes of testimonials on the results his plan has produced for others.

Ordinarily Reverend Ike suggests that one should make a beginning pledge of at least $100 to the Blessing Plan. If necessary, this can be paid in easy installments of just $10 a month. If $10 is too hard on some budgets, arrangements can be made to pay the pledge at the rate of $5 every two weeks. As soon as a pledge is paid in full, Reverend Ike counsels that a new pledge should be started immediately, to keep the flow of prosperity blessings coming in regularly. He also suggests that, whenever possible, larger gifts should be made to the Plan, since a proportionate relationship apparently exists between the amounts given and the blessings obtained. And gifts and pledges to Ike's ministry should never be considered a burden. He insists that contributors will be rewarded in turn by God: "He is rich. And He has provided a way for you to give this money, and be blessed yourself. . . ."

In such thoughtful ways Reverend Ike strives to take some of the pain out of giving, especially for beginners still grappling with the basics of the Blessing Plan. But there are times when he has taken the position that it is good for people to suffer, if only very slightly. In October 1971, when he gave the world the "Money Rake," with instructions on "How to Rake the Money In," he asked for something extra:

> I ask that you send a special offering with your request—an extra offering. Borrow it if necessary. Go to some extra effort. People borrow for the doctor and the lawyer, and save for the undertaker—but rob God! Send an extra offering. DON'T LET THIS BE YOU! Send an extra offering. And believe for EXTRA blessings . . . Whenever you give, you are working with the Blessing Plan.[2]

Reverend Ike's newsletters and magazines teem with testimonials from followers who have received diamonds, Cadillacs, unexpected money, new homes and many miracle cures. He also reserves space in his literature to share with his supporters some of his most profound thoughts on money:

> Don't be a hypocrite about money. Admit openly and inwardly that you like money. Say: "I like money. I need money. I want money

I love money in its right place. Money is not sinful in its right place. Money is good: I bless the idea of money in my mind."

In special advice to his followers, Reverend Ike counsels them not to complain about high prices. He suggests instead that they say, "I give thanks for money to pay whatever price for whatever I need." He also cautions that one should be very careful about talking or even thinking wrongly about money. If one makes such remarks as "money is hard to get," that is just the way it will be. His thoughts on the bills people owe are also unique: he suggests that one should bless the bills and bless all to whom the bills are owed.

When Reverend Ike started to broadcast his gospel of wealth from radio stations that specialize in fundamentalism, his message startled many in the regular listening audience. But he was accepted largely because his short, 15-minute radio programs rarely presented his entire philosophy and because he seemed to be a "Mr. Protestant Work-Ethic."

As support for his message grew in "middle America," Reverend Ike went on the road, holding Healing and Blessing Meetings in auditoriums and coliseums all over the country. Those who had written for his literature or those who had become users of his Blessing Plan received postcards announcing a scheduled meeting in their city. The cards generally specified that a special section would be set aside for the disabled and those on stretchers, crutches or in wheel chairs. Reverend Ike promised, "I will walk down the aisle one hour before the meeting to meet and greet you personally—as many as possible. I CANNOT TALK AFTER THE MEETING. I WILL NEED TO CATCH MY BREATH. Don't let any job or commitment keep you in slavery so that you can't attend this meeting and be blessed with health, happiness, success and prosperity." [3]

When he met some 3,000 of his followers in the Miami Beach Convention Hall in April 1971, he told them,

I can love the Lord a lot better when I've got money in my pocket. Bless Money. Money is God in action. Now I'm about to pray the prayer of success and prosperity. And as I pray I'm going to receive

the evening's offering. I don't want everyone to give—only those who
see themselves having greater prosperity.[4]

The religion editor of the Miami *News* reported on Reverend
Ike's meeting in an article entitled "Ministry of Love Made Easier
by $$." He described the New York preacher's costume as "a
black-and-red spangled double-breasted dinner jacket, pink-ruf-
fled shirt, red pants and red, white and black patent-leather
shoes." As he prepared to take the offering, Reverend Ike an-
nounced his highly unorthodox procedures:

> Now I want those of you who can give $100 right now to come up
> to the front of this altar . . . and those of you who can't give $100,
> take out $50 and bring it up . . . and if you haven't got that then
> take out a ten or a five . . . No change please . . . Hold those bills
> high, I want everyone to see your faith.

The reporter watched Reverend Ike's assistants move through
the part of the audience that remained seated. In plastic pails
they collected an offering, but they refused to disclose the amount
of money received: "That's none of your business. Our books are
open to the federal government but not to the general public."

The new Horatio Alger of radio preachers continued to spread
his message of success through hard work or good luck, in per-
sonal appearances all over the country. In December 1971 he
booked the San Francisco Cow Palace for $25,000, for a one-
night meeting. One of the biggest syndicated religion columns
called him a "comparatively new voice on the radio scene," but
was impressed enough to compare his colorful costumes to those
worn by Liberace. It also reported that Ike's money-raising meth-
ods would make "the late Sister Aimee seem shy," and his "jet-
powered healing technique" make Oral Roberts look dignified.[5]

In 1966 Reverend Ike set up his international headquarters in
a former New York City theater. He spent more than $1 million
restoring, furnishing and decorating the giant building, which
occupies a square block. Now known officially as the United
Palace, it contains the 5,000-seat United Church Auditorium, the
educational facilities of the Science of Living Institute and Semi-

nary, and the general offices of Reverend Ike's United Christian Evangelistic Association.

It is Reverend Ike's Science of Living Institute that sets him apart from most other radio and television preachers. Ike says that the Science of Living is not church doctrine, religious dogma or theology. He defines it as the teaching that equips a person

> . . . to live a positive, dynamic, healthy, happy, successful, prosperous life through the consciousness of the Presence of God—Infinite Good—already within every man. In the Science of Living, God is not "someone else, somewhere else, sometime else"; but God is the Presence of Infinite Good within you HERE and NOW . . . and this Presence is within everyone . . . The Science of Living teaches you how to become a dynamic person. You UNLEARN sickness and know health. You UNLEARN poverty and know prosperity. You learn how to break every limitation and solve every problem YOURSELF. Sickness, age, fear, worry, tension, every human torment drops away, and a NEW YOU begins to live "more abundantly."

Ike's 15-minute radio programs are usually devoted mainly to testimonials by dedicated users of the Blessing Plan. Thus, he has little time to teach his Science of Living. But on his television specials or during regular services and Science of Living Sunday School at the United Palace Reverend Ike emphasizes his philosophy. Judging from the books he sells in his bookstore, Ike's Science of Living includes metaphysical concepts related at some points to Religious Science. It also smacks here and there of Norman Vincent Peale and Dale Carnegie. But it is his own philosophy, an eclectic bundle of concepts that he put together over a period of years.

The parts of Reverend Ike's philosophy that veer most sharply from some of the traditional church concepts have brought the dynamic radio preacher under sharp attack. A *Time* magazine article hinted that another preacher might not be able to go quite so far as Reverend Ike does:

> Beyond Ike's message of the power-of-positive-greed is the ego-building, instant-divinity trip he offers his followers—far from the traditional admonitions to repentance . . . No soul-saving nonsense

for Ike . . . As for prayer, Ike issues a warning: "When you kneel down to pray, you're putting yourself in a good position to get a kick in the behind." Of course Ike would not get away with any of this if he did not have his own immense style. . . .[6]

On September 5, 1971, Reverend Ike held an International Healing and Blessing Meeting at Madison Square Garden. Ike said the crowd was never fully counted because it was packed from "floor to rafters, with countless others outside." He called it "a number that no man could number," but settled on the figure of 20,000. It was a Reverend Ike spectacular nonpareil, with movie stars, judges and bishops in attendance. Reverend Ike said even the FBI was there, because they are "always trying to find out if Rev. Ike is for real!" The Madison Square Garden extravaganza turned out just as Reverend Ike had prophesied: "one of the greatest events ever to take place on earth." Ike preached his big sermon, "How To Get What You Want Out Of Life." The central theme of his message was "if you want to experience the goodness of life, you must believe in the nowness of life. You must get rid of that pie in the sky bye and bye when you die attitude. Let your attitude be: I WANT MY PIE NOW, WITH ICE CREAM ON TOP!"

Realizing that he had many visitors in the huge Madison Square Garden crowd, Reverend Ike explained, "You're going to find that we have church perhaps a little different from what you're accustomed to." Then he proceeded to mock the old-time methods of addressing the Lord in prayer. "Some of you," he said, "have been praying all your lives and getting nothing out of it. You know why? Because your prayers have been too mamby-pamby." He demonstrated in a high-pitched voice: "Pul-eee-eze, Loord." While the crowded roared with laughter, he continued in his derisive falsetto: "Pul-eee-eze, Jeee-sus! If it's your will, Loord."

"To me," Reverend Ike declared, "this affirmation, 'I want my pie now with ice cream on top,' to me, that's a prayer, that's the way I pray . . . I know some of you good religious people are shocked to death, but that's prayer!" And he led the huge audience in repeating his special prayer. Then he dipped into some more of his unique philosophy:

You will never get any further in life than your belief about your-self . . . A lot of you are troubled and having problems because you're upset about what other people think about you. I'm going to have to upset you a bit right here and use an emphatic word that may not become a clergyman on national TV, but please listen: YOU ARE NOT GOING TO GET ANYWHERE IN LIFE—SPIRI-TUALLY, OR OTHERWISE—UNTIL YOU COME TO THAT POINT WHERE YOU DON'T GIVE A DAMN WHAT OTHER PEOPLE THINK ABOUT YOU! I'm sorry, Pharisees. As long as you worry about what other people think about you, you will be mediocre. You will be worried to death. The hair will fall out of your head . . . it only matters what I believe about myself. . . .[7]

If he alarms the more traditional with such extreme incursions into the realm of self-reliance and "God in you" consciousness, Reverend Ike mixes in parables and testimonies that please the more conservative and old-fashioned elements. For example, one of his most-used parables teaches that "unless someone has a consciousness for better things, it is impossible to even give them something better." In this parable Reverend Ike tells of a group of people who attempted to raise the standard of living of an 80-year-old woman who lived in a one-room shack. They arranged for a grant from the government and built her a new home with all the conveniences. "While patting themselves on the back for doing such a good thing, they moved her into her new home." A few weeks later they checked on her and were dumbfounded to discover that she had moved out of the new home back into her little one-room shack. Reverend Ike explains that the woman did not have the consciousness for the fine home—"she couldn't accommodate that new home in her consciousness."

I am not against having soup lines or bread lines. Sometimes people need this temporarily. Welfare has its place, but it shouldn't be a resting place. I am not against helping people. We try to help those who find themselves in a crisis, a crucial moment, but we are not going to do this forever. It is more important that we lead you to a consciousness of the Presence of God within you . . . When you know this truth . . . the Welfare will not be able to hold you. God in you is all that you need. When you know this there is no longer reason for you to depend upon anyone or anything. . . .[8]

With such statements Reverend Ike cancels *Time* magazine's concern that he might not be able "to get away with" some of his more radical remarks. He has also spent much time and money fighting drug addiction. And he opposes gambling as a vice that strikes hard at the poor, even though his critics believe he is merely trying to put his competition out of business:

About Gambling, Playing Numbers, Races, etc. These are ungodly rackets. The Bible says, "Some trust in horses. . . ." I do not deal with gambling, numbers, games of chance, or contests. Beware of False Prophets Who Do! Luck: You don't need luck. You need the blessings of God. Luck is uncertain. Luck will let you down. But the goodness of God is sure and certain.

Reverend Ike advances on many fronts. His ministry grows and his Science of Living Institute now confers degrees of higher learning. Although he preached for many years without a divinity degree, Reverend Ike did attend Manhattan Bible College in Manhattan, Kansas, for a time. But now he is Dr. Frederick Eikerenkoetter II and has recently conferred upon an associate the title of "Dr. of the Science of Living." Reverend Ike has also integrated his staff with a white associate minister, a move that should greatly expand the scope of his ministry. Apparently the more Reverend Ike boasts of material success, of conspicuous consumption, the more his congregation grows.

In his services he usually finds a way to mention that he owns three Rolls-Royces, two Mercedes and a Bentley, and has residences in both Hollywood and New York. His services continue to include features not usually associated with the activities of any church. But Reverend Ike seems to have mastered the knack of introducing new ideas with a maximum of harmony and a minimum of friction. Although his choir of 1,000 voices can make the rafters vibrate at Madison Square Garden with an old-fashioned hymn, Reverend Ike proudly includes on the same program his Rock Dancers, praising the Lord in a dance. He has conducted a "Holy Rock Service," featuring the "original Holy Rock Band." He has described his ministry as "A Swinging Church with a

Singing Pastor!" At his regular services in the United Palace Auditorium, he has dressed his ushers in nurses' uniforms and equipped his nursery with closed-circuit television so that mothers will not miss any of the service.

The critics who had viewed Reverend Ike's Blessing Plan as Oral Roberts' old Blessing Pact "writ large and run amuck" can be expected to "gnash their teeth and rend their vestments" over the latest Reverend Ike innovation—the Success Idea. The Success Idea is primarily for those among his supporters who have mastered the Blessing Plan and want to advance into even greater realms of prosperity and blessing. Each month Reverend Ike introduces a new Success Idea, but it is mailed only to those who specifically request it. Each Success Idea is named for the date on which it is issued. A good example is Number 0572, issued in May 1972. This Success Idea was further identified as Winning Combination Number 2. Reverend Ike supplied 13 words which "make up Winning Combination Number 2; take these words for your thought, your words, your prayer." "I SEE MYSELF AS A BIG-TIME WINNER IN THE GAME OF LIFE!" Using this combination of words, Reverend Ike's supporters were encouraged to practice "seeing and feeling." "Praying and begging a God-in-the-sky won't help you. You must see and feel yourself with all the GOOD you desire WITHIN your own mind," instructed Ike in Success Idea 0572. To be successful one had to "see." "As soon as you can see it, it will happen to you," promised Reverend Ike, and he outlined the seeing and feeling promises in three rules backed up by Scriptural proof:

(1) You can be whatever you can see and feel yourself being. "As a man thinks in his heart, so is he."
(2) You can have whatever you can see and feel yourself having. ". . . he shall have whatsoever he says."
(3) You can do whatever you can see and feel yourself doing. "If you have faith, nothing shall be impossible to you."

Reverend Ike felt so strongly about the seeing and feeling procedure that he advised his followers to "be full of the feeling . . . don't get hung up on 'how' . . . WHAT YOU SEE IS

WHAT YOU GET!" He even encapsulated the "seeing" in a little
poem:

> If you can see it, you can be it!!
> If you can see it, you can have it!!
> If you can see it, you can do it!!

Reverend Ike has printed as many as six million copies of his
full-color magazine, *Action!*. These are distributed free of charge.
In each issue he features the Blessing Plan and the testimonies
of people who have used it successfully. Along with photographs
of new homes or automobiles his followers have received, he
pictures huge rolls of large-denomination bills. Alongside the
testimony of a woman who claimed to have been healed of
arthritis by sleeping with a copy of *Action!*, he may feature his
interpretation of a Scripture on the subject of money: "The LACK
of money is the root of all evil." And most amazing, he now
features a little-known passage of the Scriptures from Ecclesiastes
10:19, which reads, "Money answers all things." Reverend Ike
has also thought of the impatient ones and promised, "The very
moment you believe, and begin to write me and mail your letter,
your blessings will start! You will begin to get results even before your letter reaches me."

In early 1973 Reverend Ike bought substantial amounts of advertising space in all of New York City's daily newspapers. Under
a large picture of himself, he asked the question, "Are you still
waiting for pie in the sky when you die? Get yours now with ice
cream on top!" Carefully noting that "The Church is NOT located
in Harlem," Reverend Ike invited "people of all races, religions
and those with no religion" to view his "Joy of Living" sermon
on television.

When Reverend Ike assumed the title of "Right Reverend
Father-in-God, His Divine Eminence, Dr. Frederick J. Eikerenkoetter II," one critic commented that there were few worlds
left for Reverend Ike to conquer. He observed that Ike needed
a slogan to complete the royal aspect of his ministry, and suggested a homily from a Montaigne essay: *Fortis imaginatio gen-
erat casum,* which translated to "A strong imagination begets the

event." But there was a rumor that the indefatigable Ike was already preparing the slogan. With his banner flying over a ministry that numbers over a million followers, Reverend Ike needs nothing else to establish his claim of being one of the biggest evangelistic attractions in the country.

TOM HUFFMAN

V

Carl McIntire

The Ghost of Senator McCarthy needs to ride again.
—Carl McIntire, December 21, 1972

Dean of the Far-Right
Radio Preachers

The voice is unmistakable. Every weekday morning tens of thousands of Americans are delighted to hear the husky, folksy tones boom from their radios, "Good morning! Good morning! Good morning! This is Dr. McIntire!"

He never uses a script; he just starts right out with whatever is on his mind. On some programs he may spend most of the time encouraging people to get to Washington, D.C. for the next Victory March. Sometimes Dr. McIntire talks to his supporters on the telephone, discussing a variety of subjects with patriots from all parts of the country. Usually he spends some time asking for money, but no more than most radio preachers and a lot less than some. He generally remembers to ask for the special one-million-dollar donation to help put his message on 1,000 radio stations. Several people have mailed him such checks, but they were all bogus. One of these days somebody will probably send him a real one.

For a long time he was accompanied by Dr. Charles Richter, a minister and personal friend, who sat in the studio and encouraged Dr. McIntire with an occasional amen and praise the

189

Lord. In time he seemed to be a regular part of the program, and folks started calling him "Amen Charlie." No more than once or twice during a broadcast, Dr. McIntire would turn to his friend for emphasis and approbation. A typical exchange:

". . . Isn't that right, Charlie?"

"That's right, Rev. Carl. Amen!"

"Thank you, Amen Charlie!"

Even when they travel through some of the most remote areas of the United States, avid supporters of the Reverend Dr. Carl McIntire can usually tune in one of the more than 600 stations carrying his "Twentieth Century Reformation Hour" radio program and enjoy a bit of professional high-decibel controversy delivered by one of the best-known radio preachers in the history of broadcasting.

At 66, the controversial and flamboyant McIntire is the oldest of the preachers with national radio ministries based on fundamentalist religion mixed with right-wing politics. He is unquestionably the dean of the radio preachers, having joined the forces of far-right religion back in 1936. He has helped such well-known personalities as Dr. Fred C. Schwarz and Dr. Billy James Hargis start their own anti-Communist crusades, and to a greater degree than almost any other radio preacher working the "Christian far-right" corner of the political spectrum, McIntire has been involved in the divisive religious and political controversies of the past four decades.

Like some of the other radio preachers with right-wing fundamentalist ministries, McIntire considers his activities religious rather than political, even though observers have described some of his programs as almost totally political. But such skepticism must be tempered with McIntire's special definition: "What men call politics, to me is standing up for righteousness." [1]

McIntire is the only big-time right-wing radio preacher who has centered most of his activities in the middle Atlantic states, where he can spread his religious and political nets along much of the eastern coast of the United States. To radio listeners throughout the nation his headquarters is Collingswood, New Jersey, even though he controls property and conducts schools and other projects from New York to Florida and claims supporters around the world. Some of the critics who have denounced him most vigorously as a bigoted extremist also describe him as "intelligent," "a man of unusual preaching ability," a "vivid personality," a preacher with a "voice resonant and comforting." It is interesting that a minister described in such terms would find himself almost continually involved in controversy.

The Collingswood preacher grew up straight and tall, and for many years he has been described by both friend and foe as a "husky six-footer." Today his thatch of neatly trimmed hair is gray, but it still looks as thick as when he first started preaching. His facial features are fairly regular, with light blue eyes that complement a ready smile. Although not excessively large, his nose is somewhat long and curves slightly near the tip. When he became a nationally-known political figure in 1970 and his picture and name were on most of the front pages of the major newspapers, McIntire was somewhat heavier than usual and the political cartoonists, who found him an excellent subject for caricature, drew him even larger than life. They also turned his nose into a large hawk's beak, emphasizing his strident call for victory in Vietnam. His eyes were pictured as bulging excessively. His double chin, which has become larger in recent years, was enlarged enough by one cartoonist to turn the Collingswood preacher into a man with no chin at all.

McIntire was born in Ypsilanti, Michigan, in the manse of the Presbyterian church his father pastored. He grew up in southern Oklahoma, in the town of Durant, in an atmosphere permeated with daily prayers and Gospel hymns, where strict discipline and the work ethic were considered vital rules of life. He planned to become a lawyer and studied in the State Teacher's College in his home town before transferring to Park College in Kansas City, Missouri, where he helped pay his expenses by working as a janitor and a traveling salesman. McIntire remembers those days as crucial to his later career:

Those years selling were better preparation for life than the seminary. I started out walking, then I bought me an old gray mare and rode her two summers, then a motorcycle, then an old car. It was a rough-and-tumble life, with all the hard knocks you could ask for, but I learned people, and I learned the value of a dollar, and I learned to respect the capitalist system.[2]

While earning his B.A. degree at Park College, he decided to become a minister rather than a lawyer. Said McIntire: "God gave me certain forensic and human gifts. I was aware of it and thought they could be used more fully in His service. My first collegiate sermon came from Corinthians: 'If the trumpet give an uncertain sound, who shall prepare himself to the battle?' " [3] From that day forward some might object when the outspoken preacher sounded his trumpet, but few if any would describe it as "uncertain."

He married his college sweetheart before graduation, and they headed East, where he enrolled in Princeton Theological Seminary. There he met and was strongly influenced by the outstanding fundamentalist scholar, Professor J. Gresham Machen, who was already a well-known leader in the fight against liberalization of church institutions. When the General Assembly of the Presbyterian Church reorganized the seminary under a liberal governing board in 1929, Professor Machen withdrew to found Westminster Seminary, a conservative stronghold at Chester Hill, Pennsylvania. Young McIntire followed Machen to Westminster and received his divinity degree there in 1931. Since the Westminster was still under the jurisdiction of the church, McIntire was ordained a minister in the Presbyterian Church in the U.S.A. He accepted the pulpit of the Chelsea Presbyterian Church in Atlantic City, and three years later he answered a call to the pastorate of the large fundamentalist Presbyterian Church in Collingswood, New Jersey. According to a McIntire interviewer, it was an unheard-of opportunity for a 23-year-old minister to become pastor of a congregation of 1,200 conservative, middle-class Bible-believers. The young McIntire of that day was described as "tall, lean and good-looking," a preacher who "had terrific presence . . . the old ladies just trembled when he talked." [4]

As a young minister, McIntire became very active in the Machen wing of the liberal-conservative battle, which by 1934 was considered such a threat to the good order of the denomination that the General Assembly intervened in the struggle. This had little effect on Machen and his followers, who had become so intractable by 1936 that the Presbyterian Church brought them to trial. McIntire was found guilty on three of six counts with which he was charged: (1) disapproval, defiance and acts in contravention of the government and discipline of the church; (2) lack of zealousness and faith in maintaining the peace of the church; and (3) violation of his ordination vows.[5]

McIntire appealed the synod verdict to the General Assembly of the church, but that body upheld the decision. He later alleged that he had been disciplined on mere technicalities, but an official commentary made clear that the church had disciplined the ousted ministers because they had defamed the character of some of their fellow Christians, broken certain of the Ten Commandments, and been instrumental in "causing dissension and strife" and engendering "suspicion and ill will" and "seriously injuring the peace of the Church."[6]

Following the decision of the General Assembly, the defrocked pastors sought through a series of legal battles to obtain control of their church properties. The Collingswood minister wrote of his losing battle in terms which seemed dramatic enough to guarantee he would never forget:

> Thank God, my congregation in Collingswood, the largest missionary church in the Presbytery at that time, with 1275 members, renounced the jurisdiction of the denomination. We fought for our church property and every penny we had in the bank. The congregation—1200— walked out of the beautiful Gothic structure which they had themselves built; sang "Saviour, Like A Shepherd, Lead Us," went down to an empty lot, put up a large chautauqua tent . . . took communion in paper cups, built a wooden tabernacle in which we still worship.[7]

Though officially deposed, McIntire continued to insist that he had not defied the discipline of the Presbyterian Church. His

dismissal would become the great event around which his whole
life would center; it would shape his convictions and focus his
efforts. Out of this experience he would develop his doctrine of
total separation, which required that those conforming to the
McIntire interpretation of biblical orthodoxy separate themselves from the great apostasy, to which all but a small number
of churches, a saving remnant, had already bent the knee.

Following the rejection of their final appeal, the ousted ministers proceeded to establish a new church, which they called
"The Presbyterian Church of America." But almost immediately
the leaders fell to quarreling over certain minor doctrines. Mc-
Intire disagreed with Machen and gathered enough followers
to defeat his old professor's bid for re-election to the office of
president of the mission board.

Machen died suddenly in early 1937, and with the original
leader gone, there was little hope that the factionalism within
the newly established church would subside. Finally an open
split occurred, and McIntire and his group, made up largely of
members from his Collingswood Church, departed to organize
what became known as "The Bible Presbyterian Church." The
other faction, the Westminster group, established still another
church, which they named the "Orthodox Presbyterian Church."
McIntire was free of any restraining hand; there was no board
or assembly or other authority which could issue orders to him.
Now that he was the leader of his own church, it was Carl
McIntire's turn to set the standards and issue the orders. He
and his followers formalized the bylaws, which decreed that all
who would be members of the Bible Presbyterian Church must
become total separatists. Thenceforth all churchgoers who maintained membership in any church that did not conform closely
enough to their rigid doctrines would stand condemned. In a
very special sense, it was McIntire and his tiny band of militants
against the rest of the church world. So extreme was his concept of orthodoxy that many church leaders would no longer
consider him and his followers ordinary fundamentalists. Increasingly the world would call them "ultrafundamentalists."

It is the view of the Collingswood radio preacher that the

sharp line drawn by the Scriptures is now missing from the discipline of the church, and that the concept of the broad, inclusivist church has been so thoroughly established that the truth has become relative. The Gospel is what any man wants it to be, he insists, lamenting the fact that anathemas are gone. He declares that "dialogue, rapprochement, reconciliation have become the weapons of a corrupt church to aggravate and intensify its apostasy . . . the walk of the believer must be clean and pure and separate. . . ." [8]

McIntire was aware that he and his small band of separatists could accomplish very little of his ambitious program by themselves. He approached the leaders of the Bible Protestant Church, a fundamentalist splinter group which had just separated from the Methodists. Out of their discussions came the decision to establish a council which all independent fundamentalist bodies adhering to the separatist doctrine could join. In 1941 they organized the American Council of Christian Churches (ACCC), with Carl McIntire as president. The little council, whose churches were estimated to have fewer than 50,000 members, set itself on a course of militant opposition to all churches that did not conform to their idea of orthodox Christianity. And to the indefatigable McIntire there existed no greater example of flagrant apostasy than the Federal Council of the Churches of Christ in America, a cooperative fellowship to which most of the large, affluent Protestant churches belonged.

While Reverend Carl was organizing his council, a number of other fundamentalist and conservative churches were beginning to feel the need for an agency through which they could present a cooperative witness. In 1942 in St. Louis, Missouri, leaders from a number of such churches formed the National Association of Evangelicals (NAE). This new organization of conservative churchmen agreed with many of the positions taken by McIntire's group, but some of its leaders were critical of the methods he employed in protesting the gatherings of liberal church leaders. Members of the NAE preferred not to call themselves "fundamentalists." Eventually the NAE became closely identified with the "new evangelical" movement, and most of its supporters called themselves "evangelicals." Later McIntire wrote of the issues that distinguished his ACCC from the NAE in its early days:

> At St. Louis in 1942, where the decision was made to form the National Association of Evangelicals, the body refused not merely to call for separation from the Federal Council of Churches but even so much as to mention it. Several years later, because of the militant exposures of the ACCC, the NAE did name the Federal Council of Churches but never did it call for the separation from it. It has always had a policy of dual membership; it has been inclusive.[9]

The NAE attracted a large number of conservative churches, including some Adventist and Pentecostal groups. Guided by its first president, Dr. Harold John Ockenga, it grew rapidly and by 1965 claimed a total membership of 1,654,278. Additionally, it claimed to have some affiliation with a total of ten million church members. This was still far below the more than 41 million members whose churches were said to support the National Council of the Churches of Christ in the U.S.A. (NCC), which was formed out of the Federal Council of the Churches of Christ in America in 1950; but it far outdistanced McIntire's ACCC, which was estimated at that time to have increased its membership to approximately 15 church groups with a total membership of 200,000.[10]

The NAE was strongly supported by the religious periodical *Christianity Today*, which owed its existence to Dr. Billy Graham and his father-in-law, Dr. Nelson Bell. In a similar manner, Billy Graham has worked closely with some members of the NAE, and that organization has always endorsed Graham's evangelistic efforts. McIntire gave his idea of the relationship which existed between the NAE, *Christianity Today* and Billy Graham in 1967: "Carl Henry (editor), with *Christianity Today,* has offered the Association [NAE] its degree of intellectual prestige, and Graham has been the darling of this group from the beginning." [11]

In 1948 the New Jersey preacher led the American Council of Christian Churches in active opposition to the growing Protestant church-unity movement. He began a policy of holding protest meetings wherever an ecumenical convention or gathering was scheduled. When representatives of churches from 44 countries met in Amsterdam in 1948 to form the World Council of Churches (WCC), McIntire and a small band of his ACCC leaders joined with a few foreign clergymen to establish the International Council of Christian Churches just before the World Council meeting started. McIntire's international council issued a doctrinal statement which showed that the new group had been set up expressly to harass and protest against the World Council of Churches.

What has motivated McIntire and his followers to travel to distant parts of the world to protest the meetings of the World Council of Churches? McIntire has never denied that he and his supporters have always tried to sow discord in the ranks of the NCC and the WCC; nor does the New Jersey clergyman shrink from accusing the two large councils of being sinful modernists and apostate liberals who are misleading their followers and advancing socialism. From the time McIntire organized the ACCC and ICCC until the present, his two councils have continued their practice of harassing and denouncing the ecumenical movement. Dr. John Mackay, former president of Princeton Theological Seminary, provided an evaluation of the work of McIntire's International Council:

> This group, while paying lip tribute to the Bible and Jesus Christ, represents an unbiblical Christianity. While being concerned about Communism it carries on work with Communist technique. Wherever they go and in all they say about those whom they love to malign and to traduce, they act without the slightest interest in truth. . . .[12]

The Reverend Carl McIntire did not rely heavily on radio during the early years of his ministry, but he did use some broadcasting, along with every other practical means, to expand his operations. In 1950 the Toronto Baptist Seminary, a part of the American Council of Christian Churches, bestowed an honorary Doctor of Divinity degree on the New Jersey clergyman, a title he has used unfailingly ever since. His ministry prospered, and he built a $250,000 Sunday School building adjacent to his beautiful new church in Collingswood. Later he established

Faith Theological Seminary and became president of its board of directors. He led his people in setting up a home for the aged and a summer Bible conference, and started Shelton College in Ringwood, New Jersey. As time went by, his list of organizations continued to grow. There were more schools, including a college on the West Coast, the International Christian Youth Organization and an international relief agency.

Dr. McIntire's first channel of communication was a weekly newspaper called the *Christian Beacon,* which he started publishing in 1936. He is still listed as its editor-in-chief and is said to write some of the material for each issue. The paper features photographically reproduced articles from other newspapers and periodicals. The articles are usually stories that support his own position on some issue, but occasionally they are attacks by what McIntire considers the "enemy," which he roundly denounces in an adjacent column of the paper.

The *Christian Beacon* also sponsors McIntire's "Twentieth Century Reformation Hour," a half-hour program broadcast more widely than the radio programs of any other preacher in America. It is heard on more than 600 radio stations, coast to coast, Monday through Friday. At various times McIntire has also used short-wave broadcasts to extend his outreach to foreign countries. Through speeches, rallies, pamphlets, letters, a number of books and his own newspaper, McIntire has spread his message to millions of people; but probably all of these methods combined have been less effective than his radio broadcasts in rallying support for his political and religious causes.

The New Jersey radio preacher has been saturating the air waves with attacks on a wide variety of political and religious issues. A complete list of the targets of his wrath would be impossible to assemble, but a short, representative collection might include the World Council of Churches, medical care, the Roman Catholic Church, the Revised Standard Version of the Bible, the income tax, the World Baptist Alliance, businessmen who supported changing Easter to the first Sunday in April, the United Methodist Church, civil-rights programs, the Episcopal Church, the U.S. Post Office, hippies, the Presbyterian Church in the U.S.A., the Presbyterian Church in the U.S. (Southern), the NCC, the Federal Communications Commission, women's lib and Dr. Billy Graham.

The McIntire message has varied somewhat through the years. Today, for example, even though he is still considered anti-Catholic by some critics, he does not appear to make anti-Catholic statements in the manner for which he has been heavily criticized in the past. At the end of World War II, in September 1945, McIntire summed up the Catholic threat to America in the *Christian Beacon:*

> As we enter the post-war world, without any doubt the greatest enemy of freedom and liberty that the world has to face today is the Roman Catholic system. Yes, we have Communism in Russia and all that is involved there, but if one had to choose between the two . . . one would be much better off in a communistic society than in a Roman Catholic Fascist set-up . . . America has to face the Roman Catholic terror. The sooner the Christian people of America wake up to this danger the safer will be our land.[13]

In 1945 McIntire also declared that the Catholic Church was "the Harlot Church and the Bride of the Anti-Christ," a "false religion which enslaves human souls in darkness and superstition," a church which will "sell her secret confessional system for political world power." [14] McIntire no longer considers himself anti-Catholic, but during the 1960 Presidential election the Democratic Party listed him as one of "five major anti-Catholic extremists operating in the current political campaign."

McIntire has been labeled anti-Catholic in a large number of publications, but the quotations attributed to him appear to come from an earlier period of his career. The Collingswood clergyman's indirect denial of an anti-Catholic bias included in the following quotation was published in July 1969, and some believe it represents a more mature McIntire position:

> They call me an anti-Semite. They forget I went on the air during the Six-Day War and raised $5,000 for the Jewish cause. They call me anti-Negro. Well, we have Negro students at Shelton; fine young people. They call me a Catholic-hater. Well, I oppose the appointment of an ambassador to the Vatican because it binds the church

to the state. But I'm much closer to the Catholics in my belief in the
Virgin Birth than I am to liberal Protestants who deny it.[15]

Does this represent the final position of the Reverend Dr.
McIntire on the Catholic Church? His critics insist that Mc-
Intire's definitions must always be carefully checked, and point
out that he also insists that he is not anti-Negro while taking
some curious positions on racial matters. Generally, McIntire has
held that the solution to the racial problem is to be found in
every man's accepting God and the Bible. When that day comes,
the problems will disappear, but in the meantime, he insists, the
racial problem is aiding the Communist cause. He has also
written that ". . . Segregation or apartheid is not sin *per se;*
if so, then God is a big sinner for He certainly did in His
providence segregate races and nationalities and colors. . . ."[16]
While the Communists are quick to exploit any national problem for their own gain, to label the whole civil-rights movement
a tool of the Communists is to make a mistake the late J. Edgar
Hoover warned against: "Let me emphasize that the American
civil-rights movement is not and has never been dominated by
Communists—because the overwhelming majority of civil-rights
leaders in this country . . . have recognized and rejected Communism as a menace to the freedom of all.[17]

Whatever McIntire's final positions on Catholics and blacks
may be, they will probably never rank at the top of his long
list of hates, for that honor seems destined to be reserved for
either the National Council of Churches or the World Council
of Churches, against both of which the energetic minister has
preached a modern version of the jehad, or holy war. His voluminous writings indicate that at one point McIntire had been attacking the NCC for so long that he became resentful when the
National Association of Evangelicals, rather than his own ACCC,
started to gain a reputation as a more viable religious alternative
to the National Council. It would appear an unrewarding task
for McIntire to attack the NAE, for on many issues they are as
fundamentalist as his own council. But Dr. McIntire can view
a very small departure from his doctrines as the rankest form of

soul-destroying apostasy. This can be illustrated by one of the most widely quoted appraisals of McIntire's doctrinaire orthodoxy, which has been attributed to one of his avid supporters: "You're either a Christian or you aren't. You either agree with Rev. McIntire or the Devil. Take your choice."

It was probably inevitable that McIntire's militant opposition to the National Association of Evangelicals would lead eventually to an attack on Evangelist Billy Graham, since the famous revivalist has been so enthusiastically supported by that organization. It is probably also a measure of McIntire's courage and determination—although some might judge it recklessness—that he would decide to lump the most popular preacher in America with his usual targets of compromisers, inclusivists and modernists. Believing that the NAE progressed in step with Graham's ever-increasing popularity, the Collingswood preacher has kept up a campaign against Billy Graham for many years. Perhaps he should have been concerned that once he was committed to such an audacious attack there would be no easy way to turn back, but when Graham declined to respond to his barbs and refused to dignify them with an answer, the revivalist's act of turning the other cheek seemed only to heighten McIntire's flinty determination. As the New Jersey preacher had once so correctly explained, God had given him certain forensic gifts, and he had never yet hesitated to use them. Now this most skillful of polemicists would continue his attacks on Graham with unremitting fury, year in and year out.

Why had the wily McIntire, whose tactical expertise in religious battles was reputed to be second to none in the far-right phalanxes, elected to enter the lists against such odds? Had an unrequited thirst for more power or the pangs of envy blinded his usual perspicacity? Or was it possible that he sensed that it was Graham, much more than the NCC or the WCC, who would ultimately become the most formidable impediment in the path of the councils he led? McIntire had written, "The one fact that stands out . . . is that there has already been organized a council of fundamental churches in competition with the World Council of Churches, in opposition, in open, public battle.[18] Was Graham the charismatic figure who would lead a mighty third force in Christendom that would eliminate the need for McIntire's councils?

He accused revivalist Graham of doing great damage to the cause of the true church and the true Gospel of Jesus Christ. He criticized his cooperation with Pentecostals, Jews and all manner of ecumenical groups. But it is very doubtful that many people condemned Graham on such grounds, since very few consider separation as defined by McIntire a requirement of their religion.

It was not easy to fight an opponent who did not answer pointed questions and refused to respond even to harsh criticisms. But Dr. McIntire hammered away at every opportunity. And at times he had help from the leaders of some of the most influential independent fundamentalist ministries in the country. The best-known among these extreme fundamentalists were Dr. Bob Jones, Sr., and Dr. Bob Jones, Jr., of Bob Jones University, in Greenville, South Carolina. Dr. McIntire commended the Joneses when Billy Graham held one of his crusades in Greenville in 1966, and the father and son openly challenged his whole position. Another independent fundamentalist who criticized Graham was Dr. John R. Rice, editor of the *Sword of the Lord*, an independent Christian weekly newspaper published in Murfreesboro, Tennessee. Dr. Rice had once been close to Graham, but by 1958 he was writing to McIntire and telling him that the famous revivalist was keeping company with modernists.[19]

Evangelist Graham suffered mostly in silence, responding only rarely to his detractors, and then usually with great humility. Still the chase went on.

In July 1966 a most welcome document was brought to the attention of the fiery fundamentalist preacher. The United Church *Observer*, the official organ of the United Church of Canada, had published a list of questions it had submitted to Billy Graham. It was, according to McIntire, ". . . the first replies which he has been known to give to a series of questions . . . Always Dr. Graham has said that he remained silent and would not respond to such questions, but for some reason, known only to himself, he changed that policy and put himself out in the open where men could appraise his approach and his answers." [20]

It must have seemed an excellent opportunity to criticize some of the religious views held by Graham, and McIntire made the most of it. Of the 26 questions submitted to Dr. Graham, 24 had been answered. Two were dismissed as "rather ridiculous," but McIntire answered them himself, explaining, "Dr. Graham winced and then fled. He refused to reply." [21] He then reviewed the other 24 questions, but Graham's answers proved far from satisfactory. Even in the few instances in which he agreed that Graham had fully answered a question, he added such comments as, "This is a weak and evasive answer," or "How evasive Graham is!" Graham's answer to one of the questions serves to illustrate the critique:

Question to Dr. Graham: "Do you think that churches such as the United Church of Canada and the great liberal churches of the United States that are active in the ecumenical movement and whose ministers study and respect the work of Paul Tillich and other great modern teachers are 'apostate'?"

Answer by Dr. Graham: "I could not possibly pass this type of judgment on individual churches and clergymen within The United Church of Canada—my knowledge of The United Church of Canada is too inadequate, and my ability to make such discernment is too limited. My books and writings are public knowledge but I love fellowship and work with many Christians who don't agree with me theologically in everything. As to my calling everyone 'apostate' who reads and gets help from Tillich—this is preposterous. There are too many shades of theological opinion in a large denomination to lump them all off as liberal, neo-orthodox, conservative, fundamentalist, or what have you!"

Dr. McIntire began a lengthy discussion of what makes a church apostate before coming to a direct criticism of Graham's answer:

One can understand, as he listens to Dr. Graham, how he has excluded a whole realm of unbelief and sin from his messages. He has categorized sin and has chosen only to speak of certain types of sin which will not involve him in the great struggle for the Christian

religion in the twentieth century . . . His studied effort to ignore
and avoid the realities of the apostasy and the sin of the church is
the situation that has brought upon Dr. Graham his own confusion
and compelled him to give the studied answers in this document, so
unsatisfactory to a simple Bible people.[22]

And so it went, through most of the questions. With each one
there seemed to be something wrong, something to complain
about, e.g., "What has produced Graham's dullness and his blind
spots in such matters? I believe it is his compromise." On another
McIntire commented, "Graham does not answer forthrightly."
And on still another, "At this point Billy Graham is capitulating
to the whole liberal, Communist coalition in their racial pro-
nouncements and agitation." [23]

The opportunity to comment at length on Graham's answers
was obviously a satisfying experience for Dr. McIntire; so much
so that he later published the list of questions and his comments
for his people to appreciate. But another opportunity to protest
Billy Graham was scheduled later that same year, and Dr. Mc-
Intire soon turned his attention to it.

In January 1966 the conservative religious magazine *Christianity Today* announced that a World Congress on Evangelism
would be held in Berlin from October 26 through November 4,
1966. It also revealed that five continents and all major Protestant
denominations would be represented on the 55-member sponsoring committee of the congress.

Dr. McIntire was very interested in the upcoming congress,
but he was aware that Dr. Carl F. H. Henry, noted theologian
who was chairman of the Congress and editor of *Christianity
Today*, had made it known that those of "divisive affiliations will
be sidelined." This meant to Preacher McIntire that Dr. Henry
had ". . . pointed his finger directly at the separatist testimony
of the American Council of Christian Churches . . . As a result,
no leaders of the American Council received invitations to be
delegates or observers, or anything else. They were excluded." [24]

Because neither he nor members of his American Council had
been invited to the World Congress on Evangelism, McIntire
concluded that ". . . it was natural and in keeping with the
American Council's ministry to give a testimony in connection

with the projected Congress . . . A message, therefore, was carefully prepared. . . ."

A special challenge from the ACCC would be delivered to the World Congress, but McIntire also explored another avenue into the Berlin congress. In early October he wrote to Dr. Carl Henry, informing him that the *Christian Beacon* would "cover" the Congress, and asked for a press box or press credentials. He was somewhat taken aback by an answer informing him that it was too late to honor his application. In his reply to McIntire, Dr. Henry observed somewhat icily, "As a matter of fact, it is clear from the last issue the *Beacon* published that you do not need either to attend or to get the facts in order to provide coverage of the type the *Beacon* carries. The attacks in that issue, on the ministry of Dr. Graham, and on the World Congress, contain not only half truths, but untruths."

Editor Henry also revealed that he had heard that the Collingswood preacher was planning to mount a protest demonstration in Berlin during the World Congress. On the strength of that information he issued a special challenge to McIntire:

Fulfillment of the Great Commission by protest demonstrations is something so obviously apostolic that you ought not to forego this method of saving sinners in which you excel. I urge just one thing. If you come to Berlin for a protest demonstration, as chairman of the World Congress I challenge you not to march from the Berlin Wall to the Congress Hall, but rather to march from the Congress Hall to the Berlin Wall—and then don't stop short by any means, but keep right on marching and protesting—so it will be clear to the Christian world what you are protesting against.[25]

Preacher McIntire declared he had never received a letter quite like the one Dr. Henry had sent him. He drafted a reply heavy with references to freedom of the press. Stressing that he could not submit to conditions that might regulate his reporting, McIntire remonstrated with the congress chairman: ". . . Dr. Henry, I have been covering NCC, WCC and numerous church assemblies through these many years. Never have I received a letter or have I been treated as you here write. I have gone to assemblies without ever even writing in advance for press

credentials, just presented myself, and I have been assigned a
box or given a badge and granted the privileges of the press
room. . . ."

Dr. McIntire also wrote, "Obviously, you have given credence
to rumors. We have planned no protest demonstrations in Berlin."
Furthermore, he continued, when he received such a letter from
"the editor of *Christianity Today* and a spokesman of the new
evangelicalism," it served to confirm the very things that he had
been writing about the position of clergymen such as Dr. Henry
and Billy Graham: "The evangelicals who work and hold fellowship with the modernist unbelievers are more abusive and do
more harm to the cause of the Gospel and the purity of the
church than the liberals themselves." [26]

On October 31 the group of ACCC leaders bearing the special
"message" to the World Congress met Dr. Henry, Dr. Stanley
Mooneyham and Mr. Gil A. Stricklin in the entrance to the
Congress Hall in what McIntire later described as a "confrontation." The ACCC leaders were informed that the World Congress
would not receive their message. Later McIntire wrote that
during the "confrontation," when queried by the ACCC delegation as to how the message could be delivered, Mooneyham,
"perhaps in an offhand way," said that they could "put it on the
wall." McIntire then sent a "formal communication" to Dr.
Henry, asking him to be present at the entrance on Wednesday
afternoon at three o'clock to receive the message. At the stated
time, neither Henry nor anyone representing the Congress appeared. While reporters and other passers-by watched, the ACCC
delegation taped the message to one of the glass partitions at
the entrance to the hall. Almost immediately a guard rushed out,
jerked it off and crumpled it in his hands. Another copy of the
message was then taped to the same glass, but the guard again
removed it.

By this time a large crowd had gathered, some staring, others
taking pictures. Dr. McIntire, with a tape recorder, was busy
securing a record of everything that happened. For half an hour
he remained in the area, answering reporters' questions and, as
he called it, "entering into an exchange with various church
leaders." Questions and charges were still being directed at him

and his fellow ACCC leaders as they were leaving the hall, and McIntire observed that ". . . one sweet, loving evangelical turned and yelled, 'Heil, Hitler!' " The fact that his efforts to hang a copy of the ACCC message in the hall entrance had been rebuffed was to him proof enough that the leadership of the Berlin congress was afraid the divisions already present might "scandalize the Congress in international publicity." Never had his protests been met with such firmness. "Indeed," he remarked, "this assembly was the most controlled from the top of any non-Roman religious gathering I have ever seen. Its doors were more closely guarded than any assembly, religious or political, I have ever witnessed." [27]

If the leadership of the congress had roundly rejected the message of the ACCC delegation, they were equally firm in denying press credentials to Carl McIntire. That had been made clear on October 31, when McIntire and the ACCC delegation first met Dr. Henry and his assistants in "confrontation." McIntire considered the argument that there was no room for additional press accreditation a "front" that Dr. Henry and Dr. Graham had presented. And he resented Dr. Henry's telling the press conference that he had stamped out of the hall when the credentials were denied. He knew he had retreated most courteously from the room. And he felt that the evangelicals, who were always boasting of their love, had in effect called him "poison" and told him to "go home." He counted many press boxes and reporters during the remainder of the congress and concluded, "There were always empty seats. The argument, therefore, that they were filled to capacity, and that it was impossible to accredit Dr. McIntire was simply not supported by the realities of the convention's actual operation and constitution . . . The truth is that Dr. Carl Henry and Evangelist Billy Graham decided that in their rebuking of Carl McIntire they would keep him outside of the Congress." [28]

But the Collingswood radio preacher readily admitted that while he had been denied press credentials, he had been offered the status of an observer or a visitor to the congress. He complained that the status of an observer had come in recent years to indicate that the observer held a favorable relationship with the meeting being observed. And he insisted that he had turned down the observer status only because he did not want it thought that he had a favorable relationship with the congress, and not—as Dr. Henry had tried to twist it when reporting to the press—because he did not want to be associated with Jews and Roman Catholics who were there as observers.

Dr. McIntire said he found nothing wrong with the status of visitor, except that it involved great inconvenience to obtain a separate entrance card each morning. And so he and the other members of his party were admitted to the Congress with the status of visitors. But for reasons that only became evident later, McIntire abruptly changed his mind and decided against the visitor status, preferring to remain outside the congress in "reporter status." Dr. Henry later analyzed the strange behavior of Preacher McIntire:

> It was clear from the first that what he wanted was to make the Congress itself an object of attack for the partisan purpose of promoting his own organization. This he has done ever since. It is simply untrue that he was not permitted to enter the Congress. Mrs. McIntire, and, for that matter, Dr. McIntire's entire entourage were permitted to enter and did so, attending some of the sessions.[29]

But Dr. McIntire did not see it that way. He knew when he was being kept out of a building: "No gate was ever more vigilantly guarded than the one into this meeting. My exclusion, therefore, put me in a new and special position, one occupied by no other reporter who covered the conference."

Now began perhaps the most unusual performance of the irrepressible radio preacher's career. During four consecutive evenings he took up a position of protest at the entrance to the Congres Hall, "outside the gate," he called it. He did this, he said, because he had gone to Berlin as a reporter and had been excluded in that capacity. There were sometimes as many as four guards stationed at the entrance. The first set of doors opened into a storm vestibule, beyond which another set of doors opened into the Congress Hall. Dr. McIntire reported that on the first night of his protest he was permitted to remain inside the storm vestible, where it was quite comfortable, and he could converse with a steady stream of visitors and guests who had heard he was conducting a "stand-in" protest. And he did not have to stand alone. He was always accompanied by one of his party, who acted as both bodyguard and witness.

On the second night of his vigil the guard refused him permission to continue his protest inside the warm vestibule, according to the doughty radio preacher. Now he would have to stand outside in the cold. He surmised that this turn of events had come about because his first night's protest had been too successful; too many people had seen and talked with him. Now that he was outside, it was doubtful that very many would stop to chat in such weather. Said Dr. McIntire, "It was cold, freezing weather. The snow actually was falling." And then Mrs. McIntire came out and joined him in the snow. She had left her identification at the hotel, and Dr. McIntire claimed that even though the guard knew who she was, he refused to let her enter. Instead of returning to the hotel for her identification, she joined her husband in his snowy protest. Now how did the Congress leaders feel about what they had done? The Collingswood preacher described their wintry vigil:

. . . the cold became more intense. I specifically asked the guard if we could stand inside the vestibule where I had stood the night before. He refused. I made this request several times. Others also felt that Mrs. McIntire should go in out of the cold and this stirred considerable reaction. Other members of our party who went in raised strenuous objections to this treatment of Mrs. McIntire and asked how Mrs. Billy Graham would feel, or how Mrs. Carl Henry would be treated under circumstances of this kind. How would Graham and Henry have reacted? They revealed their own lack of love or kindness! [30]

The last two nights of his protest were relatively uneventful, and McIntire took his tape recorder along and spent part of the time making tapes for his radio programs. While he was at the congress, he also recorded a program just outside the Berlin Wall, and commented that it was easier to get into East Berlin than the press room in Billy Graham's congress. He saw some ministers who had once been in his own separatist camp, but had since opted for what he called the "softer approach," joining the movement of the new evangelicals. McIntire also discussed two other well-known ministers at the congress—the Rev. Theodore Epp of the "Back To The Bible" radio program, one of the largest and most popular Gospel broadcasts in the United States, and world-famous faith healer Oral Roberts.

The Collingswood pastor described Epp as a typical independent Gospel broadcaster who had attracted support from people who were disaffected from their regular churches. McIntire believed that many of Epp's supporters had learned of the great apostasy from his own programs, which were broadcast on many of the same stations that carried the "Back To The Bible" programs. He minced no words in telling how he disapproved of Epp's temporizing and evading, and described him as one careful not to position himself so distinctly that he "stirs opposition or raises questions." But he also recognized that Epp's careful approach to the great issues of the day had attracted many cautious fundamentalists who did not want to become deeply involved in religious controversies. He acknowledged the great following that Epp enjoyed, but predicted that the position of evangelists like him would become more and more difficult to maintain. And in McIntire's view that time started running out for Evangelist Epp when he was captured by Billy Graham and the new evangelicals at Berlin.[31]

If Dr. McIntire seemed appalled by the "capture" of the Reverend Theodore Epp by the new evangelicals, it may have been because he considered Epp a Bible-believing fundamentalist whose loss had indirectly hurt the cause, even though Epp was not a part of the separatist movement. His discussion of the Reverend Oral Roberts revealed that he cared little for the Roberts ministry. He saw him as little more than a grand opportunist, a preacher of false doctrines, a man desperately hungry for respect and acceptance. When Roberts joined Graham on the platform, McIntire described the faith healer as a "curiosity," trying to "outdo all the others in his effusive praise." Furthermore, Roberts had journeyed to the World Congress on Evangelism to "exploit for healing and tongues everyone that he could, and Mr. Epp helped his cause along." McIntire believed that the Tulsa faith healer had moved in with strength to be recognized at the congress for his brand of evangelism, and would reap a bountiful harvest for Pentecostalism. And not only had the ecumenical movement been advanced with Roberts' help, "but Pentecostalism, with its error in tongues and faith-healing, received an emphasis which will make it more difficult for true evangelists to deal with." [32]

Dr. McIntire reported that Oral turned on the emotion, testifying that Billy Graham and the World Congress had "out-prayed, out-organized, and out-preached anything that he had been able to do." Thus, said McIntire, "the man who is accustomed to crowds, the world's foremost 'divine healer' and the user of tongues, elicited from the crowd prolonged and enthusiastic applause." Roberts obviously had the blessing of Billy Graham, McIntire reported, and would go back to his Tulsa headquarters to "exploit it and expound it for the advancement of his own program." Said Dr. McIntire,

> It was a new day for Roberts. He was recognized, accepted, honored, applauded by evangelical and ecumenical circles. Now the rank and file of evangelicals would also feel free to listen to the message of Oral Roberts.[33]

The World Congress was nearing an end. In a parting shot, Dr. Henry charged Rev. Carl with "ecclesiastical blackmail." [34] But Dr. McIntire consoled himself with the knowledge that he had stood up for freedom of the press. That, he said, would be a major issue hanging over the congress "and over Henry and Graham the rest of their lives. They did an evil deed that hurts." And as far as locking him outside the gate was concerned, he decided, "What Dr. Henry feels he has gained by such a strategy is of course his personal satisfaction. The Christian world will have to hold him and Evangelist Billy Graham responsible for this abuse of freedom." [35]

The Rev. Dr. Carl McIntire went home. It had been a unique experience protesting the Billy Graham Congress, he later wrote. He had gathered tapes and notes and more information, from every angle, on everyone, than he had ever before obtained on any such congress in his career.

He returned from Europe to discover that the November 25 issue of *Christianity Today* had included a paragraph about him in its review of the congress: "Halfway through the congress, evangelist gadfly Carl McIntire turned up in Berlin with an armload of mimeographed literature denouncing 'ecumenical evangelism' . . . He was invited in, however, and was offered observer and visitor badges, but he ultimately refused both."

Obviously, they were sticking with their version of the story. And they had labeled him an evangelical gadfly! He included a chapter on that subject in his new book. And he told not only his people, but people all over the world about the treatment he had received at Billy Graham's congress in Berlin. "I told it in the *Christian Beacon,* our weekly religious newspaper; in the packet which I sent out to our radio listeners who requested it; and then I told the story on the radio itself in two coast-to-coast broadcasts and short-wave around the world. I told it then so that it carries the life and the freshness of my testimony under the pressure of those strange moments." [36]

After the Berlin congress, it appeared that McIntire had delegated to his *Christian Beacon* the job of keeping a close reportorial eye on Billy Graham and the new evangelicals. But there were so many other things that he was also trying to watch that it was something of a wonder that he found time to sleep. He was concerned about the proposed merger of ten major Protestant denominations, a merger which would unite some 68,000 ministers and 25 million church members in what he feared would be a superchurch that would bring on a world government. He also was opposed to the fairness doctrine being implemented by the Federal Communications Commission. He saw it as a weapon which his enemies would use to threaten, intimidate and hail into court those stations that broadcast Gospel radio programs. McIntire also seemed to fear that President Johnson was being influenced by one of his daughters to become a convert to the Roman Catholic Church, and he was so sure that the President was conducting the military operations in Vietnam with a "tremendous fear" of the Russians that he hurriedly sent to the White House a long telegram containing information to help the President pray properly. But that positive action seemed to be offset by the news that Dr. David A. Hubbard, the president of Fuller Theological Seminary, had agreed on the church's ministry in the world with Bishop James A. Pike, and Dr. McIntire could only ask, "How far gone is Fuller Seminary?" [37]

The year 1968 was one of frenetic activity. It was one of the worst possible times for the arguments and dissension which broke out between McIntire and some of the leaders of his American Council. The problems concerned McIntire's handling of the *Christian Beacon* newspaper and his radio program. The ACCC leaders felt that McIntire had used these "personal ministries" in such a way that they had become a voice of the International Council of Christian Churches. They were also alarmed at the "increasing involvement in political issues, including the civil-rights question, the frequent criticism of the United States Government or other governments of the free world, and the participation in or endorsement of protest marches and demonstrations which are in any sense political." One leader declared that many religious separatists objected to the methods used by Dr. McIntire, to the extreme statements he sometimes made and to his involvement in political issues. Directed at McIntire, a formal statement said, in part,

> Unfortunately the president [McIntire] of the ICCC, when he writes in the *Christian Beacon*, or broadcasts over the Reformation Hour, is interpreted by our Christian brethren abroad and at home as speaking for the ICCC and its Associated Missions. When he speaks in the area of politics, race, and civil rights, this causes irreparable damage to our missionary efforts and in some cases is causing our missionaries abroad and the national churches, brought into being by them, to remain outside the ICCC.[38]

News of the battle soon reached the public, and *Newsweek* took a look at the Collingswood churchman and the noisy dispute with his fundamentalist brethren:

> Dr. Carl McIntire has long ruled the forces of the fundamentalist far right with almost papal suzerainty. An implacable foe of Communists, Catholics and all other "apostate" Christians, he has spent

more than 30 years building a movement out of his personal antipathies . . . Last week, however, there were unexpected signs that McIntire was no longer in total control of his movement . . .[39]

Observing that McIntire's real source of power was in his talent for polemics and that his editorial "we" in the *Christian Beacon* was frequently indistinguishable from a papal *"nos,"* *Newsweek* declared that it was McIntire's pervasive influence over the entire movement that was really at issue, since multiplied thousands of "Bible Belt Protestants" accepted his radio program and newspaper as the voice of truth.

Dr. McIntire responded to the *Newsweek* account of his problems in a front-page column entitled "I Was Betrayed." He accused the magazine of "telling the world that Carl McIntire has been rejected because of his 'one-man mold.' " He felt that it must have been God's will that the argument was brought into the open, but "no one knows the sting of having brethren whom you trusted betray you, to tell you one thing to your face and then say something else behind your back. . . ." He had already complained that the attack on him by the brethren was an *ad hominem* argument, that a *coup d'état* had been executed against him, and now that he was being ousted from his position of leadership, he found the ACCC leaders guilty of conspiracy.[40]

The internal squabble dragged on as McIntire fought to regain his authority in the American Council, but it was soon pushed off the front page of his paper by the press of current events. Among other things, a Russian fishing fleet was operating off the eastern coast of the United States, and that was enough to bring some 200 of his followers with their placards to Atlantic City, where they demonstrated against the Russians on a cold February day. When he spoke at the demonstration, the doughty New Jersey preacher announced he was launching an Atlantic Citizens Association to fight the encroachment of the Soviet fishing fleet. He urged the cancellation of the 1938 U.S.-U.S.S.R. treaty permitting Russian fishermen to use one-half-inch nets. And he called for the United States to extend its coastal limits from 12 to 200 miles. "We believe in God," he declared. "The Russians don't." [41]

Beginning on February 3, 1969, McIntire waged what he described as a "vigorous campaign" over his broadcast network for 24 straight days. He wanted some of the words from the Bible that the astronauts had broadcast back to earth on the previous Christmas Eve put on the Apollo 8 stamp. He also published a long attack against the registration and control of guns. And he went to Atlanta to protest COCU (Consultation on Church Union), the merger of the big Protestant churches. As a rallying call against the ecumenical movement, he published a little poem called "Row, Row, Row," which began,

> Row, row, row your boat,
> COCU down the stream
> Ecumenical, ecumenical,
> What a monstrous dream.[42]

He plunged next into an attack on Existentialism, but it was apparently forgotten when he sensed a rising grass-roots antipathy toward the upcoming 1970 census. Even though it is authorized by the Constitution itself, Dr. McIntire described the hated census in frightening language: "The citizens of the United States are confronted with one of the most direct challenges to their liberty and constitutional rights that they have ever faced." [43]

But suddenly he was forced to go on the defensive. State education officials of New Jersey recommended that Shelton College be denied a license to grant Bachelor of Arts degrees. The threat of loss of accreditation was based on a variety of inadequacies at the little school, ranging from improper heating facilities to an inadequate library. The State Higher Education Chancellor, Ralph A. Dungan, charged that Dr. McIntire and the academic dean of Shelton did not have time to direct the school, "because of commitments outside of the college." [44]

In late June of 1969 a hearing began on the 16 charges against Shelton College. McIntire sent out a call for help over his broadcast network, and some 600 of his followers joined him in a Trenton, New Jersey, auditorium, where they sang hymns and waved placards denouncing the Chancellor of Higher Education and the governor of the state. The New Jersey preacher saw the move to close his little college as a conspiracy of magnificent proportions: "Men in the highest levels in the political world and in ecumenical circles have joined hands to harm us and destroy Shelton College." He planned next for 10,000 "Bible-believers" to follow him in a march on Trenton.

Just before the march took place, Louis Cassels, well-known U.P.I. religion writer and an inveterate McIntire adversary, devoted his syndicated column to Rev. Carl's problems in a story entitled "Hard Not to Enjoy This Guy's Troubles." He described the radio preacher as a man who for three decades "has heaped vituperation upon thousands of people including liberal Protestants, conservative Protestants, fundamentalist Protestants, Roman Catholics, public officials who cross him, and some journalists. To those who oppose him, McIntire often imputes atheism, pro-Communist leanings, dishonesty, cowardice or venality." He listed McIntire's far-flung interests, in which he included some $3 million worth of real estate in the resort town of Cape May, New Jersey. After reporting that McIntire had been ousted a few months earlier from leadership of the American Council in a "palace revolution," Cassels went on to discuss the radio preacher's battle with the New Jersey Department of Higher Education over Shelton College. He also disclosed that the International Council had been weakened that month by the withdrawal of its largest U.S. affiliate, the 180,000-member General Association of Regular Baptist Churches.

But McIntire never hesitated to return the attacks of the U.P.I. columnist. He began his rebuttal by noting that "Love your enemies" was a text which Louis Cassels supposedly upheld, but the columnist was "now manifesting that love in the way in which he abuses me and completely misrepresents my position in the battle to preserve the Christian faith and the heritage of freedom in the U.S.A." McIntire placed most of the blame for the Cassels attack on the leaders of the American Council, who, he believed, were "putting ammunition in the hands of Louis Cassels and others to use against me." And in the tone of one who still expected to be completely vindicated, he philosophized that the Lord would surely deal with the American Council leadership.[45]

The Collingswood pastor had hardly completed his counter-attack against Cassels when he came under the guns of *Newsweek* once more.

In the steeplescape of American religion, fundamentalist radio preacher Dr. Carl McIntire occupies a small but special tower. Not content merely to preach his brand of Biblical literalism, he has developed over the years the reactionary American Council of Christian Churches and its international counterpart as opposite but unequal forces to the National and World Councils of Churches. Indeed, like a shadow, McIntire comes alive only when the "apostate" liberal churchmen make a move or gesture that he can mimic in reverse.[46]

Newsweek's article concluded that about all that was real about the New Jersey radio preacher was his need for funds and desire for publicity. Because of the reverses he had recently suffered, the magazine predicted, "In truth, McIntire's watch on the right may soon be over."

Far from it, the scrappy radio preacher retorted; *Newsweek* was merely giving assistance to the forces that were out to destroy his operations. Speaking of himself in the third person, as he is often inclined to do, he declared, "*Newsweek* misjudges Dr. McIntire, for he will never quit fighting."

When the Rev. Carl McIntire elevated someone's name to his first list of "enemies," that person could usually count on having his every move reported in the *Christian Beacon*. The Collingswood radio preacher missed few opportunities to attack those who opposed his doctrines and ideology. In some cases even the relatives of his enemies were not immune. And this seemed to be especially true when the paper was not involved in a major ideological struggle. In the August 7, 1969, issue of the *Beacon*, McIntire saw fit to publish an account of the death of the late Martin Luther King's brother under the heading "King's Brother Dead—Drunk." The short article noted that while an autopsy had ruled the death of King's brother an accidental drowning in a swimming pool, he was also drunk.

Dr. McIntire also remembered his differences with Bishop James Pike after the onetime Episcopal Church leader died in

the Dead Sea wilderness of Israel. In his opinion, Pike had been
an "apostate and denier of the faith," whom God had dealt with
"in a summary way." Noting that there are various passages in
the Scriptures that describe the ends of men like Pike, the minister who once had condemned Billy Graham's lack of love in
refusing him a press card, selected some verses from the Book
of Jude to describe Pike:

> These are spots in your feasts of charity, when they feast with you,
> feeding themselves without fear: clouds they are without water, car-
> ried about of winds; trees whose fruit withereth without fruit, twice
> dead, plucked up by the roots; raging waves of the sea foaming out
> their own shame; wandering stars, to whom is reserved the blackness
> of darkness for ever.[47]

McIntire is often at his best when he is parrying the attacks
of the national news media, and perhaps that is why the *Beacon*
has reported so many of his battles. In the November 14, 1969,
issue of *Time*, McIntire was called a man with a rare gift: "everything he touches turns to schism." The news magazine was referring to the action of some leaders of the ACCC convention in
Columbus, Ohio, who had repudiated McIntire by pointedly not
returning him to the council's executive committee, on which he
had served for 28 years. The convention also passed a resolution
criticizing him for "his cavalier transfer" of an ACCC relief fund
to his International Council and for then spending nearly a
quarter of a million dollars for "administrative expenses" over
eight years. *Time* also revealed that at the 1969 convention of
McIntire's own Bible Presbyterian Church, some 40 per cent of
the delegates voted for a rival candidate to replace Pastor Mc-
Intire as their moderator.

To *Time*'s remarks McIntire responded with a firm rebuke.
The article, he said, was a good example of how those opposed
to his work were seeking to discredit the whole Reformation
movement. As for the allegation that some 54 per cent of the
ACCC relief fund was spent for administrative expenses, that
was not true, and the facts in the audited report had actually
been given to the magazine.[48]

But he claimed that it was not only *Time* that was publishing false statements against him. From his description it would appear that a host of enemies was maligning him. He cited an article in the December 12, 1969, issue of *The Banner*, the official organ of the Christian Reformed Church; the article alleged that he was chummy with racists, an attack that McIntire brushed aside as "an irresponsible and false accusation." *The Canadian Mennonite* of November 14, 1969, called him an "ultra-fundamentalist," and McIntire published the article along with his letter asking the *Mennonite* to please drop the "ultra," and *Christianity Today* joined the chorus with some strong remarks.[49]

Near the end of 1969 McIntire involved himself and his followers in the political issue that in a few months made his name better known than all his years of battling "apostate" churches had done. With timing remarkable in anyone other than Rev. Carl, he committed himself to public demonstrations for victory in the Vietnam war.

McIntire had always supported all-out victory in Vietnam rather than a negotiated peace stemming from a war of limited objectives. As early as June 1967 he revealed that one of his close associates, the Rev. James T. Shaw, together with a team of ACCC leaders, had returned from a tour of the Far East. The group told McIntire they had found that the U.S. forces knew exactly why they were there and "they want to win over the Communist forces." The group was received by General Westmoreland, and Rev. Shaw said, "I told the General that I was glad to see that there were two Bibles lying on his desk. . . ."[50]

But it was not until after the November 1969 Moratorium against the war in Vietnam that he made the first announcement that ". . . Bible believers with their Bibles, the patriots with their Flags, and those who have served in America's wars, all who desire to see victory in Vietnam, will rally to the nation's capital. . . ."

Because he was editor of the *Christian Beacon* and director of the "Twentieth Century Reformation Hour" radio network, he went to Washington, D.C., to cover the Moratorium. He announced in advance on his radio network the time and place where any of his listeners could meet him if they wished to carry placards as a testimony against the demonstration. About one hundred people joined him, and while his little group was almost lost in what McIntire described as "an unending sea of hair," he considered his symbolic opposition to the Moratorium so successful that he called it a confrontation. Said McIntire, "The whole spectacle broke your heart, made you weep, and made you realize that something tragic has happened in American life." Out of that experience against the hippies and the longhairs came his announcement that in Washington, D.C., on April 11, 1970, "Christians and patriots throughout America" would join in a march which he expected to be "the largest demonstration in American history in behalf of victory over the Communists and for the preservation of a God-given heritage." [51]

All through the winter the radio voice of the "Twentieth Century Reformation Hour" and the pages of the *Christian Beacon* continued to spread word of the coming great April 11 March for Victory. There were, of course, other issues that required attention, such as the fight against sex education and the renewed effort for prayer in schools. Also, Dr. McIntire discovered that Billy Graham had appeared on the television show "Laugh-In," a fact that hardly amused the pastor from Collingswood, but which did inspire him to reproduce in his paper an article critical of the Graham performance. [52]

Suddenly, as the time for the giant march drew near, McIntire received news that the date set for his demonstration had to be abandoned. He was forced to reschedule it for April 4, because as originally scheduled his march conflicted with the Cherry Blossom Festival, and nothing could be permitted to interfere with the crowds arriving to see the cherry blossoms. Dr. McIntire called the forced reschedule "one of the most high-handed and brutal operations." [53]

With the most ambitious project of his career just a few days away, radio preacher McIntire moved at a frantic pace. Everywhere he turned he discovered difficulties. After six weeks of struggle, he had to call on a congressman to force the Washington park officials to let him set up his speakers' platform on public property. Also his group had been denied the use of the Washington Cathedral, a national shrine, for a prayer meeting the day before the march. That was especially galling to McIntire, since he claimed that hippies had used it on the evening prior to their Moratorium march. But he reported that the most "shocking development" came from the White House itself. On April 2, only two days before the scheduled march, he photographically reproduced in his *Christian Beacon* a letter written on White House stationery, announcing that the March for Victory had been postponed. McIntire quickly sent a letter to the President, protesting "the interference of the White House in our March for Victory." He hurriedly recorded special radio tapes to tell his people that the march was not postponed, and he made a determined but unsuccessful effort to reach the President himself in order to request an apology.

But he surmounted every obstacle, and the march went on as scheduled. McIntire described it as "100,000 March For Victory." He proudly announced that the marchers came from every section and state of the United States, and also from parts of Canada. They marched down Pennsylvania Avenue, Bibles in hand, with a sea of American and Confederate flags waving, and assembled around the Washington Monument. There speakers demanded that prayer and Bible reading be put in the schools and sex education be put out. They denounced the Nixon Administration's "no-win" policy in Vietnam. There were various special groups, including Indians in colorful war bonnets, and what had become a regular feature of many fundamentalist and right-wing gatherings, a young girl mawkishly testifying that she had been saved from a life of hippiedom and dope, while elderly protesters stood around wiping the tears from their eyes. *Christianity Today* reported other aspects of the march: "Here and there groups of hippies and others whooped it up, flashing the 'V' sign and, when the Americanisms got thick, bursting out with "oink oink' and 'Sieg Heil.'"

Still, Dr. McIntire was extremely pleased with the turnout and the way the program had been conducted. "The March exceeded that which had been anticipated," he said. "For one day the Capital was commanded by those who carried Bibles. . . ."

But the march was no sooner over than McIntire was hurling anathemas in a number of directions. So many barriers had been erected against his demonstration that he considered writing a book to list all who opposed him, especially many Washington officials. The premier position was apparently reserved for the news media, which he considered to be on trial. The coverage of the March for Victory was the finest example of suppression and discrimination that anyone could possibly ask for, said McIntire, contending that much of the press had ignored the march until it was over, and then they participated in what some would call the "great numbers game." Most of the major newspapers used their own guesses, ranging from 8,000 to the 50,000 estimate printed by the New York *Times*, a figure that matched that released by the Washington Park Police. McIntire would not be swayed: ". . . actually there were 100,000 or more by any way that one looked at that mass of people and sought to calculate them. And many people left believing there were far more than a hundred thousand." [54]

Christianity Today used the figure of 50,000 in pointing out that for McIntire the march was "the biggest single victory in his relentless fight against the 'international conspiracy of godless Communism.'" The magazine observed that the big newspapers had paid scant attention to the Collingswood preacher before the march and very little afterward. Few realized that McIntire's effort had been largely a one-man affair, "one man haranguing on 600 radio stations." McIntire took note of the magazine's remarks and called them shameful, little more than a personal attack." [55]

In the very shadow of his March for Victory, while congratulations from listeners in his far-flung radio empire were still coming in and discussions and arguments about the number of marchers still spiced his radio programs, the fundamentalist minister announced that he would stage a second March for Victory in Washington. He decided to schedule it for after the summer, on the first weekend in October; at the same time he announced June 13 as the date of simultaneous local rallies to be held in cities all across the country, wherever his supporters could find enough people to march around their town squares.

Dr. McIntire had never found an issue that compared with his big Marches for attracting regular notice in the national news media. But it would be unfair to imply that publicity was the primary reason for his efforts to organize demonstrations for the war, since he had a long and consistent record of calling for total victory in Vietnam. Now he apparently had become so caught up in the issue of winning the war that he took two of his associates and flew to Southeast Asia for a brief tour of Vietnam. There they met General Creighton Abrams and interviewed soldiers and airmen. Said Preacher McIntire, "Everywhere I went I found our men ready and anxious for action." He posed for pictures dressed in Army fatigues and visited the hospitals and a prisoner-of-war camp, and departed after four days to inform his people that "The American people must demand victory. This is the quickest and surest road to peace." [56]

During the hurried days of preparation for his next great march, McIntire took time to observe that he had not received an invitation to visit the White House. He decided it was something important enough to write to the President about. After all, he had complained to him about the Apollo 8 stamp and heard nothing. And in November 1969, when he and a delegation bearing a wreath for the Tomb of the Unknown Soldier were stopped by park officials, he had complained bitterly to the President, but had heard nothing. Since the successful March for Victory he had sent President Nixon a packet of descriptive articles and later a supply of bumper stickers advertising his next march. It was as if they had fallen down a deep well.

In his letter to the President Dr. McIntire recounted some of the rebuffs he had suffered. The immediate reason for writing to the White House was the news that representatives of the union "hardhats" had been invited to visit President Nixon. All of this, according to the New Jersey fundamentalist, had raised some very basic questions with him and his people. Besides the March for Victory, Dr. McIntire and his followers had ardently supported the President's decision to send troops into Cambodia. And after asking at that time to see the President, he had received no reply. He also reminded Nixon of the White House letter announcing that the April 4 March for Victory had to be

postponed, and what confusion that had caused. After that embarrassment he and his people had asked for some expression of
regret, but they had heard nothing. He also recalled that the
President had seen the representatives of various colleges, and
had even made a point of going early in the morning to the
Lincoln Memorial to talk with student strikers. Dr. McIntire
emphasized that he and his followers would not object to being
shut out if the President were not seeing a variety of other
groups: "We are wondering now if the reason that we are being
snubbed in this way is that we are calling for victory." [57]

His attention was deflected from the White House by another
development that suddenly appeared in the news. It was the
ubiquitous Billy Graham again. This time he had teamed up
with famous comedian Bob Hope to plan a Fourth of July rally
in Washington, D.C. And apparently they had the blessing of
the White House, McIntire concluded, as he revealed that the
sponsors of the rally would not call for victory in Vietnam.
Neither would the rally demonstrate against the war. The purpose of the gathering was to show national unity. To the fundamentalist preacher this was almost too much: "It is inconceivable
that the Fourth of July could be celebrated by the American
people without its emphasis being upon victory. . . ."

He struck back by announcing a balloon project for the Fourth
of July. Supporters in many cities along the eastern coast would
simultaneously release victory balloons at 10:00 A.M. on the Fourth
of July. As more information about the Graham-Hope rally became available, McIntire seemed more concerned than ever that
his efforts for victory were being "neutralized." He reproduced
a full-page promotional advertisement for the Graham-Hope
"Coming Together" rally and pointed to the slogan they were
using: "Show Your Love." It was the letter "O" in the word
"love" that excited him. It was decorated as a "hippie flower,"
he said. Furthermore, he didn't like some of the names listed
as honorary chairmen by Hope and Graham, names like Harry
S. Truman, Mamie Eisenhower and Lyndon Johnson. Nothing
could be clearer to the pastor from Collingswood: "Billy Graham
at last has positioned himself . . . It will be interesting to see

just how many are deceived by the Hope-Graham 4th of July festival." [58]

Graham had already stated that he felt the "Honor America Day" rally would attract 300,000 people. He was also quoted by the New York *Times* as deploring the widespread identification of patriotism with the political right:

> I think we have allowed patriotism to slip. We have allowed the word "patriotism" to get into the hands of some right-wingers. I don't guess anybody loves the flag more than some of the people that are against the war.[59]

It was a remark that stung fundamentalist McIntire deeply. Chagrined, he observed, "This is the characterization that has been given to those who have sought to maintain America's heritage of individual freedom, resisting the socialistic developments in the country and exposing the Communist conspiracy . . . Dr. Graham and Bob Hope must answer now to the great company of patriots. . . ." [60]

Honor America Day attracted 350,000 people to Washington, according to one source, but Billy Graham later released a figure of 400,000. Earlier, in response to an estimate of 300,000, McIntire had said he would bring in 500,000 for his upcoming October March for Victory. But he remarked that Bob Hope and Billy Graham had "received the widest and fullest possible support from the press, television, and radio." Assailing Graham as the "Apostle of Neutralism," McIntire reported bitterly that the nation's biggest news magazines, *Time* and *Newsweek*, had provided extensive coverage of the rally. Graham was quoted in *Newsweek* as denouncing "negativism" in the nation, which he blamed on a "relatively small extremist element, both on the left and the right." Then, observed the Collingswood fundamentalist, *Newsweek* had proceeded to "identify Dr. McIntire in its brief paragraph referring to a balloon action as 'the far right.'" And he had seen an article in the New York *Times* which claimed that Graham himself had referred to Dr. McIntire as the far right. That was too much! He promptly sent a telegram of protest to *Newsweek:*

Object to being called far right by you or Graham. Those of us who want to win our wars as we always have cannot be maneuvered out of our historic American position. Neither must dissent mean polarization. Our March for Victory in Washington October 3rd will exceed anything Graham produced. Don't throw America out of focus.[61]

Billy Graham seemed to be pulling ahead, and McIntire claimed to know one big reason for it: "As the facts have come in, it is clear that the Washington Fourth of July celebration was designed to support Richard Nixon's program, and he, behind the scenes, had a deciding hand in the way the whole matter was arranged. . . ."[62]

Now he swung into determined action and announced the scheduling of "booster meetings" and "cow pasture rallies" in preparation for his October 3 March. He also kept up his attacks on Billy Graham as often as possible. He published one article which said that Graham had admitted visiting a marijuana smoke-in in order to talk with the smokers. This story, observed McIntire, had caused a stir among fundamentalists. He was also aware that Graham's picture was on the cover of *Newsweek* and that the feature story described the revivalist's friendship with Presidents Nixon, Johnson, Kennedy and Eisenhower. Calling him "The President's Preacher," *Newsweek* declared that Graham had exerted considerable influence on those national leaders and "holds a passport into the world of power politics of a kind that no other U.S. preacher before him has ever been granted."[63]

With only a few weeks remaining before his second big march on Washington, McIntire announced that for the fifth time his request to see the President had been turned down. Speaking of Nixon's refusal to see him, McIntire said, "This repeated turn down by the President is a real offense in the light of his willingness to receive representatives of other positions, which he has already done. . . . Let the March be so massive and so impressive that the impact in behalf of victory will have to be felt by the President."

Dr. McIntire took time from his prepartion for the march to write to Dr. John D. Siegfried of the United Methodist Church of Germantown in nearby Philadelphia. He had learned that Father Daniel Berrigan, the Jesuit priest wanted by the law for burning military draft records, had paid a surprise visit to the Germantown Methodist Church and addressed the congregation from the pulpit. McIntire demanded equal time to express his views. When his request was refused, he attempted to enter the Germantown church during Sunday morning services, but was stopped by Dr. Siegfried. Undeterred, the irrepressible fundamentalist proceeded to deliver his message from the church steps to a handful of his followers, a police civil disobedience squad and a little group of newsmen. Assistants held umbrellas to protect his white suit from the drizzling rain while McIntire read a ten-minute speech. Then some of his assistants lifted him high enough to tape the copy of his remarks over the church door. In a few minutes the rain-soaked paper fell off. He reported the incident to his people under the heading of "Criminal Welcome; McIntire Barred." [64]

But there was little time for side issues, since there had already been so much opposition to his second march, and Dr. McIntire needed the kind of publicity that would get his story to the whole nation. Just before the march, a suitable issue presented itself. Peace groups were stunned and official Washington was shocked on September 3, when Nguyen Cao Ky, the Vice-President of South Vietnam, announced in Saigon that he had accepted the invitation extended to him by the Rev. Dr. Carl McIntire and his March for Victory Committee to speak at the October 3 rally in Washington, D.C.

McIntire was jubilant; his story of the March for Victory was on the front pages of all the leading newspapers and on broadcasts across the country. The Washington *Post* headlined the latest turn of events as "Ky Plan Shakes Washington." But most of the news media was soon warning that Washington officials were taking a dim view of Ky's speaking at a right-wing rally, and almost immediately there were rumors that he had felt the pressure and was reconsidering his decision. Alarmed, McIntire sent a telegram to the Vietnamese Vice-President, urging him to stand firm and adding that he was flying to Saigon.

Dr. McIntire returned in time for a scheduled address before the National Press Club in Washington. It was a time like no other in his whole career. Every large newspaper carried accounts of his actions and a number of his quotations. The press which had proved so elusive for so long now seemed to be almost underfoot. Speaking into banks of microphones at the Press Club, McIntire was expansive as never before. He proclaimed that the war could be won in six weeks and even had his own plan for doing just that, which he published in the *Beacon* under the title of "How To Win The War." He told the press that many of the things happening around the world were caused by the failure of the Nixon Administration to go all out for victory in Vietnam. He even declared that the skyjacking of airplanes stemmed from the negative policy in Southeast Asia.

On September 26 newspapers all over the world announced that Vice-President Ky had been persuaded not to speak at the March for Victory. The Collingswood radio preacher immediately flew to Paris, where Ky was staying. In a brief conference Ky convinced McIntire that he was definitely not planning to speak at the march. Carl McIntire returned to the United States and prepared a message to his people:

> The man who spoke there was a different man entirely than the one I had talked to in Saigon previously. He said he was canceling his trip because of the best interests of his country. Behind that statement lies a story of the most powerful pressures originating in the highest levels of the United States government . . . It was clear that misinformation and untrue statements had been given to the Vice-President by those who had sought to keep him from coming.[65]

The march was still a week away, and McIntire moved carefully to prevent casting a pall of discouragement over that event. Later on he would have more strident quotations about how Nixon had stopped Ky from coming to his march. But he was still able to attract reporters and photographers, who seemed to follow him everywhere.

The March for Victory was held as planned, with music, placards and many speeches. Six hundred and fifty newsmen and television reporters were accredited to the march. Seven television networks covered the gathering for people all over the world. Dr. McIntire called the March for Victory a "glorious success," but in the words of the Washington *Evening Star,* the crowd that marched with him was "orderly and small." The paper noted also that there were some obscene provocations during the march by a few young people, and the reaction of blind rage on the part of some marchers caused them to use their religiously-inspired signs and placards to attack any youth in sight.[66]

The New Jersey clergyman seemed reluctant to participate in the "numbers game" this time. Just before the march he also found himself in the embarrassing position of being under attack by the leaders of his American Council of Christian Churches. The Council issued a statement criticizing McIntire's march for operating on a double standard that involved major compromises. It stated that his march had violated clear and positive commands of God that His people be separate from all unbelief and corruption: "If fundamentalists are truly in control of the program and the platform as it relates to this march, how then can the chairman of the March, Dr. Carl McIntire, scripturally justify inviting a Buddhist as the key speaker and encourage others who do not share his theological views to stand with him in this crusade for God and country?"[67]

It has been said that one mark of an extremist is that he never realizes that his "just enough" has long since become "too much." That may have been the case with the doughty McIntire, for he not only proceeded to announce that a "National Victory Sunday" was scheduled for November 22, but he also scheduled a whole series of marches extending into the middle of 1971. There would be, for example, a January 30, 1971, "Patriots' March For Victory" in San Clemente, California, the location of President Nixon's vacation retreat. There would even be simultaneous marches for victory in each of the 50 state capitals.

It did not seem possible for McIntire to add more marches or any other activities to his busy schedule. He still had 600 radio stations and a newspaper to worry about. And the list of properties acquired by the councils and the reformation movement had grown considerably. In the early 1960s he purchased the old Admiral Hotel on the Cape May, New Jersey, ocean front. McIntire and his people acquired the old six-story hotel with the idea of operating it as a Bible conference center. It was renovated and renamed the Christian Admiral and advertised as "a year-around Christian and patriotic conference center with 333 bed-rooms, American plan, dedicated to the glory of God."

When Bible conferences or other special events are scheduled at the Christian Admiral, the grand old hotel is usually filled to overflowing. Many McIntire supporters spend their annual vaca-tions there; others drive long distances to hear some of the best-known right-wing speakers in the country. If people make reservations early enough, they may be able to stay in one of the rooms named for right-wing heroes like General Douglas Mac-Arthur, General Edwin Walker or Senator Strom Thurmond.

In 1967 McIntire and his people purchased Congress Hall, another large property near the Christian Admiral, for $550,000. For a while it was used as a dormitory for the male students of nearby Shelton College. In 1970 Dr. McIntire announced "an-other development in the blessed providence of God" when he purchased the Windsor Hotel in Cape May. The historic Windsor, now more than 100 years old, is located just across the street from Congress Hall. With this acquisition, the Cape May devel-opment controlled the three largest buildings in the oldest sea-shore resort in the United States. The water-front rights were acquired with the Windsor, which meant that Dr. McIntire's Bible conference had two full blocks of the finest beach in Cape May.

In December 1970 grand old patriot McIntire held a press conference to announce that his Twentieth Century Reformation Movement planned to develop 300 acres in Cape Canaveral, Florida, for a Freedom Center and Christian Conference along the lines of the Cape May development. Along with the land, the properties included the 200-room Cape Kennedy Hilton, the Cape Kennedy Convention Center, the Chrysler Building and the Boeing Building. Dr. McIntire called the multimillion-dollar complex the "Gateway to the Stars," a place that would be a "witness to His Word and a haven for patriots who put their love for God first." He had never seemed so thrilled about the future of his cause. "Only God," he said, "put the dream in the minds of top business leaders and bankers in Florida to offer the entire package to the Twentieth Century Reformation Movement." [68]

In January 1973 the treaty ending the war in Vietnam was signed, but Dr. McIntire denounced the cease-fire agreement as a "fiasco" and "a disaster." He insisted that the treaty left South Vietnam "in worse condition than when we went to her aid." [69] Acting as though the war still continued, he announced that another great Victory March would be staged in Washington on April 14, 1973. He seemed to be serving notice that he would never quit marching or fighting or carrying out his interpretation of the biblical injunction to "cry aloud and spare not."

I
BELIEVE
IN
MIRACLES
BY
KATHRYN
KUHLMAN

TOM
HUFFMAN

VI

Kathryn Kuhlman

Nothing almost sees
miracles But misery.
   —Shakespeare, *King Lear*

I . . . believe . . . in miracles!
      —Kathryn Kuhlman

Kathryn Kuhlman's
Miracle Healings

October 1971 brought mostly pleasant weather to north-eastern Oklahoma; and although October 24, a Sunday, was some-what overcast, it was still warm and bright, with just the slightest hint of a breeze, almost an Indian-summer day. All morning the sick and the anguished had been converging on Tulsa's beautiful new Assembly Center Arena from every direction. Some came from little farming communities in buses, making a "foliage trip" out of their pilgrimage, glorying in the red and brown oak trees that splashed their bands of color across the rolling hills. Others loaded their sick and crippled into automobiles and drove from cities like Blackwell, Enid or Muskogee, crisscrossing the lake country where the roadsides displayed the blood-red Oklahoma soil like the border on a landscape painting. In the distance, twist-ing lines of little creeks, where Pawnee braves once watered their ponies, were outlined by towering cottonwoods already topped out in early-autumn crowns of yellow leaves. Pilgrims from every point on the compass were traveling through some of the Lord's loveliest land, hurrying to meet a celebrated faith healer. They poured in from neighboring states and even a few foreign coun-

235

tries, to gather in the Assembly Center area around Seventh and
Denver Streets, where the older section of Tulsa tucks one shoul-
der comfortably against a big bend in the Arkansas River. They
came early and waited uncomplainingly for the arena doors to
open, for theirs was a most important rendezvous: they had come
to meet the charismatic Kathryn Kuhlman.

For many years Tulsa has been called the oil capital of the
world, but during the 1960s it also became known as the center
of the world of fundamentalism, the home for a greater number
of independent, one-preacher "denominations" in proportion to
population than any other metropolis of comparable size in the
Republic. The three largest and best-known evangelistic enterprises headquartered in Tulsa are the organizations founded and
directed by Oral Roberts, Billy James Hargis and T. L. Osborn.
There are hundreds of other independent evangelists in the Tulsa
area, and of course there are regular churches of all types, some
600 in number. Dr. Billy James Hargis observed in 1972 that
"there is a Southern Baptist or Pentecostal church on almost every
corner in Tulsa. We're considered by some as the capital of the
Bible belt in the United States." He has also called Tulsa "America's most modern, progressive, spiritual and trouble-free city." [1]
In 1970 one newspaper disclosed that just one of the three largest
evangelistic associations received more mail than all the oil companies in Tulsa combined.[2] By 1971 the largest newspapers in
the state were referring to the city as the "fundamentalist capital
of the world." [3]

And now Kathryn Kuhlman, a new leader of the faith healers,
had finally come to conduct her services in the most famous
center of the old-time-religion circuit. If she looked forward to
visiting the first city of fundamentalism, the people gathered at
the Tulsa Assembly Center were more than happy to see her.
Long before the arena doors swung open at noon, the parking lot
was packed, and more than a thousand of the faithful and the
merely curious waited patiently to be sure of a seat. An hour before the services began the 9,000-seat arena was already filled,
and the overflow had packed the 2,000-seat assembly hall upstairs, where closed-circuit television softened the disappoint-

ment of not seeing the famous healer in person. And still many hundreds were turned away. Standing near an entrance, one could experience a drama that is played out at most of Kathryn Kuhlman's services. A young father begged an usher to let his crippled son inside the arena, and an old woman who stood on one crutch and a built-up shoe stared in disbelief as the door was shut in her face.

It seemed inevitable that Tulsa and Kathryn Kuhlman would meet. Now that Oral Roberts had quit the "sawdust trail" to continue his healing ministry by other methods, and faith healers like A. A. Allen and Jack Coe had lost their last great healing contests to the grim reaper, the Kuhlman services were slowly but surely becoming one of the best-known miracle ministries in the land. But in 1971, except in certain areas, such as Los Angeles and Pittsburgh, the name of Kathryn Kuhlman was probably still not as famous as Oral Roberts. For years she has been well-known on both coasts, and able to fill Yankee Stadium or Shrine Auditorium in Los Angeles with ease. In recent years she has expanded her services to all the larger cities, and her radio and television programs now cover most of the country.

Inside the Tulsa Assembly Center Arena the audience prepared to meet the healer. In the center of the arena floor, rows of wheel chairs were lined up hubcap-to-hubcap like phalanxes of Roman chariots. To their front and on their flanks were those on crutches and canes, in metal braces and casts. And scattered here and there were little groups of the blind, the deformed and the deaf. Even the space between the entrances and the walkways dividing the upper and lower sections was filled with people obviously prepared to stand for three to four hours. One could move through the better seats near the pulpit and pick out scores of preachers from the Tulsa area. There were faith healers and fundamentalist preachers, and psychic healers from a half-dozen different occult organizations. There were healers who specialized in prayer cloths, those who preferred miracle oil, special talismans or a miracle "touch" from the Lord. Some had active ministries, and others were retired faith healers who had invested their money in local enterprises. Most were visiting the Kuhlman services to satisfy their professional curiosity, to compare their own techniques with those of the leading healer of the moment. In whichever city Miss Kuhlman appears, many preachers turn out to see her; but it is doubtful that she would ever be scrutinized by so many other professionals at one time as she was during her visit to Tulsa.

A little before 1:30 P.M., Kathryn Kuhlman walked out onto the huge platform. She paused, looked at the vast audience and walked rapidly to the center of the stage. She looked tall and very slender, with long curls of golden auburn hair that cascaded down the sides of her face. Her hair was parted in the middle, in a style that has been called early Shirley Temple. She was a striking figure in a long, fleecy white dress with huge, billowy sleeves that floated about like small cumulus clouds as she waved her long arms about her head. Her radiant smile and cheerful greeting cast their magic so quickly that the congregation was almost immediately on its feet, greeting her with thunderous applause.

Evangelist Kuhlman turned to her special guests seated in places of honor on the platform. To the sound of booming organs the most important one was brought to the microphone, but he required no introduction in that auditorium. It was none other than the onetime king of the faith healers, the Rev. Oral Roberts. As she introduced him, Miss Kuhlman told how she admired Roberts and how honored she was that he was on the platform with her. Since abdicating his throne, Oral had become a banker, university president and television star. He was also known as a Tulsa booster who welcomed many famous guests to his home town. But it is doubtful that he would deign to sit on the healing platform with any faith healer other than Kathryn Kuhlman. Her religious orientation and flamboyant style are probably more like those of Roberts than any other of the nationally-known faith healers. Emily Gardiner Neal chose Roberts and Kuhlman as the only two fundamentalist healers to be included in a 1965 book dealing with the outstanding "spiritual healers" in the large Protestant churches.

After Roberts told the audience how humbled and thrilled he felt to be there, and added that he considered Kathryn Kuhlman "a servant of God," the lady faith healer started her service. She was folksy, friendly and charming. She asked the people where they came from. And she wanted to know what church they attended. She seemed especially to enjoy pointing out how many in her audience were members of denominations that do not practice faith-healing.

No Kuhlman audience can possibly become bored. The energetic faith healer not only seems to be constantly in motion, she also displays a wide range of moods and voices. She may move in a moment from cheerful banter to the very serious subject of being filled with the Holy Spirit. In her Tulsa service, as in most of her campaigns, she constantly emphasized that she cannot heal—only God can heal. She insisted, "I have nothing to do with these miracles. I have nothing but the power of the Holy Spirit." And she reiterated that the Holy Spirit could not have chosen a more ordinary person than she:

Don't you understand, you people? Without the Holy Spirit, I haven't a crutch, I haven't anything to lean on. I don't have a thing. I don't have a thing. You see, if I had been born with talent, I might have been able to lean on that. Had I had education, I might have used that as a crutch. But I don't have a thing. I don't have a thing.[4]

While she spoke she constantly moved about the platform. Her sermon seemed to be built around an emotoinal tribute to the Holy Spirit. The full sleeves and the long, dazzling white dress billowed and wafted as she glided and turned. At first her voice seemed halting and slow, then more vibrant and mellow. Suddenly it was mixed with throaty sobs, and she was almost crying. Her audience was carried along on the tide of emotion, and many dabbed at their eyes, and more than a few wept openly and unashamedly. Her services have been described as extremely emotional and overly dramatized. But no one has called them mawkish or fanatical.

Suddenly her voice changed again. She was speaking as most of her radio and television audiences often hear her. Her sentences began with a rush that quickly stalled on the first syllable of a long word. She paused there and seemed to start once more, only to linger an extra long moment on the following syllable. Then the words rushed forth again, a new Niagara of sound in a husky, low-pitched voice: "You want me—to bare—my soul? In these great—miracle services—before I walk from—behind the wings . . . I die a—thousand deaths." Her voice became more labored; she seemed almost to be gasping for breath. "I know better than—anybody else that I have—nothing—absolutely nothing!" By then she had begun to sound as if she were crying more than talking: "Nobody in the—whole world knows it—better than I do!" [5]

As the emotion-drenched service moved toward its powerful climax, the miracles began. The evangelist suddenly announced that a person in one of the balconies had been healed of an ailment, then a second person was pointed out as being cured of an ear problem, and someone in the wheel chair section was healed of cancer. On and on the announcements continued, as her ushers moved up and down the aisles locating those who claimed to be healed in one of the ways described by Miss Kuhlman. No prayer lines like those of Oral Roberts or the late A. A. Allen are ever used in her services. Instead of a prayer line, which brings the sick to the healer, the ushers bring people who already claim to be healed to the platform to meet Kathryn Kuhlman. She greets them, interviews them briefly and congratulates them. When her hands are laid on them—when she "touches" them— they almost invariably "fall down under the power of the Spirit." To many visitors this is the most spectacular part of the Kuhlman services, but this religious phenomenon is by no means a characteristic of her ministry alone; it is a regular feature of many, if not most, Pentecostal worship services.

The campaign in Tulsa produced fewer dramatic healings than the usual Kuhlman services. Only four people out of a wheel chair section of some 300 claimed to be healed of their ailments. But more than 100 persons inside the arena attested to cures of illnesses such as sinus and ear trouble, headaches and even more severe ailments. A cancer patient who had undergone a series of operations and special treatments claimed to be completely healed. And even though most of those who journeyed to Tulsa seeking a miracle went home as ill as when they arrived, there were few complaints. Many of them said how happy they were for the opportunity of seeing Kathryn Kuhlman, and others said they had received a spiritual blessing even though they had not been one of the lucky ones who received a miracle.

The Kathryn Kuhlman entourage completed its miracle services in Tulsa and moved on to the next stop on its schedule. But few if any of the basic questions about her ministry had been answered during the campaign. Why, for example, had her ministry suddenly become so widely publicized? And how did an older woman, who logically should be nearing the end of her active ministry, continue to attract much larger crowds than any other faith healer in the country? To try to discover some of the reasons for her success, it is necessary to review the important events in her background.

Kathryn Kuhlman was born and spent her early years in the little town of Concordia, Missouri. She was not brought up in an especially religious home. Her father, whom she greatly revered, was the mayor of Concordia, a man who seems, oddly enough, to have thoroughly despised preachers. Miss Kuhlman says in her popular recording, *I Believe in Miracles,* that her father would cross the street to keep from speaking to a preacher. The evangelist continues her membership in a Concordia Baptist church. She has never attended a Bible college, but was ordained by the Evangelical Church Alliance after studying the Bible on her own for two years.[6] Today her services are very definitely nondenominational, and her doctrines are pointedly Pentecostal:

> You want to know if I'm Pentecostal? I'm more Pentecostal than the most Pentecostal person who claims to be Pentecostal today. I believe in it as it was in the early church; I do not believe in a lot of fanaticism; I do not believe in the manifestation of the flesh. But beloved, I want to tell you something: I believe in speaking in an unknown tongue, but there are still people today who speak in an unknown tongue who have never been born in the Holy Spirit.[7]

Kathryn Kuhlman underwent an intense religious experience when she was about 13 years old. Since that time, she says, she has felt an extraordinary burden to save souls. She dropped out of high school after her sophomore year and began preaching when she was 16 years old because she "felt a definite call to the ministry." [8] She became an itinerant preacher in Idaho and for almost two decades "worked in the small places, among the farmers." [9] She has not revealed the year of her birth. Indeed, one writer, Allen Spraggett, who has produced two complimentary accounts of her ministry, wrote, "The date is classified."

In a book on the occult called *The Unexplained,* Spraggett included a chapter on Kathryn Kuhlman, in which he wrote, "She says she is eighty-four years old." In 1970 the chapter was expanded into a popular paperback entitled *Kathryn Kuhlman: The Woman Who Believes in Miracles.* In this account he revised his earlier statement about her age:

> In my book *The Unexplained* I mention that the evangelist says she is eighty-four, an obviously—or so I thought—facetious remark. Many readers, however, took me seriously. One woman wrote to say that she had seen a picture of the evangelist, "and if she's really eighty-four and looks like that, that's the biggest miracle of all." A doctor wrote, demanding to know who the "impostor" was who was holding meetings in Pittsburgh under Kathryn Kuhlman's name. "You say she's eighty-four," he explained, "and this woman can't be a day over thirty-five." Let me say here that Kathryn Kuhlman, as she herself put it in a letter to an inquirer, is "a long way from eighty-four." Beyond that, my lips are sealed.[10]

It is true that Kathryn Kuhlman is far from being 84, even though she is the oldest active faith healer with a national following. She was an itinerant preacher for two decades before her special religious experience in 1946, following which she started her faith-healing ministry. Since she started preaching at the age of 16, she is now approximately 62 years old. While this may be near the retirement age in many professions, some ministers are still active at 90.

In 1946, when Miss Kuhlman was inspired by her "baptism of the Holy Spirit," she began preaching regularly about her experience. And it was after such a sermon in 1946 that one of the women from her congregation in Franklin, Pennsylvania, reported that she had been healed of a tumor. That marked the beginning of the miracles and also the beginning of a new phase of her ministry.

The following year she moved to Pittsburgh, and it has remained her base of operations since. She does not have a church or a church building. The headquarters for the Kathryn Kuhlman Foundation is located in Pittsburgh's Carlton House Hotel. Miss Kuhlman does not have a membership organization; she urges those who find salvation in her campaigns to return to their own churches. And unlike most radio preachers, she does not publish a newsletter or magazine. She is the author of two books, which recount some of her most spectacular healings. The first, *I Believe in Miracles*, has gone through many printings. Her 1969 publication, *God Can Do It Again*, is also a best seller.

As President of the Kathryn Kuhlman Foundation, a religious, nonprofit charitable organization, the evangelist from Concordia has gained the respect of many of Pittsburgh's city fathers and leading citizens through the good works of her ministry. The Foundation has done much to help the needy and the blind. Financial aid has been extended to many college students, and funds have been provided to help in the rehabilitation of young drug addicts. Additionally, a large number of missionary churches and schools in remote areas of the world have been assisted by funds from the Kathryn Kuhlman Foundation.

These good works have been accomplished since Kathryn Kuhlman received "the Power" in 1946. Her biographer wrote that "In her early days she knew the criticism that is the lot of most evangelists (and she does not completely escape it even today), but this, on the whole, has given way to positive recognition."

In the first phase she was just another itinerant evangelist, a little more eloquent and energetic than most, perhaps, but otherwise undistinguished. In some twenty years of preaching she has whistle-stopped her way across the American Midwest several times . . . The second phase of her ministry was a much different story. That initial healing was the start of an unbroken succession. Word spread about the woman evangelist who worked miracles. The sick began to make pilgrimages to her services. She took to the air waves, and the crowds grew larger still. Since then there has been no turning back.[11]

In telling of the great change that came into her religious life in 1946, Miss Kuhlman has touched on her unusual method of calling out the miracles as they occur in her services. She hated the traditional tent-healing services: "the long healing lines, filling out those cards. It was an insult to your intelligence." After visiting such a service, she reportedly cried all night.[12] She often observed that the sick were prayed for but never healed.

> . . . I knew why the evangelist asked people to fill out those cards to get into the healing line. It was to get a mailing list, that's all. I used to sit there and watch this kind of thing and I wasn't satisfied it was real. I knew this wasn't what I was looking for. Yet I knew there was something to it, that miracles could take place today just as in the Bible. But I didn't know how.[13]

Kathryn Kuhlman started the faith-healing phase of her career without the use of a prayer line. In its stead she instituted a system of diagnosing illnesses by supernatural means. She called out the healings as they occurred, and her ushers brought to her the person on whom that miraculous cure had been bestowed. But was she the only evangelist who favored using this method of handling the sick? And did the system originate with her ministry? Kathryn Kuhlman dates her first healing in 1946. In that same year William M. Branham of Jeffersonville, Indiana, was using a similar method of diagnosing diseases and ailments in faith-healing campaigns all across the country. It was Branham, more than any other evangelist, who started the post-World War II fundamentalist faith-healing revival following his encounter with an angel on May 7, 1946. The following year, Oral Roberts received power from God to heal the sick and started healing campaigns.

Branham had worked with a prayer line, but he was known throughout the Pentecostal world in the later part of the 1940s for his supernatural diagnosis of diseases. One early Branham biographer wrote,

When the angel appeared to Brother Branham, He told him he would be able to detect and diagnose all diseases and afflictions . . . Faith at the right level in any part of the great audience pulls on the virtue in the indwelling Christ, who is operating the gift; and this can't take place without Brother Branham knowing it. He feels it as distinctly as you would if I should pull on your coat, and knows the direction it is coming from; and he even points out the individual whose faith is touching Christ.[14]

According to his followers, Branham was so sensitive that he had visions of people before they received their healing. He not only provided descriptions of their diseases, but often added information about their dress, how they looked or where they came from. He was also able to demonstrate that he had mastered mass healing. Starting with the healing of nine deaf and dumb men, he progressed to the healing of an entire audience.[15]

When the first of the healings associated with her ministry took place in Franklin, Pennsylvania, Kathryn Kuhlman was not even aware that a miracle had occurred until the woman who was healed told her about it the following night. Thus, the healings started before the power to diagnose illnesses was given to her. It is now a very important part of her ministry, and some observers think it the most sensational part of her services.

Possibly because she is a woman preacher, Kathryn Kuhlman has been extremely careful in directing her ministry. She does not collect "love offerings" from her congregations as Oral Roberts did in the early part of his ministry. In her book and in interviews, it is emphasized that she draws a salary fixed by the Foundation Board. In *I Believe in Miracles* and in the Kuhlman organization's literature her charitable activities are listed in detail. When *I Believe in Miracles* was published in 1962, she had been in Pittsburgh for 14 years. Asked why she did not extend the scope of her influence by traveling, she replied, "My purpose is to save souls, and my particular calling is to offer proof of the Power of God. I feel I can accomplish this more effectively by staying in one place where I am in a position to follow through on my people, and to insist that those who claim healing procure medical verification." [16] In direct contradiction of that policy the Kuhlman services have for some time been conducted in most of the

major cities of the United States. There also exists some misunderstanding about medical verification of the miraculous cures
claimed by people in her services. More than any other nationally-
known faith healer, Kathryn Kuhlman has associated doctors and
medical specialists with her ministry. Yet a lengthy article about
her in the September 14, 1970, issue of *Time* magazine disclosed
that the Kuhlman staff "spends little time verifying healings, because Kathryn has no doubt that they are accomplished. But in
some remarkable cases . . . they attempt to document the cure
fully."

She is also aware that many Protestant denominations are
strongly opposed to women preachers. For many years a woman
in the pulpit could only be found in some Pentecostal churches.
The movement to include women in the clergy is gaining momentum, but only in the large Protestant denominations, where it
parallels and perhaps complements the women's liberation movement. And the women's lib movement draws more opposition
than support from the middle-class church members who form
one of the largest groups of Kuhlman supporters. Thus, if her
role of evangelist is viewed as supporting women's liberation, she
might lose her following among those who most strongly favor
faith-healing. On the other hand, those who are more likely to
applaud the liberation of women are often the least inclined to
believe in the efficacy of faith-healing. Kathryn Kuhlman makes
her position very clear:

> I never think of myself as a woman preacher, I tell you the truth. I
> am a woman; I was born a woman, and I try to keep my place as a
> woman. And I want to say to the women here in this auditorium:
> please, whatever you do, don't try to be a man . . . I recognize the
> fact that I was born a woman, and with it I try to be a lady. I never
> try to usurp the place of authority of a man—never! That's the reason
> I have no church. I leave that to the men. I am a woman. I know
> my place . . . I do not believe that those who know me best think
> of me as being a woman preacher. I never do. Never! [17]

As she moved from the little rural churches to the successful
career of faith healer, Kathryn Kuhlman's life-style changed somewhat, but her thinking seems to have changed very little. She

believes a preacher should live a comfortable life, and she enjoys fine clothes. On the other hand, she admits to living a lonely life when she is not at her services. She is sensitive about her lack of education:

> . . . I have no education. I said to Dr. Jarman—modernistic minister for 52 years . . . I said to him the other day, "Dr. Jarman, do you realize that we're worlds and worlds apart? You have had all your education—here you are with all your degrees, educated beyond your intelligence.[18]

A feature of the Kuhlman ministry that has attracted many reporters and writers is the number of miraculous cures claimed by those who admit to having little or no faith. If such cures are obtained in other fundamentalist faith-healing organizations, they have gone unreported. But it is a regular feature of the Kuhlman services for agnostics, atheists or the merely curious to claim dramatic healings. Miss Kuhlman has attempted to explain this little-known side of her ministry:

> When I was twenty years of age, I could have given you all the answers. My theology was straight and I was sure that if you followed certain rules, worked hard enough, obeyed all the commandments, and had yourself in a certain spiritual state, God would heal you . . . Lo and behold, my theology came tumbling down and was crushed into a thousand pieces when one day a man who had just entered the auditorium during a miracle service stood silently against the back wall, and after not more than five minutes walked boldly to the stage and freely admitted, "My ear has just opened and I do not believe!" . . . he never recanted . . . he had not been to church for more than twenty-five years and had put himself in the category of an atheist. It is possible for me to relate many cases where people have been healed who were amazed, who freely admitted that they did not expect to be healed . . . Until we have a way of defining it, all that I can tell you is that these are mercy healings. . . .[19]

Allen Spraggett, psychic researcher and former Religion Editor for the Toronto *Daily Star,* has probably done more to make Miss Kuhlman a living legend than almost any other writer. His books have introduced legions of potential followers to the Kathryn

Kuhlman ministry. He is convinced that miracles occur in the Kuhlman services, and claims that his book about her ministry is a "fully documented, impartial investigation into the powers of the greatest faith healer since Biblical times," a presentation of "scientific evidence for her miraculous healings."

His book on Kathryn Kuhlman is academically important because it demonstrates that the miracle ministry of a fundamentalist faith healer can be viewed from a parapsychological standpoint and explained in language meaningful to the psychic healer or researcher. It reveals why the miracle cures of several well-known fundamentalist healers were considered unacceptable to psychic researchers. And it provides insights into the kinds of fundamentalist ministries that can meet the standards necessary for the two principal types of miracle healing—fundamentalist faith-healing (called by some "divine" healing) and psychic healing (called "spiritual" or "paranormal" and many other names)— to be blended into a single stream of miracle healing.

Spraggett cited a 1950 survey to reveal how widespread "spiritual healing practices" have become among the pastors of such churches as the Methodist, Episcopal, Lutheran, Baptist and Disciples of Christ. He concluded, "Healing by prayer and faith, then, is moving out of the theological boondocks of the itinerant revivalist into the Protestant mainstream." [20] To help decide which of the fundamentalist faith-healing ministries might be acceptable to the psychic world, he drew upon an official report on faith-healing issued by the United Church of Canada in 1967. The document was a revision of an earlier report that had categorically asserted, "Faith healing is not a legitimate ministry of the Church and should be actively discouraged and resisted wherever it is practiced." The 1967 revision recognized the existence of faith-healing, but carefully admonished that "discrimination between the authentic and the spurious is not easy but important." Itinerant revivalists such as Oral Roberts, who was specifically mentioned, were strongly denounced. The main criticisms of what the report called "standard, revival-tent faith healing" were

(1) It is based on an inadequate theology which often assumes sickness to be a divine judgment.

(2) It has a naive view of the distinction between "natural" and "supernatural" healing.

(3) It works—when it does—usually by suggestion and hysteria and the patient may suffer a relapse that leaves him worse off than he was before.

(4) Persons who are not healed may feel that God has rejected them and suffer morbid guilt feelings and spiritual shipwreck.

Spraggett seemed to use his own experience with itinerant faith healers as the final measure of the kinds of ministries that were acceptable to the world of psychic phenomena. His encounter with the Rev. Oral Roberts, whom he described as the "high priest of contemporary big-shot faith healers," occurred in August 1963. After watching a Roberts crusade in Toronto, he bluntly told the Tulsa healer that there were many features of his ministry which he questioned. When he said his investigation had failed to reveal "even one apparent healing," Roberts referred him to one of his earlier, "irrefutable" miracles. But when he attempted to verify the supposedly classic example of Roberts' healing, he found that in a doctor's opinion it was "not in the category of a true miracle." [21]

He described his investigation of A. A. Allen's revival-tent campaign as a "most distasteful experience." When Allen took his big tent to Toronto in August 1966, Spraggett attacked the Allen ministry in an article entitled "Miracles For Sale." He described Allen's demons, his record of drunken driving, his request for pledges in return for special prosperity cloths, and his expulsion from the Assemblies of God Church. He wrote that the article had an immediate impact:

An amusing postscript to the Toronto miracle revival: A. A. Allen failed to appear at the climactic final meeting of this crusade, which took place the day after his past was revealed in *The Toronto Daily Star*. His associate evangelist did put in an appearance, however, to take a collection and explain to the congregation that the Lord suddenly had called Brother Allen back to Arizona on urgent business.[22]

Not all of the faith healers he encountered before he met Kathryn Kuhlman made such a negative impact on the psychic researcher as Oral Roberts and A. A. Allen, and he professed to hold an attitude of "open-minded skepticism" toward inexplicable healings. His study of the Kuhlman services was apparently conducted under the best of conditions. He was convinced in a relatively short time that miracles were occurring at her meetings. In taking a public stand for the presence of miracles, Spraggett confessed to be in sympathy with those who fear that to acknowledge miracles is to step back into the medical Dark Ages, when "the insane were whipped to drive the demons out of them and animal dung was used to poultice wounds."

While making his approval of Miss Kuhlman's services known, Spraggett did not disguise his interest in investigating the relationship of ESP and other psychic phenomena to the miraculous cures that reputedly occur at her meetings. He was careful to point out that Kathryn Kuhlman "knows nothing about parapsychology as such" and he also felt that she does not want to know anything about it. This attitude has apparently not affected his friendship with the Pittsburgh faith healer, nor has it discouraged him from defining and explaining the fundamentalist words and concepts used by Miss Kuhlman in terms more meaningful to the psychic healer and the parapsychologist. He acknowledged that Kathryn Kuhlman believes the healing factor is the direct intervention of God, but he was satisfied to call it "anti-chance." Holding that nothing can be defined as "supernatural," he substituted the word "supernormal," meaning beyond the normal. He also found that there was evidence that on occasions Miss Kuhlman goes into a deep trance, although he conceded that she "might object to the word trance in connection with herself." Despite its connotations of dark rooms and mediums, it was "a good biblical word." Spraggett found that when the Holy Spirit "comes upon" Kathryn Kuhlman, she experiences an "altered state of consciousness" that psychics refer to as an "out-of-the-body" experience. And he discovered "marked affinities between Kathryn Kuhlman's strange diagnostic powers and clairvoyance as the parapsychologists have come to know it." He suggested that her Holy Ghost power is a "field phenomenon" similar to an electric or magnetic field, and furnished quotations from sources inclined to interpret Miss Kuhlman's awareness of healings in terms of Jung's concept of synchronicity, which states that two events are linked meaningfully but noncausally. Carl Jung's concept of the "collective unconscious" was similarly thought to play a part in the Kuhlman healings.

Spraggett, whose work has been applauded by astrologist Jeane Dixon, the late Bishop James Pike and Norman Vincent Peale, has concluded that Kathryn Kuhlman is "one of the most extraordinary Christian mystics and clairvoyants of our time." She is not only the greatest charismatic healer of our time, but she is also a saint. He also decided that despite her sincere disclaimers, "Kathryn Kuhlman clearly does have something to do with the healings. Such phenomena do not attend every clergyman who preaches the power of faith to heal."

Perhaps many, if not most, of those who crowd her meetings also believe that Miss Kuhlman will have something to do with their chances of being healed. Otherwise many would remain at home and watch her on television. The doubters generally label the healings psychosomatic. But others take a position somewhere between the extremes of unquestioning belief and total skepticism. A recent New York *Times* article cited healings reported at a Kuhlman meeting and said they could be called emotionally-induced cures in the absence of further evidence. The article noted that there was no way to verify the healing of the people who rose from their wheel chairs, apparently suddenly relieved of pain. The author of the article interviewed a woman who announced during the services that she had been cured of heart disease, and found that the woman herself, rather than a physician, had diagnosed the ailment. Another woman, who told Miss Kuhlman that two breast tumors the size of walnuts had just vanished, said later that they were much softer. Among others who were interviewed a week after the healing service, most claimed they were still healed, but some indicated a temporary return of some symptoms. None had verified the alleged healings with a doctor.[23]

Today the Kuhlman ministry continues to grow rapidly, even though the number of critics and skeptics also seems to be increasing. The faith healer who once confined her services largely to the Pittsburgh area because she feared she might lose her power, now logs an average of 500,000 air miles each year.[24] Her daily half-hour radio programs blanket most of the nation from approximately 60 stations; her weekly television broadcasts emanate from some 65 stations. And her ministry received a little under $2 million during the last fiscal year, mostly from donations made during her services.[25]

How can the great popularity of the Kuhlman services be accounted for? Partly by publicity. The Kuhlman programs are now broadcast over a growing network of radio and television stations. Also, Kathryn Kuhlman now takes her healing services to cities all over the country, and purchases large amounts of advertising space in newspapers. And the great resurgence of interest in the occult points to an increasing climate of irrationality favorable to an increase in the popularity of magicians and miracle-workers.

The Kuhlman meetings now attract some of the largest audiences in the religious world. And more and more advertising appears in local newspapers in advance of the peripatetic Kuhlman entourage. Criticism is apparently ignored; even Spraggett's negative appraisal of the Oral Roberts ministry has been brushed aside. In 1972 Miss Kuhlman was back in Tulsa, walking with Oral under his big prayer tower and addressing his graduating university class.

CRUSADER

TOM
HUFFMAN

VII

Billy James Hargis

The Lord never called a minister of the Gospel to enter a popularity contest. He calls a minister to declare the truth and truth is sometimes unpopular. When a minister meets opposition, it proves to me that he's effective in his calling. You can almost judge the success of a man by the enemies he has . . . A clash of convinced minds is and always has been good for America. The Lord taught this principle when He said, "Woe unto you when all men shall speak well of you. . . ."

—Billy James Hargis, October 1972

Billy James Hargis and
His Christian Crusade

Radiating along a large section of the northern Atlantic coast of the United States, on 50,000 watts of power from radio station WNBC in New York City, the folksy twang that disc jockey Don Imus affects to become radio's Rev. Billy Sol Hargis greets early morning listeners to the "Imus in the Morning" program: "By special arrangement with Him, Billy Sol is offering you the chance for Heaven-Right-Here-On-Earth, say *hallelujah!* That's right, He asked Billy Sol to purchase 700 acres of land for a Heaven-Right-Here-On-Earth, and He told Billy Sol, He said, 'Billy Sol, let them in on this tremendous offer' . . . the Promised Land Development Company is making this offer for as little as $27.77 a month, VA and FHA approved. . . ." [1]

Early risers who discover the mythical radio preacher while twisting the dial for a music station may be shocked or vastly amused to hear what seems to be a scathing parody of one of the most controversial radio preachers of all time, the Rev. Dr. Billy James Hargis, founder and director of Christian Crusade. Don Imus does not explain the details of the creation of his radio reverend, however obvious it may be to listeners that his principal

257

model was the Rev. Billy James Hargis of Tulsa, Oklahoma. How much his Billy Sol skits negate the radio messages of the real Billy Hargis can only be surmised, but if measured by the popularity of the Imus program, the effect is considerable. And WNBC's clear-channel pattern reaches a wide audience in the middle Atlantic states. One listener reported that he tuned in the Don Imus program at 6:30 A.M., as he was leaving New York City, and heard this final Billy Sol message as he drove into Baltimore, Maryland:

> Glory! hallelujah! yeah! It's the Right Reverend Dr. Billy Sol Hargis here on behalf of the First Church of the Gooey Death and Discount House of Worship for the salvation of yore soul. Have you said to yourself lately, Billy Sol, boy, I'd like to get in a little fun? I mean, this being religious, it's fun, but it gets terribly depressin' sometimes . . . Would you like to raise a little cain, but—you know—not go too far? Well, sure you would and Billy Sol . . . wants you to know that He doesn't mind you havin' a little harmless fun, say hallelujah! Put yore right hand on the radio if you believe—that's right, no matter if you're drivin'. PUT YORE HAND ON THE SPEAKER IF YOU BELIEVE—say *hallelujah!* Because He'll vibrate right in yore hand through that radio. PUT IT ON THE RADIO!! Now Billy Sol has a tremendous offer for you this mornin', something that will unite yore entire neighborhood in a cause near and dear to yore heart and His heart. It's Billy Sol's battery-operated burning cross—say *hallelujah!*—patterned after those extremely popular fake fireplaces. Billy Sol's burning cross is not only realistic and scary, it burns all night long—what a shocker—say *hallelujah!* What a way to put the fear of Him in them! Send now . . . the first several hundred that send now, Billy Sol will include the Holy Land choir . . . singing "Mama, Come On and Light My Fire," say *hallelujah!!* [2]

In Baltimore the listener changed stations and tuned in the voice of the real Billy Hargis, a taped, 15-minute "For God and Against Communism" message similar to those he has beamed to all corners of the nation for many years.

Hardly a phrase used in the Billy Sol skits accurately describes the ministry of the real Billy Hargis. The Tulsa evangelist does not sell land or burning crosses, nor does he exhort those who support his broadcasts to put their hands on their radios, in the manner made famous by Oral Roberts. Certainly it is a measure of the impact that Hargis and his supporters have had on life in contemporary America that a disc jockey would select his name when creating a mythical radio minister.

It is probably also true that the use of his name in such a parody was no surprise to the Reverend Billy James Hargis; he has been involved in controversy for so many years that it is safe to say that he has by now been assailed and denounced in almost every conceivable manner: in magazine articles, in books, from the pulpits of many churches, in newspapers, on radio programs. But Billy James Hargis has his own legion of ardent followers and loyal supporters. In their opinion, Hargis has helped save the nation by attacking those in the religious and political worlds whom he thinks are subverting the security of the United States.

And by almost every index considered worthwhile by evangelists, Hargis has been a thundering success. His voice is heard on radio virtually throughout the North American continent. He is the author of a number of books and publisher of a weekly newspaper. He can be seen each week on a network of television stations that blanket the nation almost as thoroughly as his radio broadcasts. He counts among his legion of supporters many congressmen, governors, high-ranking military men and civic leaders from every point on the compåss. As the director of Christian Crusade, which he calls "the nation's largest Christian-oriented anti-Communist movement," preacher Hargis operates two youth training centers. The Summit University, set in the foothills of the Rocky Mountains at Manitou Springs, Colorado, has been the scene of seminars, conventions and summer-school classes for young people for a number of years. The Summit East, a complex of dormitories, classrooms and meeting halls on a 300-acre estate in the Berkshire Hills near Blandford, Massachusetts, will soon provide similar facilities for his supporters from the eastern part of the United States.[3]

But a staggering price tag has been tied to his position of prominence in the right-wing fringe of the political and religion worlds. Dr. Fernando Penabaz, Hargis' official biographer, has called the Tulsa radio preacher "the most maligned man I have ever known." [4] Julian Williams, director of research for Christian Crusade, claims that Hargis and his organization have long been targets for a large segment of the American press.[5] And Hargis himself makes no secret of the fact that he bitterly resents the savage attacks he has endured for many years: "I have a deep hurt in my heart; I have been wounded and my work has been almost wrecked dozens of times. . . ." [6]

What is the purpose of Christian Crusade, and what are the special qualifications that Hargis has which qualify him to lead it? The Crusade was founded as a nonprofit, tax-exempt organization, in 1948, with headquarters in Tulsa, Oklahoma. Hargis' biographer calls Christian Crusade "a pioneer in the battle for God and against Communism. . . ." Hargis has said that he is following the will of God in fighting Communism and religious apostasy.[7] His message has been distributed by letter, pamphlet, weekly and monthly newsletters, magazine and newspaper, radio and television. Of these, radio has probably reached the largest number of people.

The founder and director of this vast enterprise can claim very little formal schooling and has never based his leadership on academic qualifications. He explains that he was placed in the leadership role as the result of a miracle: "God called me for this service. I did not choose it; God called me. It is nothing short of miraculous the way the Lord has used my friends and my enemies to create the ministry of Christian Crusade . . . Without proper educational background [sic], God has used me in the movement which I inspired, Christian Crusade, in a marvelous way to get His truth out to a slumbering generation." [8]

According to Hargis, it was very difficult to accept the call of God and give up the pulpit of a Sapulpa, Oklahoma, Christian church, which he described as a comfortable pastorate with a good salary and many other benefits, an enviable position many pastors labored a lifetime to obtain. He asked himself, "Would I volunteer to God as a prophet and crusader or would I remain as a comfortable pastor? . . . God bear me witness, I had rather win souls to Christ than fight Communism any day, but a man has to do what God calls him to do. When God calls a man to a specific ministry, he had better do it." [9] It was neither the first nor the last time he would leave such hard decisions to God.

Billy Hargis was born August 3, 1925, in Texarkana, Texas, the only child in a poor family whose whole life seemed to center around their church and its teachings. Many evenings his father read the Bible aloud to the family, and at one time young Billy made it a practice to read at least one chapter from the Bible every day. At an early age young Hargis had some very fixed ideas about the church, so much so that at the age of nine, without consulting his parents, he presented himself to his pastor for church membership and asked to be baptized.

The following year, his mother faced a serious operation, and Hargis, who often sang his favorite hymns while doing farm chores, suddenly became a very worried young man. He has written that while cleaning out the cow barn one day he promised that if his mother lived, he would do anything God commanded. Then and there, he made the first of his solemn promises to God, an arrangement he would employ again and again until he found himself the head of a worldwide ministry.[10]

Young Hargis' enthusiasm for church activities did not extend to his regular schoolwork. He has said, "I never was willing to really study in school, either in elementary school, junior high school, or senior high school." He explains this was because his mind was "too energetic," and he wrote that he was able to graduate from high school only "by the skin of my teeth."

Shortly after graduation, in response to an answered prayer, he made a sudden, almost overnight decision to become a preacher. With the small amount of financial help his family could give him, Hargis entered Ozark Bible College in Bentonville, Arkansas, on March 15, 1943. The little college had opened its doors only a few months before he arrived. With little money, few facilities and an enrollment of 16 students, it was a school based almost solely on hope. Its ministerial students made extra money by holding revivals or preaching in nearby communities. Hargis dropped out of school after completing approximately one year and three months of training, and a short time later the Bible college moved to Joplin, Missouri, where students could find more part-time jobs and more churches to preach in.

After a few weeks at school Hargis returned to Texarkana long enough to be ordained by the pastor and elders of the Rose Hill Christian Church. There was some criticism that he was too young at age 18 to become an ordained minister. He wrote later, "Whether I should have been ordained so early or not, I do not know."

Arrangements were made during his first summer at Bentonville for Hargis to preach a revival at Uniontown, Arkansas, a country town so small it lacked bus or telephone services. He preached the revival in an antiquated two-story wooden building which housed a Masonic Lodge upstairs, a church sanctuary downstairs and a pigsty under the building. He noticed that the pigs were often able to drown out even the loudest parts of his sermons. It was here that he baptized his first convert, in a stream just outside Uniontown, under a quaint old Ozark bridge.

During that same summer he preached a revival at New Hope, Arkansas. There he roomed with an old widower, whose wife, a member of Jehovah's Witnesses, had died a few months earlier. Hargis revealed in the paperback book he sells as an official story of his career that he committed "my one and only experience as a 'book burner.'" Although he was later to repent, he gathered up all the copies of the *Watchtower* and burned them while his host was away from the house. He repented. And he would not oppose the Jehovah's Witnesses again for more than 25 years, when he would turn thumbs down on their struggle for religious freedom in Africa.[11]

The summer was not quite over, and he moved on to preach for a few weeks at the Christian Church in the town of Ozark, Arkansas. Apparently he fell heir to a feeling of authority that sometimes overcomes ardent young ministers, for he set out to reform certain objectionable practices in the community. He had not only learned that the principal of the local school was having an affair with a teacher, he had also discovered that there were elders and deacons in the church who frequented motion-picture shows. On Sunday morning he denounced the principal of the school from the pulpit and that night he exposed the guilty elders and deacons. He was promptly asked to leave. Some students were so infuriated by the outrage done their principal that they decided to "rotten egg" Billy Hargis out of town. His bus left just ahead of the delegation of irate students.

He rode the bus to a crossroads stop some 20 miles out of Ozark, where connections could be made for Ozark College. While he waited he reviewed his disappointing efforts to become a preacher. Saddled with a young man's heavy burden of remorse for the mistakes he had made, he entertained serious doubts that he was meant to be a minister. Finally he was moved to present still another of his either-or decisions to God. If the bus going south to Texarkana arrived at his stop before the one going to Bentonville and Ozark College, he would know that God wanted him to go home and forget all about the ministry. He waited a long time in the cold before headlights cut through the roadside darkness. He climbed on the crowded bus and found himself headed north to Ozark College. He was meant to be a preacher.

The college president met him, bringing news that a church in Sallisaw, Oklahoma, had an opening for a full-time pastor. He would be leaving Bible College just when he was finding a deep interest in studying. But his financial resources were all but exhausted; now at least he would have a job.

During the next four years he was pastor of little churches in Sallisaw, Oklahoma, and in Granby, Missouri. Then quite unexpectedly came the opportunity to pastor a rather large Christian Church in Sapulpa, Oklahoma, a small city a few miles south of metropolitan Tulsa. Hargis had been given a chance to become the neutralizer in a church he described as being "split a dozen ways." The handsome church building, with its pipe organ and stained glass, represented a rapid elevation in prestige and status for such a young minister, and Hargis remained there in the midst of the intrachurch controversies until he announced that he had heard a call from God.

Hargis considered the mission to fight Communism and religious apostasy a sacred calling. He said it was such a heavy responsibility that he shrank from it as Moses did after he was

called by God.[12] Thousands of anti-Communist organizations had
been formed in the United States since the end of World War I.
Scores of new ones appear each year—often organized by fundamentalist preachers prepared to lead the forces of light against
those of darkness and evil—only to run aground financially when
they are unable to compete successfully for the much sought-after
"anti-Communist crusade dollar." Many fundamentalist preachers
who burn with a passionate zeal to sound God's alarm and waken
the sleeping brethren, leave their little rural churches to make a
brief appearance on the fringes of the established religious and
political worlds, equipped with little more than a mimeograph
machine and a wife who can type a monthly newsletter. The religious apostasy they inveigh so heavily against usually turns out
to be nothing more than a continuation of the old modernist-
fundamentalist controversy that has been generating more heat
than light since the latter part of the nineteenth century. Thus it
is not difficult to understand why Hargis encountered a sea of
troubles almost as soon as he embarked on his crusade. He wrote,
"After leaving Sapulpa, my world fell apart. As soon as I started
fighting Communism, churches didn't understand my motivation
or my message. Revivals were cancelled; speaking appearances
were cancelled. . . ."[13]

He had married after leaving Sapulpa and was in deep financial
trouble. He turned to some right-wing fundamentalist leaders for
advice and instruction. Years later he came under attack for these
early associations, especially that with the late Gerald Winrod,
the onetime head of a right-wing organization whose publications
were so favorable to Hitler's Germany that the Nazi propaganda
organ *World Service* recommended his literature. Winrod, who
became widely known as the "Jayhawk Nazi," was indicted for
sedition three times during World War II, but was never convicted. Since Hargis was not a part of the Winrod organization,
his response to such accusations was to denounce his attackers for
using guilt-by-association tactics.[14]

Despite some setbacks, the new Hargis organization started to
grow. Christian Echoes Ministry, Inc., was the formal title he
used for his corporation, but later he adopted the more popular

name of Christian Crusade. He got his first taste of nation-wide publicity in 1953, when he headed up an overseas project for Carl McIntire and the International Council of Christian Churches. McIntire was already a leading figure in right-funda-mentalist circles and had established a reputation for flamboyant activities that showered a maximum of publicity on the groups he was associated with. For some five years Billy James Hargis directed an ingenious effort to send the Gospel to peoples of Russian satellite countries. More than a million balloons, each approximately six feet in diameter when filled with gas, carried portions of the Bible translated into seven languages behind the Iron curtain. Through what became known as the Bible Balloon Project, Hargis made his name known to many of the leaders of the right-fundamentalist movement.

During the 1950s Hargis worked at a frantic pace. He spent much of his time traveling about the country and speaking at dinners, rallies and in churches. He continued to add stations to the radio network carrying his daily 15-minute programs. Only the lack of money prevented his organization from growing faster. He has often declared that donations to his work come chiefly from small contributors; however, he has revealed that he owes much to the late W. L. Foster, a Tulsa oil man, for gifts and loans without interest that allowed him to get Christian Crusade started.

His message was typical of that preached by a large segment of the far right in the 1950s. He attacked the United Nations and the National Council of Churches in almost every issue of his *Christian Crusade* magazine. He preached that Communists were involved in promoting civil-rights agitation. And he sold tracts, pamphlets and books produced by his and a number of other far-right organizations.

Although he received a great deal of publicity from the Bible Balloon Project and from the articles he wrote for well-known rightist magazines, it took another incident to put his name solidly on the right-wing map of America. This affair occurred in early 1960, when the United States Air Force published one of its manuals for the training of noncommissioned officers of

the Air Force Reserve. The technical writer assigned to prepare
the article on Communism found his own knowledge of that
subject so limited that he asked the pastor of his church for
help. His minister suggested that he contact Billy James Hargis
for information, and he obtained a routine Hargis mailing con-
sisting of two pamphlets entitled "Apostate Clergymen Battle
for God-Hating Communist China" and "The National Council
of Churches Indicts Itself on 50 Counts of Treason." Material
from these documents concerning Communist sympathizers alleged to have infiltrated the churches was published in the Air
Force manual. This documentation was also used to attack a
new translation of the Bible by claiming that "The National
Council of Churches of Christ in the United States of America
officially sponsored the Revised Standard Version of the Bible.
Of the 95 persons who served in this project, 30 have been affiliated with pro-Communist fronts, projects and publications."

The National Council of Churches almost immediately lodged
a complaint with the Department of Defense, and the Air Force
apologized and quickly withdrew the manual from distribution.
But some congressmen supported the Hargis-documented allega-
tions, and the furor created headlines resulting in a publicity
windfall of the first magnitude for Billy James Hargis and Christian Crusade. In the April 1960 issue of his magazine, the Tulsa
radio preacher used large red and black headlines to announce
his joy: "Air Force Manual Controversy . . . a God-Send!"

At the beginning of the 1960s, following the Air Force manual
controversy, one observer noted that Christian Crusade had
grown so rapidly that it had clearly become the leading group
in that segment of the far right often called the "Christian right."
In one detailed survey of the right wing, Christian Crusade's
budget for the year 1962 was said to be $1,250,000. Hargis was
reported to be broadcasting some 400 programs each week over
200 radio stations in 46 states and was viewed on more than a
dozen TV outlets servicing 20 states. The survey concluded, "His
is a big business." [15]

The activities of Christian Crusade were so widespread that
they were beginning to be noticed by various national publications. The *Saturday Evening Post* was one of the first periodicals

to investigate Christian Crusade's operations in an article entitled "Doomsday Merchant on the Far, Far Right."

The *Post* attacked almost the entire range of Christian Crusade activities, but reserved the most biting criticism for what it implied was flagrant opportunism on the part of Hargis:

> Doctor Hargis does not want this money for his own use, of course. Last year, out of the nearly $1,000,000 that came in as payment for his lectures, books, pamphlets and in the form of outright gifts, he took only $12,000 for himself . . . his nonprofit, tax-free corporation paid his salary and expenses and provided him with a $43,000 parsonage and a $50,000 bus, fitted out like a yacht to travel in . . . Someday, of course, he would like to do a little better for himself. He is trying to work out a corporate setup through which he can retain some of the royalties his books and writings bring in and some of the lecture fees he earns. A man with a wife and four children . . . must give some thought to the future. Last year, for example, he was paid $145,000 for speaking at various rallies, plus $50,000 in royalties . . . In a few more years, he says, he hopes that his work will be done. America will be awake to its danger. The Communist conspiracy will be under control. He can then pay off the $45,000 he still owes on his 700-acre ranch near Tulsa and retire. . . .

The Rev. Billy James Hargis was quick to respond to the slashing attack of the *Saturday Evening Post,* and someday that response may be accorded its proper place in the pantheon of right-wing faux pas, for he could hardly have planned an answer that would have done his cause more damage. It is not clear why a resourceful field general of Hargis' capability would use his own magazine to thank the *Saturday Evening Post* for some of the most negative publicity possible. But Hargis actually announced in a rather exultant manner, "During its 14 years of anti-Communist activity, Christian Crusade seldom has had an opportunity to thank a great national magazine for its valuable and cooperative publicity." In the midst of his unalloyed praise for the article Hargis reserved space to compliment the *Post* as a "shining pillar of genuine Americanism." And as if anticipating that some might point to the criticism the article contained, he added, ". . . we are not going to look a gift horse in the mouth."

He emphasized that he was not about to reject $207,760 worth
of publicity in a circulation of 6,624,866. And he implied that he
would be willing to be publicly denounced again for still more
publicity: ". . . If only *Life, Look,* and the New York *Times*
could now do as well by us, we've got it made." [16]

When letters of protest poured in to Christian Crusade and to
the editor of the *Saturday Evening Post,* it was obvious that
Hargis had committed a serious tactical blunder. He waited a
few weeks before boldly attacking the *Saturday Evening Post* in
the September 1962 issue of his monthly magazine:

> Among the "past-masters" at vicious, tongue-in-cheek smear, we
> must admit the *Saturday Evening Post* has the greatest effect. Since
> Christian Crusade was the object of such treatment several weeks
> ago, we feel qualified to pass on to our readers many of the re-
> actions to their unfairness. It is truly a testimony to the potency of
> an aroused citizenry. *Christian Crusade* herewith presents excerpts
> from many of the letters written regarding the *Saturday Evening
> Post* abortion.

Three years later in a biography published by *Christian Crusade*
a Hargis associate wrote that even the headline of the *Post* article
reeked "with vicious desire to ridicule, downgrade and destroy
Hargis as an effective preacher of the Word of God and a foe of
Communism. What the headline almost desperately attempts
to convey is that the subject of that article, Hargis, lucratively
peddles baseless warning on a non-existent threat . . . Throughout the *Post's* artful masterpiece of half-truths, innuendoes and
lies, the entire purpose of their article is always clearly discern-
ible." Even more hateful than its words was the picture the *Post*
published of the Tulsa preacher. The *Christian Crusade* writer observed that most of Hargis' detractors referred to him as "che-
rubic," "pleasant faced," "disarming" and "baby faced." "But the
Post's full-page Hargis pictures were at an angle which completely
distorted his features. They made him look like an over-sized
turtle with a grafted, brutish, semi-human face." [17]

An increasing number of books and articles about Christian
Crusade appeared in the early 1960s, most of which viewed the
Tulsa radio preacher as something less than a savior of the na-

tion. Hargis and his associates were extremely sensitive to some criticism. They denounced one book, a 1964 publication called *Danger on the Right*, for trafficking in some of the sensitive areas; first, they said, for ". . . portraying Dr. Hargis as a money-crazed opportunist, living in great opulence off the bemused supporters of Christian Crusade," and second, for wallowing "in the mire of derogatory descriptive writing and picturing Hargis as 'pudgy.' " [18]

Billy Hargis is a heavy man, but not objectionably obese. He always appears at public functions conservatively dressed in fashionable attire of unquestioned good taste. But it is possible that his reaction to any mention of his physical proportions has attracted some writers to the subject.

In addition to the mountainous load of correspondence involved in soliciting contributions, follow-up pleas, or selling books, pamphlets, recordings, tapes and souvenirs of the Holy Land, Hargis and his staff conduct a vast amount of correspondence in rebutting articles, editorials and letters to the editors of many newspapers and magazines. Often enough the comments directed toward the Tulsa evangelist and his associates are couched in biting, satirical language, and Hargis almost always replies in kind. He usually spices his letters with some ideological scare words. Nothing has made him more controversial than his leveling of the charge of pro-Communism against individuals, groups or publications that have been critical of him.

This counterproductive policy is nowhere better exemplified than in his response to an article in the August 17, 1963, issue of *Time* magazine, which estimated Hargis' weight at 275 pounds and indulged in a gratuitous discussion of his physical proportions by picturing him with ". . . rolls of fat that start at his jowls and balloon into an elephant-sized waistline." Infuriated, Hargis detracted from an otherwise effective riposte by dipping his brush in a bit of red paint: "There is an old adage among Communists that says, 'When you can't answer a man's charges, ridicule him. Make fun of his appearance. Make him look like a fool.' " [19] Hargis' protest probably caused very few Americans to consider *Time* pro-Communist just because it had discussed his weight.

When *Life* magazine included Hargis in an article called "The Fearmongers," which also discussed a wide variety of extremists, he wrote to *Life,* accusing the editors of making charges against him which were "unfair, un-American and are intended to smear and destroy Christian Crusade." He added, "These same charges have appeared only in the Communist *Worker.* I have never read them any place else. I must assume then that you are using the Communist *Worker* as your research source."

In his turn the editor of the magazine replied, "*Life* didn't say Hargis was a Communist, Klansman, anti-Semite or anti-Catholic. *Life* did say he is a segregationist."

Unsatisfied, Hargis wrote to the president or general manager of every company that had advertised in the objectionable issue of *Life.* He explained how he had been attacked, and protested the advertiser's "financial sponsorship of this vicious smear publication. . . ." By making it possible for *Life* to attack him, the big companies had sealed their own doom: "Through advertising in the February 7 issue of *Life* magazine, you have helped finance the undermining of the Free Enterprise System." When all but one of the companies indicated they would stick with *Life,* Hargis suggested that they would continue to advertise in the magazine "even if the editorial comment came out of Moscow." [20]

Hargis also objected to being labeled a "hate monger" in an article written by Tom Braden for the October 28, 1963, issue of *Look* magazine. In a long letter of protest to the author, he recommended that Braden refrain from using guilt-by-association tactics in his future articles. He added, "Certainly you must know that this is an aged Communist trick and not worthy of an American." [21]

But it was not only national publications that Hargis engaged in constant battle. It was also newspapers large and small all across the country. In a February 1965 issue of the Nashville *Tennesseean* the editor commented that Billy James Hargis and Robert Welch had no more business trying to fight subversion and Communism "than Jesse James has heading a United Fund drive." Hargis found that statement was not only libelous, but indicated that the editor had definite criminal instincts. And when reporter Don McGaffin of the San Jose *Mercury* wrote in his coverage of a Christian Crusade lecture that there had been a "wave of tsks, tsks and murmuring" at the meeting, Hargis interpreted that and other comments as "heckling" on the part of the reporter and suggested that "Mr. McGaffin may think this type of reporting will merit him the Pulitzer Prize, but I would suggest that if he is determined to smear anti-Communists and conservatives with such unobjective reporting, he is more qualified for the Lenin Prize." The Tulsa Crusader also became terribly upset with the Boise, Idaho *Observer* for reporting in its April 2, 1964, issue that Christian Crusade had distributed some 40,000 pamphlets labeling President Kennedy a Communist. Without explaining that he had called the Kennedy administration "pro-Communist" on many occasions, he roundly assailed what he characterized as "your little smear sheet": "Now, you people are claiming to be objective. You either have an uninformed nut for a reporter or an outright Communist sympathizer because he knows this is not so if he has any facts at his disposal . . . I thank God for anybody who fights Communism, instead of people like you who are apparently in sympathy with it." [22]

Hargis has also had his arguments with religious publications such as the *Baptist Program*, organ of the Executive Committee of the Southern Baptist Convention. He complained that he and Carl McIntire had been "attacked viciously and unfairly and in an un-Christian and untruthful manner" in the *Program*. He objected to the their describing his and McIntire's radio programs as "poison," "onesided" and "vitriolic hatred." "Do you call this Christian?" the Tulsa evangelist wanted to know.[23]

He hardly had time for an answer before discovering that the "vicious lies and untruths" contained in the *Baptist Program* had been reprinted in another Southern Baptist publication called the *Baptist Message*. And off he went after that magazine. There would always be others. In fact three years later, in November 1967, he was still involved in a correspondence battle; this time with the Southwest Texas Conference of the Methodist Church.

When he was not busy counterattacking the articles that assailed Christian Crusade, he was often refuting critics who wrote about the privileges he enjoyed as head of a nationally-known organization. Much was said in the early 1960s about his $44,000 home, $7,500 automobile and $200-per-week allowance for domestic help. There was also criticism about the $50,000 bus in which he traveled about the country fulfilling his speaking engagements. Many people do not think the director of a religious organization should enjoy the same leadership perquisites that the director of a large corporation does. In recent years most of the criticism of his fringe benefits has been forgotten, and inflation has increased prices so much that by the end of the 1960s Hargis could tell an interviewer that even the house he lived in did not cost much more than a shack in Tulsa.[24]

Hargis' lack of formal education led him, early in his career, to seek a degree through correspondence schools. Critics charged that both his honorary Doctor of Divinity and Doctor of Laws degrees were bestowed on Hargis by diploma mills. But this criticism subsided after he was presented with another honorary Doctor of Laws degree in 1961 by Bob Jones University in Greenville, South Carolina.

During the 1960s Christian Crusade grew rapidly. In 1966 Hargis moved out of his rather cramped organization headquarters in downtown Tulsa into a beautiful and spacious new building in the suburbs. He named the building the Cathedral of the Christian Crusade. It was a long-time dream come true. He also secured adjoining land for a college he planned to establish, and he set up new quarters for expanding departments such as shipping, circulation, mail processing and printing. It was a big business growing bigger. He now had a headquarters large enough for the many seminars, leadership schools and conventions that he conducted each year. Once opened, the Cathedral was a veritable mecca for an ever-increasing array of military and governmental leaders, educators, nationally-known ministers and outstanding conservative spokesmen, who came from all parts of the nation to participate in Christian Crusade activities.

Although he has always guarded the independence of the Crusade, Hargis has long cooperated with many leaders on the far right. He has even made one serious but unsuccessful attempt to bring about a coalition of right-wing groups. Very few organizations on the right hold identical political and religious beliefs, but those promulgated by Christian Crusade are fairly typical of most of the far right. Hargis does not dispense anti-Semitism or make overt anti-Negro or anti-Catholic positions a part of his Crusade. But his organization has still supported most of the vast collection of sometimes curious political attitudes that are generally included in a catalogue of right-wing causes.

The Rev. Billy Hargis has often emphasized that his purpose in establishing Christian Crusade was to fight Communism and apostate religion. He has also condemned other philosophies. He has written, "From this day forward, my friends, it [Christian Crusade] will equate liberalism and socialism with Communism. . . ." [25] Hargis resented being placed on the same side of the political spectrum with such home-grown Nazis as the late George Lincoln Rockwell. He solved the problem very neatly by placing Nazism in the far-left camp with Communism. While most political scientists would probably agree to a totalitarian kinship between the two ideologies, they would hardly call them the same thing, and they might be somewhat taken aback to learn that Hargis has on several occasions placed the ideology of Christian Crusade smack in the center of the spectrum. Still, the spectrum belongs to Hargis just as much as it does to the political scientists. In 1970 he announced on a broadcast, "There are only two ideologies abroad in the land: one is Marxism; the other is Christian freedom. Take your choice. . . ." [26]

What are the sources of far-right fundamentalism? Who applauds the right-wing leaders, listens to their broadcasts and contributes to their programs? Interestingly enough, not even the Rev. Dr. Billy James Hargis knows all the answers to these questions. Early in 1969, after he conducted his own poll, he announced that for the first time in 22 years he knew what "Mr. and Mrs. Christian Crusaders are really like!" The Hargis poll revealed nothing about the educational background or income level of his supporters, but did show that the average Crusader is more than 50 years old and is very concerned about the threat of Communism, changing religious values and public immorality. Many Crusaders worry about taxes, inflation, the breakdown of family life, and sex education in the schools. But this poll may not accurately reflect the thinking of the entire far right, since Christian Crusade places great emphasis on being a religious-oriented protest group. For that matter, even some Crusaders apparently do not consider very fine ideological distinctions important. One Hargis associate failed to choose among the various issues when he described Christian Crusade's mission in rather simplistic language: "The job of Dr. Billy James Hargis is to yell, 'Fire, fire, fire, fire' till America awakens and realizes that there really is great danger to our way of life." [27]

But Hargis has not pleased everyone in his role of national watchman. In 1966 the Internal Revenue Service revoked the tax exemption of Christian Crusade, alleging that the organization had attempted to influence legislation.[28] Hargis appealed the ruling, and in June 1971 a Federal court in Tulsa ruled in his favor. But a Denver appeals court later reversed the Tulsa ruling and at the same time prohibited tax-exempt organizations from "direct and indirect appeals to legislators and the public in general." Hargis had heavily criticized the IRS over his network of radio stations and in his newspaper. The court did not reveal how much the Hargis attacks had helped to bring on the sweeping restriction, but many churchmen considered it a denial of their right to speak out on public issues and therefore unconstitutional. Their concern became so great that it even affected the generation-long feud between Hargis and the National Council of Churches. On January 22, 1973, *Time* magazine reported that because of the mutual concern over the court restriction, lawyers from the two organizations had planned a strategy against a common crisis. Christian Crusade, backed by the NCC and other groups, is now carrying the case to the Supreme Court.

Throughout much of his career radio preacher Hargis has developed more new programs to stir up the wrath of "middle America" and capture space in national periodicals than any other leader on the right. Often enough he has been the first to sense that many people are distressed about a particular issue. In a short time he may publish a booklet on the subject and begin to attack it on his radio network. If the response is great enough, and listeners contribute to further attacks on the issue, it may well become a regular feature on his lecture circuit.

But of course not every popular right-wing issue originates at Christian Crusade. And in some respects, each new issue or grievance must be handled in a different manner, since each one may appeal to a slightly different group of people. This, at least, has been true of most of the outstanding right-wing issues of the past decade. Still, the Hargis organization has been flexible enough to handle them all very well and, in many cases, to set the pace for the whole movement. No right-wing organization has been more effective in attacking the United Nations or the National Council of Churches. The same can probably be said about his fight against the Federal Communications Commission's fairness doctrine. This policy, which made it financially hazardous to criticize or attack people by name on a broadcast, seemed especially to infuriate the Tulsa Crusader. One of his many attacks on the FCC fairness doctrine took the form of a popular booklet called *The Death of Freedom of Speech in the USA.* This was backed up with hard-hitting radio broadcasts which probably did much to stimulate widespread criticism of the FCC.

Christian Crusade's efforts on such staple far-right issues as opposition to gun registration, modern art, busing and mental health programs were extremely effective, but they did not appear to be backed with the level of commitment that was demonstrated in the Hargis support of the governments of Rhodesia, South Africa and Greece.

Probably no other right-wing issue of the past decade has generated more sound and fury than the fight to remove sex education from public schools. And no campaign shows Hargis and his Christian Crusade operating at a more effective level. It has been widely reported that Billy James Hargis started the drive against sex education programs in the schools. This is true only in a special sense. The movement first made news in 1968 in Anaheim, California, where a local newspaper started a battle to remove a sex education program from a school. Articles describing the struggle over sex education in various schools appeared in a number of periodicals. And the *Saturday Evening Post* did much to alarm parents by suggesting that a 26-year-old program in San Diego might be causing children to be overly preoccupied with sex.

But it was a Christian Crusade booklet called *Is the Little Red Schoolhouse the Proper Place to Teach Raw Sex?* that really got

the issue off the ground. In that sense, it is true that Hargis started
the anti-sex-education movement. But the Tulsa Crusader has only
claimed credit for defeating "SIECUS-type" sex-education programs. By this he referred to the materials or curricula developed
by a private group, the Sex Information and Education Council
of the United States. Hargis denounced this organization as "a
small but powerful group of humanists who don't believe in
God . . . trying to inject their humanistic and amoral attitudes
towards sex and human behavior into the educational stream."
He claimed to concentrate his fight against the materials produced
by SIECUS for youngsters in elementary schools. It was Hargis'
little booklet, backed by a sustained and blistering attack over
his nationwide network of radio stations, that spread the early-
warning message to every hamlet in the nation. He was joined
by many others—the Birchers, Carl McIntire, C. W. Burpo and
Dan Smoot, to name a few of the best known—but it was the siege
guns of Christian Crusade that cut down SIECUS and a host of
other sex-education programs throughout the United States.

Two years after the battle was joined, the *Pediatric News* for
August 1970 published the remarks on the anti-sex-education
movement made by Dr. Alfred Auerback, of the University of
California, before the American Psychiatric Association. Noting
that the "two-year effort of right-wing groups to curtail sex education in the public schools has been singularly successful," Dr.
Auerback pointed to the legislation to curtail or eliminate sex-
education programs that had been introduced or passed in nearly
every state. Observing that anti-sex-education groups had termed
sex-education programs part of a Communist conspiracy, Auerback cited many well-established programs that had been elimi-
nated and the moratorium placed on new programs everywhere:
"Any school district hoping to initiate a program in family life
and sex education can anticipate a well-financed, well-organized
attack. . . ."

The "Communist Conspiracy" cry was heard in every phase of
the sex-education battle, but Hargis claimed in the September 20,
1970 issue of his paper, "We did not say that SIECUS was a com-
munistic movement." He did state, however, that ". . . the cause
of international Communism would be served with a sex revolu-

tion or the growth of amorality and immorality in the United States." Thus, a sex-education program that survived would represent a victory for Communism.

Hargis took credit for a portion of the sex-education victory, perhaps even less than he could properly claim. And he thanked other groups which helped him in the fight. He estimated that his victory had cost less than a quarter of a million dollars because "we were able to get our views in every leading magazine in America such as *Look, Time, Life, Newsweek,* and *Reader's Digest* and to be the subject of national television programs on NBC and CBS."

Billy Hargis may still have to crank up his anti-sex-education machine again. The New York *Times* of January 17, 1973, reported that despite considerable public opposition, some states are quietly promoting sex education in public schools to curb increasing rates of illegitimate births. One of the states mentioned in the Department of Health, Education and Welfare report quoted by the *Times* was Hargis' own state of Oklahoma.

The Rev. David A. Noebel, one of Hargis' associate ministers, has often been described as the man nearest the throne at the Crusade. He is Dean of The Summit, Hargis' anti-Communist youth university in Colorado; he has directed a number of the Christian Crusade attacks against institutions of the liberal establishment and authored a number of publications, including books on the Communist use of music. When he announced a few years ago that he had uncovered a Communist master music plan, he was heavily ridiculed by much of the regular press, and even leaders in the far right who have distributed the wildest type of propaganda believed he had gone too far. It was a difficult assignment, to be sure; while he was able to attack the Beatles unmercifully, he was forced to skirt carefully around Elvis Presley, a hero in some parts of "middle America." And the use of questionable documentation in some of his works on music also hurt his credibility as a right-wing author. But he still has much to contribute to a far-right organization, even though he has caused Dr. Hargis to spend a great deal of time and effort defending his work. When, for example, the Dallas *Times Herald* published an editorial entitled "Nyet, Nyet, Nyet," ridiculing Noebel's book

Communism, Hypnotism and the Beatles, it was Hargis who rushed to Noebel's defense.

On February 15, 1965, Hargis wrote to the *Times Herald* and set the paper straight in his usual no-nonsense style: "Contrary to your editorial, gentlemen, my associate evangelist, David Noebel, did not suggest that the Beatles were Communists. Instead, his thesis is that the music of the Beatles 'like more innocuous-sounding rhythms heard daily by American children,' is in actuality part of a systematic plan geared to making a generation of American youth mentally ill and emotionally unstable, a scientific plan geared to using the destructive qualities of music for the degeneration of American youth."

The Tulsa radio preacher went on to explain to the editors that exhaustive and time-consuming research had been performed for almost a year in order to announce the Communist master music plan that Noebel had uncovered, a disclosure that included the facts on the Communist-controlled record companies which had been established in the United States to distribute hypnotic music in American homes and schools. Hargis continued, driving home his argument with even stronger words, "Now, I realize it is too much for the minute brains that write the editorial pages of the Dallas *Times Herald* to recognize the threat of Communism internally or internationally, but for your readers who would like to know the facts instead of your interesting objection entitled, 'Nyet, Nyet, Nyet,' which at the most is based on hearsay, they can obtain the entire printed piece, complete with sources, for 50 cents by writing to Christian Crusade. . . ." [29]

He had no sooner put the *Times Herald* in its place when *Newsweek* heard of Noebel's new theory. In an article called "Beware of the Red Beatles" *Newsweek* said, "Fluoridation, mental health programs and the United Nations are, as every right-thinking fundamentalist well knows, insidious Communist plots to soften up America for the Bolshevik take-over, but by dint of 'hard intelligence,' a 28-year-old Wisconsin preacher on tour for Billy Hargis' Christian Crusade says he has unearthed the most subtle Communist ploy—the Beatles."

Newsweek quoted part of the Rev. David Noebel's lecture before the members of a Claremont, California, Baptist church: "You listen to this, Christians," he shouted. "These Beatles are completely anti-Christ. They are preparing our teenagers for riot and ultimate revolution against our Christian Republic. It's all a part of the Communists' master music plan." According to the news magazine, Noebel revealed that "The drum is the key—little Ringo," and added that these young people will do anything they are told to do. "One day when the revolution is ripe, they could put the Beatles on TV and could mass hypnotize the American youth. This scares the wits out of me!"

Against such an article even Hargis found it hard to counter-attack, but he did cite some errors as he protested against the story, explaining that "the truth found in this paragraph is set in such a manner as to make the reader feel it is something that is half-cocked or worse. . . ." But he was able to clear up any misunderstanding about the Beatles and their reputation: ". . . David Noebel has never called the Beatles 'Red.' He has, however, on the authority of the Beatles' press officer, called the Beatles 'rude, profane, vulgar, anti-Christ, atheistic, agnostic, anti-Pope and anti-Christian.' " [30]

As a speaker, Billy James Hargis has received a wide variety of ratings. Some observers have praised his informal style as interesting enough to shrink a two-hour speech into something that seems like a 20-minute sermon. Unquestionably he finds many who enjoy his colorful use of colloquialisms, and others claim that he is able to keep any audience laughing with his collection of jokes and stories. British writer Alan Bestic was so impressed with Hargis' humor that he thought the Tulsa Crusader's aggressive phrases were teetering constantly on the slippery brim of slapstick. He likened Hargis to a dinosaur pup lashing its tail dangerously, but at the same time hilarious in its wild, brash abandon.

At least one Master of Arts thesis has been written on Hargis as an orator, and an issue of *Language and Style*, published by the University of Colorado has featured an analysis of his speeches. Most of these works delve deeply into the stylistic traits employed in Hargis' speeches, but do not describe the audience's reaction to him when he is at his tension-building best. A strong case can be made for claiming that Christian Crusade has been built largely on the eloquence of its leader.

On February 1, 1968, Billy James Hargis addressed an audience of loyal followers from Oklahoma City. The newspapers had revealed two days earlier that the United States had suffered its most disastrous reverses of the Vietnam struggle, and Hargis, a strong advocate of military victory, had journeyed to the capital city of Oklahoma to speak informally about world conditions.

The Tulsa Crusader came in a little late, after most of approximately 150 people were already seated. He paused in one of the aisles and deposited his topcoat and some papers with three of his children who were seated in a back row. He walked slowly up to the dais and stood behind a little pulpit looking around rather casually at the crowd in the auditorium. He continued staring until it grew so quiet that the heavy breathing of an older man in the middle of the small auditorium was audible to those sitting near the back. Finally Hargis began to speak. Slowly at first and in a low-pitched voice: "We have lost the war in Vietnam."

That was all he said. And it grew very quiet again while Hargis fussed around with one of his cuff links for a little while and then seemed to study the ceiling at the back of the auditorium as if he were all alone. Finally he began speaking again, softly, evenly. "Things that have happened the last two days in Vietnam prove we have lost the war. All we need is the funeral." He stopped talking again, but now there was a slight murmuring throughout the auditorium, a low response that seemed to be saying, Yes, that's true, we have lost the war, but why? Hargis waited until it grew quiet once more, almost as if he were listening to the voices. His coal-black hair was combed down tight against his scalp, and his dark eyes looked especially fierce; little points of darkness that stared laserlike straight ahead. From the back row of the theater his solemn visage glowered down at the troubled listeners like that of some Old Testament prophet about to announce the great day of wrath.

Suddenly his right hand flashed downward and his open palm struck the top of the pulpit WHAM! with the force of a bolt of lightning. Right behind that sound came his voice, now a high, almost unnatural cry: "WE PATRIOTS WILL NEVER STAND FOR THIS DEFEAT!" As the last word came pealing out, his palm slammed down against the pulpit again WHAM! and he almost screamed: "*Never!*" Again and again and again his hand crashed down against the pulpit, followed each time with a crescendo of thundering nevers that pierced every ear in the auditorium. NEVER, WHAM! NEVER, WHAM! *NEVER, WHAM! NEVER, WHAM! NEEVEERRR!!*

In the auditorium some heads were pushed back against the seats, but mostly the people were staggering to their feet like shell-shocked troops coming out of a trench. Some still waved their hands as if synchronized to the rhythmic pounding that no longer thundered from the platform. One old man in the audience showed signs of having a heart attack; his eyes gleamed brightly and he breathed heavily through his mouth, mumbling, ". . . my God . . . oh, my God. . . ." Caught without so much as a pencil in his hand, a reporter from the Associated Press wrestled with his tape recorder in case Hargis should release another burst of oratorical pyrotechnics.

In a short time everyone was back in his seat waiting for more thunder from the pulpit. But Hargis did not repeat his electrifying performance. He began instead to discuss the war. He told in a casual voice how he had just come from Boston and Chicago and how people were so shocked about the recent turn of events that they seemed to be in a daze. He even progressed to the point of injecting into his talk some of his famous folksy expressions, a "listen, brother," and a "that bird in Congress." But there were no jokes, no laughter. It was not a time for laughter. The most powerful speaker of the far right and perhaps in all of America, could hardly joke on such an occasion. He was there to make his report on the American defeat in Vietnam and to pass a few moments of solemn rapport with his people, true believers to a man.

During that same spring of 1968 the Rev. Oral Roberts was enduring a gethsemane trying to metamorphose from the larva of a Pentecostal faith healer into a Methodist pupa while the whole world watched. Critics could be heard on every hand, but none was more vocal than the Rev. Billy James Hargis. In his headquarters across town from Oral's lush campus, Hargis cut the tapes for his nationwide broadcasts and printed his monthly magazine. In the *Christian Crusade* Hargis reported that Oral Roberts had read some 50 volumes on existentialism written by men with names like Søren Kierkegaard, Rudolph Bultmann, Albert Camus and Jean-Paul Sartre. And on his radio broadcasts Hargis confirmed the rumors of a "no-love-lost" relationship between him and Roberts:

> . . . He's head over heels in debt and therefore he's trying to make peace with the National Council of Churches crowd. He's left the Pentecostal Church that he's been affiliated with all his life and joined one of the big liberal Methodist churches in Tulsa. Now he's to be ordained by the Methodist Bishop of Oklahoma. As I said, this has broken my heart because I saw another evangelist do this—he's dead now, and I'm not going to mention his name . . . he joined one of the big denominations of America and he died a natural death —literally—that man started going down from the time he united with that liberal denomination . . . finally he quit the ministry in disgust and frustration. He quit the ministry and for the last two years he turned to drink before the man died. A young man, a handsome young man, a powerful evangelist, whose whole ministry was ruined because he compromised his convictions. Oral Roberts has repudiated the Pentecostal people who have supported him all these years. I've got men working for me here who used to work for Oral Roberts. They claim that sixty percent of his support is Pentecostal people. And after all these years of accepting this support—Pentecostal people died and left everything they had . . . After all these years, he feels he has to make peace with the big denominations—the Methodist Church—and in so doing with the National Council crowd. . . .[31]

A onetime Roberts employee was quoted on the cause of the faith healer's problems, which seemed to stem from a leaning toward Christian Existentialism. Dr. Hargis explained to his listeners, ". . . Christian Existentialism—that means modernism, my friend. Christian Existentialism is the newest modernist attack on the fundamental faith of Jesus Christ."

While Billy James Hargis was telling the world about Oral

Roberts, a book was published which would soon play an important role in the activities of Christian Crusade. The author, John H. Redekop, was a professor of political science at Pacific College in Fresno, California, and his book was entitled *The American Far Right: A Case Study of Billy James Hargis and His Christian Crusade.*

At an early date the book was reviewed by Gerald Pope, editor of *Christian Crusade* magazine. Editor Pope was none too happy with the book, observing that the author was guilty of ". . . an abundance of condemnation, ridicule, misinformation and the customary practice of dismissing 'Rightists' as anything but intelligent and honest people." Still, he was willing to concede that Redekop did not attack Hargis in quite the same manner as most of his critics. He thought that Redekop's rebuttals to the Hargis stands on many issues were tainted with the same old liberal arguments. To Pope, Redekop's charges that Hargis was inconsistent, inaccurate, illogical, naive, guilty of unwarranted generalizations, of outright errors, and of ignoring the most basic distinctions, showed that the professor was guilty of "engaging in invective."

But Chapter Eleven came as something of a surprise. Editor Pope was pleased to discover that the author realized the Communist threat was real. And when the professor decided that Hargis was not totally outside the American tradition, the editor even began using a few exclamation marks. Then came the clincher: is Hargis a racist as characterized by some of his critics? "This accusation is not founded in fact," declared Dr. Redekop. Editor Pope concluded that, except for some negative comments in the earlier part of the book, Professor Redekop had actually achieved a noteworthy analysis of Hargis and Christian Crusade.[32]

In June Hargis revealed that he had made some plans for the new book and its author. The Tenth Annual National Convention of Christian Crusade was scheduled for the following month in the Tulsa Cathedral. Some of the best-known speakers of the far-right circuit would be assembled, including General Edwin A. Walker, soldier-hero of the University of Mississippi riots in 1962. Dr. Gordon Drake, Director of Education for Christian Crusade, would provide some hard-hitting disclosures on the National

Education Association and on sex education in the schools; and Dr. and Mrs. Bob Jones III of Bob Jones University would star in a dramatization entitled "Savonarola—Crusader." Dr. James Bales, whose prolific writings, unknown to the literary world of many Americans, had sold more widely than those of Hemingway and Faulkner combined, would be a featured speaker, along with Colonel Curtis Dall, author of the Hargis publication, *FDR—My Exploited Father-in-law*.

As exciting as this program promised to be to the Crusaders, it was only a bill of supporting players. The main attraction, apart from Dr. Hargis himself, would be what the Tulsa Crusader glowingly described as "The Great Debate." It was to be Professor Redekop, a "representative of the Liberal Establishment," who would debate the Crusade's own David Noebel. Hargis' announcement was presented with all the restraint reserved for the opening of a world's fair or a trip to the moon:

> Dr. John Redekop, political science professor at Pacific College, Fresno, California, and author of the best-seller "anti-Hargis" book, *The American Far Right: A Case Study of Billy James Hargis and His Christian Crusade*, has kindly consented to face Pastor David A. Noebel, brilliant spokesman for Dr. Hargis and Christian Crusade, in a scholarly debate on the subject . . . "Can Christians support the Philosophy and the anti-Communist activity of Christian Crusade?" . . . As a spokesman for liberalism, John Redekop will argue that Dr. Hargis and Christian Crusade are harmful to America and the cause of Christ, while David Noebel . . . will argue that Billy James Hargis and Christian Crusade have been singled out by God to help preserve the Christian faith and maintain freedom in the U. S. A.

In the July issue of *Christian Crusade* the build-up for the "Great Debate" continued. It had now become "the debate of the year," in which liberalism per se would be pitted against conservatism. Despite protestations from Dr. Redekop, who considered himself a conservative, Hargis insisted on featuring the professor as a standard-bearer for liberalism. In the past Hargis and his associates had generally placed anyone who disagreed with their philosophy on the left side of the political spectrum.

On the night of August 3, 1968, the central auditorium of the Cathedral of the Christian Crusade was packed to overflowing. People were standing all along the long entrance passageway that served as a museum displaying Hargis' collection of Billy Sunday memorabilia, General Walker's military medals and various God-and-country masterpieces. There was an air of excitement and expectancy. People had come from several states to enjoy the Great Debate. Fundamentalists from Kansas and Arkansas shook hands with Christian Crusaders and John Birchers. Nondenominational preachers from Texas greeted radio preachers from Sand Springs and Oklahoma City, and Governor Wallace backers seemed to be everywhere. Visiting time was over when Dr. Hargis and General Walker took their seats: it was time for the debate to begin.

The Rev. David Noebel is a tall, ruggedly handsome man, with short blond hair and a firm jaw. He took the affirmative side of the question, "Can Christians support the philosophy and anti-Communist activity of Christian Crusade?" Oddly enough, he began by discussing what he called "Christian Crusade's Biblical Theology of Evil." He ranged in his discussion from Satan to Aristotle, from Christ to St. Paul. For 20 minutes he surveyed the high points of the Bible.

Dr. Redekop, a tall, slightly-built man with dark, wavy hair and deep-set eyes, turned a serious countenance to the audience. He seemed somewhat perplexed, and said so:

Ladies and gentlemen, I must say, I'm a little perplexed by the initial statement of my opponent—and really I don't like to use the word "opponent," because I do feel we have a lot of things in common, as just was evidenced. I would agree, I think, with virtually everything that was said. That's not why I'm perplexed. I'm perplexed because it seems to me it didn't deal really with the topic . . . The topic is: "Can Christians support the philosophy and anti-Communist activities of Christian Crusade?" And I would like to address myself specifically to that topic . . . I will not refute, I think, anything he said in the first 20 minutes, but rather endorse it wholeheartedly and thank him for the clear presentation. But I'd like to stick more specifically to the subject.

Noebel looked stunned. But Redekop was already establishing his anti-Communist credentials. He denounced Communism until it seemed impossible that anyone would ever get to the political right of him on that subject. Then he examined Christian Crusade's belief that America is the greatest gift that God had ever given man outside of the Christ and the Bible. The Christian's first allegiance, he pointed out, is to God, and that should be expressed through an international church. Why not try the slogan, "God and Church," he asked, rather than "God and Country," which was almost the identical slogan of the Nazis, who wore belts inscribed with "For God and Fatherland."

Redekop's voice was full of warmth and friendliness. He documented all quotations he used against Christian Crusade. He constantly reiterated that he could be wrong, that his mind was open, that he would appreciate being corrected on this and that. When he jarred the Crusaders with a discordant note, he was off on a new subject before their scowls hardened into hate. Now he was suggesting that they open their eyes and see Russia as it really was: a "lousy" system to be sure, and he wanted none of it, but was that any reason for believing the picture painted by Hargis and Christian Crusade? Then he quoted from a Crusade document: "The Soviet Union has the worst educational system in world history." What kind of statement is that, he asked. If they really had the worst educational system in the history of the world, we wouldn't be scared nearly witless about their success in the space race. No matter how well-meaning one may be, this kind of characterization does nothing but harm to the battle against Communism. We must see things as they really are, otherwise critics will write this movement off as irresponsible. And so it went. Quote after quote. This is wrong; that is simply not true. How can you believe this—I have been there, I know that is incorrect; please consider. . . . Constantly he pleaded with them not to weaken their case through overstatement or distortion. Then he was suddenly explaining that Christian Crusade had real potential, only to lower his voice somewhat and mention their intolerance: "I hesitate to say this, because I might be misunder-stood. But I think there's a tendency toward intolerance of a kind. Not a personal kind—I've had nothing but friendship and coop-eration from the people here. But a kind of an ideological intoler-ance . . . I suggest to you that in the approach of Christian Crusade there isn't a place for a political moderate. This bothers me. . . ."

As the persuasive Redekop came to the end of his allotted time, he forced the audience to consider the Hargis position that "Those who oppose this conservative effort are not fighting us; they are fighting God." Wasn't that just a little bit presumptuous? It is the church that is the modern equivalent of ancient Israel—not a country, not a movement, not a group. There was not, he de-clared, a place for a Christian, not even a conservative Christian, in the total political perspective of Christian Crusade. And that bothered him, he said, because he very much wanted to fit in.

Noebel rose to take his second turn at the podium. He acknowl-edged Dr. Redekop's criticisms and explained they would be dealt with during the question-and-answer period. Then, most amazingly, he proceeded to launch once more into a prepared philosophical discussion he called "Christian Crusade's Philosophy of History as it Pertains to the United States of America and International Communism." Starting with the premise that the American heritage is a Biblical heritage, Noebel developed the theme of a Christian America, quoting Lowell Thomas, Alexis de Tocqueville, Whittaker Chambers and Dean Manion, among others, to support his thesis.

Dr. Redekop observed without irony that he did not know whether to compliment or criticize David Noebel:

The first 20 minutes he gave us a lecture on theology and history, which was, I think, outstanding, and I'm certainly going to keep it for my records . . . but it was hardly . . . relevant to the topic. The bulk of the second lecture dealt with the fact that Communism is evil and we should oppose it. Again, I think it was one of the clearest presentations . . . I have no problem with it. But I suggest to you that over half of his statements had nothing to do with the topic . . . Who will quarrel—certainly I won't—that Communism is evil? This isn't what we're talking about . . . Who will quarrel with the notion that we should resist it? Why waste time talking about it? This we assumed—this we have in common . . . again I thank him for his very eloquent statement as to the evils of Communism and why we should resist it . . . Now let's continue.

He was off again in a dazzling array of words, statistics and questions. He challenged the Crusaders to get their history straight. Of course the Bible played a large role in American history, but American history was largely a continuation of British history, he said, and virtually all of the freedoms this country has were borrowed from the British. Then the professor examined Hargis' much-used phrase, "Christian Americanism." He asked, if this country has been totally Christian, how can we explain such things as slavery?

Now they were near the end, starting into the question-and-answer period. It would be Noebel's last chance, and he began by noting that of all the critics who had attacked Christian Crusade, John Redekop was the most Christian. But he added that Christian Crusade had discovered many people who claimed they were "Christian." So a few questions were in order. Noebel wanted to know, ". . . what are your feelings toward the deity and humanity of our Lord? Was His death and resurrection vicarious? Also, I would appreciate your reaction to the inspiration of the Scriptures . . . do you feel there is a Heaven to gain and a Hell to shun? Or is everything of value in the here and now, as Arthur Schlesinger Jr. contends . . . is Satan to be considered mythological, as many liberal theologians contend today?"

There was an almost palpable tension in the auditorium, and some of the Crusaders were leaning forward in their seats. This, obviously, would be the moment. No more airy phrases, no more neatly stacked bits of logic, no more history that almost left one dizzy. These were questions that separated Christian Americans from the Marxist world. For a moment Redekop studied his notes, then he looked up, smiled and said he would be happy to answer all of the questions:

I stand firm on what I would like to call an evangelical Baptist tradition. I believe in the inspiration of the Bible, the Virgin Birth of

Christ, His death and bodily resurrection, the propitiation of our sins. I believe in the Second Coming, a literal Heaven and Hell. I think I could agree with every one of the theological emphases which we heard about last night in the first part of Reverend Hargis' fine message. I have spelled this out in several periodicals. . . .[33]

Then it *was* true! Redekop was a theological conservative, as he had claimed all along. By twisting the political spectrum to suit himself, Hargis, who liked to be called a conservative, had placed himself in the awkward position of debating a real conservative. There would be a few more questions, but Redekop's last sally had for all practical purposes put an end to the contest.

At Redekop's request, Dr. Hargis promised to inform his followers in a future issue of his magazine that the professor had always considered himself a conservative. Ordinarily that would have been the end of the story, but a few weeks later *Christianity Today,* the conservative periodical so closely linked with Billy Graham, decided to take a close look at Redekop's book.

In the August 16 issue of *Christianity Today,* Lieutenant General William R. Harrison (Ret.) reviewed Redekop's *The American Far Right* in a column entitled "Is Hargis's Crusade Christian?" After studying the professor's documented analysis of the far right, Harrison was driven to conclude that ". . . Christian Crusade is not actually Christian," and he declared that "it may be as dangerous to the country as the radical left or Communism." [34]

When word of Harrison's review reached Christian Crusade headquarters, it caused the next issue of the *Weekly Crusader* to be set aside for Billy James Hargis' sizzling reply, entitled "Why I Am Concerned About the New Billy Graham." Hargis prefaced his report with a review of past attitudes toward the famous revivalist and *Christianity Today:*

As the listeners, readers and supporters of Christian Crusade know, this organization has never attacked Billy Graham, although we have been concerned over his ever-increasing support of the National Council of Churches and World Council of Churches and his failure to speak out against Communism, internationally and internally.

However, because we were convinced that Billy Graham was winning souls to Christ and was being mightily used by the Lord, we
refused to criticize him and speak out against him. . . ."

Dr. Hargis reviewed a bit of the history of *Christianity Today,*
noting that it had been established by Billy Graham and his
father-in-law, Dr. Nelson Bell. He observed that *Christianity
Today* had never published any articles particularly friendly to
him, but neither had there been any anti-Hargis stories until the
August 16 issue. Hargis emphasized that it was the "most devas-
tating, hatchet book review against me and Christian Crusade
which has been written by anyone in the last 12 months, including outright Communist writers. It is inconceivable to think that
this tirade was published in Dr. Billy Graham's and Dr. Nelson
Bell's *Christianity Today.*"

Hargis found the book reviewer's conclusion—that Christian
Crusade was not Christian—"horrifying." But what he described
as the "horrendous part of the book review" was the author's
feeling that Christian Crusade might be as dangerous as the radical left or Communism.

It is not difficult to appreciate Hargis' concern over the article.
The March 1967 issue of his monthly *Christian Crusade* magazine
had carried an article entitled "Billy Graham and the NCC,"
which was far from flattering, but could hardly be considered an
attack on the famous revivalist. In striking contrast to McIntire's
Christian Beacon, Hargis' newspaper carried very few articles
about Graham. Indeed, nothing more graphically illustrated the
difference between Christian Crusade and Carl McIntire's Twentieth Century Reformation Movement than their public positions
on Graham.

Hargis called upon his friends to write to Dr. Bell and evangelist Graham to express their dissatisfaction and "heartache" for
the "satanic treatment" dealt him. His own letter to the editors
of *Christianity Today* was rather a masterpiece of restraint compared to those he often wrote to publishers of anti-Hargis articles.
Although his language was courteous, he did not fail to explain
why he was so grieved. He noted that no publication had ever
dared suggest that his ministry was as bad as Communism. He

asked, "How can a brother in Christ so viciously attack another brother in Christ who believes the same faith? Is it jealousy?" The Tulsa Crusader promised to take the problem to his followers, and to "pray every day that God will forgive Billy Graham, Nelson Bell, William R. Harrison . . . I can only say, 'Father, forgive them. They know not what they do.' "

While the Hargis response to the book review could hardly be described as irenic, it was also no slashing counterattack. But in the final three pages of his newsletter he printed a summary of Graham's career that definitely pictured evangelist Graham in a critical light.

The 1964 elections proved in most respects to be an unmitigated disaster for Hargis and his Crusade. His man lost the race for the presidency, and because Hargis was alleged to have involved himself in the election, the Internal Revenue Service revoked Christian Crusade's tax exemption. As the 1968 elections approached, the Tulsa evangelist surveyed the coming political battle for his followers. Writing in the October 13, 1967, issue of the *Weekly Crusader,* he noted, "Even when all of us united behind one candidate, Senator Barry Goldwater, there were not enough of us to elect a President." Since the conservatives were limited in numerical strength, Hargis counseled that they could not afford the luxury of division and should unite behind one man. With what seemed an awareness that the Internal Revenue Service might be watching, he explained his new election policy. Noting that he was prevented from endorsing a candidate, he shrewdly observed that there was nothing in the law that prevented him from opposing one.

These observations were made at a time when most observers assumed that President Johnson would stand for re-election, and few could foresee the impact of Governor Wallace on the race. As election day approached, the Crusaders were split into Nixon and Wallace camps. Reminding his followers that he was prevented from endorsing any candidate, Dr. Hargis published a special letter in his monthly magazine shortly before election day. Writing in the vein of you-know-who-I'd-endorse-if-I-could, he created a masterpiece of ambiguity that apparently pleased both wings.

Those who view the American far right as a monolithic force are generally unaware of the disputes and disagreements that have always divided the gigantic rightist movement into hundreds of petty duchies and fiefdoms. All attempts to consolidate the hundreds of such organizations into a viable political force have failed. But Christian Crusade and some of the other large rightist groups have shown a willingness to cooperate with each other as long as their leaders run no risk of losing control of their organizations.

Hargis has invited many leading rightists to speak at his Cathedral and has endorsed or supported other right-wing leaders and organizations, thereby strengthening the movement and helping to build a circuit of far-right lecturers and speakers. Nowhere is the organizational autonomy among these groups better illustrated than in the relationship between Hargis' Christian Crusade and the John Birch Society. Long before the Birchers became a nationally-known organization, their leader Robert Welch was addressing Hargis' audience in Tulsa. And some of those highest in the organization of Christian Crusade have officially endorsed the Birch Society.

Organizational independence can be seen in the positions the two far-right leaders have taken on Richard Nixon. The President long ago denounced the Birch Society, and Robert Welch and his Birchers have repaid Nixon by promoting him to the rank of "Insider," the very highest order of evil politician. Insiders are national leaders who covertly manipulate governments and use Communism in their long-range efforts to bring about a one-world slave state. Insiders are never called Communists, but are described as directing and using Communists; thus, the term is actually a novel way of calling many leading Americans traitors.

But the Tulsa radio preacher has seldom burned a political bridge behind him, a feat the Birchers have performed with great regularity. His position on Richard Nixon has been far different from that of Robert Welch. In 1968 Hargis explained that he had originally been convinced by the late Senator Joseph McCarthy that Nixon was a true conservative. In the early 1950s, when Hargis was playing host to McCarthy and his wife in Tulsa, Nixon was quoted by the press as having criticized the senator.

When Hargis protested, McCarthy proceeded to counsel him against unnecessary criticism of Nixon. According to Hargis, McCarthy liked Richard Nixon:

> Be slow to criticize Dick Nixon. I know him. He is one of the best friends that I have in Congress. He is as anti-Communist as I am. It was not Nixon that criticized me today, it was Eisenhower. Eisenhower made him do it; he had no other choice. If Nixon can ever get rid of the Eisenhower influence, he will be a good President. You will see it if he ever gets a chance to prove it. He will be a good conservative and anti-Communist leader.[35]

It was this feeling about Nixon that was reflected in Hargis' 1968 postelection report to his Crusaders. He called it "The Nixon-Wallace Victory" and analyzed the contribution of Governor Wallace to the Nixon victory. He concluded that the nation definitely owed a "debt of gratitude" to Wallace, and he thanked "God in Heaven that Hubert Humphrey was defeated." But in the same breath he conceded that Humphrey was "one of the most consistent politicians who has come down the pike in a long time":

> When Humphrey went into politics, he was a Socialist; midway in his political career, he was a Socialist; today, in the year of his bid for the Presidency, he is a Socialist. He is not a political hypocrite like Lyndon B. Johnson—a man who was a segregationist in 1949 and a militant integrationist singing "We Shall Overcome" in 1968 for his own political aggrandizement. I have often said that Mr. Johnson is neither a conservative nor a liberal. He is a Johnsonian. He would go any way, adopt any political philosophy, support any cause that would help him politically.[36]

Pleased with the results of the 1968 presidential election, Dr. Hargis returned to his many labors. Between Nixon's triumph in 1968 and his re-election in 1972, the Tulsa crusader involved his organization in a variety of projects and causes. He completed a series of tours and participated in conferences in many foreign countries. He established a missionary foundation, hired Dr. Jess Pedigo from faith healer T. L. Osborn's organization to administer its activities, and proceeded to set up orphanages in Korea, India and Mexico. Pedigo started a separate radio program, called "Reaching Out," to solicit funds for the orphanages. He also established an agency which arranges the adoption of Korean children. For less than $1,000 a Korean child can be rapidly processed for a qualified American family. Hargis also helps finance his operations by leading tour after tour to Greece, Rhodesia and the Holy Land. He established the American Christian College in Tulsa. Soon he had a choir of college "kids" accompanying him on a musical tour of the United States, singing a repertoire of sacred, patriotic and "fun" songs in a production called "An Evening with Billy James Hargis and His Kids." He modeled his little college as much as possible on Bob Jones University and refused to solicit federal school grants or loans, and denounced all private colleges that did. Early in February 1972 he broadcast his first nationwide television program, an outreach that added some $100,000 to his monthly operating costs. But Christian Crusade could afford it; while other far-right organizations were losing support or even going out of business, Hargis' programs were attracting more new supporters every month. In addition to his many schools, conventions and special seminars, he offered a financial program that paid a good interest rate on investments, and offered counseling services to his followers in estate planning, wills and trusts. He was pastor of a local church at his Cathedral and lectured or preached almost constantly in all parts of the country. He kept a number of teams busy taking his message all over the nation, and turned out a constant stream of publications.

Despite such a heavy schedule of activities, Dr. Hargis still found time to battle his traditional enemies and tormentors. Indeed, he even came to welcome the slings and arrows of his detractors and revealed that attacks on his ministry actually resulted in positive gains: "Incredibly, every time this ministry is either attacked in the national news media or mentioned favorably, it results in a net gain. In our case, every knock is a boost. . . ." [37]

Dr. Hargis also had time to ferret out and attack all kinds of religious apostasy. In April 1970 he exposed a Southern Baptist Convention seminar on morality. He wrote that he found it "difficult for Bible-believing Christians to understand the twisted and perverted thinking" of the officials of the Southern Baptist Convention, who would invite a speaker from *Playboy* magazine. In reply the *Alabama Baptist,* an official church publication, called Hargis a "mischief maker," and remarked, "It is difficult for Bible-believing anybodies to understand the half-truthed kind of reporting done by Hargis. . . ."[38]

Nor were the Methodists neglected. When a Methodist church member from New York wrote to him and reported that his pastor had called Christian Crusade a fascist organization, the Tulsa preacher published his answer in his newspaper: the United Methodist Church, he said, is one of the strongest supporters of pro-Communist causes in the United States.[39]

The following month he blew the whistle on the United Presbyterian Church. In bold headlines he accused the Presbyterian General Assembly of approving for study a report that "repudiates the Biblical view of certain sexual practices as sin." In the same issue of his newspaper he noted that *Look* magazine was in dire financial trouble, and he explained why it deserved to go under: "In my opinion, there is no national magazine which more consistently advocates the Communist position regarding internal affairs than *Look* Magazine. By no stretch of the imagination can one conclude that *Look* is either pro-American or pro-Orthodox Christianity."[40] More than a year later, Hargis announced that *Look* would cease publication that month. He took the occasion to denounce a number of the other national magazines:

> Do not lament the passing of *Look* Magazine. I think it is a good thing for America. I just wish *Newsweek* and *Life* and *Time* would follow suit, as quickly as possible. It was encouraging to me when the *Saturday Evening Post* perished in February, 1969. . . .[41]

Dr. Hargis had long used these magazines as a source of quotations for his newspapers, magazines and books. He had even used quotes from some of them to document his conservative and anti-Communist positions. If they were bad for America, what, asked his critics, did that do to the integrity of his publications?

In 1971 Dr. Hargis made the important decision to change the mission of Christian Crusade. His announcement was included in an Associated Press story in the largest newspapers of Oklahoma, under the title, "Tulsa Now Called Fundamentalist Capital of World."

> Evangelist Billy James Hargis, an anti-Communist crusader who says his emphasis no longer is "concerned with conspiratorial problems but internal moral problems," operates from his base here, convinced the influence in the "Fundamentalist Capital of the World," as he calls it, has meant the city "has been virtually free of unemployment, racial tension, student dissidents or other Communist agitation." . . . Hargis now strikes hard at drug use, the "sexual revolution," X-rated movies and Satan worship. "We're convinced Satan worship is on the rise in this country," he says. . . .[42]

But he was still interested in politics, and during the first two years of the Nixon administration he experienced little difficulty in explaining the President's problems to his Crusaders. At times he was able to defend Nixon by denouncing members of Congress: "Many of us tend to make President Nixon a scapegoat, blaming him for all the problems that confront America. Actually, this nation is still run by the Congress of the United States and not by the President." What, he asked, had happened to the nation? "The Fulbrights, Hatfields, Kennedys, McGoverns, the Hartkes of the United States have forced our President into decisions in the field of foreign affairs that are both un-American and unlike the traditional thinking of the American people."[43]

A little later he wrote, "Regardless of our personal opinion regarding President Richard M. Nixon, we all must agree that he has made an honest effort to stem inflation and to restore some economic sanity to the government which had been left bankrupt by the left-wing, Liberal Democrat administration that preceded it."[44]

But as the President adopted more and more of the political positions that Hargis and most of the far right had long denounced, the Tulsa Crusader was apparently forced to begin criticizing the administration's policies. He started using a quotation he attributed to General Curtis LeMay, a frightening prediction that seemed to catch the fancy of many right-wing leaders. According to Hargis, LeMay said in mid-1971 that "within 18 months Russia would demand our total surrender or would threaten to bomb us off the face of the earth." Dr. Hargis claimed he was becoming increasingly alarmed that the United States was disarming while the Soviet Union continued to stockpile arms. In the July 18, 1971, issue of his newspaper he headlined that fear and explained that what frightened him so much was the fact that the Nixon administration was now acting just like the Kennedy and Johnson administrations had and was suicidally trusting the Communists: "I am not a prophet nor a son of a prophet, but I am here to tell you that if President Nixon trusts this disarmament treaty with the Soviet Union and cuts back on our U.S. Safeguard Anti-Ballistic Missile System, this can amount to commiting suicide as far as the United States is concerned."

The following week he went so far as to call the Nixon policy toward Chile "stupid," and on August 8, 1971, he used red headlines to inform his Crusaders that "Nixon Swallows Red Chinese Bait." This meant the President was going to China, and Hargis assumed that Nixon was prepared to recognize mainland China and see it admitted to the United Nations. He called it a "betrayal of Free China" that would serve as "an example of U.S. perfidy in the 20th Century." By the middle of August, when it had become known that the President had accepted Chou En-lai's invitation, he seemed very concerned and published an article by a Bircher congressman from California, John Schmitz, that was openly critical of the President's proposed "normalization of relations" with the Chinese Communists.

Even though the Birchers were punching the President pretty hard in October 1971, calling him an "Insider" and accusing him of protecting Mao's heroin trade, they still put a lot of effort into a drive to halt his trip. Carl McIntire headlined the fact that many were praying that Nixon would not go to China. All of this may have influenced Dr. Hargis to print a special protest-to-the-President letter for distribution to his followers. The letter was entitled "Please, don't go, Mr. President" and was followed by a list of reasons why he should cancel his trip to Peking. Each of 50 letters in a packet was to be signed by a concerned citizen and forwarded to the President or a member of Congress. Hargis had long since become famous in far-right circles for the dramatic appeal letters he sent quite regularly to those on his mailing list. The "Please don't go, Mr. President" letter was no exception. Using his automatic typewriter equipment, Dr. Hargis included in the body of each letter the name of the person who received it, a personal touch that no doubt convinced many people that they had received a personal letter from Dr. Hargis. He also included an appeal to cover his personal needs:

> . . . I must ask a personal favor of you. When you write for your packet, please consider the needs of Christian Crusade this month . . . over and above the regular operating expenses for October, I must meet three contract accounts and annual payments amounting to $64,395. I must ask you to go an extra mile with me . . . to help meet this extra obligation . . . by sending a contribution of $100, $75, $50, $25, $10, $5. Even $2 or $1 will help . . . For God and Country. . . .[45]

A few weeks later Dr. Hargis published a three-page supplement to his newspaper to present his views on the course of national events. He called this lengthy article "The Suicide of a Nation—Ours!" but its contents hardly measured up to such a sensational title. He admitted that he had arrived at a point where he no longer believed in the purity of Richard Nixon's right-wing ideology and described him as a politician in search of votes. But when he assailed the President, the slashing attack that had become a Hargis trademark was missing. He had savagely denounced other Presidents for implementing far less radical policies than those Nixon was supporting. This seemed to indicate that his powerful supporters were upset by the new Nixon, but were nowhere near the point of losing complete political faith in the President.

> Can you imagine this? The President of the United States, who became famous politically because of his anti-Communism, will not only favor bringing the aggressor, Communist China, into the United Nations, but has consented to kicking Nationalist China out of the Security Council and giving her strategic seat to the Communists

. . . What an interesting man our President is. The extremes a politician will go to to be re-elected. . . .[46]

Dr. Hargis closed his three-page report by calling for support for Christian Crusade: "We have bared our breasts to the bullets of the enemy and to the attacks of the Liberal news media to get the truth out, and we are deserving of your support. This movement which presents God's side of the news . . . is deserving of support. . . ." [47]

Dr. Hargis continued to agonize over Nixon's political deviation, and late in February 1972, under a headline that cried, "Politicians Mislead the People," he summarized the sins of Richard Nixon:

His enthusiastic support for unilateral disarmament; his suicidal Red China policy; his blundering mistake in supporting pro-Red Chinese Pakistan in the Indian-Pakistan War; his determination to send military aid to avowed enemies, such as Communist Yugoslavia and Communist Chile, prove that the man had something in mind besides what benefits the nation.[48]

The Tulsa Crusader made it clear that he believed the President's "accommodation of the left-wing element and its goals" was a political maneuver. He wrote he was sorry he had not lived in the days of Teddy Roosevelt or other *nonprofessional politicians.* Said Hargis, "It would have been good to live in an era where the national president was dedicated to America's interest and not his own political future." [49]

President Nixon proceeded to journey to Peking very much as if he had never read Dr. Hargis' editorials. Associate minister David Noebel penned Christian Crusade's reaction to the trip in an article entitled "Fateful Week Changes Destiny of Mankind." We are witnessing, he wrote, the most unbelievable spectacle in history:

President Nixon, who just a few short years ago was involved in exposing Communist subversion in high places, is now seen applauding Chinese Communist theatrical performances where the Red flag (hammer and sickle and all) waves victorious over the dirty land-lord, and drinking toast after toast to Red leaders and "profound" Chou who stated at the Bandung Conference, "we Communists are atheists" and who helped assassinate and murder millions of fellow Chinese who did not wish to give up their lands and families to new god-Mao . . . Would our President wine and dine with Hitler? . . .[50]

Suddenly a new factor was added to the story of Nixon's ideological dereliction in the person of Dr. Henry Alfred Kis-singer. There had been copious hints that the leaders of Christian Crusade had long viewed Kissinger's influence on the President in a most baleful light. Much of the far right had already cast Kissinger in the role of a sinister Metternich, and the Birchers had fitted him for an Insider's shroud and referred to him as "Rasputin in the White House." On March 30, 1972, 36 con-servative Protestant church leaders were briefed at the White House by Dr. Kissinger. Soon after, Hargis announced that Christian Crusade had published a new book, *Henry Kissinger— Mystery Man of Power*. The new publication was really only a 32-page booklet; but it endorsed the idea that Kissinger's in-fluence was harmful to the Nixon administration.[51]

If Dr. Hargis was concerned about Henry Kissinger, he seemed doubly alarmed that the Presidential adviser was briefing the leaders of many of the conservative Protestant bodies that en-joyed the friendship of evangelist Billy Graham. And a very important group of evangelicals it was that gathered in Wash-ington, D.C. Even Oral Roberts was there, using his new title of "Doctor." The White House called the meeting a "foreign policy briefing," but Hargis noted that some observers had used other names to describe the gathering, among them "brain-washing":

A Bible-believing Christian Conservative, by definition, is anti-Communist, and therefore anti-Red China. (Mao, Chou, et. al.) And this effort by the White House and Dr. Kissinger is clearly geared to neutralize the strong, consistent, Conservative anti-Communists. Otherwise, why weren't the Hargises, McIntires, Noel Smiths, John R. Rices and Bob Joneses invited? In this hour, we need more Elijahs and fewer Obadiahs; more Amoses and fewer Amaziahs.[52]

What could Dr. Hargis do? Obviously he wanted very much to be invited to the White House briefing. The Rev. Carl Mc-Intire was literally screaming on his radio programs that Billy Graham could get into the White House almost any time he desired, while his own requests to see the President were ignored. But McIntire could hardly publish an issue of his *Christian Beacon* without at least mentioning and often criticizing Billy Graham. That was not true of Dr. Hargis' paper. There were usually very few references to the famous revivalist in Christian Crusade's literature. Not until after Dr. Hargis accepted McIntire's invitation to participate in the October 1970 march in Washington did Graham's name appear with any regularity in his newspaper. The atmosphere of competition between McIntire's march and the "Honor America" gathering organized by Billy Graham and Bob Hope had no doubt generated feelings that intensified the poor relationship between fundamentalists and evangelicals. The Tulsa radio preacher let his feelings appear in print a few weeks after Billy Graham made some remarks about rightists during his revival in New York City on June 24, 1970. Graham deplored the identification of patriotism with the political right, and said that the flag belonged to all Americans and that the word "patriot" had been taken over by the rightists. Dr. Hargis' strong rejoinder indicated that he had been stung rather sharply by Graham's observation:

Billy Graham knows, if anybody does, that the militant Left Wing in this country does not love our flag. Why he would side with the Left-Wing element in this country to attack the Conservatives and Right-Wingers because of their defense of the stars and stripes I do not know. However, I do know this—in order to get national favorable publicity on television, radio and the news media, you have to identify yourself with the middle-of-the-road or left-of-center. Once a man is outspokenly anti-Communist or Conservative, he can never expect privileged treatment from the Liberal news media again. Some people are willing to compromise with the Liberal news media in return for a kind word in the press, but I am not one of them." [53]

The rightist opposition to the presidential visits to China and Russia was becoming increasingly strident. But could the President be criticized without alienating those conservatives who remained loyal Nixon supporters? On May 14, 1972, Hargis' newspaper called Nixon's visit to China the political blunder of the twentieth century. But he noted that he had learned it was Chou En-lai's great respect for Henry Kissinger that got Nixon the invitation:

> As you recall, Kissinger worked out the details with Chou En-lai. In fact it was Henry Kissinger who, on the night before Nixon's departure from Red China, actually wrote the draft of the statement that betrayed Chiang Kai-shek and Taiwan. The press says he shuffled back and forth between the apartments of Chou En-lai and Richard Nixon with the draft (or joint declaration) until both men agreed to the terms. The result: a betrayal of Chiang Kai-shek. That is the only conclusion one can make of the matter.

Hargis now saw Kissinger in a more important position than the Secretary of State. In fact to the Tulsa evangelist he had become "the unconfirmed and unconstitutional prime minister of the United States." [54] On July 30 Hargis' paper contained about the last of his political speculating for the season. After that he appeared to go into a self-imposed ban on any political reporting that might be interpreted as the endorsement of a candidate. The Democratic Convention in Miami Beach was over, and Dr. Hargis took a look at their nominee. He found, for the most part, that McGovern's Miami Beach followers were some "clenched-fist fanatics with a few tired old ward healers thrown in for front dressing." "As far as the Democrat Party is concerned," said Hargis, "wiser and more mature heads have been replaced by anarchists, liberal Marxists and clenched-fist fanatics." As far as the Republican Party was concerned, he thought it was "headed by a well-intentioned man who sincerely wants to satisfy the public demands by insuring a decade of peace. . . ." He did not like Nixon's handling of the disarmament program, but "In all fairness, President Nixon has done everything he can do to prevent inflation and recession, and to give us wise and capable men on the United States Supreme Court . . ." [55]

From August until after the November elections, Dr. Hargis'

paper carried nothing that could be construed as a Christian Crusade endorsement of President Nixon. He was apparently still following the strategy he had adopted in 1964, since he attacked McGovern with vigor. He applied the Nixon treatment to John G. Schmitz, who had replaced the wounded George Wallace as spokesman for the American Party. A Bircher and personal friend of Dr. Hargis, Schmitz's articles had often appeared in the *Christian Crusade Weekly.*

At the national nominating convention of the American Party in Louisville in August 1972, a group of John Birch Society members demonstrated that they had effectively gained control of the party machinery. No attempt was made to "draft" the ailing Wallace, and Schmitz was nominated to head the American Party ticket. He had earlier lost his seat in the House of Representatives when he was defeated in a primary by a candidate who reportedly quit the Birch Society to cling to the President's coat tails. Publisher Tom Anderson was nominated to be Schmitz's running mate. Anderson has long been one of the most popular Birch writers and speakers.

The takeover of the American Party might have proved at least a temporary embarrassment to Robert Welch, who has always insisted that his Society is an educational rather than a political organization. It did not appear to have a similar effect on Dr. Hargis; his Christian Crusade literature was prominently displayed in the lobby of the convention headquarters.

But the most sensational publication at the Louisville convention was a book by Birch writer Gary Allen called *None Dare Call It Conspiracy.* Allen's book accused President Nixon of being a tool of "leftist international bankers," just as five other Presidents before him, both Republican and Democrat, were also alleged to have been controlled.

Earlier Dr. Hargis' bookstore had stocked Allen's *The Man Behind The Mask,* an anti-Nixon tome which advised Republicans to "swallow their pride and realize that they have been conned" about Richard Nixon. Dr. Hargis had once posed on the hump of a camel to advertise his overseas tours, but that was nothing compared to the delicate balancing performance he carried out during election year 1972. He appeared to attack

Kissinger enough to please his Nixon people. At the same time he successfully subscribed to the Bircher attack on the President, and even dared to invite author Gary Allen to speak in his Cathedral.

After election day the scope of the new Nixon trade policy with the Soviets became clear. There was the great sale of wheat, followed by a whole series of trade agreements between American businessmen and the Russians. Trade with the Soviets has always been viewed as something close to treason by most of the far right. Certainly it had been regarded as such by Dr. Hargis, who also taught that the free-enterprise system was ordained by God.

In November 1972 Nixon was reported to be in favor of Clarence Streit's old Atlantic Union idea, a proposal that the United States abrogate its sovereignty and join a political union with Western Europe. This would run counter to all that Dr. Hargis held dear in his Christian nationalist concepts. Hargis admitted, "Bible scholars are persuaded that formation of such a Union is nothing less than preparation for antichrist." With all that had happened, would Dr. Hargis still support the President?

In early December 1972 Dr. Hargis completed his analysis of the presidential election. After a world tour and talks with certain heads of state, he happily announced that the "Nixon landslide and historic world actions indicate an international move to the right." [56]

While Dr. Hargis refrained from direct political action during a large part of 1972, there was more than enough happening to keep him and his staff of Crusaders busy. One task that has never been completed is the mailing out of appeals for contributions. What is a routine procedure at most institutions that appeal to the public for support has been raised to the level of an art form at Christian Crusade. It is doubtful that any organization in the United States has focused such a wealth of time, effort and ingenuity on the problem of achieving maximum returns from postal solicitations. Even the most ordinary types of letters sent out by Christian Crusade are minor form-letter masterpieces. Most of them load down the opening sentences with shocking, attention-getting information; for example, a typical one may begin,

> Dear Mrs. Smith, I have just received some information about the security situation in this country . . . and believe me it is alarming. Since this matter concerns you and your loved ones, your future and theirs, I feel obligated to pass it on.

A few paragraphs later the Hargis letter may proclaim, "It's useless to make any plans beyond the next four years. You and I face the prospect of either being dead or behind barbed wire enclosures. That is, of course, unless something is done . . . unless the situation is reversed. ALARMING BUT TRUE. I HAVE THE PROOF."

Then comes the moment of truth: he has just published a book which he will send to the reader for any contribution to help carry on the work. "I must ask you to please MAKE A SACRIFICE, to please give. . . ." [57]

Another type of appeal by mail contains a flyer labeled "Free Book." To secure the free book one must complete and return the bottom portion of the flyer, which is worded in such a way that few people could send for the book without enclosing a contribution. The following quotation is an extract from a letter in which a heavily emotional plea is included: "I face a combined deficit for the two months of $73,322.28. THIS IS SERIOUS . . . If you don't help me NOW, I don't know what I'll do. A businessman in Tulsa told one of my associates, 'I appreciate what Brother Hargis is doing. Few men would be willing to take the knocks he has to take.' " [58]

Dr. Hargis uses different colors on his envelopes, and sometimes he may mail an appeal marked in bold red letters: "URGENT." On rare occasions he may send out first-class certified appeals, and has even resorted to mailing special delivery letters. Another refinement, placing him forever in the professional class, involves his use of yellow ruled tablet paper for correspondence. Sometimes the edges of this paper are torn or frayed. If a recipient of a Hargis special delivery letter dislikes being put to some trouble only to discover it is merely a request for money, his feelings may be assuaged somewhat by the sight of the ragged yellow paper. Has this poor man written on the last piece of paper left in his office? The opening sentence reaches out and rivets the reader's eyes to the page: "Dear Mrs. Smith: Please, for our Lord's sake, hear me out. Because of an emergency here, I have had to QUICKLY turn to my dearest friends."

Almost any frightening headline can be an excuse for Dr. Hargis to rush to the post office with another appeal for funds. Long-lasting national issues often call for more attention. The Tulsa Crusader may decide to publish one of his 30-page "books" on the subject.

A good example of the Hargis touch can be seen in his handling of the ecology issue. In general the whole far right was suspicious. Did the Earth Day ecology celebration on many campuses "just happen" to fall on Lenin's birthday? At the height of the controversy, Carl McIntire summed up the issue as most rightists saw it:

> Generally, it has been thought that the great emphasis upon ecology was a diversionary tactic to turn people's minds away from the war and what the Communists are doing throughout the world to take over. But now it is seen to be even deeper than that; it involves the rejection of Christianity and what is called the "Protestant ethic." [59]

Long before McIntire had even begun to sound the alarm about the ecology movement, Dr. Hargis had already very shrewdly discerned that the issue was going to be around for a long time and that most Americans did not put a left-wing or right-wing tag on clean water or unadulterated food. While McIntire was using headlines to announce that ecology was anti-Christian and mailing out literature to show that it was a one-world trap, Dr. Hargis had already put a hold order on certain anti-ecology remarks on his radio program and in his newspaper. Of course evangelist Hargis took a much narrower view of ecology than some environmentalists. He did not include over-population as part of the problem. And he did not rush out to call for the closing down of industries that pollute rivers and streams. He seemed to concentrate on good, healthy food. On that issue he even claimed a conservative priority:

It irritates me no end to see the left-wing element in our country all of a sudden claim that they initiated the concern for our natural resources. This has long been a Conservative objective. Conservative organizations have fought pollution and the poisoning of the atmosphere, and argued for the preservation of our wildlife before the Liberals were ever aware of what was happening.[60]

By July 1971 Dr. Hargis' radio programs were advertising an ecology program as part of the upcoming thirteenth annual Christian Crusade convention. And he was still protesting that ecology was a conservative issue. The speakers he invited were experts on nutrition and organically-grown foods, subjects of great interest to many of his older supporters. In a little while his bookstore would be stocked with a complete line of vitamins.[61]

If the Tulsa radio preacher's view of ecology was extremely limited, the very thought of the women's liberation movement was enough to bring his organization to alarm status. When momentum increased for ratification of the Equal Rights Amendment to the Constitution, he rallied his forces in opposition to women's lib. His headlines screamed a warning to "Beware of the Equal Rights Amendment," which he described as a move that would signal man's ultimate revolt against God and nature. "The ER Amendment will annul all laws against rape and white slavery which now apply to men," he wrote. In 1972 he assigned four of his leading associates to sum up his warning in a 29-page booklet called *Women's Lib: One-Way Street to Bondage.* There is no way to estimate how effective his crusade against the amendment has been, but Oklahoma was one of the first states that refused to approve it. He has mounted a big campaign against the ER Amendment and has made strong pleas for funds, as the following letter illustrates:

Dear Mrs. _____: I am writing you at this time about 24 words that could bring this nation to the brink of Hell. My language is strong, I know, but I am incensed. I wrote you previously about the sinister attack on the family. It is even more dastardly and coming sooner than I thought. How do you think I will react if my two younger daughters are drafted into military service when they reach

18, forced to live in the same barracks with male recruits and eventually assigned to combat duty? . . . .

Almost any topic having to do with sex has proved a popular subject with Dr. Hargis. Much of his concern centered on X-rated motion pictures, sex education in schools and the "sexual revolution." He was also concerned for some time with hair styles and the length of men's hair. When he called God's blessing down on the overthrow of Greek democracy in 1967, he applauded the orders by the dictatorship that banned miniskirts and forced young men to cut their hair. When writer Alan Bestic interviewed him in the early 1970s, he asked about Christian Crusade's famous stand for "soap and water, haircuts and dresses." Dr. Hargis explained, "Beards and long hair today represent another radical departure. Even dress has become revolutionary . . . Those who wear long hair and beards are aping Fidel Castro and Che Guevera."

As late as November 1971 he was still concerned about hair and served notice in his newspaper. "There is solid evidence from the ancient world which undercuts the degenerate idea abroad today that Jesus was a welfare case looking like a shiftless 'hippie.' If anyone can find any Biblical evidence that Jesus had long hair, please send it along." [62]

When the controversial rock musical *Hair* arrived in Tulsa, Christian Crusade launched a noisy campaign against the show. Associate Minister David Noebel got the nod from Dr. Hargis to supervise the effort, and so much clamor was generated by the combined voices of Christian Crusade, the local newspapers and a great many Tulsa preachers that outsiders were attracted to the battle. A "bawl and stomp" radio preacher from Ft. Smith, Arkansas, even journeyed to Tulsa to enter the lists against *Hair*. Noebel turned out another of the "sudden" Christian Crusade "books," an eleven-page publication he called *God's Answer to Hair*. Preacher Noebel, a devotee of the exotic theory that rock music kills house plants, while devotional music played in their presence makes them grow at a faster-than-normal rate, got off to a good start with his attack on *Hair*. But suddenly the local Ku Klux Klan unit outflanked him in the local press by trying to make citizens' arrests of cast members. Oddly enough, by August 1972, when Hargis was complaining about the "bearded weirdos" who supported Senator McGovern, one could visit the fourteenth annual Christian Crusade convention and see some strange sights. With the hair on his neck almost touching his collar and his huge sideburns down to his ear lobes, Dr. Hargis supervised a question-and-answer session led by Phillip Abbott Luce. Luce, a onetime Communist who is now a popular speaker on the far-right circuit, sported a mustache and bushy beard and wore his hair hippie-style, almost down to his shoulders. He delivered his speech to the convention dressed in a simple T-shirt. Even more shocking was an October 1972 report that one of Dr. Hargis' closest friends, General Edwin Walker, had grown a beard, a mustache and long hair.[63]

Christian Crusade was the first of the large organizations mixing right-wing politics with fundamentalist religion to react to the occult revival in America. Almost from the beginning of his fight against the metaphysical subculture, Rev. Hargis blamed the resurgence of interest in psychic phenomena and other elements of the occult on the liberals' cynicism toward God and disregard for Bible morality. He wrote, "The established churches (the National Council of Churches affiliates) and their preacher spokesmen are to blame for not checking the growth of the satanic occult by a truth exposure and a revival of the Christian fundamentals." [64]

The Tulsa Crusader published one of the biggest of his little books to kick off his opposition to the occult movement in 1971. He had assigned the writing task to the Rev. Jess Pedigo. Pedigo explained in his foreword that the millions of souls involved in the study of the occult included even professing Christians, ministers and religious leaders. Because of this crisis,

Dr. Billy James Hargis, Crusader extraordinary, has made known his own deep concern that this monstrous delusion should so engulf his beloved America, and should so invade his beloved church . . . Moved mightily by the spirit of God to strike hard at the forces that loom menacingly on the horizon, Dr. Hargis is determined that the horror shall be exposed, that the guileless cloak assumed by this new experimentation with the occult shall be pulled back strongly to reveal clearly the terror, the sure destruction of that one unfortunate enough to become involved.[65]

From the beginning of his book, Pedigo made clear that the whole range of the occult would come under the guns of Christian Crusade. All forms of extrasensory perception, or ESP, such as clairvoyance, precognition and telepathy would feel the ban, along with fortunetelling, palmistry, phrenology, magic, soothsaying, hypnotism, necromancy, spiritualism, witchcraft, the use of ouija boards and crystal balls and anything that paraded under the title of "psychic." For research and documentation in his little book, Pastor Pedigo relied on many sources, including *Time, Esquire,* the Los Angeles *Times,* and the New York *Times*—the kinds of publications that Dr. Hargis has attacked for years. But of course they were not to be considered harmful publications in his anti-occult book; there they are used as sources of truth.

Although Hargis began by attacking the whole occult movement, he very early concentrated his efforts against devil worship—Satanism. Although it is surrounded by frightening and sometimes secret rituals that have brought it much publicity, Satan worship actually constitutes one of the smallest elements in the entire occult movement. It may be that the Tulsa Crusader chose it because he felt it could more easily be allied to Marxism, even if he could effect such an alliance only through his own prediction:

> The ultimate in these black arts is Satan worship, which I predict will become the state religion of the youthful militant Marxist. Since Satan is undoubtedly the initiator of the antichrist Marxist revolution with its inherent atheistic, amoral, anarchistic philosophy, it stands to reason that Marxist devotees will ultimately accept a mass Satan worship attitude.[66]

Thus Pedigo's book opposing the occult was entitled *Satanism— Diabolical Religion of Darkness.* It struck hard at the devil worshipers and at almost all the other well-known dabblers in the occult. While it made mention of seeress Jeane Dixon, it also alluded to her regular church attendance and mentioned that she claimed to look to God for her knowledge. Apart from that brief passage only one other reference was made to the Washington, D.C. crystal-ball gazer and it was flattering. In a discussion of the many new participants in occult rites, Pedigo wrote, "Of course, any of them would give much to be in Jeane Dixon's category and have the world-wide acclaim that has been given to her for her predictions." [67]

Dr. Hargis has advertised Pedigo's anti-occult book by radio, mail and in every other possible way. He emphasized to his followers that he is terribly frightened of the rapidly mushrooming occult movement: "I didn't realize the devil had such a hold." His newspaper continues to carry articles that stress the danger to the church from the growing interest in things psychic, particularly Satanism. But he has never brought himself to attack the best-known figure in the whole occult movement, Jeane Dixon. Fundamentalist preachers all across the country have denounced her; Carl McIntire has attacked her. Even when newspapers revealed that one of the members of his American Christian College Board of Regents had publicly verified one of her predictions, Dr. Hargis remained silent. He continued to publish articles about witchcraft or Satanism cults that were springing up in New Jersey and California. At the same time Jeane Dixon was addressing overflow crowds in many cities of Dr. Hargis' home state. And not only did he remain silent, he even published an article about the activities of Martha Roundtree in the April 2, 1972, issue of his newspaper. Journalist Roundtree was closely allied with Jeane Dixon at one time and helped to publicize her psychic abilities. Dr. Hargis has even continued to publish articles by an Oklahoma City preacher who has distributed material on pyramidology and flying saucers, both bona fide elements of the occult. Ever more fiercely Dr. Hargis continues to warn of Satanism, even though there are still no organized devil worshipers in Tulsa. But down the street one of his favorite conservative newspapers carries Jeane Dixon's daily horoscope and features articles favorable to the growth of astrology. And all around his Cathedral the occult movement continues to flourish while the mighty scourge of apostate religion holds his fire. A little way from his headquarters are Rosicrucians, members of the Self-Realization Fellowship, Edgar Cayce's Association for Research and Enlightenment, the Japanese occult religions of Oomoto and Seicho-No-Ie. How long could he pretend to be fighting the occult?

Apart from his problems with the occult, Dr. Hargis has been extremely successful in many other phases of his work. If he is so inclined he can point to many of his once-virile enemies who are now little more than toothless tigers. The United Nations that he has inveighed against for a quarter of a century sits senescent and senile in its ivory tower on the East River. And early in 1973 one of his favorite papers, the Tulsa *Tribune,* examined the condition of the National Council of Churches and called it a "once powerful inter-church organization" that is now clinging to existence in a highly attenuated form, with "so little real power left it can't even stir up much controversy anymore." And from time to time on his radio broadcasts Dr. Hargis still refers indirectly to Oral Roberts and all the federal money invested in Oral Roberts University. He discovered that a professor from ORU had written an article in a Pentecostal periodical claiming that religious worship was being conducted freely and openly in Russia, Poland, Yugoslavia and several satellite countries. Hargis attacked that claim as most disturbing, noting that "Even the National Council of Churches, whose orientation is generally pro-Communist, has never to our knowledge, gone this far." He did not seem to be critical of Oral's television specials, unlike Carl McIntire, who called the Roberts shows "an offense to many since it manifests real swing and seeks to present Gospel rock." But Dr. Hargis devoted a large part of a radio program to covering an evangelical youth meeting held at Oral Roberts University. He bitterly condemned it. Among other things, he was displeased that the young people wanted the penalties relaxed against the use of marijuana. They also affirmed that modern war and the militaristic policies of national and international powers are un-Christlike.[68]

After so many years on the firing line, Dr. Hargis seems to be taking life just a little bit easier. And more and more he is receiving recognition from people and institutions in his adopted state. He was called upon to install the famous western singer

Bob Wills in the National Cowboy Hall of Fame. And in 1971 the Oklahoma Secretary of State officially bestowed on him the title of Oklahoma's Ambassador-at-Large. As a spokesman for "Christian Americans" he is considered by one of the leading Oklahoma City newspapers to be "a potent force in state politics." [69] He has always claimed that he has no political ambitions, but on his July 14, 1971, radio broadcast he disclosed that he has had offers in the past from two political parties to be a candidate for Vice-President. He is now grooming his son for the future leadership role at Christian Crusade. If the predictions of some analysts come true, and the United States moves still farther to the right, the professional politicians may need a man with Dr. Hargis' charisma and unique background. In terms of national politics he is still relatively young. Perhaps he will be available a few years from now.

Not long ago Dr. Hargis complained that of the 28 books that have had something to say about Christian Crusade, all but one were critical. And he did not seem very pleased that Pulitzer Prize-winning David Brion Davis had classified him as a "paranoid of American history." These were probably low moments when he had momentarily forgotten about telling the public that he welcomed adverse criticism.

But in other ways he is obviously happier and more content than ever. It even appears that Dr. Hargis has decided to settle down in his beloved Tulsa. In the early 1970s he told an interviewer, "The house we live in belongs to the Crusade. It cost only $40,000 and in the United States that's a shack. The average home in Tulsa costs $70,000. My wife's tired of living in someone else's house. We'd like to have a home of our own. We really would, you know, somewhere we could change the color of the wall, if we felt like it." [70] And he finally found a house. The Oklahoma *Journal* disclosed that the Church of the Christian Crusade had purchased a home for its president and founder, Dr. Billy James Hargis. The unusual hilltop house, located in Tulsa's Executive Estates, had been listed at $500,000, but records indicate that a sale had been effected at a lower cost. The multilevel home has a white marble exterior, 11,000 square feet of floor space and four complete bedroom suites with separate entries. The *Journal* also revealed that the home offers a heated, indoor swimming pool, a 40-foot game room and an 85-foot sundeck. Also included are two basements, a fallout shelter and more than 90 telephone outlets.[71]

From time to time visitors traveling through Tulsa stop to look at Dr. Hargis' beautiful Cathedral of the Christian Crusade, just off busy Sheridan Boulevard. Early in 1973 some visitors browsing through the Christian Crusade bookstore discovered that the controversial anti-Nixon book, *None Dare Call It Conspiracy*, was still for sale. But the main topic of interest had shifted somewhat from politics. Dr. Hargis was excited about finding Noah's ark high upon a mountain in Turkey.

Across the road they could see Dr. Hargis himself. His long black hair was blowing in the Oklahoma wind as he consulted with some of his staff about the big buses parked in the Cathedral driveway. He smiled and waved and then shook hands. He seemed very happy indeed.

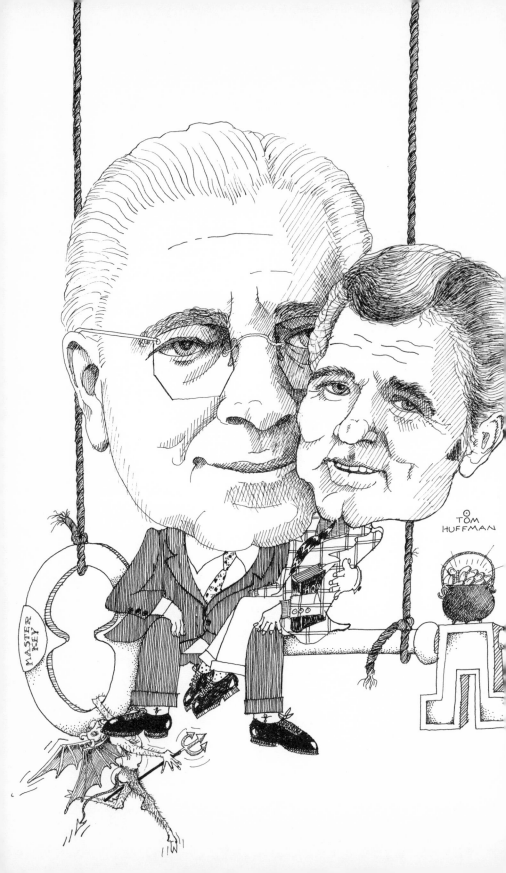

MASTER KEY

TOM
HUFFMAN

VIII
The Armstrongs

"Lean-look'd prophets whisper fearful change."
—Shakespeare, *Richard II*

The Pasadena Prophets

"What's it all coming to? I've been telling you that world-renowned scientists say publicly that they are frightened when they look into the future . . . And they say now that it is possible to blast all life—all plant life, animal life and all human life—off the planet that you live on. Now, my friends, we're coming to the place that unless something happens to stop it, your children, your grandchildren, won't be existing on this earth, nor will you, very much longer. . . ." [1]

That doomsday message was broadcast to a significant part of the world's population in early March 1972 by Herbert W. Armstrong, Chairman of the Worldwide Church of God, one of the largest religious organizations ever established by one man during his lifetime. Through radio, television and large-space advertising in mass-circulation magazines and newspapers, Armstrong claims to be reaching 150,000,000 people with what he calls "the inspired message of the way of life that is the cause of all good—of peace, happiness, prosperity, abundant well-being —the truly successful life." [2] The dynamic Herbert Armstrong and

319

his handsome and articulate son, Garner Ted, direct the world-wide outreach of a rapidly growing church whose annual budget is counted in tens of millions of dollars. The Armstrong operating fund is perhaps twice that of the huge Billy Graham Evangelistic Association, and several times that of the Oral Roberts empire, the only two independent evangelistic organizations of comparable size.

While Herbert Armstrong and his son hurry about the world with their message of a wonderful new world waiting just around the corner, other preachers are busily engaged in attacking the Gospel according to Armstrong as a radical deviation from orthodox evangelical Protestantism. But many of them find Armstrong *père* and *fils* so interesting and parts of their message so attractive that the pages of their reviews are often laced with as much praise as condemnation. One minister confessed, "Humanly speaking, if I were not a Christian, I would quickly join the Armstrong Radio Church of God and attend his college. For it has everything this world has to offer." [3] Another preacher strongly opposed to Armstrong's religious views wrote, "It is plain that Herbert W. Armstrong is no ordinary man. It is plain that he must not only be a man of extraordinary business acumen and administrative abilities, he must also be a man of fiscal integrity and responsibility. He is certainly a man I should like to have as a customer were I a businessman and sold products or services that he used." [4] And one of the leading evangelical periodicals devoted almost as much space to praising the virtues of Armstrong as it used to show that his prophetic role is a rejection of the wise counsel of Christianity's greatest interpreters: "In a time of cynical repudiation of moral values, Armstrong has vigorously affirmed the old-fashioned Christian and American virtues of honor, reverence, patriotism, thrift, integrity, chastity, and temperance. Thus he has gained the sympathy and support of vast numbers of the so-called silent majority." [5]

The man whose work is so widely respected that critics often find him as likable as do his supporters, is now in his eighties. He has turned over most of the regular radio and television broadcasting duties to his son, Garner Ted. But compared to most men half his age, Herbert Armstrong is still a human dynamo; he constantly travels about the world, visiting heads of state and directing his church programs in some of the farthest corners of the world.

Armstrong's seemingly magic formula for attracting followers in almost unheard-of numbers is actually quite simple: a gloom-and-doom message supposedly prophesied in the Scriptures, delivered with an urbane professionalism that moves all but the well-informed and the very sophisticated to the edge of despair. This is followed with the promise of a "wonderful world of tomorrow," a bright and shining utopia without poverty, war or disease, which lies only a few short years ahead, so near that most of those receiving his message can be assured that they will live to see this promised land. Many people are first attracted to Armstrong's radio and television messages by the articulate, highly polished manner in which the problems of the world are discussed. In recent years it has been almost exclusively Garner Ted who broadcasts the daily alarms: wars and rumors of wars, worldwide changes in weather patterns, including floods, tornadoes and droughts, ecological disasters, overpopulation, earthquakes, famines, spiritual degeneration, moral decay and the decline of the church's influence in everyday life. The 30-minute programs are delivered by the father or son in a fast-paced discussion spiced with just enough statistics and humor to make them lively, entertaining periods of learning. They are short capsules of information served up in a highly enjoyable manner by the Armstrongs, two of the finest voices in broadcasting.

Another impressive feature of the Armstrong radio and television programs is the absence of any appeals for money. Pleas for financial assistance from all kinds of charitable organizations pour forth continually from radio and television spokesmen, and radio preachers are sometimes regarded as the modern counterpart of the mendicant friars. The Armstrongs not only refuse to ask for contributions on the air, they also offer their monthly magazine, numerous booklets and a Bible correspondence course without charge. Indeed, the Armstrongs advertise that you cannot pay for literature under any circumstances. Says Armstrong senior, "Our mail-opening staff is instructed to return your money if you try."

Herbert W. Armstrong was born in Des Moines, Iowa, on July 31, 1892. He grew up in the Quaker Church of his parents, and at age 16 he first felt the urge to "become somebody important." Before that he had been only an average student, but after his awakening he started spending extra hours at the public library, forming a lifelong habit of study. At age 18 he decided to forego formal education for a career in advertising.

During the next 16 years he enjoyed several periods of success in business. He traveled, became a successful copywriter and rubbed elbows with some of the elite of the literary and business worlds. But at the end of those 16 years, he found himself in Portland, Oregon, with his third business failure behind him, unemployed and on the brink of poverty. In such circumstances he soon lost the last vestiges of his "cocky and self-confident" attitude. Years later he decided that he was being "softened" for an unconditional surrender to God:

> It seemed, indeed, as if some invisible and mysterious hand were causing the earth to simply swallow up whatever business I started. And indeed, that is precisely what was happening! God was knocking me down! But I was not yet out!

A little earlier, while visiting his parents in Salem, Oregon, his wife had become acquainted with an elderly lady who was an avid student of the Bible. Mrs. Armstrong had been an active Methodist most of her life and retained a deep interest in Bible study. Under the aegis of the elderly scholar she learned, among other things, that she had been worshiping on the wrong day of the week. Saturday, she discovered, was the true Sabbath.

Mrs. Armstrong was delighted with the results of her study, but Herbert decidedly was not. It was a clear case of religious fanaticism, he concluded. In his business world such attitudes carried a stigma. What would his friends and former business associates think? Unable to convince his wife of her error, he determined angrily to prove by the Bible that all the big churches couldn't be wrong about the Sabbath. Temporarily out of a job and with little to do but read, he set out on a "virtual night-and-day, seven-days-a-week study" of the Bible. Six months later he emerged from his labors to concede that he had failed to prove his wife wrong. To those who consider his training in the Bible rather brief, he points out,

> I studied the Commentaries. I studied the Lexicons and *Robertson's Grammar of the Greek New Testament.* Then I studied history. I delved into encyclopedias—the Britannica, the Americana, and several religious encyclopedias. I searched the *Jewish Encyclopedia,* and the *Catholic Encyclopedia.* I read Gibbon's *Decline and Fall of the Roman Empire,* especially his chapter 15 dealing with the religious history of the first four hundred years after Christ . . . I left no stone unturned.[6]

He had not only discovered that Saturday was the Sabbath; he had also found that the theory of evolution was false. And he had proved the divine inspiration of the Bible and found absolute proof of the existence of God. Now that he had made these discoveries, he was faced with the "greatest inner battle" of his life. He had to accept these truths, and that meant cutting himself off from all his former friends, acquaintances and colleagues:

> I had come to meet some of the independent "Sabbath-keepers" down around Salem and the Williamette Valley. Some of them were what I then, in my pride and conceit, regarded as backwoods "hillbillies." None were of the financial and social position of those I had associated with . . . My associations and pride had led me to "look down upon" this class of people. I had been ambitious to hobnob with the wealthy and the cultural [*sic*] . . . To accept this truth meant to throw in my lot for life with a class of people I had always looked on as inferior. . . .

The great change in Armstrong's life as a result of his study occurred in early 1927. After more study and work he was ordained by, and under the authority of, the Oregon Conference of The Church of God.

In 1933 the Rev. Herbert Armstrong lectured to little groups in a country schoolhouse near Eugene, Oregon. He started a radio broadcast early in 1934, and he began to turn out a little mimeo-graphed publication called *Plain Truth*.

Early in his career Armstrong disclosed that he was a devotee of the quasi-historical theory known as British Israelism. Belief in this creed did more to shape Armstrong's career than anything else in his life. The British-Israel theory travels in various parts of the world under a variety of names, such as Anglo-Israelism, Destiny of America, Celto-Saxon and the Kingdom Message. British-Israelism holds that the Anglo-Saxon peoples are the descendants of the ten lost tribes of Israel, and as such are heirs to the biblical promises God made to ancient Israel. The ten tribes were taken captive by the Assyrians in the eighth century B.C. and thereafter disappeared from history. What happened to them? Were they gradually assimilated into the Assyrian population? No, insist the British Israelites, who through the years have advanced a number of complicated theories to account for the disappearance of the ten tribes. Armstrong holds that after several generations of slavery, during which time they lost their national identity, the descendants of the ten tribes migrated to Europe along with the Assyrians sometime before 604 B.C. They moved through what is now the Ukraine and Poland into the territory of modern Germany. Armstrong teaches that the descendants of those Assyrians are the Germans of today. He also believes that the Israelites did not remain the slaves of the Assyrians in Europe; they migrated to Western Europe, the Scandinavian peninsula and the British Isles.[7]

The Armstrong doctrine holds that descendants of the ten tribes retained some marks of their Hebrew culture. He points out that "berith" or "b'rith" in Hebrew means "covenant," and "ish" means "man." Thus, in Hebrew, "British" is said to mean "covenant man." He claims also that the House of Israel was prophesied to lose its identity and its name. From the Old Testament he cites God's promise to Abraham, "In Isaac shall thy seed be called," and in Amos 7:16, a reference to "the House of Isaac." Thus, the descendants of the ten tribes were Isaac's sons. By dropping the "I" from "Isaac," Armstrong discovered "Saac's sons," or in more modern spelling, "Saxons."

As further proof that the ten tribes migrated from ancient Assyria to northwest Europe, Armstrong points to the signs and "waymarks" left along the trail by the tribe of Dan. Observing that the word "Dan" might be pronounced in English as "Dan," or "Den," or "Din," or "Don," or "Dun," he claims that the tribe left its calling card in the Spanish peninsula in "Me-*din*-a Si-*don*-ia." From Irish annals and history he purports to demonstrate that the settlers of Ireland were called "Tuatha de Danaans," meaning "Tribe of Dan." He points to the tribe's mark in such names as "*Dans*-Laugh," "*Dun*-drum," "*Don*-egal Bay," "*Don*-egal City," "Lon*don*-derry," and "*Din*-gle." Along the tribe's route near the Black Sea he finds their mark in Mace-*don*-ia and Dar-*dan*-elles, and in the names of rivers like the *Dan*-ube and the Don. In the British Isles he locates E-*din*-burgh and Lon-*don*, along with a host of other Dans, Dons and Duns.[8]

Another important part of Armstrong's version of British Israelism is based on the Biblical promises God made to ancient Israel. If Israel obeyed His ordinances, its people would inherit the Birthright blessings. God would bless their land; they would become prosperous and powerful. Armstrong interprets a number of Scriptural passages to show that the House of Israel was not Jewish. The term "Jew" was a nickname for "Judah"; it applied only to the people in the southern kingdom of Judah. The people of the ten-tribed northern kingdom, the House of Israel, were not Jews. Therefore, he contends,

> . . . It is wrong to call the Jews of today "Israel." They are not Israel—they are JUDAH! And wherever ISRAEL is today, remember that ISRAEL does not mean JEW! Whoever the lost ten tribes of ISRAEL are today, they are not Jews! Wherever you see the name "Israel," or "House of Israel," or "Samaria," or "Ephraim," used in prophecy, remember this—IT NEVER REFERS TO THE JEWS. . . .[9]

Armstrong deftly turns a people into two different races: those of the southern kingdom are Jews and those in the northern kingdom become Gentiles. "This distinction is vital, if we are to understand prophecy. Because most so-called Bible students are in ignorance of this basic distinction, they are unable rightly to understand prophecy!"

Having turned ten tribes of Jews into Gentiles and marched
them thousands of miles from the Black Sea to the valley of the
Thames, Preacher Armstrong still needed to explain how these
Anglo-Saxon people could be ruled by a continuation of the bib-
lical House of David. Through biblical interpretation he postu-
lated that the prophet Jeremiah and his secretary Baruch made a
trip to Ireland. Accompanying the prophet was the daughter of
King Zedekiah of Judah, "and therefore heir to the throne of
David," who was given in marriage by Jeremiah to the son of the
King of Ireland. Thus was the throne of David established in
Ireland. Armstrong shows that the throne was later overturned
and replanted in Scotland, in keeping with prophecy. Still later
another prophecy was fulfilled when the throne was established
once more in England. Armstrong boldly states that "this same
dynasty continues today in the reign of Queen Elizabeth II." He
goes on to assert that "when Christ returns to sit on that throne,
He shall take over a live, existing throne, not a nonexistent one." [10]
Armstrong's procrustean historical and genealogical manipulation,
that places the Queen of England on the throne of the House of
David, requires some documentation. And he is able to offer a
most singular genealogical chart that not only supports the claims
made for the royal family of Britain, but also shows that Armstrong himself is descended from British kings:

> The Royal Family of the British Commonwealth possesses a chart
> showing its ancestry, every generation, back . . . to Zedekiah, on
> back to David, and thru the scriptural genealogy clear to Adam!
> The writer has a copy of this chart, and also his own genealogy for
> each generation back into the line of ancient British kings, and
> therefore has the complete record of his genealogy thru the House
> of David clear to Adam—believe it or not! [11]

Herbert Armstrong contends that the Birthright blessing was
withheld for 2,520 years because of the disobedience of Israel.
It was bestowed once more on the descendants of the ten lost
tribes, the Anglo-Saxon peoples, in 1800 A.D. Specifically, it was to
go to the descendants of the tribes of Ephraim and Manasseh.
And further study of the Old Testament convinced Armstrong

that Ephraim is the Biblical name for England and Manasseh stands for the United States.

Having identified Ephraim and Manasseh as Britain and the United States, he announced that "the lost master key has been found." The missing key, he said, was the identity of the great world powers in biblical prophecy. Now that he had found that key he could make known the secrets locked in the prophecies of the Bible.

> . . . approximately a third—*grasp this!* an entire third—of our Maker's revelation to mankind is devoted to infallible prophecy—writing the history of future events, before they occur. These foretold future events reveal the Great Purpose being worked out—being brought to its completion!

The heads of state, news analysts and the great minds of our times do not comprehend the real meaning of world events, declared Armstrong. But world conditions are "plainly described in the voluminous prophecies of the Bible." With his key he can discover the advance news of what is certain to occur. But are these old prophecies, addressed mainly to the ancient nation Israel, applicable to our times and problems? Yes, insists Armstrong. "The plain truth is, these prophecies were written for our people or our time, and for no previous people or time! They pertain to world conditions of today, and could not have been understood until today!"

Where did Herbert Armstrong find the "lost master key" that he believed unlocked the secret identity of the great nations in biblical prophecy? It may be easily verified that the British-Israelite theory had been in existence for more than a century when Armstrong began his Bible study in the 1920s.

Mysteries such as the supposed survival of the lost tribes have an almost hypnotic appeal for the human mind. Over the centuries the tribes have been "discovered" in innumerable guises and countries—as Tartars and Indians, in the Sahara and Afghanistan, in Japan and China. "No race has escaped the honor, or suspicion, of being descendants from the subjects of Jeroboam," wrote the British historian A. M. Hyamson. They were even supposedly involved in the destruction of Atlantis. Such names as Cotton

Mather, William Penn, Czar Nicholas I and Joseph Smith appear among those who have given credence to the tales about the lost tribes. Some remarkable stories have been told. Eldad Hadani, the ninth century charlatan, set his contemporaries agog with tales about the tribe of Dan. He told of the Sabbath River, which imprisoned the Levitical descendants of the tribes. This river flowed six days of the week only and was impassable because of its breadth and ferocity. On the seventh day, when it was still, it was ringed with fire and was unapproachable. The historian N. McLeod "proved" in his *Epitome of the Ancient History of Japan* that the Shinto religion was a lineal development of the Israelite religion and that the first king of Japan, Osee, was none other than Hoshea, biblical king of Israel, who had gone into exile. Thus, claimed McLeod, the Japanese were descended from the ten lost tribes.[12]

Movements and groups claiming to be the ten lost tribes have existed on every continent since the Middle Ages. One that is still active is the Ahmadiya sect in Pakistan, founded by Mirza Ghulam Ahmad, who was born in the Punjab in 1839. In the West Indies another movement, the Ras Tafari, teaches that Negroes are the descendants, or at least reincarnations, of the lost tribes.[13] One of the most interesting theories holds that Christopher Columbus was a converted Jew who went to America to seek the ten lost tribes of Israel. And an occult group, the Light Affiliates of British Columbia, publishes messages received by "telethought" for members of the ten lost tribes.

The basic doctrines of the British-Israelite creed can be traced to a book written in 1649 by an Englishman named John Sadler. Although he did not fully develop the theory, he planted the idea that the people of England might be descended from the ten lost tribes of Israel. Some scholars point to another Englishman, Richard Brothers, as the man who did more than anyone else to start the Anglo-Israelite message around the world. Brothers was born in Newfoundland in 1757 and served in the British navy until he was 30 years old. In 1787 he began distributing pamphlets in London that marked him as a religious fanatic. As a self-styled "Prince of the Hebrews," Brothers demanded that George III abdicate the throne in his favor. He was arrested for treason, but was judged to be insane and was committed to a London asylum for a number of years. Although he died in poverty, his ideas captured the imagination of several people in positions of influence, including at least one member of Parliament. Brothers' ideas were modified and embellished for another century before they found their way to Herbert W. Armstrong.

Today the people best known for their genealogical claims on the ten tribes are those affiliated with the British Israel World Federation. With headquarters in London, it has branches in Canada, the United States, Australia, New Zealand, Rhodesia and South Africa.

There was no significant British-Israel movement in the United States until the late 1920s, when Howard B. Rand, a New England Bible scholar, started to propagate an Anglo-Israel message.[14] As the creed moved throughout the country it gained tens of thousands of adherents, especially in the South, along the Pacific coast and in western Canada. Although many new organizations were formed, the Anglo-Israelite movement—many preferred to drop the word "British"—grew mainly as a movement of individual converts. Many fundamentalist ministers adopted the Kingdom Message and used it in their interpretation of the Scriptures. But some Anglo-Israelite pastors have embraced the chosen-people theory so fiercely that they have sometimes been accused of lending support to organized bigotry.

During the late 1920s and early 1930s, the years when Herbert W. Armstrong was shaping his eclectic religious philosophy, the British-Israel creed took strong root in the Pacific Northwest. It fell on fertile ground in Oregon and Washington, and dozens of Anglo-Israel organizations sprang up. Spreading the Kingdom Message almost in Armstrong's back yard was the Anglo-Saxon Christian Association of Portland, Oregon. And nearby were large Kingdom Message congregations in Tacoma and Spokane, Washington. These groups published magazines, tracts and pamphlets and sponsored radio broadcasts to disseminate a racist Anglo-Israelite message. Although some of these organizations sponsored broadcasts in Armstrong's area, there is no evidence that he became acquainted with British Israelism from these sources. It should also be made clear that racism has never played a part in

the ministry of Herbert W. Armstrong. Indeed, it is probably because he has generally avoided arguments and discussions about
race and politics that he now broadcasts over the world's largest
Gospel network, while those who supported overt racism have
long since been forgotten. On the other hand, his message has
always been strongly conservative, and he emphasizes that white,
English-speaking people are God's chosen people:

> On the world scene NOTHING is so important, right now, as to know
> where the white, English-speaking peoples are identified in scores
> and hundreds of prophecies—prophecies which describe vividly our
> sudden rise to national power and reveal the causes of that great-
> ness . . . It is our peoples who have been like a "lion" among the
> other nations of the earth—preserving in two great World Wars the
> peace of the world and stability for all human life on this planet! [15]

Even though he considers the white, English-speaking peoples
the chosen of God, Herbert Armstrong has never vilified other
races: "God is concerned about the people and races we have
called 'heathen.' They, too, are human. They, too, are made in
God's own likeness, with potential of being molded into God's
spiritual and character image."

Armstrong and his son Garner Ted insist that they do not
propagate the theory of British Israelism. On his July 10, 1971,
broadcast over the powerful Mexican station XEG, Garner Ted
Armstrong denied that he was "a British Israelite, whatever that
is." He added that he had not looked into what a British Israelite
stood for. An inquiry directed to the personal correspondence
department of the Armstrong organization in Pasadena, California, elicited a response that did include a definition of the British-
Israel creed:

> . . . Those who adhere to British Israelism believe that the English-
> speaking peoples of Britain and America are the modern-day de-
> scendants of Joseph [father of Ephraim and Manasseh] . . . Many
> people who know the identity of modern Israel believe that they
> are especially favored by God simply because they are His people.
> While we know that America and Britain are God's chosen people,
> the Bible also shows that God will punish us all the more because

we should know better than to disobey Him. Therefore, the only
thing we have in common with British Israelism is knowing the
identity of modern Israel.[16]

The supporters of the bizarre British-Israel theory are seldom
dissuaded by the opinions of reputable scholars. Historians have
called their arguments for the Kingdom Message everything from
highly improbable to fantastic. Ethnologists have pointed out that
ancient Israel's most distinctive customs of ritual cleanness and
seventh-day worship were not observed by the Angles, Saxons,
Jutes or Normans. Expert philologists have shown that there are
no possible links in vocabulary, grammar or syntax between the
Semitic language of the ten tribes and the Low or High German
of the Teutons. Use of the Oxford English Dictionary is the quickest method of exploding the philological balloons of the adherents
to the Anglo-Israel theory.[17]

Many years after Armstrong discovered the Kingdom Message,
a critic referred to his British Israelism as "the calliope of Herbert
W. Armstrong's carnival of religion." [18] But that was hardly true
in the early days of his ministerial career. The Church of God,
with headquarters in Stanberry, Missouri (now Denver, Colorado), the original parent body of the Oregon Conference of the
Church of God, rejected Armstrong's British Israelism. He claimed
later that the Stanberry headquarters privately confessed they
were teaching an error after he sent them proof of his argument.
He also maintained that Elder A. N. Duggar of that church admitted that the truth of United States and British identity had
been revealed to Armstrong.[19]

Following his ordination in June 1931, the Rev. Herbert Armstrong conducted evangelistic campaigns with other ministers.
His disillusionment with the tactics employed by some of his colleagues in these services became so great that he finally decided
to leave the church. One preacher he worked with was a secret
believer in Pentecostalism, and another deserted him in the midst
of a campaign. He was plagued by Pentecostals interrupting his
services, turning one meeting into a bedlam of din and confusion
created by women "who wailed and shrieked like a fire siren,
audible for three or four blocks," huge fat women who jerked in
staccato steps, or danced a jig, arms floundering wildly overhead,

"fat hips waddling and shimmying." There was also a plot to discredit his wife with a false accusation. And another minister tried to prevent Armstrong's articles from appearing in a church magazine. Finally he was accused by ministers of baptizing converts before they were properly instructed and warned about eating pork. In August 1933 he severed all direct connection with the Church of God and entered the independent evangelistic field.

A few weeks later, on October 21, 1933, a new, independent Church of God was organized by approximately 20 of his friends, who named him pastor. Even though they were passing through the worst part of the Depression, the energetic Armstrong began to expand his new ministry. Earlier he had taken advantage of an offer of free radio time on the local 100-watt station KORE in Eugene, Oregon. Armstrong was determined to put his message on radio, and he soon found eight "co-workers," who pledged a total of $5.50 to help him start. It was the tiny mustard seed from which a mighty work would grow. And it was not an inconsiderable sum for those Depression days: the average monthly cost for broadcasting each Sunday was $10.83. On the first Sunday of 1934, at 10 A.M., he started the "Radio Church of God" program. It has been on the air continuously ever since.

On his first broadcast Armstrong invited listeners to write for a copy of *Plain Truth* magazine. Like most independent evangelists, he considered a magazine one of the most important parts of a successful ministry. However, he had to be content with a few copies of a rather amateurish product for a while. Sometime later in 1934, he was able to spend $10 for an old hand-operated neostyle, a predecessor of the mimeograph, which he used to turn out copies of his little magazine.

The third part of Armstrong's "Three-Point-Campaign" started in April 1934 with an evangelistic service in downtown Eugene, Oregon. His ministry had begun, however shaky and insecure its financial underpinning might be.

Church members who volunteered to support Armstrong's work were called "co-workers." One exception to that rule was made for those radio listeners who sent in offerings or tithes at least twice during a six-month period. He also considered these people co-workers and made them acquainted with the financial needs of his work.[20]

But few of the many listeners to his programs became co-workers. Early in his radio ministry he discovered "a peculiar paradox." He learned that people would listen to radio sermons which they would not tolerate from their own ministers. They would listen avidly to such preaching, but they would not support it. There are millions, Armstrong says, who will never listen to "the last Gospel warning" in any way except over the radio. And through the years his programs were molded to broadcast a message "pointed toward the non-church-going public—people who are not religious and may never attend church."

Herbert Armstrong's message to his radio audience was in his discussions of where the world stood in the march of prophesied events. His master key enabled him to predict these events in advance. His detractors generally described Armstrongism as an eclectic amalgam of British Israelism, Seventh-Day Adventism, Mormonism and Russellism (Jehovah's Witnesses).

The spread of British Israelism in the United States during the 1920s increased the interest in such biblical prophecy. Armstrong went on the radio less than a year after Hitler's rise to power in Germany, a time when many preachers already believed that Mussolini was the Antichrist. Armstrong wrote in 1936 that Fascism was merely ". . . Romanism—the once mighty Roman Empire—being revived and brought once more to life under the satanic leadership of the world's most dynamic personality, Benito Mussolini." [21] He had warned his radio listeners about the prophesied resurrection of the Roman Empire since his first years on the air. In the February-March 1939 issue of *Plain Truth*, Armstrong's master key allowed him to explain how the United States and Britain had received the Birthright, the blessings God promised Abraham. But the Anglo-Saxon peoples had sinned since receiving the inheritance—they had turned from God, and now, said Armstrong, God would punish Britain and America at "the hand of this coming resurrected Roman Empire, with invasion, captivity and slavery." He called Mussolini's fascist state a partial fulfillment of the prophecy, but later, in 1961, he wrote,

This tremendous prophecy was fulfilled, in the form of the insignifi-
cant "sixth head of the Beast," by Mussolini . . . But the all-
important seventh and last "head" is being formed, today, before
our very eyes! It is rising out of the Common Market in Europe—
out of which ten nations or groupings of nations will combine to
form a new U.S. of Europe.[22]

During 1935 Armstrong continued to turn out his tiny *Plain
Truth* magazine for a mailing list that grew along with his radio
audience. He also conducted more evangelistic meetings, often
some distance from his home. His income was very small during
those years. Often he lived near the edge of poverty. In the latter
part of 1935 he had an estimated listening audience of 10,000, but
his income was only about $45 per month.[23]

In November 1936, almost three years after he started on the
air, Armstrong expanded his radio outreach by securing a telephone connection to stations KXL in Portland and KSLM in
Salem, Oregon. Soon he made plans to extend the broadcast into
the state of Washington, and in September 1937 he went on
KWJJ, a 500-watt station in Portland.

His ministry was growing, but he was still in "the lean years."
He complained that only one in ten of those on his *Plain Truth*
mailing list ever sent him a contribution. This ratio would remain
about the same throughout his career. In 1961, when the number
of people receiving *Plain Truth* had grown to approximately
300,000, the number of co-workers supporting him was only
29,000.[24]

When World War II broke out, Armstrong speculated that one
of two things might happen. Either the Allies might go on to
smash Hitler, possibly with the help of either or both the United
States or Italy; or Armstrong thought that Italy might yet enter
the war on the side of Germany—the battle sector shifting at once
to the Mediterranean, especially Egypt and Palestine.[25] He apparently could not use his master key, for he stated that World
War II was not specifically mentioned in the Scriptures. It is
somewhat puzzling that Armstrong's prophecies contained so
much detail about the Anglo-Saxon peoples, but did not refer to
the greatest war in history.

In 1942 Armstrong's radio ministry expanded north to Spokane

and south to Hollywood. And he started broadcasting for the first
time on a superpower, clear-channel station, WHO in Des Moines.
One of his programs over that station brought in a record 2,200
letters from listeners. Next he arranged to broadcast from another
clear-channel, 50,000-watt station, WOAI in San Antonio. By
1943 Armstrong's message was heard from coast to coast.

With his increasing prosperity, Armstrong reported a wave of
persecution. He claimed that the persecution came mostly from
"organized religion." [26] But it was not the last time he would report such opposition. He wrote in his autobiography,

> I am going to be forced to recount for my readers some of the great
> amount of opposition and persecution that has been thrown at me
> and at God's work by preachers, ministers, and evangelists. I do not
> wish to defame their characters. Yet the facts must be related . . .
> I actually believe that some of the lying, deceitful, underhanded and
> dirty political tricks that have confronted this Work since I was
> plunged into it have been instigated by men who had somehow con-
> vinced themselves that they were "doing God service." . . . I won-
> dered what I would do when I came to this part of my life history
> where church officials and preachers began using deceitful and foul
> means to discredit the work God was doing through me—to steal the
> "flock" or, like hungry wolves, to devour the sheep God had given
> for my labors, and spiritually kill the shepherd. . . .[27]

By 1944 the circulation of *Plain Truth* had increased to 35,000,
and the magazine had virtually outgrown the facilities of the local
printing company in Eugene, Oregon. This problem plus the
availability of top-quality sound recording facilities in Hollywood
caused Armstrong to begin thinking about moving his headquarters to southern California.

In August of that year he put his program, now called "The
World Tomorrow," on the 100,000-watt station XELO in Juarez,
Mexico, across the Rio Grande from El Paso, Texas. At night
XELO could reach every state and even into Canada, but Arm-
strong worried about going on the station. One of the partners
who ran XELO had once operated the 250,000-watt station in
Mexico that broadcast the programs of the notorious goat-gland
specialist, Dr. John Brinkley.

I was not very happy about the company I was going to have to keep
on this Mexican station—programming which never would have been
acceptable on most United States stations—and religious programs of
a nature I most certainly did not want to be identified with.[28]

His audience continued to increase at the rate of 30 per cent
each year. The year 1945 was very important for Armstrong, but
1946 was called the "year of Beginnings as an organized major
national and world-wide work." It was the year in which he
started his own printing department, and when three superpower
radio stations blanketed the entire United States and parts of
Canada and Alaska with his message. And it was the year in
which Armstrong founded Ambassador College in Pasadena, California.

More and more he was finding it necessary to make trips to
Hollywood. Often he stayed as long as two weeks or a month.
Hollywood and New York were the two main centers for radio,
where special recording equipment and facilities were available.
Some of the church members at Eugene were opposed to an
Armstrong move to southern California. When he revealed that
he had signed a lease-and-option contract to purchase what later
became part of his college campus, church members screamed,
"Armstrong extravagance!" He felt that he had outgrown Eugene,
and no doubt the attitude of many church members had contributed to that feeling.

> . . . about half of the church members at Eugene opposed the
> founding of the college. Actually two or three leading families in
> that group felt that this entire growing work ought to be operated
> on an expenditure about equal to their own frugal individual family
> expenses. These people were farmers. They spent pennies like most
> people would spend dollars.[29]

Ambassador College in Pasadena started small, in a building
that had been a private residence. Armstrong later stated that God
founded the college through him: "I had no help from our church
in Eugene. Rather, I met with disapproval and criticism." [30] The
tiny college had no dormitories or facilities of any kind. Despite
its small and unpretentious beginning, the college survived and

grew rapidly. It was a dream on which Herbert Armstrong lavished sweat, tears and a great deal of love. He claimed to have set out to found a completely new kind of college—God's college. It was not a Bible school, nor was it a special kind of "religious" institution. It was, according to Armstrong, a liberal arts coeducational institution "based on God's revealed knowledge."

Even after the end of World War II Herbert Armstrong continued to cry danger: "We need to wake up and realize that right now is the most dangerous moment in the United States' national history, instead of assuming we now have peace!" On his radio broadcasts and in virtually every issue of his *Plain Truth* magazine he reminded his followers that he had been proclaiming his great prophecy since 1927. It was the end-time revival of the Roman Empire, which would be permitted by God to attack, invade and take into slavery Britain and America unless they repented and turned to God. This basic prophecy was the central core of his message. But he also made many other predictions, short-range prophecies of world events.

After World War II, with Europe destitute, the idea of a United States of Europe gained great currency. Such a vision coincided with Armstrong's old prophecy of a resurrected Roman Empire, a dictatorship that would be led by Germany. In November 1962 his son Garner Ted, who had become as instrumental as his father in proclaiming the Armstrong prophecy, wrote in *Plain Truth*, "We Told You So!":

> Even though in the U.S. Navy from 1948 through 1952, I remember well how my father, Mr. Herbert W. Armstrong, was constantly preaching and writing that Russia would NOT attack the United States or Britain, that poverty-stricken, beaten-down, cold, starving, helpless Germany would begin to rise again to a position of real dominance and power in central Europe. He even went so far as to say Germany would head a United States of Europe, beginning as an economic union, and finally becoming an ultimate union of ten nations, completely unified in political, economic, military and religious ties! Along with multiple thousands of others, I scoffed, too.[31]

With his master key Herbert Armstrong proceeded to unlock the long-hidden prophecies of the Old Testament. Germany

loomed large on his prophetic horizon. In September 1948 he
proclaimed,

> Even before the end of this war, I revealed to you the Nazi plans for
> a Nazi underground movement, to go underground as a secret or-
> ganization the very moment they lost the war—to lay low a few
> years during allied and Russian military occupation, then to come
> forth when least expected, RESTORE GERMANY TO POWER,
> and go on to finally accomplish their aims in a World War III.

Armstrong trumpeted a shrill warning that time was short:
world events, he proclaimed, were moving swiftly toward the
climax, when Great Britain and the United States would be attacked, conquered and destroyed. By restoring Western Europe
to economic prosperity and then to military power, a dictator
would emerge and gain control of a United States of Europe.
Britain and America would wake up, too late, to realize that "we
shall have restored our Fascist enemy to power to destroy us!" [32]
    If Germany would lead the ten-nation European union, who
would be the great dictator? At one time Armstrong believed
that this would be Hitler and that World War II would be the
time of the fulfillment of the great prophecy he had been preaching about since 1927. After the war he wrote, "For a while I
though Hitler might organize it [the United States of Europe]—
especially when he tied up with the Roman Mussolini." Had his
master key failed to unlock the prophecy? Or was it possible that
Hitler was not dead and that he could still lead a new Roman
Empire against Britain and America? In 1948 Herbert Armstrong
still clung to the possibility that Hitler was the "Beast" prophesied
in the Scriptures:

> I doubt seriously that Hitler committed suicide. He may have
> escaped, alive. And now, underground, Hitler may pull a fake resur-
> rection, claiming to have been dead, and resurrected from the dead
> by a European religious leader who will then claim power to perform
> miracles, resurrecting also the ancient Roman Empire, by uniting
> ten nations in Europe.

By "European religious leader" Armstrong meant the Pope,
since he had often proclaimed that no group of nations could suc-

cessfully combine into a United States of Europe unless it was "headed and ruled by the Pope." [33] The role of the Pope was amplified by Garner Ted Armstrong in a November 1962 article in *Plain Truth*. An English weekly news magazine, *Topic*, had published an article on the Common Market, providing what Garner Ted called "one of the most shocking, one of the most truly startling, one of the most vitally significant quotations, and one of the most direct fulfillments of prophecy in all recent time. . . ."

> If the "Pact of Rome" which created the Common Market had been signed within the Vatican walls it could not have favored the Church more . . . Small wonder, then, that the Roman Church is smiling benignly over the formation of what one Vatican official defined as the greatest Catholic super-state the world has ever known.

In the early 1960s Herbert Armstrong appeared for a time to have abandoned his long-held notion that Hitler was destined to lead the resurrected Roman Empire. Was he ready to admit that his master key had failed to unlock the Scriptures? No such admission was forthcoming. Instead he turned to an analysis of the strategy employed by the Germans in World War II. Beginning with the premise that reputable historians recognized that "it took a miracle to save England from certain defeat," an article in *Plain Truth* discussed "Hitler's seven fatal blunders." The article contended that God caused Hitler to make an incredible blunder each time he had certain victory within his grasp. There had to be a very important reason for God to use miracles to thwart Hitler and block the fulfillment of a prophecy:

> It may shock you to realize that God kept Hitler from winning World War II because He planned to have "The World Tomorrow" broadcast give YOU one final opportunity to believe in the Gospel of the Kingdom of God! And a chance to have a part in the work of spreading that Gospel as a final witness—including Germany.[34]

But Armstrong still maintained that the prophecy he had proclaimed since 1927 would be fulfilled. In 1961 he boldly stated, "The astounding union of a German-dominated United States of

Europe with a great Church at its head is the next thing proph-esied to occur." If America and Great Britain did not turn to God and repent, He would very shortly send them "into captivity." Europe would soon have hydrogen bombs and guided missiles. And World War III would start with hydrogen bombs being dropped on every major city of England and the United States —without warning.

Just when it semed that Herbert Armstrong had finally gotten Adolf Hitler out of his prophecies, a spate of articles questioning Hitler's death appeared in the press. Armstrong also questioned the reported suicide, and published a series of articles on the Führer.

In April 1965 *Plain Truth* published evidence "from responsible persons" which showed "clearly that Adolf Hitler *did not die*, as supposed, in his Berlin bunker." Supportive quotations were marshaled from General Walter Bedell Smith and Russia's Mar-shal Georgi Zhukov to buttress the theory that the infamous Führer still lived. The article revealed that various investigators found German crews ready to fly the Führer to some remote part of the world and that an entire flotilla of Nazi U-boats left a secret base about the time of Hitler's supposed suicide. Since they were never seen again, it was surmised that they may have "headed for a secret Nazi Shangri-La in Antarctica!" Supposedly that would explain Adolf Eichmann's bellowing as he went to his death, "Long live Hitler! Long live Germany!"

The *Plain Truth* article claimed that Hitler did not die. It speculated that the Führer, with Martin Bormann, might have become the evil genius behind a worldwide Nazi underground. But what did all this mean to a supporter of "The World Tomor-row" radio program? The answer was that prophecy and "docu-mented evidence" showed that Germany was ripe for another dictator, and would not have to conquer continental Europe before turning its attention to the United States and Britain. This time, "she will already have the awesome, industrial, financial and military resources of Europe on her side to begin with!"

Even though Hitler had been gone for 20 years, he was in-volved in the great prophecy. From Justinian to Napoleon, there had been five revivals of the Roman Empire dominated by a world-ruling church. The sixth was described as the "little half-baked Hitler-Mussolini" one, which had occurred during World War II. After all, Mussolini had officially proclaimed Italy and its possessions the "Holy Roman Empire." But now there was to be a seventh revival, a final "Beast" prophesied in the Book of Revelation. Could Hitler yet turn out to be the final "Beast"? Suppose the great religious leader, the "coming false prophet," were to pretend to resurrect Hitler from the dead—perhaps from purgatory itself? What greater miracle could be claimed? The German people would be electrified! Political changes and alliances between nation and nation, between church and state, could be effected with lightning speed!

> If a fake resurrection of Adolf Hitler is claimed by the "great whore" of Revelation 17 and her false prophet, the electrifying sensation produced by the return of Adolf Hitler to power could quickly bring about a full-scale revival of the "Holy Roman Empire" or United States of Europe far sooner than is already called for by plans now being put into effect. This time guaranteed by religion sitting in the top seat.[35]

Armstrong's timetable for the fulfillment of the great prophecy and the attack on Britain and America was set up in accordance with his theory of cycles. He believed that the earth, the sun and the moon came into almost exact conjunction only once in 19 years. Nineteen years marked off what he called one complete time-cycle. God had used two time-cycles for originally proclaiming his message. Thus, Armstrong believed he was also given two time-cycles to get his warning to the world. He wrote, "God has marked off two 19-year time-cycles just before Christ returns for the restoring of the knowledge of the same Gospel!"[36] His second time-cycle would be up in 1972. The German government had extended the statute of limitations for prosecuting Nazi war criminals to January 1, 1970. But there was still time for the prophecy to be fulfilled.

> . . . Bible prophecy indicates that the final attack on the U.S. and Britain by this coming "Beast" power could easily be launched perhaps as early as the spring of 1972 . . . Thus, if Hitler is still alive,

he would legally be able to appear at the last moment—electrifying all Europe—and still have a year and more to consolidate his power before launching the attack against the Western democracies! [37]

If Herbert Armstrong was experiencing some difficulty with the great prophecy he had been warning about since 1927, it did not discourage him from announcing a continuous stream of shorter-range predictions. Prophecy, he said, was merely history in advance, "headlines in advance of the natural consequences of sin." With his master key he could interpret the Scriptures to provide tomorrow's news today! "You will find today's and tomorrow's headlines written in advance in God's revelation to man —the Holy Bible. Let me show you these very headlines." Mostly he showed the bad news, but of course most headlines contain only bad news. It was the threat of war or violent weather or disastrous drought. It was the death-ray bomb, earthquakes, volcanic disaster or disease epidemics. In the June 1956 *Plain Truth* he proclaimed,

> The heathen, Jeremiah says, are dismayed at the signs in the heavens, but not God's people. To us, earthquakes, flying saucers, rumors of war are the signs of an approaching event, one which we await with joy, not fear.

In the early 1950s Herbert Armstrong began warning of natural catastrophes. There were unusually bad floods and droughts, which he predicted would worsen. Also some of the coldest winters of the twentieth century were occurring in parts of the world. But people hardly noticed that they were being punished. Armstrong's magazine served notice that God was about to add something far worse. In April 1956 *Plain Truth* warned of plagues:

> God means what He says! A few doctors and scientists and public officials know what is in the offing. We are already beginning to bring upon ourselves man-made diseases. But that is not all! Plagues are coming—and, according to this prophetic warning, *in about two years from now!* Our cattle have already suffered from the drought. Soon we shall find that the hoof-and-mouth disease *will spread out of control!* Rabid foxes, squirrels, muskrats will attack our children.

The plagues that were to strike in two years' time would ultimately reduce the population by one-third. Almost as frightful, it was also predicted that drought and floods would drive destitute farmers into the cities in search of jobs. This would lead to a crisis far worse than the Depression of the 1930s. And it was prophesied that the sword of Communism and a revived Fascism in Europe would begin to bring America and Britain to their knees. By 1965 Communist terrorism would be so terrible that it would be unsafe for Anglo-Saxons to live in Asia or in Africa.

In December 1959 Armstrong's magazine contained an article warning that "Red China Plans Spring Invasion of India!" After a spring 1960 thrust to the Bay of Bengal and the Indian Ocean, China was said to be ready to begin devouring the rest of Asia with Russia's secret military backing! But if Russia was surreptitiously aiding China, how could one account for stories about a rift between the two Communist giants? The answer was part of the same *Plain Truth* article: "Many are saying today that the Chinese Communist leaders may pull 'a Tito.' *Prophecy says this will not happen!*" In September 1963, after China and the Soviets had gone their separate ways, *Plain Truth* presented another view of the two powers in a report entitled "The Russian-Chinese Split —Hope for the West?" There was no mention of the earlier prophetic declaration that Russia and China would not split. Instead the controversy was viewed as a continuation of "an historic hostility." "Moscow and Peking are divided by racial animosity which would persist even if their ideological differences could be squared away." No scriptural prediction concerning the Russian-Chinese split was included in this article.

The exploration of outer space was not the most appealing subject to Herbert W. Armstrong, and he did not pay an unusual amount of attention to it. In June 1961 he wrote an article explaining that the Russian cosmonaut Gagarin was not the first human being in outer space. He had received reports that a Russian celebrity, a Col. Ilyushin, was actually the first man in outer space. But some type of malfunction occurred and the Russians were unable to bring him back to earth.

To Armstrong the attempt to conquer outer space was a sign

that the age was near its end. He claimed that God would not
allow man to control space.

God Almighty gave mankind dominion over the solid earth, the
oceans, and the air—but not over outer space. When men started to
build a tower to get to Heaven—up into outer space—God stopped
them! He did not stop them before they got well started. He allowed
them to get a good start. He has allowed a start once again—this
time actually into outer space. He will, undoubtedly, let men get a
little farther. But not much farther!

Although members of Armstrong's church do not vote, they
still are interested in economic conditions that affect their standard of living and their future. Through his radio programs and
in the pages of his magazine, Armstrong has discussed the economic outlook many times. He has provided free booklets on
"Ending Your Financial Worries" and "How to Get Out of Debt."
His booklet on the laws of success is one of his most popular pieces
of free literature. In September 1963 *Plain Truth* carried the
prophecy of the soon-coming greatest economic crash in history.
Quoting an economist who said that by 1970 "the U.S. will go flat
broke," Armstrong's magazine predicted that there was no escape;
already on hand were the explosive ingredients of a crash that
would make the Great Depression seem like a minor slump.

Of all the subjects of prophecy that Herbert Armstrong and his
staff have examined with the master key, none has figured more
prominently or consistently in his prophetic utterances than Germany. In a 1958 article distributed by the Radio Church of God,
Germany's role in the continuing Middle East crisis was analyzed.
Armstrong's magazine announced that the invisible force behind
the Arab problem was Nazism. This prophecy unlocked with the
master key proved to be one of the most amazing and most
mistaken:

. . . Germany—not atheistic, communist Russia—is ultimately going
to support an Arab union against the Jews and against Israel—Britain
and America! This is what prophecy foretells. This is God's warning
to us today. The West's intervention may temporarily save certain
Arab countries from Nasser, but the very countries we are now trying
to rescue are yet to turn upon us!

When the Congo crisis erupted, Armstrong's magazine found that German aspirations in Africa had gone unreported by the press. Indeed, "the Germans, in the name of a United Europe, are out to carve a new economic empire," proclaimed *Plain Truth*.

The constant harping on Germany as the leader of an imminent great dictatorship seemed out of place in a time when hundreds of anti-Communist organizations were working constantly to distribute a somewhat similar warning about Russia and international Communism. Even though he has long proclaimed that Russia would not attack the United States, Herbert Armstrong has always been strongly anti-Communist. Often he has prefaced his remarks about Germany by saying something like, ". . . yes, Communism is an enemy, but there is another, greater enemy. . . ." Another approach is, "Yes—inconceivable as that may sound to your ears—we are now threatened by an even greater enemy than Communism! This by no means infers Communism is not to be looked upon as an enemy, nor Communist domination to be feared as the most detestable thing that could befall a free people —but Communism is not the ONLY enemy!"

From time to time, Armstrong included the subject of Communism in his radio programs and his magazine. He strongly opposed Communism, but at the end of his messages he usually added that Communism would not conquer the world or even attack the United States. Communism, he insisted, would "be buried" by Christ in the early 1980s, when the Red hordes attack Palestine. In 1962 *Plain Truth* exposed the basic philosophy of Marxism-Leninism in an article entitled "Who Will Bury Communism?" Unfortunately, the opportunity to stress Armstrong's opposition was weakened by the article's poor research. Two of the principal quotations used were fraudulent. One of these, the so-called Lenin Overripe Fruit quotation, was the central theme around which the article was constructed. This quote, falsely attributed to Lenin, says, "First we will take Eastern Europe, then the masses of Asia, then we will encircle the United States of America which will be the last bastion of capitalism. We will not have to attack it, it will fall like an overripe fruit into our hands." Experts on Communism have searched in vain for the origin of the quotation for many years. Research scholars at Stanford have

searched for it in Lenin's works, and so has the curator of the
Slavic Room at the Library of Congress. In the *Communist Line
Bulletin* of March-May 1959 the quotation was described by the
late Louis Budenz as one of the many questionable quotations
attributed to Lenin or Stalin that are floating around ill-informed
anti-Communist circles. Armstrong also used another fraudulent
quotation, one attributed to a certain Dimitry Manuilsky. Some
scholars have called it the "Manuilsky clenched-fist quotation."
Armstrong's was not the first organization to be taken in by these
fake quotes. Scores of them were being used by conservatives who
often failed to verify their sources because the quotations seemed
"so real"; they seemed to describe "what's happening" in the
course of historical events.

✿   ✿   ✿

The problems associated with money—generally the lack of it
during the early days of Armstrong's ministry—probably caused
him more worry than anything else. During the initial years of
Ambassador College, he was so desperate for money that he had
to pray for a miracle. And his income immediately tripled. By
1969, long after the organization had become a worldwide operation, the financial structure was so sound that Armstrong
published one of his most optimistic reports:

> Virtually every phase of our operations has increased on an average
> of 30% each year over a 35-year period—save one factor. That is the
> number of Co-Workers who make it possible. It costs money to con-
> duct this Work. Our operational expenditures have had to increase
> at the rate of approximately 30% every year over the year before.
> That means it doubles in approximately 2 years and 7 months—less
> than 3 years. I know of no enterprise—whether commercial or non-
> commercial—that has grown so consistently so long. And of course
> that means the income for the Work from the Co-Workers has in-
> creased on an average of 30% each year—for we do pay our bills and
> therefore our financial standing today is quite strong.[38]

The one outstanding feature of the Armstrong message that
has distinguished it from the ministries of all other radio
preachers has been the lack of financial appeals. Most first-

time listeners to an Armstrong broadcast are delighted to discover a nonprofit organization that seems clearly nonmercenary. There are never any pleas for contributions on the broadcasts; indeed, all literature is offered free, and the promise is repeatedly made that there will be no "follow-up"—no one will call at a person's home after he has requested a free subscription to *Plain Truth* or other literature. Each program usually emphasizes that "We have absolutely nothing to sell!" The whole Armstrong effort is described as an educational work. "There are no gimmicks in our Program."

Some critics view the Armstrong technique as one of the most effective methods of advertising. This "soft-sell" approach has attracted legions to the Armstrong message. But one radio preacher believes Armstrong is using "psychology" to sell his product:

> Anyone who has studied psychology realizes the fine use of reverse selling in this approach. The very mention of the fact that (a) you can't pay for your . . . it is priceless . . . coupled with the idea (b) there are no gimmicks and (c) I'm holding these for you and (d) let me know in the enclosed self-addressed return envelope if you want them . . . is enough to send multiple thousands of Christians and non-Christians alike rushing to include a check in the mail along with their request. And they do! . . . With many born-again people saying, "All those Christian groups do is beg for money" . . . is it no wonder they find this approach not only disarming but appealing? [39]

Armstrong's free literature is one side of a glittering coin that some radio preachers now emulate by sending out free monthly magazines. To see the other side one can examine the articles on tithing that appear frequently in *Plain Truth* magazine. Here one finds Armstrong's "hard-sell" approach. New co-workers are always needed. Even in 1972 there were only about 75,000 of them.[40] Readers of *Plain Truth*, 98 per cent of whom are not members of the Worldwide Church of God, are threatened, cajoled, challenged and promised blessings in order to convert them to tithing. An Old Testament Scripture is frequently repeated to show that those who do not tithe are robbing God and are cursed. But if they will tithe, God will bless them "in many physical and material ways." Each article generally ends with a paragraph or two devoted to the subject of "Where Should You Pay God's Tithes?" The tithes should go to the "true ministers of God." And the reader is advised to "check up and prove whether or not The World Tomorrow broadcast isn't the only work on earth which is fulfilling Christ's commission!" [41]

Armstrong has recounted an early experience that seems to have fixed his ideas about tithing. A farmer near Vancouver, Washington, built the outside shell of a house. Over a period of three years, he saved $40, with which he planned to buy lumber to complete its interior. In response to an Armstrong broadcast he contributed the $40. Armstrong attempted to return the money, explaining, "I just couldn't take this money when you have struggled so long to save it so you could have a home to live in." When the family insisted, Armstrong kept the money. He realized, he said, that it was really God's will that he use it. [42] Since that time he has missed few opportunities to advertise for support. He has even directed articles on tithing to non-Christians: "Yes, strange as it seems, you—even if a non-Christian— can prosper and be free from debt if you make God your financial partner. In this partnership God gives you 90 percent of the income. Think of how much the U.S.A. or the British Commonwealth would have saved if each had made God a national partner!" [43] In the personal column of his magazine and in the semiannual letters to readers of *Plain Truth*, Armstrong often compares his own financial program with that used by others:

> The world is full of gimmicks, come-ons, deceptions—always to get your money. But we never have been, never will be, guilty of any such practice. Your *Plain Truth* subscription comes to you FREE— already paid. YOU have never paid for it. You never heard us begging for money over the air. You never will. [44]

At other times Armstrong has become almost lyrical in describing how there has never been a program such as his, giving away literature to thousands and thousands of people year in and year out. Sometimes he becomes almost rhapsodic in his praise:

Was there *ever* such a program, purely and unselfishly in the interest of the listening public, with no axe to grind, no sponsor or wealthy philanthropist or Foundation back of it—*starting out with NO MONEY*—never begging for funds over the air or in literature offered *free*—ABSOLUTELY NO VISIBLE SOURCE OR ASSURANCE OF FINANCIAL BACKING, yet growing constantly for 33 years until it became the MOST POWERFUL PROGRAM ON RADIO—WORLD-WIDE? [45]

In 1953 Armstrong's financial structure was strong enough to extend his radio ministry to Europe. Later he discovered that it was exactly 19 years to the day from the time his preaching career began until he started broadcasting over Radio Luxembourg. As previously mentioned, nineteen years equals one Armstrong time-cycle. This was very important because now he was beginning the "second and last remaining 19-year cycle!"

In 1955 Garner Ted Armstrong began broadcasting the radio messages of "The World Tomorrow" program. The youngest of the four Armstrong children, Garner Ted was four years old when his father started broadcasting in Eugene, Oregon, in 1934. Approximately 22 years later he began broadcasting the message in a voice that sounded so much like his father's that many people could not tell them apart. As a young man, Armstrong had been hostile to the mission of his father. He said later that he was ashamed of his father's work and had never read even one of the many Radio Church of God booklets. He finally ran away and joined the Navy. He served four years during the Korean conflict and returned to Pasadena to take a temporary job in the Ambassador College mailing office. He apparently had no plans to remain with his father. He was on the waiting list for a job as page boy at the Columbia Broadcasting System in Hollywood and had auditioned twice for television talent shows. His goal was either television or motion pictures, or even nightclub entertaining.

But while he was waiting for a call from the entertainment world, he enrolled in a few courses at Ambassador College and continued to work in the mail room. But a scriptural contradiction discovered in a Bible course piqued his interest in learning, and he soon became a dedicated student. He went on to obtain a

Doctorate in Child Psychology and Education. He does not hold a Doctorate of Theology, although he is a Professor of Theology at Ambassador College.

He was a success almost from the beginning of his broadcasting career. Earlier, his older brother, Richard David Armstrong, who was killed in an automobile accident in 1958, had broadcast some of the programs, and Garner Ted has insisted that his brother's radio delivery was superior to his own, which is rapid and well-modulated. His father believes that he obtained this wonderful gift through a miracle. He explained that little Garner Ted was unable to speak until he was two and a half years old. He had fallen out of his crib-bed when he was less than a year old, and his father attributed his inability to talk to this fall. Then the child was stricken with pneumonia. Herbert Armstrong anointed him and prayed for his recovery. The fever fell quickly, and three days later Garner Ted was talking. According to Armstrong senior,

> Words have been pouring like a torrent out of his mouth every since, as millions of radio listeners on every continent around the world well know! God gave him his voice by an unusual divine miracle. And I am well pleased, as God was with His Son Jesus, that he is now an instrument in God's hands.[46]

Increasingly Garner Ted's work was backed up by a growing research facility at Ambassador College. A well-organized News Bureau and a trained staff now support the broadcasts. It is equipped with both A.P. and U.P.I. teletypes. In addition, the Armstrong broadcasts are aided by workers who scan and clip important news magazines like *Time, Newsweek, U.S. News and World Report, Paris Match, Der Spiegel* and many others. They also review important newspapers, including the *New York Times,* the Chicago *Tribune,* and the London *Daily Times.* All of these improvements as well as many others have caused both the broadcasts and *Plain Truth* magazine to improve year after year. But certain practices from earlier days have been retained. Garner Ted continues to thunder warnings about world conditions and periodically repeats the old prophecy about the revived Roman Empire that his father has been repeating since 1927.

After Ambassador College was established in Pasadena, Herbert Armstrong felt the need for branch colleges in other parts of the world. In 1959 property was purchased for a campus in Britain, a few miles north of London, near St. Albans. The school opened in 1960.

Although Armstrong's message was broadcast from Radio Luxembourg as early as 1953, with separate transmissions in English, French and German, he was unable to saturate England with his message.

> The British government would not allow any broadcasting facilities within its jurisdiction that might be used by God's servants to proclaim God's Message of this hour to the British peoples! But God was determined to get His Message to the British! So, the first week in 1953, God's Message started getting in to Britain from Europe—when "The World Tomorrow" program began going out on the superpowered voice of Radio Luxembourg! When Radio Luxembourg was no longer effective for this Message, God raised up broadcasting stations on ships anchored just outside Britain's jurisdiction. "The World Tomorrow" was then thundered over all of Britain daily, on seven of these ships. They were NOT illegal. They violated no law of man. They did proclaim faithfully the Law of GOD! But the British authorities falsely called them "pirate" ships. They were not pirates. They were not marauders. They did not invade the land and pillage or steal. They harmed no one! [47]

But the British authorities were strongly opposed to broadcasts from the "pirates," and in 1968 the Armstrong message no longer radiated from the antennas of stations like Radio London, Radio Caroline North, or Radio Scotland. The September 1, 1967, issue of the *Catholic Herald*, published in England, noted in an article entitled "Temporary Silence for Prophet of Doom" that the "sword and thunder broadcasts" of Herbert Armstrong might be a fulfillment of the "famine of hearing" of the word of God that Armstrong had prophesied some ten years earlier. The Pasadena preacher replied that the magazine was mistaken. The radio silence over Britain, said Armstrong, was not a prophecy fulfilled.

He claimed even then to be making final arrangements to "cover the entire British Isles, beginning either December 1st or January 1st." But five years later Britain was still not blessed with his radio broadcasts. His message now goes out from Radio MANX, on the Isle of Man. But this signal does not reach London, the heart of his Ephraim-Manasseh kingdom.

One British observer noted that the two Armstrongs had made several thousand converts in England during the 1960s. But some English church leaders warned the public to steer clear of the Radio Church of God. In 1970 the BBC also warned the public, in a program that explained the dangers to family life that association with the Radio Church could bring. Armstrong's doctrine called for

> . . . strict discipline and obedience in the home; wives had to call their husbands "sir," children were forbidden to attend parties. It exerted its hold on members by means of fear and suspicion: predicting the end of the world and hell on earth within a few years, it exhorted them to "pay their debt to God" (i.e. to the Radio Church) even *before* paying their rent or putting money aside for their children. The sect, by the way, also claimed to represent the famous lost tribes of Israel, and one of its predictions was that the Pope would soon move his headquarters from the Vatican to Jerusalem.[48]

Armstrong claims that he does not reply to such criticism, but earlier he had written that the British government and the national Church of England "would legalize the revolting perversion of homosexuality! They would condone heinous sins, but no door inside the U.K. is open to broadcasting God's Message! But God did get His Message to Britain."

Armstrong's early visits to England, especially in connection with the branch of Ambassador College he opened there, made a profound impression on him. As a descendant of British kings, he could have expected better treatment from the English, whom he found to be somewhat snobbish, full of pride and disdainful of their sins. He wrote in his autobiography,

> The English tell us that we Americans are just now starting to go through the stage of development they did 200 years ago—that we

are that far behind the times. They really think they are ahead of us! They are smugly ahead of what they *suppose* us to be—yet they know nothing of America, actually. I was particularly impressed by their pride. They feel they are superior, morally, to all the people of the earth. Yet it is quite apparent that their morals have hit a toboggan slide since the war! They are surely a long way from realizing their sins, nationally and individually, and of repenting of them—and they don't even dream, and would never believe, that they are to be punished and conquered. . . .

England, Ephraim of the grand United States of Europe prophecy that undergirded the Worldwide Church of God, proved more troublesome to Herbert Armstrong than Manasseh, Reuben, Dan and the remainder of the tribes thrown in. In the latter part of the 1950s the European Economic Community, or Common Market, moved rapidly ahead. Herbert Armstrong stepped up his warnings about the impending United States of Europe. Suddenly a new turn of events disturbed his outlook for the future. Britain was trying to get into the Common Market. This definitely posed a problem, for if Britain should join the EEC, it would leave Armstrong's prophecy in shambles. How could Ephraim attack and invade itself?

In 1961 Herbert Armstrong carried on as usual, warning about the coming European dictatorship. It was 34 years since he first sounded the alarm. Now that some of the public was beginning to take his warning seriously, he remembered how long some had scoffed at him. He had his eye on West Berlin as a key that could trigger the sudden reemergence of the Roman Empire. And he had not dropped the requirement for the Roman Catholic Church to be the "Supreme Authority" which alone would be able to weld together a political and military union of the ten nations. But Armstrong still felt that "in all probability" Britain would not be a part of the United States of Europe.

In September 1961 Armstrong began complaining that of all nations, it was Britain and America who seemed to be doing the most to foster the EEC: "Yes, paradoxically, the very Frankenstein Monster that prophecy warns is to destroy us has been proposed, encouraged, aided and abetted by both the U.S.A. and Britain!" He also faced the prospect that his prophecy was in trouble. He asked, "Will any of these Israelitish nations become members of the ultimate Ten-Nation prophetic 'Beast'?" Armstrong's answer indicated that he might be prepared to hedge the prophecy with an alternate interpretation:

> In the past years I have thought not. Prophecy does not say, specifically. But in Revelation 18:4 we read the warning, "Come out of her, my people." The "her" is this modern Babylon, the resurrected Roman Empire! God's spiritual people, converted Christians, could not be converted if they still were "in Babylon." So it must be speaking of God's national people, Israel. This, therefore, may indicate that *some* of the Israelitish nations of northwestern Europe will become a part of the coming United States of Europe. At least, France, Belgium, and the Netherlands already are in this "Big Six." And right now, even Britain and other nations are trying desperately to get in!

In July of the following year Herbert Armstrong wrote a long article for *Plain Truth* which indicated he had been studying the Scriptures. He entitled his report "Britain's Doom Prophesied for Seeking Common Market Membership." The title clearly showed that in Herbert Armstrong's view Britain was going to get it and get it good for even trying to get into the Common Market. He made that statement because he had located the prophecies that "pinpoint specifically Britain's decision to join the EEC." He reminded his readers that Ephraim was Britain, and Assyria, Germany. And he led them to several passages of the Scriptures, including one in the eighth chapter of Hosea which indicated that Ephraim had "gone up to Assyria, a wild ass alone by himself." That, said Armstrong, showed that Britain, instead of trusting in God, had gone begging help from the Germans.

During 1963 and 1964 Armstrong kept up his warnings. He announced no new prophetic answer concerning the final disposition of Britain vis-à-vis the Common Market, except to say, "Prophecy reveals that there will be no 'happy ending' to this situation." He seemed encouraged that De Gaulle held Britain at bay. In fact, he observed that "no longer is France alone in her wish to keep Britain out of the Common Market."

In 1969 President De Gaulle resigned, and Herbert Armstrong noted that the French president's "release of power removed the one block that has been delaying political union in Europe. After a period of confusion, it will now fit together rather quickly— possibly within two years." He expected Britain to make immediate new overtures in a renewed attempt to enter the Common Market. But he claimed that the general consensus was that Britain would not make it. In fact he felt it was now certain that she would not be one of the ten nations in the coming United States of Europe.[49]

In February 1970 Armstrong took a modified tack. He asked, "Will Britain ever be admitted into the Common Market? And, if she does enter the European Economic Community, will she remain in this union?" He answered that it was not clearly revealed in Bible prophecy whether Britain would ever be admitted to the Common Market, but the "prophetic indications" were that it was more likely she would never be allowed to join the EEC at all. He did not define "prophetic indications," but he declared positively that prophecy showed that England would not be one of the ten nations comprising the "final" United States of Europe.

On October 28, 1971, Parliament voted to enter the Common Market. The following December a *Plain Truth* writer discussed the event in an article that omitted any reference to the great prophecy of a resurrected Roman Empire. But oddly enough, the emphasis was on how much control Britain might be able to exert as a member of the Common Market:

> By joining the Common Market, Britain hopes to help shape and control the destiny of Western Europe—from the inside. Many in Britain (and in other nations of Europe) shudder to think of a powerful, united, federal Europe—without Britain. They know full well that in the past, leaders have arisen in Germany, France, Italy and other European nations—leaders whose power-mad schemes took them on rampages throughout Europe. Great Britain hopes to forestall any such dangerous union—by making sure she is on the inside . . . This makes Britain's future in the Common Market of extreme importance. . . .

This new view of Britain and the Common Market, and the absence of warnings about a new Roman Empire, appeared to be related to a very long but extremely significant statement by Herbert W. Armstrong. Writing in the February 1972 issue of *Tomorrow's World,* his new publication devoted mainly to religious topics, Armstrong observed that January 7, 1972, had come and gone. On that date the second 19-year time-cycle was completed, and according to statements made in the past, his work was to be completed and the voice of the movement stilled. Armstrong re-examined his time-cycles.

First of all, he stated that while he had been chosen for a very definite commission in God's service, he definitely had not been called to be a prophet, "except as that work, Biblically used, does sometimes refer to a minister or speaker—one who proclaims the Gospel of Jesus Christ." He continued,

> Emphatically I am NOT a prophet, in the sense of one to whom God speaks specially and directly, revealing personally a future event to happen or new truth, or new and special instruction direct from God —separate from, and apart from what is contained in the Bible. And I never have claimed to be. There is no such human prophet living today! The Bible is the written Word of God—and for our time now, it is complete! Never have I believed or claimed that God reveals to me new truths not contained in the Bible—in addition to, or apart from the Bible.

This interesting explanation startled some observers, who could point to page 505 of Herbert W. Armstrong's *Autobiography,* where he wrote that "new Biblical TRUTH had been revealed to me." Had he not written on page 2 of the April 1956 issue of *Plain Truth,* "I personally SEE what lies ahead!"? Had he not declared that the knowledge necessary to understand the true meaning of the world news could only be obtained by those who had the key which could unlock the closed doors of biblical prophecy? And that he, Herbert W. Armstrong, had that "master key"?

But Armstrong seemed to forget such statements as he rushed on, explaining that there are no prophets, except false ones:

> Now a word about what my Commission is NOT. It is not to become an infallible expert on, or to preach, chronology. I feel at present that

the whole question of chronology is in confusion, and no one can be positively sure of dates. As of the present I, and a majority of our historians in Ambassador College, and reseachers in the School of Theology, feel that it is utterly unsafe to try to set dates in regard to future prophesied events. . . .

Next he defined "our main purpose, or Commission—which is to proclaim Christ's announcement of the advance good news of the coming Kingdom of God to rule all nations—and the message commonly called salvation—and the fact we may be born again through Jesus Christ—born into that Kingdom."

But such a Commission differs little from that of any independent evangelical organization. What happened to the Armstrong mission to warn the world that a resurrected Roman Empire was going to invade, conquer and destroy Britain and America? Had he not claimed to know tomorrow's news today through the use of his master key? That was one of the main reasons people had supported him for almost four decades with untold millions of dollars.

Herbert W. Armstrong had always been so sure, so certain. In October 1962 he wrote in the *Plain Truth*, "Other groups may talk in vague generalities about the coming world cataclysm or tribulation or 'the Lord's return some day,' but no other religious work on earth understands specifically what is happening!" And as recently as January 1969 he wrote, "I know whereof I speak, for no organization on earth has a more knowledgeable grasp and understanding of world conditions, trends, and causes, than ours. We know where the world is heading. . . ."

But now, at the end of the last of his allotted time-cycles, he sounded strangely different. Now, referring to the dedicated six-month study that launched him on the road to fame and fortune, he said,

In my study, I did not receive everything perfectly all at once. There were instances where, having felt I had come to understand the true Biblical teaching on a certain subject, other Scriptures discovered later put a different light on it. I *had, on occasion, to confess I had been in error,* and to correct it.

Of course there had been mistakes, but

Let me ask you this question. Do you know of any large, established, well-recognized professing Christian denomination which has PUB-LICLY confessed it had been wrong in what it had been teaching, and which then corrected the error, and turned to the truth? No, the big established churches and denominations feel they cannot afford to admit having had any error—having ever mis-taught the people.

Yet Armstrong was willing to recognize that these established churches are filled with humans. They are all subject to error, he observed, and "so are you—and so am I—and so is this Work of God." . . . all of us are subject to mistakes! "You may ask, do I, then, feel that we in this Work are full of errors, misleading the people? MOST EMPHATICALLY NO! We have not had to correct error many times. But each time we have corrected an error, we have had one fewer error left."

Now he was ready to talk about the time-cycles: ". . . I want to tell you the truth about the two 19-year time cycles, ending January 7, 1972, with a frank, straightforward explanation of where we were mistaken—and where we were RIGHT!" He still felt strongly about the 19-year cycles, but admitted that to some extent it was an "emotional revelation." But it has never been his intention to set dates! "Yet in our human zeal and enthusiasm for getting this greatest mission on earth done, we have a few times come close to it or appeared to—and that we deeply regret. . . ." After all, scientists set dates for the times they hope to accomplish certain breakthroughs. But, he asked, "Does anyone discredit them, if they set the wrong date? Of course not!"

He provided a number of examples to prove his point. There was Sir Philip Noel Baker, Nobel Prize winner in 1959, who said, "I believe that within ten years we will all be dead and the earth will be an incinerated relic." Sir Philip's ten years were up three years ago, observed Armstrong. There also was John Platt of the University of Michigan, who said, "We may have even less than a 50-50 chance of living until 1980." And Armstrong went on to quote other leaders and scholars, before adding,

The point: Because these men add a date to their concerned comments regarding mankind's future, does it mean that their concern, and all the overwhelming facts which cause that concern, are wrong? No! When the house is on fire no one seems interested in the exact number of minutes one might have before he is finally consumed!

If scientists could miss *their* predictions, why couldn't he? Sir Philip Baker had been incorrect when he prophesied the end of the world by 1969. "But no one calls Sir Philip a false prophet." Armstrong was correct: no one had called Sir Philip a false prophet, probably because he did not buy radio time around the world to tell whoever would listen that he had a "master key" that could unlock the Scriptures, with which he could tell in advance what was going to happen.

Armstrong continued with his explanation of the time-cycles, quoting from the *Plain Truth* of October 1965: "But we know that the time is soon coming—probably at the end of the second 19-year time-cycle of this work—when our voices shall be stilled—our printing presses stopped!" Said Armstrong, looking back at his words, "The main statement remains as certain today as then —only the 'probably' by 1972 has proved to be premature . . . scores and scores of times we have said, 'we do not set dates.' Yet, in our zeal, we have used 'possiblies' and 'probablies' and even appeared to set dates we really didn't intend to set."

Through page after page Armstrong continued his confession, but without ever saying that he had ever definitely set the date of January 7, 1972, or the end of two time-cycles as the date his Work would end. But he did make such statements. For example, on page 2 of the April 1956 issue of *Plain Truth*, Armstrong wrote, ". . . after one 19-year time-cycle, God opened another great Door and His last warning Message began to be thundered all over Europe—and . . . He has revealed that there remains only the one more 19-year cycle (of which we are well into the 4th year already)—after which it will be TOO LATE!!!"

Armstrong was doing far more to excuse his old errors than he was to confess them, but then in the space of a paragraph he made an astounding revelation.

. . . after June, 1967, and the six-day war between Israel and the Arab nations, just when world events *could have* plunged suddenly by that impetus to a climax in a few short years, world events, in-

stead, began to slow down. But we could not discern that for a year
or more. De Gaulle, in France, began to slow down the Common
Market moves toward political union in Europe . . . In the Vatican,
in Jerusalem, in Germany and Europe, in United States economy,
affecting this Work, the pace slowed! But we were so impressed with
what already had happened in the 19-year time-cycle, that we failed
to divorce actual contemporary world events, as they were slowing,
from our time-cycle analogy. During the past two or three years, the
realization came upon us more and more that events were slowing—
that the world crisis would not be reached by January, 1972. All this
has happened since the 1967 edition of the *U. S. and British Commonwealth in Prophecy* book came out: This book contained statements that seemed justified in 1967. . . .

Here Armstrong reveals that he had been frantically trying to
guess the future all along. He does not even mention the master
key that he had once claimed categorically could unlock prophecies and reveal tomorrow's news. Still, things could have been
worse. It was the date he had set—the end of the second time-
cycle on January 7, 1972—that people remembered. As yet no
one seemed to be complaining about the many little prophecies
that had backfired or fizzled. And somewhere in the future the
Worldwide Church of God still had to face up to the failure of
Herbert Armstrong's great prophecy concerning the resurrected
Roman Empire. The little prophecies were hard to remember.
How many of his loyal co-workers studied the in-depth article
on the Middle East crisis in the November 1971 issue of *Plain
Truth?* Did they remember that in 1958 Armstrong had predicted
that it would be Germany, rather than Russia, that would support the Arabs against the Israeli government? How many would
check on the numerous short-range predictions he has made
about world events, and discover that he could probably have
predicted the future just as accurately had he blindfolded himself and thrown darts at a world map?

Armstrong closed the article that explained his "mistakes" by
observing that all great men occasionally erred: "Moses made
mistakes, Abraham made mistakes, David made mistakes, Elijah
made mistakes, Peter made mistakes, and so have all men God
has ever called and used."

Herbert Armstrong was not about to shut down his far-flung empire on January 7, 1972, no matter what he had said in the past. A reported 150,000,000 people were being served by Ambassador College programs and literature in the early 1970s. His message went by radio into every country in the world, from some 400 stations, using more than 50 million watts of power. Only in England, the most important center of British-Israelism, was his radio coverage poorer than he desired. His television network of more than 50 stations in the United States covered most of the country each week. He was Chancellor of the very posh college in Pasadena, with a reported enrollment of some 700 students. His school in England had 350 enrollees, and his newest college, with its 4,000-acre experimental farm, at Big Sandy, Texas, had 550 students. His educational facilities included three schools of the liberal arts and sciences, a school of education and a graduate school of theology.

The Armstrong empire is supported by an estimated 75-80,000 co-workers, from the approximately 250 congregations of the Worldwide Church of God. The semisecret congregations meet in rented halls and carefully screen newcomers who express a desire to join an Armstrong group. Although new converts may come from among the acquaintances of Armstrong co-workers, the congregations do not advertise or actively proselytize for new members. Instead, special teams of superintendents or ministers move through the country, conducting series of evening "Bible Lectures." A series of these talks usually runs through one week, and according to Garner Ted Armstrong, consists of in-depth analyses of prophecies and doctrines "above and beyond anything we're free to say on television, over the radio, or in our magazines." Those who have shown a continuing interest in *Plain Truth* or *Tomorrow's World* or other literature advertised on "The World Tomorrow" radio and television programs are informed by mail when a series of lectures is scheduled for their area or city. At the Bible Lectures there are no collections, no invitations to join the church, no altar calls or requests for "decisions." But it is from these very serious lectures and discussions that many new co-workers are added to the Armstrong rolls. Those who wish to be associated with the Worldwide Church of God are introduced

to the local "Representative of The World Tomorrow and Ambassador College," if they have not already made his acquaintance
during the lecture series. Only a wealthy organization such as the
Worldwide Church, with its estimated annual income of $55
million, could make a success of this quiet method of recruiting
new members. The Armstrong empire is a giant, globe-encircling
complex that has reached what its founder calls a position of
"worldwide power and scope."

In early 1972 the Armstrong father and son suddenly became
news items in the regular press. Especially was interest focused
on Garner Ted Armstrong, who had been broadcasting "The
World Tomorrow" radio and television programs so long that he
was far better known to the general public than his father.
Rumors of a split between Chairman Herbert and his son started
growing after Garner Ted was removed from his leadership position in the church, as Vice-Chancellor of the Ambassador Colleges and as executive editor of the two Ambassador College
magazines. His radio programs were replaced by taped messages
the elder Armstrong had recorded years earlier.

After Garner Ted had been missing for several months, the
press bombarded Ambassador College for information, but the
public relations department did little to clear up the mystery and
issued vague statements about Garner Ted's personal problems
and his need for a long rest. In April 1972 a minister of the
Worldwide Church revealed to the religion editor of the Seattle
Post-Intelligencer that a confidential memorandum from Herbert
Armstrong to his congregations (with instructions to immediately
destroy after reading) disclosed that Garner Ted was "in the
bonds of Satan." Although Chairman Armstrong denied the allegation, the minister also revealed that Garner Ted confessed
that he had sinned, and following this confession father and son
went to their knees and prayed for the archangels Gabriel and
Michael to loose Satan's bonds. The exact nature of Garner Ted's
alleged sin was not explained to the co-workers. But the rumor
persisted that he had criticized the lavish spending of his father
and other leaders of the organization. The spending was rumored
to be for costly suits and jet trips, with not enough money for
"the widows."

As the mystery deepened and radio listeners all around the country placed calls to stations inquiring about Garner Ted, the press published statements of former members of the "Armstrong cult." Some articles mentioned that world champion chess player Bobby Fischer was an Armstrong co-worker. *Time* magazine reported that the doctrines of Armstrongism included observance of kosher laws set forth in the Old Testament, the celebration of Passover but not of Christmas or Easter, and the denial of the Trinity. It also reported that co-workers were expected to set aside three tithes, or tenths, of their gross income. The church was said to monitor the tithes by computer, and a member caught cheating was sentenced to tithe double for the rest of his life.

Small wonder that the church's annual income is estimated at around $55 million. Or that Founder Armstrong zips round the world . . . in a Grumman Gulfstream jet that gobbles up at least $1.5 million a year. Former Worldwide Church of God members charge that the Armstrongs live like kings while members often live in poverty in order to pay their tithes. They maintain that each of the two Armstrongs has elegant homes in Texas, California and England; that Herbert sports a $1,000 watch and bought a $2,000 set of cuff links and tie tack for a Jerusalem trip.[50]

The press also published the reports of ex-members who had come into conflict with some of the arcane and unyielding Armstrong doctrines. One told of being refused permission to undergo medical treatment. Another complained that the sect refused to recognize a civil divorce. Severe punishment of children was also cited. One father was said to have disciplined his child by whipping him like a horse at a church meeting.

In May Garner Ted returned to his microphones. Herbert Armstrong promised that the work would stress prophecy and repentance in a great new move forward. And he revealed that the movement was in serious financial difficulty and asked his co-workers for more help. *Christianity Today* speculated that the Worldwide Church's drop in income due to Garner Ted's disappearance was in the neighborhood of 40 per cent.

In July 1972 Chancellor Armstrong wrote, "In the past two years, I have flown five times around the world. I have had personal conferences with many heads-of-state, discussing domestic and world problems. . . ." His new magazine, *Tomorrow's World*, now carried most of the religious articles, leaving *Plain Truth* free to publish articles about governments and world conditions, articles such as "Can Our Oceans Feed the World?" and "Can Our Cities Be Saved? and "Why People Commit Suicide." His failure to guess what was going to happen on the world scene no doubt played a part in altering the type of articles he printed on prophecy. Even the regular monthly column called "Prophecy Comes Alive in Today's World News" was dropped in the late 1960s in favor of "Advance News in the Wake of Today's World Events." Armstrong's many anti-evolution articles and radio programs have doubtless contributed indirectly to the efforts now in progress to introduce the divine-creation story into the officially approved textbooks used in California.

There are indications that Armstrong will soon begin to emphasize some form of miracle healing. He believes that he was the instrument through which God performed a number of miraculous healings during his early ministry. He thinks it possible that an angel took control of his automobile to guide him to the home of a sick person. But healing by the Armstrongs will not resemble an Oral Roberts campaign. Garner Ted emphasizes that ministers of the Worldwide Church of God pray "quietly" for the healing of others:

> I do not believe in this commercialized business. I don't believe in great public meetings where you advertise in advance, you get long lines of people—bring your sick down here. Why aren't these healers out in the middle of graveyards, why don't they walk along the graveyards, saying, "rise up, rise up, rise up." Why don't they visit the hospitals? They could find lots of sick people. . . .[51]

Chairman of his church, Chancellor and President of his colleges, Editor and Publisher of two magazines, and Director of radio and television programs—these are the principal titles of Herbert W. Armstrong. Now 81 years old, the amazing preacher hurries about the world, visiting heads of state, writing for his magazines and overseeing his vast empire. At the age of 16 he first realized that he "wanted to be somebody." Now he can chat with premiers and presidents, with kings and prime ministers. A short, slightly stocky little man with snowy white hair and big eyes, he grins happily from pictures in *Plain Truth* as he extends his standard gift of beautiful Steuben crystal to Mrs. Indira Gandhi of India or Israeli Prime Minister Golda Meir. He no longer thunders at every opportunity about the resurrected Roman Empire, the prophecy that his career was built on. He may yet be forced to face that greatest of all his prophetic failures. But if he does not, the handsome Garner Ted will inherit the burden of the master key. In many ways, Herbert W. Armstrong is the outstanding religious innovator of our times. He has demonstrated conclusively for almost 40 years that the fable of the shepherd who cried "Wolf!" taught an incredible falsehood.

IX

Billy Graham

To his credit, however, he [Graham] has no truck with blessing pacts or prayer cloths. His magazine, *Decision*, which outstrips in circulation all its rivals, boasts of no miracles. He has never said: "Come and join me and you will be cured of your physical and mental ills, freed from your creditors and loved by all."

—Alan Bestic, 1971

Evangelist Billy Graham
and His Critics

He plays golf with presidents and famous Hollywood stars; he has counseled prime ministers and conducted private church services for the Queen of England. Some of the world's biggest bankers and business executives have helped sponsor his crusades, and a famous Roman Catholic Cardinal once summoned reporters to praise his work. He has called the Archbishop of Canterbury "brother," and Emperor Haile Selassie closed the schools and opened the royal stadium for his rally. Around the world he is the best known American Protestant churchman, and at home he is the foremost, if not the only, authentic clergyman celebrity. A leading news magazine recently declared that he "holds a passport into the world of power politics of a kind that no other U.S. preacher before him has ever been granted."[1] He is William Franklin "Billy" Graham, the voice of evangelical Christianity to many millions of Christians.

For a preacher who has reached the very pinnacle of fame and success, Billy Graham's road to the top began in the midst of some of the most unlikely circumstances. He was born November 7, 1918, in a farmhouse a few miles outside of Charlotte,

369

North Carolina. His father was a hard-working dairyman, a stern family patriarch, and a devout Christian. At an early age young Graham began to assume a share of the responsibility of running the farm. Throughout his high school days he milked twenty cows before he went to school and again every evening. He soon decided there must be other things to do in life besides milking cows. But he once explained that he had not become a preacher just to escape the chore: "Before I went into the ministry, I had often said that there were two things that I'd never do—one, be an undertaker and the other, be a clergyman. I put them both in the same category." [2]

Young Billy Graham was highly regarded by his high school classmates. And with his wavy blond hair, sparkling eyes and tall, slender figure, he was especially popular with the girls. In 1934 he was sixteen years old, an age when social activities were fast becoming more attractive than the regular family worship periods. In May of that year his father loaned a pasture to a group of local businessmen for an evangelistic campaign to be preached by the Reverend Mordecai Fowler Ham of Louisville, a fire-and-brimstone preacher whose tendency to expose scandal and attack other ministers cost him the support of most of the Charlotte Ministerial Association. In later years Ham became increasingly controversial by associating himself with a group of ministers who promoted hatred for the Jews, but in 1934 he enjoyed the support of many fundamentalist Christians in the South for the conversions that flowed from his powerful preaching.

After attending the Mordecai Ham services for several evenings, young Graham was much impressed with the preaching and contemplated dedicating his life to the Lord. He later recalled that on the evening he went forward to accept salvation Ham had begun his sermon by saying, "There's a great sinner in this place tonight." Billy said he concluded that "mother's been telling him about me." When evangelist Ham gave his altar call, Billy hesitated. But after he was urged to go forward by a counselor whom he knew and respected, he turned to Grady Wilson, a young man who would later become his associate minister, and said, "Let's go." Later he remembered that "there were no tears, no blazing vision, no gift of tongues." [3] If young Graham registered no great emotion there was still joy aplenty in the Graham household. His father crossed from the opposite side of the tabernacle to throw his arms around him and offer thanks to God.

With yet another year of high school facing him, Billy, together with his friend Grady Wilson, spent the summer of his sixteenth year as a traveling salesman for the Fuller Brush Company. Graham outsold every Fuller salesman in North Carolina that summer, a happy experience that probably played an important part in his later success as an evangelist. Graham said,

> . . . I was naturally sort of a shy fellow and I didn't particularly like to meet people. That [selling brushes] got me over that. It allowed me to talk with people and to sell people. I never took a speech course in my life. I never have read a book on speech. Because the way I speak in the pulpit is my natural form of speaking, except before a big crowd, I speak a bit louder. . . .[4]

Billy Graham grew up with the dream of becoming a professional baseball player, and he actually spent the summer of 1936, the year he was graduated from high school, playing semiprofessional baseball for a team in Charlotte. But following his conversion his parents increasingly made known their hope that he would enter the ministry. Being Presbyterians they believed strongly that ministers should be college educated. They were conservative people and strongly favored a fundamentalist college. The family purse also had to be considered. In the end they chose Bob Jones College in Cleveland, Tennessee (now Bob Jones University in Greenville, South Carolina). The late Bob Jones Sr., a one-time itinerant evangelist who founded the college, backed up his stringent rules and regulations with a stern disciplinary code and a cadre of monitors. The school specialized in training ministers, missionaries, evangelists and other Christian workers. As the Graham parents were later to discover, it was not an accredited institution. John Pollock, authorized biographer of Billy Graham, described Dr. Bob Jones Sr. as a man who "knew exactly what was true and false in faith, ethics and academics. He often stated publicly that his institution had never been wrong. Independent thought was so discouraged that many alumni say in retrospect that there was thought control." [5] At the end of his first semester young Graham announced he was withdrawing and received a gratuitious warning from Dr. Jones: "Billy, if you leave and throw your life away at a little country Bible School, the chances are you'll never be heard of. At the best, all you could amount to would be a poor country Baptist preacher somewhere out in the sticks. [6]

Graham enrolled in tiny Florida Bible Institute located a few miles outside Tampa. It was housed in a one-time country club, part of which had been refurbished to accommodate its small group of students. Another part of the building functioned as a resort hotel, and most of the students paid their way at the Institute by working as waiters, bellhops and errand boys. Young Graham cut grass, washed dishes and caddied on the nearby golf course. He remembers his three and a half years at the Institute as a happy period in which he learned to preach even though he sometimes had to use tree stumps and alligators as a substitute congregation or preach on the street in front of a saloon. It was during his stay at the Florida Bible Institute that he changed his church membership from Presbyterian to Southern Baptist and made the decision to spend his life preaching the Gospel as an evangelist. In early 1973, 71-year-old Dr. W. T. Watson, president and founder of the Florida Bible Institute, had occasion to tell reporters that when Billy Graham enrolled in his school in 1937 he was more interested in baseball and girls than in preaching the Gospel, but "he got down to business and started preaching to tree stumps along the Hillsborough River. We never had to ask Billy to preach twice—he'd go anywhere." The little Institute has changed its name to Trinity College since Billy left, and moved a few miles down the Gulf Coast. Watson commented about Graham: "Wherever he goes, he gives Trinity College a good plug." When asked if he had thought of renaming the college in honor of its most famous alumnus, he replied: "Billy wouldn't want it and, besides, Billy's so big now he belongs to the world." [7]

Graham left the Florida Bible Institute in 1940. He enrolled at Wheaton, a Bible college near Chicago that his mother approved of most highly. It was a reputable school with very high academic standards, and young Graham learned to his sorrow that most of his work at Florida Bible Institute could not be transferred for credits at Wheaton. He had become a dedicated student in Florida, and at Wheaton he found an ideal place to quench his new-found thirst for knowledge. He was graduated in 1943, the same year he married Ruth Bell, another alumnus of Wheaton. Dr. Nelson Bell, her father, would later play an important part in Billy's ministry.

During that same year Graham became a full-time pastor for the first time, at Western Spring Baptist Church not far from Wheaton College. The following year the first members of what would later be called the Billy Graham team started working together. George Beverely Shea sang and Billy Graham preached for 45 minutes each Sunday on a radio program called *Songs in the Night*. They had been able to take over the program because of the Reverend Torrey Johnson, a well-known radio voice in the Chicago area. He was the minister who would later bring Graham into the Youth for Christ movement. After World War II, Billy worked in Europe for Youth for Christ, an experience that helped mature his judgment and hone his preaching technique. It also gave him the opportunity to develop a deep friendship for the English people.

In early 1945 Dr. William Bell Riley, a controversial fundamentalist minister who founded the Northwestern Schools in Minneapolis, asked Billy Graham to become his successor as president of his schools. A series of refusals by Graham only seemed to make Riley, then in his late eighties, more determined. Although Graham was flattered by the offer, he did not want to accept. Biographer Pollock asserted that Billy was "not sure that he wished to be so closely identified with midwest 'Fundamentalism,' because of the unfortunate connotation of the word." [8]

It was against Graham's better judgment that he finally agreed to accept the post as interim president in case Riley died. And then he agreed to serve only until a new president could be found. Pollock also wrote that for the first time Graham tasted failure. He noted the "constant thwartings" induced by jealousy that not even Graham's winsomeness and great charm could overcome. Graham turned increasingly to evangelism. He appointed capable men to some of the leadership positions at Northwestern and left most of the management in their hands.

During the latter part of the 1940's, Billy Graham poured most of his energy into old-style evangelism. He continued to give some of his attention to the Youth for Christ movement, but his efforts were mainly devoted to revivals in auditoriums, theaters and canvas tents. He conducted campaigns around the country, from Grand Rapids to Miami, from Baltimore and Altoona to Modesto, California. Unlike some of the faith healers who were roaming the land in great numbers during that same period, Graham's name was all but unknown to the general public. But all of that was about to change. Late in 1949 he headed for Los Angeles to begin a three-week tent campaign. He did not know that he was moving toward a fateful rendezvous with history.

The story of Graham's Los Angeles crusade is now so well known that only the highlights bear repeating. Near the end of the third week the evangelist pondered whether to extend what had been a rather ordinary campaign. Stuart Hamblen, a race-horse owner, gambler, and local cowboy figure who composed his own songs for his popular radio program, had interviewed Billy on his show and promised to attend the revival. After some stormy scenes Hamblen was converted. When he informed his radio audience that he had "hit the sawdust trail," and gave testimonies at Billy's tent, it made the type of sensational news that attracted crowds to the tent revival. Suddenly, Billy found himself besieged with reporters and photographers from some of the largest daily newspapers. He was informed that he had been "kissed" by publisher William Randolph Hearst, whose papers were printing banner headlines about the Graham crusade.

Soon the packed tent was the scene of another astounding conversion, that of ex-convict Jim Vaus, whose name was linked with a much-publicized gangster syndicate. Vaus was followed a few days later by Louis Zamperini, a track star of the 1936 Berlin Olympics and a hero of the Pacific fighting in World War

II who had suffered brutal treatment as a prisoner of war. Even after the revival campaign was extended through a seventh week, the meetings continued to be crowded with lines of people that blocked the streets around the tent. When Graham closed the campaign on November 20th and departed for Minneapolis, his name had become a household word. He had become a genuine preacher celebrity.

Evangelist Graham received invitations to preach from almost every point on the compass. An era of great crusades that would eventually reach cities all over the world had begun. The Billy Graham Evangelistic Association, Inc., with headquarters in Minneapolis, was formed a short time later. Now grown into a multimillion dollar colossus with an annual budget of approximately $20 million, it oversees and directs a vast array of programs, such as the Billy Graham "Hour of Decision" broadcast on approximately 1,000 stations each week; television programs of the crusades televised on a nation-wide network of hundreds of stations; publication of many books and some four million copies of the monthly *Decision* magazine, including editions for the French, the Germans, the Spanish, the Japanese, and two in English for the British and the Australians. The complex also includes a counseling department, a mailing department to receive and answer thousands of letters each week, a separate division to produce films, even a photographic department.

How has the wavy-haired preacher from the hills of North Carolina built such an empire? No single answer would satisfy all who have raised the question, for Graham does not employ any of the widely used gimmicks. His association owns no property except that which its religious work requires. It has no special investments in stocks, bonds, parking lots, garment factories or mines. It makes no pleas for funds to support orphans in foreign countries only to skim off most of the donations in the name of promotional costs. There are no prayer cloths, no blessing pacts or plans, no special "key" to unlock Biblical prophecy, no seed-faith money arrangements, no miracle healings, no holy oil, no miracle pocketbooks, no pictures that glow in the dark, no miracle pieces of red string, no miracle soil from Jerusalem. To his dedicated followers there is only Billy Graham, standing tall behind the pulpit, his eyes glowing fiercely, limp-back leather-bound Bible flopped over his left hand while his right hand slices through the air in majestic arcs in cadence with a voice filled with conviction and delivered in staccato bursts that seem to turn the most commonplace phrases into Scripture-like commands. He brings a message that is orthodox—straight from the Bible—to millions of Protestants. To them and millions of others, some of whom may not be especially religious, he comes across as a person who can be believed. In a world that seems to have lost its moorings for many people, a world bristling with confidence men, charlatans, false advertising and lawsuits, his simple but forthright message is eminently believable. It helps that he stresses the old values, the tried and tested ways of America's past. But perhaps the principal reason for his great popularity derives from his strict avoidance of controversial issues, especially those which tend to divide the nation. Graham originally adopted this policy of tolerance on the advice of the President of Wheaton College. He made it a firm rule never to answer his critics. On those rare occasions when he has responded, he has usually chosen the soft answer, in humility and an irenic spirit. His ability to maintain close friendship with ministers who hold widely differing religious views without compromising his own beliefs is a logical extension of his turn-the-other-cheek policy. As his official biographer makes clear, it is a policy that has paid handsome dividends:

> Nevertheless, one of the most significant developments of the early nineteen fifties was the widening range of church support behind him. Like D. L. Moody, Graham accepted gratefully the goodwill and aid of any who let him uninhibitedly preach his message. He insisted that the executives of a crusade be men in full sympathy with his objectives, but he welcomed all, whatever their theology, who would co-operate with his platform. Thus Graham, by 1952 the most widely heard preacher in America, was spearhead of a new ecumenicity, breaking down barriers raised by a generation or more of theological bitterness.[9]

In 1960, the foremost authority on revivalism, Dr. William G. McLoughlin, Jr., of Brown University, looked at the "new ecu-

menicity" Billy Graham was leading. He considered the North
Carolina evangelist a spokesman for a newly consolidated and
articulate pietistic movement that was challenging the old Protestant church system. In his book *Billy Graham: Revivalist in a
Secular Age* he described the kinds of organizations that were
coming together in Billy Graham's cooperative evangelist movement:

> Theologically this movement is an amalgamation of the mellowing
> fundamentalism of the 1920's and the maturing pentecostalism of a
> much older date. Whether it is called "the new evangelicalism" or
> "neofundamentalism," this theology represents a middle ground be-
> tween the fanatical or ultrafundamentalist fringe groups (the follow-
> ers of Carl McIntire, the Holy Rollers, the faith healers, the snake
> handlers) and the liberalism or modernism that is associated with the
> major denominations. Ecclesiastically it seems to have found a center
> in the National Association of Evangelicals. Socially the bulk of its
> followers are among a lower-middle-class group with predominantly
> a rural background which is trying to break through to suburban re-
> spectability without yielding too much of the religious pietism it
> cherishes.[10]

By 1973 Graham's interdenominational amalgamation had become one of the strongest religious forces in the land. As it increased in size, he continued to widen the outer limits of his
middle-ground movement until he embraced both faith healers
and an ever-increasing stream of discontented modernists. He
announced that he liked everybody, and almost everybody seemed
to like him. He has been called the President's preacher; others
see him as the nation's religious father-figure, and Governor John
Connally has even called him the conscience of America. Without
doubt Graham is widely considered the epitome of morality. His
life is an open book, and there has never been a hint of scandal
about his personal life. He is also honest. Although there was
some criticism of the crusade's financial arrangements during the
early part of Graham's career, by 1960, even Dr. McLouglin, who
has been critical of many aspects of Graham's work, did not
hesitate to state that the revivalist's corporation was honestly
operated and that

Graham's personal financial honesty is beyond reproach. He does not, as Billy Sunday did, claim that "the laborer is worthy of his hire" and consequently enrich himself . . . Although he lives comfortably, he does not live lavishly . . . He has few expenses outside of his home and has received many expensive gifts from friends and admirers. But he has not made one-tenth of the money he could have made out of his evangelism and has in fact refused to use for himself much of what he has made.[11]

Because of his impeccable reputation for honesty and morality and because he is the leading symbol of religion in America, Graham can do things and go places no other preacher would dare consider. While spokesmen for other large conservative religious organizations are wringing their hands about the "generation gap," Graham can put on a cap, a sweat shirt and dark glasses and interview young people at their gatherings and their love-ins. While Garner Ted Armstrong has denounced the "Jesus Freaks," Billy has separated what was faddish from the "Jesus Revolution" and found in the remainder a mighty force for evangelism. Unlike some conservative ministers, Graham does not have to be afraid to quote approvingly from the works of liberals, anti-establishment sources or members of the avant-garde. It is also a measure of his secure leadership position that he can still retain his magnetic-like hold on the loyalty of millions of Southern Baptists while he roams the world gathering groups of Christians of quite different belief into his great international movement. Securing the cooperation of the Reverend Oral Roberts and his evangelical association is one of the best illustrations of the masterful Graham recruiting technique possible, for many Southern Baptists dislike professional faith healers and are often strongly opposed to speaking in tongues.

It was September of 1950 when Graham first arranged for Roberts to visit one of his crusades. Some twenty-two years later Oral's name was one of the thirty-six on a select list of churchmen to be briefed at the White House by Dr. Kissinger. According to Oral Roberts, who included an account of the Graham-Roberts friendship in his latest autobiography, he first saw Billy in the late 1940's, when the then unknown revivalist was conducting his tent revival in Los Angeles, but it was about ten years later be-

fore the two met face to face. Oral's big tent had been destroyed
in a storm in Amarillo, and he and his wife visited an old friend
in Tacoma while waiting for a replacement. Oral's friend had
visited the Billy Graham crusade that was being conducted in
Portland, Oregon, at that time, and he relayed Billy's invitation
for Oral to visit his services. Roberts flew to Portland, where
Graham immediately insisted that he sit on the pulpit platform
and also lead the audience in prayer. Oral wrote: "I was struck
then that Billy wasn't aware of the controversy over my ministry.
Feeling this, I told him, 'Billy, are you sure you want me to do
that? A lot of people don't understand my work.'"

Billy reassured Oral, explaining, "God has not given me that
kind of ministry, but He has given it to you. I want you to lead
in prayer."

When they met again Roberts was in Washington, D.C. to
address a Full Gospel organization. He was surprised to learn
that he and Graham were staying in the same hotel. Through a
mutual friend Billy invited Oral to his room. But the Tulsa faith
healer woud not go:

> Suddenly deep negative feelings washed over me. In the interim
> since our last meeting I'd been to Australia where I had experienced
> the greatest defeat of my ministry. My Melbourne crusade had to be
> closed midway because of the opposition from the press. Billy went
> for a crusade there later and scored a great success. Mine had por-
> trayed me as a fraud and a villain.[12]

Billy insisted, and when Oral continued to refuse, he sought
permission to come to Oral's room. Roberts agreed: "If Billy wants
to come to my room, I would be glad to have him."

A little later Graham was in the room, radiating his charm and
complimenting the Roberts ministry. Oral was listening but not
responding:

> It hurt me down deep that the media had built him up as an honest
> man and me as a dishonest man . . . While he was talking, I just
> blurted out, "Billy, you've never seen the day when you were more
> honest than I am . . . Every article about you is about how honest
> you are and the great work you're doing. Everything said about me

is the opposite. My ministry is vilivied. I'm painted as a villain and my ministry is ridiculed. But, Billy, I want you to know my office and my life are conducted in the highest ethical manner." [13]

Who could be more qualified to assuage the pain of a broken heart or a wounded ego than Dr. Billy Graham? In a instant the famous magic was at work. He commiserated with the Tulsa healer, explaining that he also had problems, different from those that plagued Oral to be sure, but every bit as hurtful.

Later, as previously mentioned in other chapters, Oral Roberts accepted Graham's invitation to attend the Berlin Congress on Evangelism in 1966. Then in 1967 Billy was the dedicatory speaker at Oral Roberts University. In 1972 Roberts was one of the thirty-six chosen to attend the special White House briefing. And shortly before election time in 1972 the cover of Oral's magazine featured Oral Roberts with the President of the United States.

Although Graham is almost universally acclaimed, it would be a mistake to assume that he has no critics. W. David Lockard, a sympathetic biographer of Billy Graham, explains this apparent paradox:

> It is doubtful whether an evangelist in recent times has been more constantly praised as a man. Not that he is not criticized; criticisms are many and varied. But they are invariably aimed at Graham's message or methods rather than Graham. Many of those who reject his theology still strongly admire the man.

Often enough critics have charged that Graham does not say the same thing year after year. Vietnam and the late Senator Joseph McCarthy have been cited as examples of subjects on which Graham has held conflicting views. Several magazines have published quotations made by Graham in 1966 that make him appear quite hawkish on Vietnam. At that time a majority of the nation probably felt much the same way. But that situation had changed quite drastically by the time the U.S. military effort in Vietnam ended. Many who had never felt dovish about the war hoped never to hear of the divisive war again. Regardless of one's position, it was a very controversial subject. When the bombing of North Vietnam was resumed shortly before the end of the war, Graham was asked by *Newsweek's* Jane Whitmore how he felt about the military action. According to *The New Republic*, his answer was:

> . . . The whole world has a great deal of violence going on which doesn't occupy the headlines. There are many people being killed in this country by drunken drivers and crime. Man is prone to violence and there will be no cessation of that, not until the Christ of our Kingdom comes . . . I deplore the killing in the war and I pray it can be ended as soon as possible. But we also have to realize that there are hundreds of thousands of deaths attributed to smoking. . . .

Such criticism of the famous revivalist may not be entirely fair. On several occasions he has described how his thinking has changed through the years. In 1960, writing on the topic "What Ten Years Have Taught me," he said:

> Ten years ago my concept of the church tended to be narrow and provincial, but after a decade of intimate contact with Christians the world over I am now aware that the family of God contains people of various ethnological, cultural and class and denominational differences. In groups which in my ignorant piousness I formerly "frowned upon" I have found men so dedicated and so in love with the truth that I have felt unworthy to be in their presence.[16]

When people are told that Billy Graham can change his mind like anyone else, some, oddly enough, take the attitude that a man doing God's work, a man of Graham's stature, somehow ought not be wrong in an opinion.

Evangelist Graham has often pointed to both the extreme left and the extreme right as irreconcilable elements of the political spectrum. Much of the criticism directed at him emanates from these political polar regions. The far left has probably captured more news space in this respect, mainly because most of the threats to kidnap celebrities and national leaders have been attributed to such groups. Unquestionably the far left has no love for Graham and attacks him in their publications at every convenient opportunity. But the extreme right is the source of more attacks on the revivalist, if only because it is numerically so much

larger and publishes much more literature. Billy's troubles with
the religious far right began in the early part of his career.
Biographer Pollock has described Graham's concern about being
identified with the midwest fundamentalists when he pondered
going to the Northwestern Schools in the late 1940's:

> Billy Graham, trusting with all his heart the living Christ, believed in
> the "fundamentals of the faith" . . . But the term "fundamentalist"
> which only about thirty-five years earlier had been adopted by many
> evangelicals in the United States . . . had developed regrettable
> overtones. It had been annexed especially by those who prolonged
> the unnecessary nineteenth-century conflict between science and re-
> ligion, who tended to mistrust scholarship and, too often could not
> find it in them to be charitable towards those who disagreed.[17]

Biographer Lockard is another who has written of Graham's desire
to shed the label of fundamentalist:

> During the Scotland Crusade of 1955, for instance, he expressed his
> desire to break away from the "fundamentalist" label. Though the-
> ologically fundamental in many ways, he wanted to avoid the aura of
> bigotry and narrowness sometimes associated with the term. When
> asked to define "fundamentalist," he declined. He substituted the
> term "Constructionist" and explained that he was seeking to rebuild
> the church.[18]

Graham's authorized biographer has listed Dr. Carl McIntire
and Dr. John R. Rice, editor of *The Sword of the Lord,* a fundamentalist newspaper, as two ministers who have attacked Billy
Graham for associating with men of false beliefs about the Bible.
McIntire has made almost a career of attacking Graham, as discussed in detail in an earlier chapter. Indeed, there does not seem
to be another example of such sustained attacks on one religious
leader by a single newspaper. Dr. John Rice has supported Mc-
Intire through *The Sword of the Lord* newspaper. And both Rice
and McIntire have been closely linked with the leaders of Bob
Jones University.

Although Billy did not remain long at Bob Jones University, he
has always felt a spiritual debt to Dr. Bob Jones Senior. In March

of 1966, when Graham took his crusade to Greenville, South Carolina, the home of Bob Jones University, he found his campaign boycotted by the students and faculty of the school. Dr. Bob Jones Senior, at 82, was Chairman of the Board of Trustees. His son, Dr. Bob Jones Jr., the President of the school, had attacked Graham as a false teacher who "is doing more harm to the cause of Jesus Christ than any living man." Jones was upset because Graham's crusade was sending people who had made decisions for Christ back to their own churches instead of directing them to fundamentalist churches. In Jones' words, Graham was sending them "back to unbelieving churches, to false teachers and Unitarians." What was even worse to Jones was the way Graham had betrayed the Scriptures by integrating his rallies and by accepting support from liberals and modernists. Billy Graham repaid them: "I really do love Bob Jones Senior, and Junior too," he explained.[19]

Graham had taken the position that God had used Bob Jones, and since he was "the Lord's anointed," he would not attack or refute him. When Billy conducted his 1957 crusade in New York, Jones was reported to have said Graham was too immature for a New York campaign. He wrote letters announcing that no Bob Jones students would be permitted to hold a prayer meeting to ask blessing on Graham in New York. A young Graham convert was expelled for standing up for Billy.[20]

Graham has been attacked for his position on social problems by both the far left and far right, by both liberals and conservatives. In many parts of the country he is considered a liberal because of his stand on the race issue.

The more sophisticated segment of the right also takes an occasional slap at Billy, although it is usually done in the form of lampoon or ridicule. Here is Francis Russell remembering Billy Graham in *National Review*:

I first encountered Billy Graham in 1950 when he came to Boston for a week's revival. Fresh from Bob Jones College, he then held to the literalness of the King James Version with a fundamentalist fervor that he would later modify in favor of Madison Avenue. Heaven was still to him the four-square city of jasper and gold like unto glass, twelve thousand furlongs in length and breadth, dimensions that he conveniently transcribed for us into modern equivalents. By his calculations the Heavenly City was 1,500 by 1,500 or 2,250,000 square miles—with an urban density of about ten thousand inhabitants to the mile . . . Aureoled by the spotlight, Billy looked the embodiment of church, home and country. The square jaw, the carefully marcelled hair, the engaging smile seemed to suggest Mother's Day even as the mobile lips spoke of Heaven. Yet there was something curiously archaic about him that I, in the balcony watching his highlighted cures, could not quite place. Then suddenly it came to me. Billy was the poster male I used to see on the billboards of the Dudley Street elevated station on my way to the Roxbury Latin School, a type that was later superseded by the more knowing Esquire gent. Billy was the Arrow Collar man! [21]

The Christian Century and a variety of other liberal periodicals have attacked Graham with vigor and some regularity. Sometimes it is about his crusades, as the following quotation illustrates: "Ministers evaluating a Billy Graham crusade held last year in Oakland, California, have estimated that approximatedly one-third of the 21,670 who registered 'decisions for Christ' gave false names and addresses." [22]

In more recent years the attacks mounted against Graham have to do with politics, a subject that holds a great deal of fascination for evangelist Graham. Since July 14, 1950, when Graham was invited to meet President Truman at the White House, the North Carolina preacher has been a friend of every occupant of the White House. Indeed, Graham has sought since he emerged on the national scene in 1951 to "be with and influence a presidential candidate." [23] His long friendship and high regard for Richard Nixon brought him perilously close to involvement in party politics, says biographer David Lockard. The evangelist remained abroad for much of 1960 because he did not wish to become involved in a partisan way in the Nixon-Kennedy campaign. Billy summed up his feeling about some Presidents to television commentator David Frost:

I have been friends with two or three men who became President years later—after our friendship began. I knew Mr. Johnson for many years and I knew Mr. Nixon for many years . . . And through the years our friendship grew . . . And he has told me many times, "Billy, at all costs, you stay out of politics." And in 1960, he said, when there was some pressure on me to endorse him, and I had no intention of getting into politics if I could avoid it, but he told me at that time, he said, "Your ministry is more important than my election." . . . And he would never, never try to use me politically. And neither did President Johnson. . . .[24]

In 1960, after remaining abroad throughout the presidential campaign, Billy Graham indicated to Henry Luce of *Life* magazine that he would like to call attention to Nixon's merits without becoming involved in partisan politics. Luce suggested that he could write an article for *Life*. After Graham gave Luce his article, he was not happy about it, but he agreed to let it be published. On the night the magazine went to press, Billy and his wife got on their knees and prayed that God would stop the article if publication of it was against his will. The next morning two Democratic governors called Graham to tell him they had heard about the article and hoped he would not let it be published, since it would put him in politics. When Luce called to say the article had not been published, Graham was said to be so relieved that he shouted.[25]

After the 1964 elections, Graham revealed that he had received 1.2 million letters asking him to support Barry Goldwater for President. But he said that not even his wife knew who he voted for. In an article entitled "Billy's Political Pitch," the Religion Editor of *Newsweek* magazine reported shortly before the 1968 elections that "Graham may decide to reveal his choice for the White House." The article quoted Billy as saying, "This country is going through its greatest crisis since the Civil War. Many people who just don't know how to cast their vote might accept what I have to say." [26]

Long after the elections were history, *Newsweek* revealed how Graham had fared during the campaign period:

When Johnson pulled out of the 1968 Presidential race, Graham was again faced with the dilemma of whether publicly to endorse Richard Nixon, a friend of two decades. "He was prepared to do it if necessary," says Presidential assistant Harry S. Dent, the red-haired Baptist

deacon who helped organize Mr. Nixon's campaign in the South. In
the end, Billy made no public endorsement, but he was a conspicuous
member of the audience in several of the televised question-and-
answer shows produced for Mr. Nixon's campaign. Then, only one
week before the election, the wire services carried a report that Mr.
Nixon's name was on Billy Graham's absentee ballot. "That was all
I needed," admits Dent. "I used it in our TV commercials right to the
end." [27]

It was not only members of the far right like Dr. Carl McIntire
who were screaming about Billy Graham getting into the White
House. From the liberal religious organs came the cries of other
critics: "Billy Graham is an apt example of how millennialist
predictions and conservative political views combine. One moment
he describes ours as an evil age which Jesus Christ will come
again to redeem; the next he is in the White House sanctifying the
Vietnam War and the domestic status quo." [28] And the retiring
General Secretary of the World Council of Churches gave his
opinion on the same sensitive subject in October 1972. In answer
to the question, "Do you think President Nixon's relation with
religionists like Billy Graham has strengthened a regressive form
of Christianity?" Secretary Eugene Blake responded:

> I'm very concerned. It is quite clear that President Nixon has religious
> advisers who have no respect for the mainline Protestant leadership.
> From the beginning, the actions of the Nixon White House have
> worked to downgrade the basic mainline Protestant leadership. And
> that is because this leadership was critical of the government's Viet-
> nam policy—was critical before Nixon came in and still is. That is the
> issue.[29]

In *The Social Contract* Jean Jacques Rousseau wrote: "There
is therefore a purely civil profession of faith of which the Sover-
eign should fix the articles, not exactly as religious dogmas, but
as social sentiments without which a man cannot be a good citizen
or a faithful subject." More and more, it has been said, Billy
Graham's God resembles Rousseau's God of civil religion. And
Robert Bellah, the sociologist of religion who has pioneered in
the study of the American form of civil religion, finds its diety

more related to law and order than to salvation and love. In one of the strongest charges yet made against the famous evangelist by a national news periodical, *Newsweek* asserted that Graham in his larger effort to justify the ways of God and government had "fashioned a common-denominator faith which hews almost doctrine for doctrine to the 'positive dogmas' Rousseau outlined for his civil religion 208 years ago: the existence of a mighty, intelligent and beneficent Divinity, possessed of foresight and providence, the life to come, the happiness of the just, the punishment of the wicked, the sanctity of the social contract and the laws."

And by lending his own powerful voice to the civil religion in America, Graham, "albeit unwittingly, may have sharpened the religious aspects of the conflicts that currently rack the body politic." [30] Whatever view one takes of Billy Graham, it is impossible not to admire the smoothness with which he runs his vast organization and the gracefulness with which he avoids all controversy. The Armstrongs are more successful financially, and even Rev. Ike has as large a mailing list. But Graham has succeeded where all of the other preachers have failed. His roots are in southern fundamentalism, but he has built upon this foundation and adapted his views as the social and political climate in America changed. In the process, he has not only established himself as a preacher of international repute, he has aided his evangelical colleagues in their quest for that most precious commodity: respectability. As High Priest of America's civil religion, Billy Graham is at once the least colorful and most powerful preacher in the United States.

Notes

THE CONTROVERSIAL MIRACLES OF A. A. ALLEN

1. *Miracle Magazine,* July 1970.
2. A. A. Allen and Walter Wagner, *Born to Lose, Bound to Win,* Doubleday, 1970.
3. *Ibid.,* pp. 68, 74.
4. *Miracle Magazine,* February 1968, p. 22.
5. A. A. Allen and Walter Wagner, *Born to Lose, Bound to Win,* 1970.
6. Knoxville, Tennessee, *News-Sentinel,* October 22, 1955.
7. Letter from Research Secretary of the General Council of the Assemblies of God, August 31, 1971.
8. Sacramento *Bee,* April 6, 1956, p. 1.
9. Sacramento *Bee,* April 6, 1956, p. 8.
10. Sacramento *Bee,* April 26, 1956, p. 1.
11. "Faith Healers," *McCall's,* February 1957, p. 39.
12. A. A. Allen, *My Cross,* undated.
13. The *Age of Reason,* published by the Freethinkers of America, New York, August 1958.
14. *Miracle Magazine,* February 1964, p. 3.

15. *Miracle Magazine*, March 1968.
16. *Miracle Magazine*, September 1964.
17. *Miracle Magazine*, October 1965.
18. *Miracle Magazine*, May 1966.
19. *Miracle Magazine*, July 1965.
20. *Miracle Magazine*, July 1965 and August 1965.
21. *Miracle Magazine*, July 1965 and August 1965.
22. *Miracle Magazine*, July 1965 and August 1965.
23. *Miracle Magazine*, September 1967.
24. *Miracle Magazine*, November 1967.
25. *Time*, March 7, 1969.
26. *Miracle Magazine*, March 1968.
27. *Miracle Magazine*, November 1967.
28. *Miracle Magazine*, November 1967.
29. Miami *Herald*, November 2, 1969.
30. Don Stewart with Walter Wagner, *The Man From Miracle Valley*, The Great Horizons Company, 1971.
31. Oklahoma *Journal*, June 13, 1970.
32. Los Angeles *Times*, June 13, 1970.
33. New York *Times*, June 13, 1970.
34. *Miracle Magazine*, August 1970.
35. Don Stewart with Walter Wagner, *The Man From Miracle Valley*, The Great Horizons Co., 1971.
36. *Miracle Magazine*, February 1971.

UP FROM FAITH HEALING:
THE MIRACLE MINISTRY OF ORAL ROBERTS

1. T. L. Osborn, *Healing the Sick*, Tulsa, T. L. Osborn, 1955, p. 207.
2. Gordon Lindsay, *William Branham; A Man Sent from God*, Jeffersonville, Indiana, William Branham, 1950, p. 113.
3. *Time*, February 7, 1972, p. 62.
4. Oral Roberts, *The Call*, Garden City, Doubleday and Company, 1972, p. 52.
5. *Ibid.*, p. 13.
6. *Ibid.*, pp. 13–14.

7. *Ibid.*, p. 14.
8. Hayes B. Jacobs, "Oral Roberts: High Priest of Faith Healing," *Harper's* magazine, February 1962, pp. 37–43; and Oral Roberts, *The Call*, Garden City, Doubleday and Company, 1972, p. 155.
9. Oral Roberts, *My Story*, Tulsa, Oral Roberts, 1961, p. 73.
10. *Ibid.*, p. 93.
11. *Ibid.*, p. 93; and Oral Roberts, *The Call*, Garden City, Doubleday and Company, 1972, p. 154.
12. Oral Roberts, *My Twenty Years of a Miracle Ministry*, Tulsa, Oral Roberts, 1967, p. 10.
13. Hayes B. Jacobs, "Oral Roberts: High Priest of Faith Healing," *Harper's* magazine, February 1962, pp. 37–43.
14. Oral Roberts, *My Story*, Tulsa, Oral Roberts, 1961, p. 2.
15. *Ibid.*, p. 33.
16. *Ibid.*, p. 34.
17. *Ibid.*, p. 37.
18. *Ibid.*, p. 71.
19. *Ibid.*, p. 71.
20. *Ibid.*, p. 71.
21. *Ibid.*, p. 33.
22. Oral Roberts, *My Twenty Years of a Miracle Ministry*, Tulsa, Oral Roberts, 1967, p. 7.
23. Oral Roberts, *My Story*, Tulsa, Oral Roberts, 1961, pp. 71–97.
24. *Ibid.*, p. 78.
25. *Ibid.*, p. 79.
26. *Ibid.*
27. *Ibid.*, p. 92.
28. *Ibid.*, pp. 87–89.
29. Gordon Lindsay, *William Branham: A Man Sent from God*, Jeffersonville, Indiana, William Branham, 1950, p. 206.
30. Oral Roberts, *My Story*, Tulsa, Oral Roberts 1961, p. 90.
31. *Ibid.*, p. 94.
32. *Ibid.*, p. 94.
33. Oral Roberts, *Oral Roberts' Life Story as Told by Himself*, quoted in John Kobler, "King of the Faith Healers," *American* magazine, May 1956, p. 21.
34. Oral Roberts, *The Call*, Garden City, Doubleday and Company, 1972, p. 40.
35. James L. Dwyer, "Elijah the Third," *American Mercury*, July 1927, pp. 291–298.

36. Aimee Semple McPherson, *This is That*, Echo Park Evangelistic Association, Inc., 1923, p. 13.
37. T. L. Osborn, *Healing the Sick*, Tulsa, T. L. Osborn, 1955, pp. 207–208.
38. Gordon Lindsay, *William Branham: A Man Sent from God*, Jeffersonville, Indiana, William Branham, 1950, pp. 76–79.
39. Julius Stadsklev, *William Branham: A Prophet Visits South Africa*, Minneapolis, Julius Stadsklev, 1952, p. 39.
40. *Ibid.*, pp. 38, 43.
41. Gordon Lindsay, *William Branham: A Man Sent from God*, Jeffersonville, Indiana, William Branham, 1950, pp. 93, 206–A, photograph and caption no. 14A.
42. *Ibid.*, pp. 102–103.
43. Oral Roberts, *My Story*, Tulsa, Oral Roberts, 1961, p. 151.
44. *Ibid.*, pp. 39–40.
45. Hayes B. Jacobs, "Oral Roberts: High Priest of Faith Healing," *Harper's* magazine, February 1962, p. 42.
46. John Kobler, "King of the Faith Healers,"*American* magazine, May 1956, pp. 88–89.
47. John Kobler, "King of the Faith Healers," *American* magazine, May 1956, p. 89.
48. John Kobler, "King of the Faith Healers," *American* magazine, May 1956, pp. 89–90.
49. John Kobler, "King of the Faith Healers," *American* magazine, May 1956, p. 89.
50. John Kobler, "King of the Faith Healers," *American* magazine, May 1956, p. 21.
51. Hayes B. Jacobs, "Oral Roberts: High Priest of Faith Healing," *Harper's* magazine, February 1962, p. 42.
52. "Deadline From God," *Time*, July 11, 1955, p. 41.
53. James W. Fernandez, "Zulu Zionism," *Natural History* magazine, June-July 1971, p. 44.
54. Oral Roberts, *My Story*, Tulsa, Oral Roberts, 1961, p. 172.
55. *Ibid.*, p. 173.
56. *Ibid.*, p. 173.
56. *Ibid.*, p. 173.
57. *Ibid.*, p. 174.
58. *Ibid.*, pp. 176, 177.
59. *Ibid.*, pp. 177, 178.
60. *Ibid.*, p. 186.

61. *Ibid.*, pp. 187, 188.
62. "I'm No Fraud, Says Evangelist," Sydney *Sun-Herald*, January 15, 1956, p. 1.
63. "Trouble for Oral," *Time*, February 13, 1956.
64. "Evangelist Roberts is Taking it Easy," Sydney *Daily Telegraph*, January 17, 1956.
65. "Crowd Chases, Abuses Faith Healer," Melbourne *Argus*, February 9, 1956, p. 5.
66. "Healer's Strong-arm Men Get a Warning," Melbourne *Argus*, February 6, 1956, p. 7.
67. "Sinful, Faithless City Too Much for Oral," Melbourne *Argus*, February 11, 1956, p. 3.
68. "Minister Finds Australia Tough," Sunday *Oklahoman*, April 30, 1972, Section A.
69. Jack Gould, "On Faith Healing," New York *Times*, February 19, 1956.
70. "Travail of the Healer," *Newsweek*, March 19, 1956, p. 82.
71. "Faith-Healing Over TV," *America*, March 17, 1956, p. 652.
72. "Coe's Cures," *Newsweek*, February 27, 1956, p. 56.
73. "Faith Healers," *McCall's*, February 1957 p. 39.
74. Quoted in Jhan and June Robins, "The Strange Facts About Faith Healing," *Redbook* magazine, July 1960, pp. 80–81.
75. Quoted in John Kobler, "King of the Faith Healers," *American* magazine, May 1956, p. 91.
76. W. E. Mann, "Supersalesman of Faith Healing," *The Christian Century*, September 5, 1956, p. 1020.
77. "Faith 'Cure' Kills Her," Miami *News*, July 6, 1959.
78. Oral Roberts, *The Call* (Garden City: Doubleday and Company, 1972), pp. 53–54.
79. "Faith Healers," *McCall's*, February 1957, p. 39.
80. The American Medical Association, quoted in "The Miracles of Faith Healing,' *Cosmopolitan*, December 1958, p. 37.
81. Jhan and June Robins, "The Strange Facts About Faith Healing," *Redbook* magazine, July 1960, p. 80.
82. Oral Roberts, *My Story*, Tulsa, Oral Roberts, 1961, pp. 97–130; and Oral Roberts, *My Twenty Years of a Miracle Ministry*, Tulsa, Oral Roberts, 1967, pp. 25–46.
83. Oral Roberts, *My Story*, Tulsa, Oral Roberts, 1961, p. 168.
84. Gordon H. Fraser, "Oral Roberts Visits the Navajos," (Minneapolis, Religion Analysis Service, Inc., undated tract.

85. Oral Roberts, *My Story*, Tulsa, Oral Roberts, 1961, pp. 169–170.
86. *Ibid.*, pp. 170–171.
87. *Ibid.*, p. 170.
88. Oral Roberts, *The Call*, Garden City, Doubleday and Company, 1972, pp. 156–157.
89. *Ibid.*, p. 157.
90. *Ibid.*, p. 157.
91. *Ibid.*, p. 159.
92. *Ibid.*, p. 159.
93. *Ibid.*, p. 160.
94. "Keys To a Healer's Kingdom," *Life*, August 3, 1962, p. 17.
95. Oral Roberts, *The Call*, Garden City, Doubleday and Company, 1972, p. 178.
96. *Ibid.*, p. 179; and Oral Roberts, *My Story*, Tulsa, Oral Roberts, 1961, pp. 160–161.
97. Hayes B. Jacobs, "Oral Roberts: High Priest of Faith Healing," *Harper's* magazine, February 1962, p. 43.
98. Oral Roberts, *My Story, Tulsa*, Oral Roberts, 1961, pp. 88–89.
99. Oral Roberts, *God's Formula for Success and Prosperity*, Tulsa, Abundant Life Publications, 1966, pp. 86–87.
100. "The Laying on of Hands," *Cosmopolitan*, February 1956, pp. 78–83.
101. Oral Roberts, *The Call*, Garden City, Doubleday and Company, 1972, pp. 199–200.
102. *Ibid.*, pp. 199–200; and Oral Roberts, *God's Formula for Success and Prosperity*, Tulsa, Abundant Life Publications, 1966, p. 127.
103. Oral Roberts, *God's Formula for Success and Prosperity*, Tulsa, Abundant Life Publications, 1966, pp. 202, 210.
104. Tulsa *Tribune*, April 2, 1971, quoted in Oral Roberts, *The Call*, Garden City Doubleday and Company, 1972, p. 214.
105. Tulsa *World*, April 2, 1971, quoted in Oral Roberts, *The Call*, Garden City, Doubleday and Company, 1972 pp. 214, 215.
106. Curry Kirkpatrick, "A Time to Bless the Beasts and Freshmen," *Sports Illustrated*, November 27, 1972, p. 38.
107. *Sport* magazine, Vol. 53, No. 5 (May 1972), p. 20.
108. Oral Roberts, *The Call*, Garden City, Doubleday and Company, 1972, pp. 107, 159, 199, 203.
109. *Ibid.*, p. 134.
110. "Interview with Oral Roberts," Texas *Methodist*, March 24, 1971.
111. David Craighead, "Evangelist Seeking 'To Open Wider Door' For Ministry," Oklahoma *Journal* March 23, 1968.

112. Oral Roberts, *The Call,* Garden City, Doubleday and Company, 1972, pp. 127, 134.
113. *Ibid.,* p. 129.
114. *Ibid.,* pp. 138–146.
115. *Ibid.,* p. 142.
116. *Ibid.,* p. 145.
117. Richard Rhodes, "Heaven on Earth," *Harper's* magazine, May 1970, p. 121.
118. All information on Oral Roberts' University Village Retriment Center was obtained in 1972 through brochures and pamphlets provided by University Village and through interviews with retirees at the Village and with some applicants for retirement apartments there.
119. Louis Rose, *Faith Healing,* Middlesex, England, Gollancz, 1968, p. 176.

DR. BURPO AND HIS BIBLE INSTITUTE OF THE AIR

1. Apache, Arizona, *Sentinel,* October 12, 1967.
2. October 24, 1970, Broadcast, KSKY, Dallas, Texas.
3. Letter from B. Edgar Johnson, General Secretary of the Church of the Nazarene, November 9, 1971.
4. Letter from B. Edgar Johnson, General Secretary of the Church of the Nazarene, February 22, 1972.
5. Letter from W. E. Opie, International Ministerial Foundation, Fresno, California, November 1, 1971.
6. Letter from Rolf K. McPherson. D.D., President of the International Church of the Foursquare Gospel, February 23, 1972.
7. The Bible Institute *News,* December 1966.
8. The Bible Institute *News,* October 1966.
9. The Bible Institute *News,* October 1966.
10. The Bible Institute *News,* December 1966.
11. *Ibid.*
12. Irving G. McCann, *Case History of the Smear by CBS of Conservatives,* Washington, D.C., McCann Press, 1966, p. 51.
13. *Ibid.,* pp. 72–74.
14. *Ibid.,* p. 74.

15. *Ibid.*, p. 74.
16. Speeches by Senator Thomas H. Kuchel, U.S. Senate, May 2 and 28, 1963.
17. *Ibid.*
18. Section 4 of Special Report No. 16, Group Research, Inc., Washington, D.C.
19. The Bible Institute *News*, January 1967.
20. The Bible Institute *News*, January 1967.
21. The Bible Institute *News*, February 1967.
22. The Bible Institute *News*, April 1967.
23. The Bible Institute *News*, July 1967.
24. The Bible Institute *News*, July 1967.
25. The Bible Institute *News*, August 1967.
26. The Bible Institute *News*, December 1966.
27. Transcript of Bible Institute of the Air Program, Radio Station WFAX, Falls Church, Virginia, September 27, 1967.
28. The Bible Institute *News*, February 1967.
29. The Bible Institute *News*, April 1967.
30. The Bible Institute *News*, May 1967.
31. The Bible Institute *News*, October 1967.
32. The Bible Institute *News*, October 1967.
33. The Bible Institute *News*, October 1967.
34. The Bible Institute *News*, October 1967.
35. The Bible Institute *News*, March 1968.
36. The Bible Institute *News*, January 1968.
37. The Bible Institute *News*, August 1968.
38. The Bible Institute *News*, May 1968.
39. The Bible Institute *News*, September 1968.
40. The Bible Institute *News*, November 1968.
41. The Bible Institute *News*, September 1968.
42. The Bible Institute *News*, February 1969.
43. The Bible Institute *News*, special, undated edition, headlined: "Which Way, America?"
44. September 22, 1970, Broadcast, XEG, Monterrey, Mexico.
45. *Ibid.*
46. February 20, 1967, rally, Little Theater, Municipal Auditorium, Oklahoma City, Oklahoma.
47. The Bible Institute *News*, June 1968.
48. September 23, 1970, Broadcast, XEG, Monterrey, Mexico.
49. The Bible Institute *News*, March 1971.

50. December 8, 1971, Broadcast, KSKY, Dallas, Texas.
51. March 2, 1972, Broadcast, XERF, Ciudad Acuña, Mexico.
52. August 5, 1970, Broadcast, KSKY, Dallas, Texas.
53. August 7, 1970, Broadcast, KSKY, Dallas, Texas.
54. September 18, 1970, Broadcast, KSKY, Dallas, Texas.
55. February 18, 1972, Broadcast, KSKY, Dallas, Texas.
56. The Bible Institute *News*, September 1970.
57. Seventeenth Anniversary Letter, December 1970.
58. The Bible Institute *News*, January 1971.
59. Special Personal Report, March 3, 1971.
60. Special Personal Report, December 1963.
61. June 4, 1968, Broadcast, KSKY, Dallas, Texas.
62. Special Personal Report, March 3, 1971.
63. *Ibid.*
64. The Bible Institute *News*, March 1971.
65. The Bible Institute *News*, May 1971.
66. The Bible Institute *News*, July 1971.
67. Letter from Representative Wright Patman, Democrat of Texas, October 14, 1971.
68. March 16, 1972, Broadcast, KSKY, Dallas, Texas.
69. The Bible Institute *News*, April 1972.
70. The Bible Institute *News*, January 1973.

REVEREND IKE—APOSTLE OF GREEN POWER

1. Reverend Ike's Blessing Plan, undated newsletter mailed in 1972.
2. Reverend Ike, Newsletter, October 15, 1971.
3. Reverend Ike, Postcard announcing January 2, 1972, Healing and Blessing Meeting in Macon, Georgia.
4. Bob Wilcox, "Ministry of Love Made Easier by $$," Miami *News*, April 1971.
5. Lester Kinsolving, Abilene *Reporter-News*, February 26, 1972.
6. Timothy Tyler, "That T-Bone Religion," *Time* magazine, December 11, 1972, p. 97.
7. Reverend Ike, "Joy of Living" Television Program, Station WPIX-TV, Channel 11, New York, January 24, 1973.
8. Reverend Ike, *Action!* magazine, August-September 1971, p. 11.

DEAN OF THE FAR-RIGHT RADIO PREACHERS

1. Ann Beierfield, "McIntire: A Man of Wrath Defies New Foes," Trenton *Evening Times,* July 15, 1969.
2. *Ibid.*
3. *Ibid.*
4. Rose DeWold, "The Sunday Preacher," *The Greater Philadelphia Magazine,* August 1964.
5. Ralph Lord Roy, *Apostles of Discord,* Boston, The Beacon Press, 1953, p. 188.
6. *Ibid.,* p. 189.
7. *Ibid.,* p. 190.
8. Carl McIntire, *Outside The Gate,* Christian Beacon Press, 1967, pp. 34, 36.
9. *Ibid.,* p. 311.
10. *Christianity Today,* January 29, 1965, pp. 3–5.
11. Carl McIntire, *Outside The Gate,* Christian Beacon Press, 1967, p. 311.
12. Ralph Lord Roy, *Apostles of Discord,* Boston, The Beacon Press, 1953, pp. 193–195.
13. *Ibid.,* p. 166.
14. George Thayer, *The Farther Shores of Politics,* New York, Simon and Schuster, 1967, p. 239.
15. Ann Beierfield, "McIntire: A Man of Wrath Defies New Foes," Trenton *Evening Times,* July 15, 1969.
16. Carl McIntire, *Outside The Gate,* Christian Beacon Press, 1967, p. 61.
17. New York *Herald Tribune,* December 13, 1964.
18. Carl McIntire, *Outside The Gate,* Christian Beacon Press, 1967, p. 310.
19. *Ibid.,* pp. 277, 279.
20. *Ibid.,* p. 69.
21. *Ibid.,* p. 72.
22. *Ibid.,* pp. 75–76.
23. *Ibid.,* pp. 80, 90, 91.
24. *Ibid.,* p. 106.
25. *Ibid.,* p. 115.
26. *Ibid.,* p. 118.

27. *Ibid.*, pp. 108, 125.
28. *Ibid.*, pp. 122–123.
29. *Ibid.*, p. 127.
30. *Ibid.*, p. 135.
31. *Ibid.*, pp. 184–193.
32. *Ibid.*, pp. 184, 200.
33. *Ibid.*, p. 200.
34. *Ibid.*, pp. 138–139.
35. *Ibid.*, pp. 138–139.
36. *Ibid.*, p. 131.
37. Carl McIntire, *Christian Beacon*, May 18, 1967.
38. Carl McIntire, *Christian Beacon*, December 12, 1968.
39. *Newsweek*, December 2, 1968.
40. Carl McIntire, *Christian Beacon*, December 5, 1968.
41. Carl McIntire, *Christian Beacon*, February 27, 1969.
42. Carl McIntire, *Christian Beacon*, March 20, 1969.
43. Carl McIntire, *Christian Beacon*, April 24, 1969.
44. Carl McIntire, *Christian Beacon*, May 29, 1969.
45. Carl McIntire, *Christian Beacon*, August 7, 1969.
46. Carl McIntire, *Christian Beacon*, August 14, 1969.
47. Carl McIntire, *Christian Beacon*, September 11, 1969.
48. Carl McIntire, *Christian Beacon*, November 13, 1969.
49. Carl McIntire, *Christian Beacon*, December 25, 1969.
50. Carl McIntire, *Christian Beacon*, June 29, 1967.
51. Carl McIntire, *Christian Beacon*, November 20, 1969.
52. Carl McIntire, *Christian Beacon*, January 29, 1970.
53. Carl McIntire, *Christian Beacon*, February 19, 1970.
54. Carl McIntire, *Christian Beacon*, April 9, 1970.
55. Carl McIntire, *Christian Beacon*, May 7, 1972.
56. Carl McIntire, *Christian Beacon*, May 14, 1970.
57. Carl McIntire, *Christian Beacon*, June 4, 1970.
58. Carl McIntire, *Christian Beacon*, June 25, 1970.
59. New York *Times*, June 24, 1970.
60. Carl McIntire, *Christian Beacon*, July 2, 1970.
61. Carl McIntire, *Christian Beacon*, July 16, 1970.
62. Carl McIntire, *Christian Beacon*, July 16, 1970.
63. *Newsweek*, July 20, 1970.
64. Carl McIntire, *Christian Beacon*, August 27, 1970.
65. Carl McIntire, *Christian Beacon*, October 1, 1970.
66. Washington *Evening Star*, October 5, 1970.
67. Carl McIntire, *Christian Beacon*, October 15, 1970.

68. Carl McIntire, *Christian Beacon,* January 7, 1971.
69. Carl McIntire, New York *Post,* January 26, 1973, p. 5.

KATHRYN KUHLMAN'S MIRACLE HEALINGS

1. Billy James Hargis, *Christian Crusade Weekly,* March 5, 1972, and August 1, 1971.
2. *Sunday Oklahoman,* November 22, 1970, p. 12.
3. Dennis Eckert, "Tulsa Now Called Fundamentalist Capital of the World," *Sunday Oklahoman,* August 1, 1971, p. 6.
4. Kathryn Kuhlman, "I Believe in Miracles," Logos International Recording, Undated.
5. *Ibid.*
6. Blau, Eleanor, "Evangelist Draws the Sick and Anguished," New York *Times,* October 20, 1972, p. 45.
7. Kathryn Kuhlman, "I Believe in Miracles," Logos International Recording, Undated.
8. Eleanor Blau, "Evangelist Draws the Sick and Anguished," New York *Times,* October 20, 1972, p. 45.
9. "Miracle Woman," *Time* magazine, September 14, 1970, p. 48.
10. Allen Spraggett, *Kathryn Kuhlman: The Woman Who Believes in Miracles,* New York, The World Publishing Company, 1970, p. 111.
11. *Ibid.,* p. 139.
12. "Miracle Woman," *Time* magazine, September 14, 1970, p. 48.
13. Allen Spraggett, *Kathryn Kuhlman: The Woman Who Believes in Miracles,* New York, The World Publishing Company, 1970, p. 111.
14. Julius Stadsklev, *William Branham: A Prophet Visits South Africa,* Minneapolis, Julius Stadsklev, 1952, pp. 38, 43.
15. *Ibid.,* p. 45.
16. Kathryn Kuhlman, *I Believe in Miracles,* New York, Prentice-Hall, 1962, pp. 11–12
17. Kathryn Kuhlman, "I Believe in Miracles," Logos International Recording, Undated.
18. *Ibid.*
19. Kathryn Kuhlman, *God Can Do It Again,* New Jersey, Prentice-Hall, 1969, pp. 254–255.
20. Allen Spraggett, *Kathryn Kuhlman: The Woman Who Believes in Miracles,* New York, The World Publishing Company, 1970, p. 63.

21. *Ibid.*, p. 30.
22. *Ibid.*, p. 33
23. Eleanor Blau, "Evangelist Draws the Sick and Anguished," New York *Times*, October 20, 1972, p. 45.
24. Tulsa *Daily World*, October 24, 1972.
25. Eleanor Blau, "Evangelist Draws the Sick and Anguished," New York *Times*, October 20, 1972, p. 45.

BILLY JAMES HARGIS AND HIS CHRISTIAN CRUSADE

1. Mike McGrady, "Radio Therapy: Shock Treatment in the Morning," *New York* magazine, April 3, 1972, p. 29.
2. "Imus in the Morning," March 28, 1972, Broadcast, WNBC, New York.
3. Billy James Hargis, *Christian Crusade Weekly*, January 23, 1972.
4. Billy James Hargis, *Crusading Preacher From the West*, Tulsa Christian Crusade, 1965, p. 13.
5. Billy James Hargis, *Christian Crusade Weekly*, December 6, 1970.
6. Billy James Hargis, *Distortion By Design*, Tulsa, Christian Crusade, 1965, p. 10.
7. Billy James Hargis, *Crusading Preacher From the West*, Tulsa, Christian Crusade, 1965, pp. 56, 221.
8. *Ibid.*, p. 62.
9. *Ibid.*, pp. 55–56.
10. *Ibid.*, pp. 42–43.
11. Billy James Hargis, *Christ and His Gospel*, Tulsa, Christian Crusade, 1969, p. 3.
12. Billy James Hargis, *Crusading Preacher From the West*, Tulsa, Christian Crusade, 1965, p. 63.
13. *Ibid.*, p. 55.
14. Ralph L. Roy, *Apostles of Discord*, The Beacon Press, 1953, pp. 30, 33.
15. H. K. Thompson, Jr., "A Survey of the Right Wing," New York, *The Independent*, 1962.
16. Billy James Hargis, *Christian Crusade* magazine, May 1962.

17. Billy James Hargis, *Crusading Preacher From the West,* Tulsa, Christian Crusade, 1965, pp. 258–260.
18. *Ibid.,* p. 73.
19. Billy James Hargis, *Distortion By Design,* Tulsa, Christian Crusade, 1965, p. 280.
20. *Ibid.,* pp. 274–279.
21. *Ibid.,* pp. 282–283.
22. *Ibid.,* pp. 284, 286, 287.
23. *Ibid.,* pp. 264–269.
24. Alan Bastic, *Praise the Lord and Pass the Contributions,* London, Cassell and Company, 1971, p. 65.
25. Billy James Hargis, *Weekly Crusader* newsletter, April 13, 1962.
26. Billy James Hargis, May 19, 1970, Broadcast, KBYE, Oklahoma City.
27. Jess Pedigo, *Yes, Ginger, Communism is Your Enemy,* Christian Crusade, Tulsa, Oklahoma, 1970, p. 42.
28. Billy James Hargis, *Distortion By Design,* Tulsa, Christian Crusade, 1965, p. 239.
29. *Ibid.,* pp. 250–252.
30. *Ibid.,* pp. 253–256
31. Billy James Hargis, April 26, 1968, Broadcast, KBYE, Oklahoma City.
32. Billy James Hargis, *Christian Crusade* magazine, April 1968.
33. All quotations and paraphrases related to "The Great Debate" are taken from notes transcribed during the actual debate. The notes have also been checked against a magnetic tape recording of the debate purchased from Christian Crusade.
34. William R. Harrison, "Is Hargis' Crusade Christian?" *Christianity Today,* August 16, 1968, pp. 38–40.
35. Billy James Hargis, *Weekly Crusader* newsletter, November 22, 1968, p. 8.
36. Billy James Hargis, *Weekly Crusader* newsletter, November 22, 1968.
37. Billy James Hargis, *Christian Crusade Weekly,* November 12, 1972, p. 1.
38. Billy James Hargis, *Christian Crusade Weekly,* April 12, 1970.
39. Billy James Hargis, *Christian Crusade Weekly,* June 7, 1970, p. 4.
40. Billy James Hargis, *Christian Crusade Weekly,* July 5, 1970, p. 1.
41. Billy James Hargis, *Christian Crusade Weekly,* October 31, 1971, p. 1.

42. Dennis Eckert, "Tulsa Now Called Fundamentalist Capital of World," *Sunday Oklahoman,* August 1, 1971, Section A, p. 6.
43. *Sunday Oklahoman,* November 3, 1970, p. 1.
44. Billy James Hargis, *Christian Crusade Weekly,* November 22, 1971.
45. Billy James Hargis letter dated September 28, 1971.
46. Billy James Hargis, *Christian Crusade Weekly,* October 17, 1971, pp. 6–7.
47. Billy James Hargis, *Christian Crusade Weekly,* p. 7.
48. Billy James Hargis, *Christian Crusade Weekly,* February 20, 1972, p. 1.
49. Billy James Hargis, *Christian Crusade Weekly,* February 20, 1972, p. 1.
50. Billy James Hargis, *Christian Crusade Weekly,* March 26, 1972, p. 1.
51. Billy James Hargis, *Christian Crusade Weekly,* April 23, 1972, p. 1.
52. Billy James Hargis, *Christian Crusade Weekly,* April 23, 1972, p. 1.
53. Billy James Hargis, *Christian Crusade Weekly,* October 11, 1972, p. 10.
54. Billy James Hargis, *Christian Crusade Weekly,* May 14, 1972, p. 1.
55. Billy James Hargis, *Christian Crusade Weekly,* July 30, 1972, p. 1.
56. Billy James Hargis, *Christian Crusade Weekly,* November 19, 1971, p. 1.
57. Billy James Hargis, Excerpts from a Christian Crusade letter dated May 21, 1971.
58. Billy James Hargis, Excerpts from a Christian Crusade letter dated January 31, 1972.
59. Carl McIntire, *Christian Beacon,* June 17, 1971, p. 2.
60. Billy James Hargis, *Christian Crusade Weekly,* January 17, 1971, p. 4.
61. Billy James Hargis, July 7, 1971, Broadcast, KFMJ, Tulsa.
62. Billy James Hargis, *Christian Crusade Weekly,* November 28, 1971, p. 2.
63. Group Research Report, October 26, 1972, p. 59.
64. Billy James Hargis, *Christian Crusade Weekly,* August 29, 1971, p. 1.
65. Jess Pedigo, *Satanism—Diabolical Religion of Darkness,* Tulsa, *Christian Crusade,* 1971, p. 3.
66. Billy James Hargis, *Christian Crusade Weekly,* August 29, 1971, p. 1.

67. Jess Pedigo, *Satanism—Diabolical Religion of Darkness, Christian Crusade,* Tulsa, 1971, pp. 5, 47.
68. Billy James Hargis, June 28, 1971, Broadcast, KBYE, Oklahoma City.
69. *Daily Oklahoman,* November 21, 1967, p. 16.
70. Alan Bastic, *Praise the Lord and Pass the Contributions,* London, Cassell and Company, 1971, p. 65.
71. Oklahoma *Journal,* December 19, 1971.

THE PASADENA PROPHETS

1. Herbert W. Armstrong, March 13, 1972, Broadcast, KBYE, Oklahoma City.
2. *This is The Worldwide Church of God,* Pasadena, California, Ambassador College Press, p. 13.
3. Salem Kirban, *The Plain Truth About The Plain Truth,* Huntingdon Valley, Salem Kirban, Inc., p. 4.
4. Noel Smith, *Herbert W. Armstrong and His World Tomorrow,* Springfield, Missouri, Bible Baptist Tribune, 1964, p. 10.
5. Joseph Martin Hopkins, *Christianity Today,* December 17, 1971, p. 7.
6. Herbert W. Armstrong, *The Autobiography of Herbert W. Armstrong,* Vol. 1, Pasadena, California, Ambassador College, 1967, pp. 285–295.
7. Herbert W. Armstrong, *The United States and British Commonwealth in Prophecy,* Pasadena, California, Ambassador College, 1967, pp. 164–166.
8. Herbert W. Armstrong, *United States and the British Commonwealth in Prophecy,* Radio Church of God, 1954, pp. 16–19.
9. *Ibid.,* p. 7.
10. Herbert W. Armstrong, *The United States and British Commonwealth in Prophecy;* Pasadena, California, Ambassador College, 1967, pp. 123.
11. Herbert W. Armstrong, *United States and the British Commonwealth in Prophecy;* Radio Church of God, 1954, p. 20.

12. Alan Crown, "The Myth of the Ten Lost Tribes," *New Humanist*, October 1972, p. 233.
13. Egon Larson, *Strange Sects and Cults*, London, Arthur Barker Ltd., 1971, pp. 86–87.
14. Ralph L. Roy, *Apostles of Discord*, Boston, The Beacon Press, 1953, pp. 92–107.
15. Herbert W. Armstrong, *The United States and British Commonwealth in Prophecy*, Pasadena, California, Ambassador College, College, 1967, pp. 10, 194.
16. Letter dated April 28, 1972, signed by W. Ronald Reedy, Personal Correspondent, Ambassador College, Personal Correspondence Dept., Pasadena, California.
17. Horton Davis, *Christian Deviations*, The Westminster Press, 1965, p. 83.
18. Noel Smith, *Herbert W. Armstrong and His World Tomorrow*, Springfield, Missouri, Baptist Bible Tribune, 1946, p. 27.
19. Herbert W. Armstrong, *The Autobiography of Herbert W. Armstrong*, Vol. I, Ambassador College, 1957, p. 505.
20. Herbert W. Armstrong, "The Autobiography of Herbert W. Armstrong," *Plain Truth*, March 1961, p. 14.
21. Herbert W. Armstrong, "The Autobiography of Herbert W. Armstrong," *Plain Truth*, September 1961, p. 14.
22. Herbert W. Armstrong, "The Autobiography of Herbert W. Armstrong," *Plain Truth*, November 1961, pp. 8, 21.
23. Herbert W. Armstrong, "The Autobiography of Herbert W. Armstrong," *Plain Truth*, March 1961, pp. 14, 31.
24. Herbert W. Armstrong, "The Autobiography of Herbert W. Armstrong," *Plain Truth*, November 1961, p. 5.
25. Herbert W. Armstrong, "The Autobiography of Herbert W. Armstrong," *Plain Truth*, p. 21.
26. Herbert W. Armstrong, "The Autobiography of Herbert W. Armstrong," *Plain Truth*, May 1962, p. 17.
27. Herbert W. Armstrong, *The Autobiography of Herbert W. Armstrong*, Vol. 1; Ambassador College, 1957, p. 306.
28. Herbert W. Armstrong, "The Autobiography of Herbert W. Armstrong," *Plain Truth*, August 1962, p. 16.
29. Herbert W. Armstrong, "The Autobiography of Herbert W. Armstrong," *Plain Truth*, February 1964, p. 43.
30. Herbert W. Armstrong, "The Autobiography of Herbert W. Armstrong," *Plain Truth*, July 1963, p. 13.

31. Herbert W. Armstrong, "The Autobiography of Herbert W. Armstrong," *Plain Truth*, November 1962, p. 9.
32. Herbert W. Armstrong, "Will Russia Invade America?", *Plain Truth*, November 1948.
33. Herbert W. Armstrong, "The Autobiography of Herbert W. Armstrong," *Plain Truth*, September 1962, p. 20.
34. L. E. Torrance, "Hitler's Seven Fatal Blunders," *Plain Truth*, July 1961, p. 11.
35. Roderick C. Meredith, "Hitler's Germany to Rise Again?" *Plain Truth*, May 1965, p. 45.
36. Herbert W. Armstrong, *The Autobiography of Herbert W. Armstrong*, Vol. I, Ambassador College, 1957, p. 408.
37. Roderick C. Meredith, "Hitler's Germany to Rise Again?" *Plain Truth*, May 1965, p. 45.
38. Herbert W. Armstrong, *Plain Truth*, January 1969, p. 31.
39. Salem Kirban, *The Plain Truth About The Plain Truth*, Huntingdon Valley, Salem Kirban, Inc., 1970, p. 44.
40. "Garner Ted Armstrong, Where Are You?" *Time*, May 15, 1972, p. 87.
41. Roderick C. Meredith, "The Blessings of Paying God's Tithe!" *Plain Truth*, May 1963, pp. 13–15.
42. Herbert W. Armstrong, "The Autobiography of Herbert W. Armstrong, Vol. I," *Plain Truth*, November 1961, pp. 23–24.
43. Herman L. Hoeh, "Should A Non-Christian Tithe?" *Plain Truth*, February 1967, p. 17.
44. Herbert W. Armstrong, Semi-Annual Letter dated November 18, 1965.
45. Herbert W. Armstrong, Semi-Annual Letter dated November 1966.
46. Herbert W. Armstrong, *The Autobiography of Herbert W. Armstrong*, Vol. I, Ambassador College Press, 1957, pp. 449–450.
47. Herbert W. Armstrong, *The United States and British Commonwealth in Prophecy*, Ambassador College, 1967, p. 208.
48. Egon Larsen, *Strange Sects and Cults*, London, 1971, Arthur Barker Ltd., p. 174.
49. Herbert W. Armstrong, "Personal From the Editor," *Plain Truth*, May 1969, p. 1.
50. "Garner Ted Armstrong, Where Are You?" *Time*, May 15, 1972, p. 87.
51. Herbert W. Armstrong, January 30, 1972, Broadcast, WMCA, New York.

EVANGELIST BILLY GRAHAM AND HIS CRITICS

1. "The Preaching and the Power," *Newsweek* magazine, July 20, 1970, p. 30.
2. Frost, David, *Billy Graham Talks With David Frost;* Hodder and Stoughton, 1972, p. 19.
3. Lockard, W. David, *The Unheard Billy Graham;* Word Books, Waco, 1971, p. 14.
4. Frost, David, *Billy Graham Talks With David Frost;* Hodder and Stoughton, 1972, p. 20.
5. Pollock, John, *Billy Graham,* Hodder and Stoughton, London, 1966, p. 28.
6. Ibid., p. 29.
7. "Tree Stumps were Billy's First Audience," *The Stars and Stripes* newspaper, March 12, 1973, p. 2B.
8. Pollock, John, *Billy Graham,* Hodder and Stoughton, London, 1966, p. 67.
9. Ibid., p. 128.
10. McLoughlin, William G., Jr. *Billy Graham: Revivalist in a Secular Age;* The Ronald Press Company, New York, 1960, p. 205.
11. Ibid., pp. 202–203.
12. Roberts, Oral, *The Call;* Doubleday & Co., New York, pp. 116–117.
13. Ibid., p. 118.
14. Lockard, W. David, *The Unheard Billy Graham;* Word Books, Waco, 1971, p. 29.
15. "Quote of the Week," *The New Republic,* January 6 & 13, 1973, p. 11.
16. Henry, Carl F., "The Theology of Billy Graham," *The Churchman,* March 1954, p. 6, Quoted in *The Unheard Billy Graham,* by W. David Lockard, Word Books, Waco, 1971, p. 33.
17. Pollock John, *Billy Graham;* Hodder and Stoughton, London, 1966, p. 67.
18. Lockard, W. David, *The Unheard Billy Graham;* Word Books, Waco, 1971, p. 33.
19. "Boycotting Billy," *Time* magazine, March 18, 1966, p. 66.
20. Pollock, John, *Billy Graham;* Hodder and Stoughton, London, 1966, pp. 227-228.

21. Russell, Francis, "Billy and Aimee," *National Review*, June 29, 1971, p. 716.
22. *The Christian Century*, September 13, 1972, p. 891.
23. Graham, Billy, "Program for Peace," sermon, 1951, p. 1. Quoted in Lockard, David W., *The Unheard Billy Graham*, Word Books, Waco, 1971, p. 146.
24. Frost, David, *Billy Graham Talks With David Frost;* Hodder and Stoughton, 1972, p. 66.
25. Pollock, John, *Billy Graham;* Hodder and Stoughton, London, 1966, pp. 282-283.
26. "Billy's Political Pitch," *Newsweek* magazine, June 10, 1968, p. 62.
27. "The Preaching and the Power," *Newsweek* magazine, July 20, 1970, p. 34.
28. Schmiechen, Peter M., "What do you Want for Christmas?" *The Christian Century*, December 20, 1972, p. 1297.
29. Rose, Stephen C., "Eugene Carson Blake: A Welcome-Home Interview," *The Christian Century*, October 18, 1972, p. 1037.
30. "The Preaching and the Power," *Newsweek* magazine, July 20, 1970, p. 35.

Index